Global governmentality

Foucault's thoughts on governmentality have made a significant impact on studies of power and governance in modern societies. However, most studies of governmentality confine themselves to the exploration of power within nation-states. *Global Governmentality* extends Foucault's political thought towards international studies, exploring the governance of the global, the international, the regional and many other extra-domestic spaces.

Combining historical and contemporary outlooks, this book offers innovative interdisciplinary explorations of such issues as international peacekeeping, refugees, political rationalities of security and neoliberalism, the spatiality of globalization, the genealogy of development, and the ethical governance of corporate activity.

At a time when many of the geopolitical and economic certainties which framed international affairs are in flux, *Global Governmentality* is suggestive of new territories and lines for international analysis. It will be of interest to students and researchers of both governmentality and international studies.

Wendy Larner is a Senior Lecturer in Sociology, University of Auckland. Her research interests are in the areas of globalization, governance and gender. **William Walters** is Associate Professor in Political Science at Carleton University, Ottawa. His current work explores questions of citizenship, borders and im/mobility in the context of European integration.

D1614539

Routledge advances in International Relations and Global Politics

Global governmentality

Governing international spaces

**Edited by Wendy Larner
and William Walters**

Routledge
Taylor & Francis Group

LONDON AND NEW YORK

First published 2004

by Routledge
2 Park Square, Milton Park, Abingdon, Oxon OX14 4RN

Simultaneously published in the USA and Canada
by Routledge
270 Madison Ave, New York, NY 10016

Routledge is an imprint of the Taylor & Francis Group

Transferred to Digital Printing 2006

© 2004 Wendy Larner and William Walters for selection and editorial
material; individual contributors their contribution

Typeset in by Baskerville by Taylor & Francis Group

British Library Cataloguing in Publication Data
A catalogue record for this book is available from the British Library

Library of Congress Cataloging in Publication Data

Global governmentality: governing international spaces/ edited by Wendy
Larner and William Walters.
p. cm.
Simultaneously published in the USA and Canada.
Includes bibliographical references and index.
1. International organization. 2. Globalization.
3. Power (Social sciences) 4. Authority. I. Larner, Wendy.
II. Walters, William, 1964-

JZ1318 .G5575 2004
327.1'01--dc22

2003024373

ISBN10: 0–415–31138–1 (hbk)
ISBN10: 0–415–40680–3 (pbk)

ISBN13: 978–0–415–31138–0 (hbk)
ISBN13: 978–0–415–40680–2 (pbk)

Contents

Contributors

Andrew Barry is Senior Lecturer in Sociology at Goldsmiths College, University of London. He is author of *Political Machines: governing a technological society* (Athlone Press, 2001) and co-editor of *Foucault and Political Reason: liberalism, neo-liberalism and rationalities of government* (Chicago UP and UCL Press, 1996). He is currently working on a book on invention and social theory.

Carl Dahlman is Assistant Professor of Geography at the University of South Carolina and an Associate in the Walker Institute of International Studies. Recent publications address political identity in the Kurdish diaspora and the geopolitical visions of civil society organisations. His current research focuses on the politics of identity and displacement among Kurds from northern Iraq, and the international effort to reverse ethnic cleansing in Bosnia.

Roger Dale is Professor of Education at the University of Auckland and Academic Coordinator of the EU Erasmus-funded Globalisation and Europeanisation Network in Education, which is based at the University of Bristol. He has written extensively on the relationship between the state and education, and is currently working on the development of European education policy.

Mitchell Dean is Professor of Sociology and Dean of Division of Society, Culture, Media and Philosophy, Macquarie University, Sydney. Author and editor of several books including *Governmentality: power and rule in modern societies* (Sage, 1999), his current interests include questions of sovereignty, international order and notions of power.

Michael Dillon is Professor of Politics at Lancaster University. Co-editor of the *Journal for Cultural Research* (Routledge), his current research interests concern the changing nature of the life sciences and their impact on governance and security.

Barry Hindess is Professor of Political Science in the Research School of Social Sciences at Australian National University, Canberra. He has published widely in the areas of social and political theory. His most recent works are *Discourses of Power: from Hobbes to Foucault* (Blackwell, 1996) and

Governing Australia: studies in contemporary rationalities of government (Cambridge UP, 1998) and numerous papers on democracy, liberalism and empire, and neo-liberalism.

Gavin Kendall is Senior Lecturer in Sociology at Queensland University of Technology, Brisbane. Recent books include *The State, Democracy and Globalization* (Palgrave Macmillan, 2003, with Roger King), *Understanding Culture* (Sage, 1999, with Gary Wickham) and *Using Foucault's Methods* (Sage, 1999, with Gary Wickham). His current research interests include the sociology of organisations and cosmopolitanism.

Wendy Larner is Senior Lecturer in Sociology at the University of Auckland. Her published work can be found in journals such as *Environment and Planning A*, *Review of International Political Economy* and (with William Walters) *Theory and Society*. She is currently working on a book called *After Neoliberalism?* Her research interests are in the areas of globalisation, governance and gender.

Richard Le Heron is Professor of Geography in the School of Geography and Environmental Science, University of Auckland. Recent articles appear in *Journal of Rural Studies*, *Journal of Economic Geography* and *Australian Geographer*. He recently co-edited a book on *Knowledge, Industry and Environment* (Ashgate, 2002). Research interests include the geographies of agri-food regulation, governance and governmentality in the context of globalising economic processes.

Robyn Lui is a Research Fellow at the Centre for Ethics, Law, Justice and Governance, Griffith University, Brisbane. Her research interests include refugee protection, humanitarianism and the good governance project. She is currently the co-ordinator of a series of dialogues between Indonesian Islamic and Western scholars on governance values in South-East Asia.

Michael Mopas is a PhD student at the Centre of Criminology, University of Toronto. His research interests are in the areas of policing, science and technology studies, and the governance of cyberspace. His doctoral dissertation examines government responses to illegal and offensive content on the Internet in Canada, Australia and New Zealand.

Gearóid Ó Tuathail is Director of the Masters of Public and International Affairs at Virginia Polytechnical Institute's campus in the Washington DC metro region. He is the author of *Critical Geopolitics* (Routledge, 1996) and a co-editor of *A Companion to Political Geography* (Blackwell, 2002) and *The Geopolitics Reader* (Routledge 1998) among other works. He also serves as Associate Editor of the journal *Geopolitics* (Frank Cass). He is currently working on a manuscript on the international community and returns in Bosnia.

Cristina Rojas is an Associate Professor at the Norman Paterson School for International Affairs, Carleton University, Ottawa. Her research interests include international social policy, Latin American politics and global governmentalities. Her most recent publications include *Civilization and Violence. Regimes of representation in nineteenth century Colombia* (University of Minnesota Press, 2002).

Mariana Valverde does work in social and legal theory, and empirical research in the sociology of law. Recent publications include two books, *Diseases of the Will: alcohol and the dilemmas of freedom* (Cambridge UP, 1998), winner of the Herbert Jacobs book prize of the Law and Society Association, and *Law's Dream of a Common Knowledge* (Princeton UP, 2003). She is currently beginning a research project on municipal law and urban order that is both empirical and legal.

William Walters is Associate Professor in Political Science at Carleton University, Ottawa. His current work explores questions of citizenship, borders and im/mobility in the context of European integration. Previous publications include *Unemployment and Government: genealogies of the social* (Cambridge UP, 2000).

Acknowledgements

This project began its life as a workshop on International Government and Social Spaces which we convened at the University of Auckland in 2001. We thank the International Council for Canadian Studies for funding this event through their Programme for International Research Linkages, and all those who attended for their helpful comments. Many of our chapters were first presented at the workshop while others were developed for panels at the 2002 International Studies Association meeting in New Orleans, and the 2002 International Sociological Association meeting in Brisbane.

We thank Anna Paris (University of Auckland) for her excellent editorial work, and Grace McInnes and Heidi Bagtazo at Routledge for their patience and encouragement. In addition, Wendy Larner would like to acknowledge the University of Auckland and the Royal Society of New Zealand Marsden Fund for financial support, and to thank her colleagues, particularly Richard Le Heron, for their encouragement of the project. William Walters is grateful to Canada's Social Sciences and Humanities Research Council (grant #410–2000–1415) for research funding. He would also like to thank Christina Gabriel for her constant support.

Wendy Larner
William Walters

Introduction

Global governmentality: governing international spaces

Wendy Larner and William Walters

Nothing is so firmly beleeved, as that which man knoweth leest.
(Michel de Montaigne 1965: 230)

Global Governmentality is a book about international studies. Like other such collections, our authors address many of the themes which have long preoccupied students of international affairs, such as international security, world order, war and peace, economic development, and the plight of refugees. But what makes this collection somewhat novel is the fact that all our contributors share in some form or other an interest in what Michel Foucault (1991) called 'governmentality'. Each chapter seeks to demonstrate how concepts and themes drawn from what has now become a wide-ranging debate on governmentality, often in combination with theories from other intellectual trajectories, offer new perspectives on the governing of international spaces.

At the same time *Global Governmentality* pushes Foucauldian studies of governance 'outside' the nation-state and onto new theoretical and political territories. One of the most notable features of governmentality research has been its investigation of power 'beyond the state', that is, with the tactics, techniques and technologies which configure apparently 'non-political' sites like the firm or the school as spaces of power (Rose and Miller 1992). But while such studies have offered an innovative framework to undertake empirical research in the modalities of power and rule in modern societies, they have nevertheless remained largely focused on political, social and economic life 'inside' nation-states. Questions regarding the constitution and governance of spaces beyond the state have not been pursued as fully as they might. It is this challenge of relating governmentality to the international, the global, the supra-national, that our contributors take up. In the process, they seek to unsettle a series of 'self-evidences on which our knowledges, acquiescences and practices rest' (Foucault 1991: 76).

This introductory chapter briefly frames the idea of governmentality by relating it to some of Foucault's other, perhaps better known, work. Then we discuss some of the paths along which scholars have taken governmentality research and highlight some of its strengths and weaknesses. Finally, we survey the various contributions to this volume, placing them in context and suggesting their wider significance.

Before we take up this introductory work, a word about our title is in order. More specifically, we want to explain our choice of the word 'global'. It is not our intention to identify a new regime of power. For instance, Fraser has recently juxtaposed a 'globalized governmentality' to the disciplinary societies of modernity which, she argues, were Foucault's principal concern. For her, globalized governmentality refers specifically to our present, to a multilevelled system of power, 'a complex edifice in which the national state is but one level among others' (Fraser 2003: 167).[1] We do not intend anything this specific in our reference to global governmentality. Certainly one might analyse contemporary rationalities and programmes of 'globalization' or 'global governance' as elements within a global governmentality. A number of our contributors do precisely this. However, global governmentality can equally encompass earlier attempts to govern extended social and economic spaces. What we understand by global governmentality includes not just studies of today's 'globalism', but the political rationalities and technologies of imperialism, internationalism, cosmopolitanism and much else besides. In sum, we use global governmentality as a heading for studies which problematize the constitution, and governance of spaces above, beyond, between and across states. Naming is itself an act of power. Our use of the global signifies a space the nature of which shouldn't be assumed in advance. It remains the task of empirical inquiry in any given case to determine whether the space in question is governed as 'international', 'global', or as something else.

Governmentality beyond borders?

The term 'governmentality' has been used in two distinct senses within the literature (Dean 1999: 16). In its wider sense, governmentality prompts us to consider how governing involves particular representations, knowledges and often expertise regarding that which is to be governed. Here one sees significant continuity with Foucault's better-known observations about power/knowledge (Gordon 1980). This understanding of governmentality draws attention to the complex relationship between thought and government. Whether it is the government of a business, a state, or of ones own health and wellbeing, the practice of government involves the production of particular 'truths' about these entities. In seeking out the history of these truths, the literature on governmentality offers critical insights about the constitution of our societies and our present.

But governmentality also has a more specific reference to a new way of thinking about and exercising power, whose historical emergence Foucault dates to the eighteenth century in Europe. Governmentality in this second sense refers to:

> The ensemble formed by the institutions, procedures, analyses and reflections, the calculations and tactics that allow the exercise of this very specific albeit complex form of power, which has as its target population, as its prin-

cipal form of knowledge political economy, and as its essential technical means apparatuses of security.

(Foucault 1991: 102)

Here governmentality can be compared with other forms of power, such as sovereignty. If the problematic of sovereign power concerns how to perpetuate one's rule over a given territory and its subjects; and if law, violence and pageantry figure amongst its most privileged instruments, then governmentality is a different regime of power, even if it combines with sovereignty in complex ways. Governmentality is dispositional, concerned with ordering people and things. In its widest sense it concerns all those attempts to 'apply economy, to set up an economy at the level of the entire state' (Foucault 1991: 92). We are dealing not with the defence of territory so much as 'the imbrication of men and things', 'men' in their myriad relations with climate, wealth, resources, the territory and so on (1991: 93).

This defines the field of governmentality. It is of course a field which has seen profound transformations in its methods and its rationality. Foucault theorizes some of these, such as the shift from the governmentalities of police and cameralism to those of liberalism. Nevertheless, it remains a field whose horizon continues to define our contemporary forms of political reason – be they neoconservative, neoliberal, or Third Way.

While they formed only a minor part of Foucault's *oeuvre*, his reflections on governmentality have come to exercise a significant influence in the political and social sciences, at least in the English-speaking world. The theme of governmentality has been taken up enthusiastically in many fields and the 1990s witnessed an impressive flourishing of research, influenced by two widely cited collections (Burchell *et al.* 1991; Barry *et al.* 1996) and a seminal article by Rose and Miller (1992). Rather like the Gramscian notion of 'hegemony' – an idea that was to have a profound impact on critical political analysis during the 1980s and which remains important for numerous scholars in fields such as international political economy, development studies, and economic geography – governmentality has become a core concept within a wide range of studies of power, order, subjectivity and resistance.

There are several reasons why governmentality has arisen to such prominence. First, it offers a line of investigation that has appealed to researchers frustrated with the enduring positivism of the social sciences, but not content either with the textualism of certain poststructuralisms. Governmentality certainly has significant affinities with poststructuralist approaches: a view of power as fragmented; an insistence on the constitutive nature of language; and a view of agency in terms of contingent rather than fixed subjectivities. But unlike much work in poststructuralism, governmentality research has been more historical and more avowedly empirical in its orientation. This has much to do with an aspect of governmentality we have not yet mentioned – a concern with power in its multifarious practical, technical manifestations. One of the foremost accomplishments of governmentality studies is to foster research into power that is always local and provisional. Eschewing the overly dramatic and sometimes apocalyptic posture of many theories of the risk society, postmodernity or late capitalism, governmentality has, as Barry *et al.* (1996: 4) point out, evidenced a more modest role for theorizing, preferring a series of mid-range concepts (strategies, tactics, programmes, techniques, and so on) that can be used heuristically to interrogate specific configurations of power.

But a second factor has to do with how we make sense of a changing world. The proliferation of discourse concerning globalization, global governance and post-Westphalian politics are surely symptoms of serious transformations in the form and content of economic, political and social relations. Such changes have proved highly troubling for the social sciences, wedded as these often are to an understanding of social totalities and bounded spaces. Favouring a view of power which is dispersed, in which the state is not a necessary or logical centre but one amongst many historical configurations of government, studies in governmentality have proved themselves particularly adept at the analysis of contemporary transformations, at least inasmuch as these have reshaped Western states. At the centre of this undertaking has been a novel understanding of liberalism and neoliberalism, innovative because it has grasped (neo)liberalism not as an ideology or philosophy, nor as the most recent political form of the capitalist agenda, but in terms of certain arts, tactics and practices of governing. Without denying that neoliberalism has implied all manner of social exclusions, these studies have drawn our attention to the many and varied ways in which it operates, not as a negative force either wielded by the state or reshaping the state itself in the interests of global forces, but through the way we are implicated in all manner of practices that enjoin us to exercise certain forms of freedom. In this way, governmentality has marked a significant advance in our grasp of the rationalities and modalities of power configuring our political present.[2]

If governmentality studies have made significant advances in these respects, they are not without their problems. Notably, Hindess (1997) has criticized these studies for their failure to distinguish adequately between the governmental and the political. On a similar note, O'Malley (1996) and O'Malley, *et al.* (1997) stress that governmentality studies, through their emphasis on the programmatic and rationalizing aspects of governance, tend to greatly understate not just the incoherence of power, but the extent to which government is frequently invented from below. This, in turn, explains a frequently made criticism of governmentality research, namely that it describes political processes without identifying actors – either hegemonic or oppositional (Kerr 1999). Against those who would maintain a cautious distance between governmentality research and sociology, Garland (1997) has argued that some of these conceptual oversights could be addressed through a more prominent role for sociological investigation – as opposed to textual analysis – within studies of governmentality.

While these pressing questions will doubtless continue to shape the future direction of governmentality research, they are not the pretext for this volume. Rather, our questions concern the domains of such work. A noticeable feature of governmentality research is its domestic orientation. Overwhelmingly, these studies have taken the nation-state as their analytical locale. A glance at the contents of the major collections in this area reveals but a handful of contributions which consider the government of processes beyond or across political borders (for example, Barry 1996; Hindess 1998).

No doubt there are good reasons for this striking asymmetry. One factor is perhaps the disciplinary location of many scholars working in this area – sociology, education and criminology. At the risk of overgeneralization, these are disciplines that traditionally focus on local and national systems of rule. They have concerned themselves with issues on the home front, as it were, while leaving the distant, international 'outside' to international relations, diplomatic history and other such programmes. As much as governmentality research has challenged the lines and demarcations of these disciplines – indeed, it has argued that they play a constitutive role in the exercise of modern power – it has nevertheless tended to respect their division of domestic and international.[3] A second factor has already been touched upon, namely a justified scepticism regarding the claims of grand theories. Nevertheless, the paradox remains that governmentality studies proliferated during the 1990s, precisely at a time when the fascination with globalization exploded across the social sciences. Yet to date there has been very little intersection between these two developments. This is peculiar not least because, unlike fields such as comparative politics or even sociology, whose very conceptual architecture has been shaped by the idea of state and society as more or less bounded interiors, governmentality is not conceptually committed to such prior objects.

It is a major concern of this volume, then, to address this imbalance, the relative neglect of the global by governmentality scholars. We do this not simply for reasons of balance and completeness, but also because the global is increasingly central to the way in which economic, political and social relations are thought about and acted upon. If the ambition of governmentality studies is to develop a 'history of the present' (Barry *et al.* 1996: 2), then the relative lack of attention to international and global topics is indeed a strange omission. But a note of caution: as we stressed above, our use of the term global governmentality is not intended to signal a commitment to the position that today, as never before, we inhabit a 'global world'. Our ambition is to identify a relatively open intellectual space and to stress the need for studies of a range of mentalities of international rule hitherto largely ignored. It is perhaps better regarded as an empirical rather than a conceptual matter; a question of focusing more fully on the various ways in which governance at the level of the world has been problematized; a history of arts of international government (Lui-Bright 1997; see also Larner and Walters 2002).

In calling for this extension of governmentality to international concerns we do not claim to be pioneers charting a hitherto unexplored territory. While we noted above that governmentality studies have been overwhelmingly oriented towards the domestic, it is possible to identify lines of investigation which connect analytics of government to questions of international life, war and peace, and world politics. Indeed, one need look no further than Foucault himself. For instance, in his 1975–1976 lecture series entitled *Il faut défendre la société*, and as part of his engagement with modern political theory, Foucault investigated the 'discourse of war' (Foucault 1997; Marks 2000; Pasquino 1993). With this genealogy of conflict Foucault was able to demonstrate the precarious-ness and recentness of inside/outside distinctions. He shows that in the idea of battle modern societies will find not just an image of their external relations with other states, but – as modern ideas of racial and class conflict confirm – the very diagram of their internal constitution. Following Nietzsche, Foucault suggests that war is woven into the very fabric of our social peace.

Perhaps the one area where governmentality and other Foucauldian approaches have been pushed most consistently 'outside' the nation-state is with the study of colonial power. Studies of colonial governmentality have explored new aspects of imperial rule (Kalpagam 2000; Scott 1995; Mitchell 1988; Rabinow 1989; Kendall 1997). These have shown that colonial power worked not by repressive mechanisms alone, nor through a combination of economic power and cultural hegemony. In addition, there is the whole exportation of an infrastructure of knowledge, installing particular ways of counting and forms of expertise that reconstitute the colony as the site of such new spaces as 'the economy' and 'civil society'. In a similar vein one could mention Escobar's path-breaking work in the field of development, and the broader Foucauldian-inspired debates occurring under the label 'post-development' (Escobar 1995; Crush 1995). These accounts depict the development project as a discursive formation and set of governing practices which assume the cultural and technological supe-riority of the 'West'. As Stoler (1995) demonstrates, such encounters are significant not least because they force studies of governmentality to deepen their understanding of 'race'.

If these studies suggest new ways of understanding historical power forma-tions, there are also scholars who have sought to map contemporary global spaces and the power/knowledge networks through which they are constituted. Hindess (1998) investigates how classical economic thought presupposed a specif-ically national economic space. He compares this with new forms of calculation that not only presuppose a 'global economy', but make it calculable and effec-tive. In the context of the European Union countries, Bigo (2000) has examined the blurring of boundaries that previously separated the fields of domestic and international security. In the wake of growing fears about terrorists, immigrants and other mobile threats – fears that are socially and politically constructed – he outlines the emergence of a transnational security field that he likens to a 'Möbius strip'. Thrift (2001) explores the invention of the so-called 'new economy', exemplifying the empirical tracing needed to explore the movement of discourses and practices through networks of academics, professionals and technocrats. Or consider the work of Salskov-Iverson *et al.* (2000) which tracks the movement of New Public Management ideas and techniques through networks and their assimilation into the practice of local government in different countries. Most recently, Ong and her anthropology colleagues have focused on the 'new spatial articulations of science, bureaucracy and technocracy, capitalism and governmentality' that together constitute 'globalization' (Ong and Collier forthcoming). More generally, the work of Taylor, Agnew, Dalby, Ó Tuathail and others within critical geopolitics offers a wealth of insight and comparative perspective on the various ways in which geopolitical thought, past and present, has divided, coded and territorialized the world.

If historical and empirical engagement with economic, social and political spaces beyond the nation-state represents one line through which governmentality has engaged with the global, a second is through studies which have interrogated its core assumptions. Michael Dillon has examined the particular intersections of sovereignty, governmentality and biopolitics which characterize the post-Cold War problematic of 'new world order' (Dillon 1995). In his view a Foucauldian understanding of power has an important contribution to make to our practice of international political theory. Particular mention should be made of the recent work of Hindess (2000a, 2000b, 2002). In a series of essays he has explored how the inter-state system, and its norm of territorialized citizenship, constitutes a dividing practice at the level of the greater human population. As such the inter-state system is not merely the sovereign framework within which the arts of governance have developed, but is itself an art of governmentality.

If Hindess has drawn attention to the political division of the world's population as a condition for its governance, Barry's suggestive work on the European Union has explored more recent problematics of international space, such as European integration, and its arts such as harmonization (Barry 1993, 1996). Here the international division of population and territory becomes a problem rather than a solution, raising the question of how to govern when flows of population cannot be contained by the political boundaries of the state.

While we acknowledge the important contribution of these studies, they are at present somewhat scattered, divided by discipline and theme. One of the aims of *Global Governmentality* is, then, a concentration of effort. By gathering together various engagements with this theme we open up the possibility of stronger resonances and new connections. What might governmentality bring to the various practices of international studies? Conversely, what might it learn from them? How might governmentality offer a different way of understanding such phenomena as inter-state violence, global commerce, regionalization, international debt or humanitarian disasters? Does the intersection of governmentality and the global require us to invent new concepts? If nothing else, the chapters collected here suggest ways of answering such questions. This provides the context for understanding what we mean by global governmentality. We intend it to signal a question of emphasis, focus, and an opening towards new empirical objects and concerns.

Governmentality and the 'global'

This collection is divided into two parts. The first section ('Rethinking key concepts') engages the global through an interrogation of the adequacy of concepts and categories which international studies has relied upon. Addressing the themes of neoliberalism, world order, security and globalization, the chapters in this section challenge us to critically reconsider the content of terms we have come to take for granted. In addition, they demonstrate how governmentality analysis can be usefully combined with concepts from other critical traditions, a move that is especially important if it is to grapple with questions of global power. The chapters in our second section ('Problems, practices, regimes, assemblages') share a similar dissatisfaction with many of the theoretical assumptions of international studies. Where they differ is in their approach. Each is constructed around a particular case study. The net result is to capture some of the variability and express the contextual specificity of international rule.

Rethinking key concepts

With the possible exception of globalization, few terms have captured the social and political sciences quite like that of neoliberalism. Here we note that the term is used in quite different ways in different areas of international studies. Perhaps the first use of neoliberalism was within mainstream international relations during the early 1980s (Katzenstein *et al.* 1999). Whereas realists and neorealists insisted upon the persistence of realpolitik, neoliberals emphasized that in such areas as trade, finance, and energy, under conditions of heightened socio-economic interdependence, one could point to enduring 'regimes' of institutionalized international cooperation. In other words, the outlook for world politics was not as gloomy as most realists implied. There could be lasting, positive-sum systems of cooperation amongst states.

But by the late 1980s a second understanding of neoliberalism had emerged, one that is surely the dominant interpretation today. It is not an academic position within international relations that this second understanding names but a particular political-economic project. This time it is defined in opposition, not to realism, but to projects of domestic governance – most notably the post-war regime of Keynesian welfarism. Here neoliberalism is associated with a series of developments across the fields of economy, society, politics and culture. These include policies such as privatization, deregulation, trade liberalization and marketization; economic phenomena such as the rise of transnational corporations and the power of global financial markets within capitalism; institutional developments such as the growing prominence of international economic institutions (IMF, WTO, etc.); and ideological shifts such as the valorization of the market over the state. Today, neoliberalism is used to denote nothing less than a fundamental restructuring of the world political economy over the last thirty years (Peck and Tickell 2002). Hence, we now see frequent references to the term 'neoliberal globalization'.

Barry Hindess (Chapter 1) suggests the possibility of a different understanding of neoliberalism, in terms of a genealogy of liberalism. Following earlier governmentality analysis, he insists that we can regard liberalism not just as an ideology or political philosophy, but as a rationality of government. However, he also takes issue with Foucault and others who imply that liberalism is only concerned with the government of intra-state relations. By promoting the rule of territorial nation-states over populations, looking to treaties and commerce as the principal means to regulate the interrelations of such states and the conduct of the population within them, Hindess contends that liberalism also governs at a supra-national level. This move allows him to locate contemporary neoliberalism within a wider political field which he calls 'post-imperial liberalism'.

Seen in this light, contemporary neoliberalism is less a response to a generalized crisis of capitalism, and more a mutation within liberal political reason. The emphasis on global markets and the new prominence of international institutions can be seen as a response to the problem of how to govern the world when even the poorest are no longer dependants or subjects but 'citizens' of formally independent states. Whereas the systems of indirect rule that characterized colonialism saw colonial peoples as incapable of development, or in need of strict rule and gradual civilization, such notions have largely been discredited. Under neoliberalism, the policy lexicon of 'good governance' offers a less offensive way to address the question of poverty while at the same time perpetuating a relationship in which the poor are the objects of intervention. By placing the policies of global governance in a line which emerges once colonial forms of rule are no longer politically viable, Hindess suggests a less benign account of these contemporary measures.

If the genealogy of liberalism offers one way to enhance the critical intelligibility of our 'global' present, our next two chapters undertake this task by a different route. In very different ways, Mitchell Dean (Chapter 2) and Gavin Kendall (Chapter 3) challenge the way we understand world order. Like Hindess, Dean urges us not to lose sight of the more coercive forms of power that characterize our present, the co-presence of globalized consumerism with tactics of force, violence, genocide and territorial struggle. But whereas Hindess calls for a wider definition of liberal government, one that retrieves its older associations with the international and pays more attention to its authoritarian aspects, Dean's chapter makes a different move. Like many of our contributors, he suggests that governmentality studies can be usefully combined with other approaches. In this respect, Dean looks to Carl Schmitt – albeit with great caution given Schmitt's highly unsavoury political associations – to help him develop the concept of *'nomos'* or world order. Dean argues that if Foucault offers us a lineage of domestic arts of government then Schmitt names and provides a genealogy of the international order that frames these arts.

Amongst the potential themes Dean draws from this encounter is the profoundly and persistently territorial aspect of rule. There is a marked tendency for theorists of globalization – certainly the first generation of such research – to see a movement towards an informationalized world of speed, networks and compression that involves the transcendence of space. But to think at the level of *nomos* enables us to grasp globalization as only the latest way in which the world has been named and coded, integrated and divided, appropriated and populated. As Dean insists, global markets do not simply spread according to their own dynamic. Instead, there are always the prior acts of force and demarcation which clear the ground for the subsequent operation of 'free market' forces. For Dean, the recovery of the concept of *nomos* is an important antidote to the active forgetting of the violence, coercion, obligation and appropriation that characterizes not only imperialism but also the present.

For Kendall the path to an alternative understanding of global order passes not through the conceptual territory of geopolitics, but through that of 'actor network theory' (ANT). In developing his argument for a more nuanced understanding of global networks, he confronts what many would regard as the heartland of the globalization literature. The question he poses is this: how is it possible to act globally? He insists that we should see the global activities of particular firms or states as sociotechnical accomplishments. Rather than global networks being a new type of generic social arrangement, he argues for an analytical focus on the spatial specificity of networks, exploring how each is constructed from the ground up in ways that always involve human and non-human elements. Globalization is, then, understood as an effect of the piling up of these networks to the point at which they acquire the appearance of order. In making this argument, Kendall does not offer an explicitly 'political' understanding of globalization in the sense of seeking to disclose its silences, its partiality or its less palatable underside. But his observations do have political repercussions. In drawing attention to the constant work of linkage that is required to hold large actors together, Kendall reminds us that the power we associate with global actors is not assured but quite provisional. One sees this clearly with the US-led occupation of Iraq where many of the networks that comprise the US war machine, not to mention the networks which might connect it to a wider 'international community', seem highly frayed and uncertain. Dependent on the maintenance of countless networks, global actors and big powers are more vulnerable than we often suppose.

Questions of security have long been at the heart of the academic discipline of international relations. As the US-led 'war on terrorism' unfolds along unpredictable pathways, and with ramifications we can still barely grasp, we can expect issues of security to remain central preoccupations not just of international experts, but of the media and public. What place exists for an analytics of security? In his lectures on governmentality Foucault discussed at some length the ways in which modern societies were not disciplinary societies so much as 'societies of security' (Gordon 1991: 20). But as Michael Dillon (see Chapter 4) observes, while security may have been a 'pivotal term' in these lectures, it never became an object of sustained analysis for Foucault in the way that, for instance, sexuality did. To this end, Dillon asks what a Foucauldian reading of security might look like. His answers to the question are varied, but at its centre, and setting it apart from both conventional and constructivist understandings of security, would be questions of how the biopolitical and the geopolitical are intertwined in particular discourses of security. Dillon pursues this question in terms of the shifts in the 'specification' of the human. He notes how contemporary geopolitics may have abandoned the explicitly racial 'dogmas' of earlier moments. However, like Hindess, he maintains that the seemingly benign geopolitics of 'global governance', despite its themes of partnership and inclusion, is no less implicated in dividing practices, no less committed to distributing and dispersing population across 'grids of utility and value'. Of particular interest to Dillon, however, is the issue of what happens to politics when humans are understood as information or code. He argues that once power takes the whole of species life as its strategic field of operations, then discourses of security go 'hyperbolic'. Enemies are now those identified as antipathetic to the promotion of the species as a whole, giving rise to a new rationalization for punishment and war.

These four chapters seek to unsettle key terms and concepts within international affairs. They might be placed alongside other studies which have sought to expose other critical terms of international life – such as sovereignty (Bartelson 1995), developmentalism (Escobar 1995) or new regionalism (Larner and Walters 2002) – to genealogical analysis. Moreover, they could fruitfully be complemented by other studies, perhaps of internationalism or cosmopolitanism. In each case, it would be a matter of exploring the different ways in which world space has been made knowable and acted upon. In this way we might begin to see globalism itself as a particular (geo)political rationality rather than a condition, fate or *telos* of humankind (Larner and Walters forthcoming). In other words, we might begin to grasp its particularity.

Problems, practices, assemblages, regimes

The chapters in our first section could be read as contributions to a genealogy of the international. But this is by no means the only way to unsettle some of the assumptions we hold about systems of global power. The chapters in our second section are indicative of another way in which governmentality analysis might fruitfully engage with questions of global power. Each of the chapters in this section deals with a particular zone of problems – development, peacekeeping, crime, refugees, etc. We hesitate to name these as 'policy areas' because in many cases it is the constitution of these issues as sites of policy which is at stake. While the subject matter of these chapters is extremely diverse, they nevertheless share a certain orientation. Instead of conventional approaches which identify a field of interests, institutions, agents, ideas and ideologies, these studies take a different approach. If there is a linking theme it is with the aspiration to identify the regimes and assemblages within which particular agents, practices, objects and subjects are assembled at different locales. In this way they avoid substantializing the international as a domain of forces and dynamics. Instead, they seek to account for the emergence of domains at the level of their practices.

More than the other chapters, the essays by Cristina Rojas (Chapter 5) and Robyn Lui (Chapter 6) exemplify the benefits of an historical perspective for denaturalizing present forms of international order. It is the practice of aid that provides the thread for Rojas' narrative. Paying particular attention to changing problematizations, conceptual spaces, objects and subjects, she charts a series of significant transformations within the governance of global poverty. Her study emphasizes that this is not the story of a timeless poor, or simply the exploitation of the Third World, but of how practices of aid have connected themselves to particular apparatuses of development to produce spatially and temporally differentiated governing subjects. She begins by showing how, early in the twentieth century, the problem of poverty shifted from being one of disease to one of population, and how this shifting problematization in turn shaped, and was shaped by, the involvement of private philanthropists. It was only during the Cold War that aid came to be linked to security, and so became an instrument for the governing of nation-states. By the 1970s aid was understood as a means of promoting nation-state-centred social and economic development, and its management framed within multi-lateral institutions. It was the debt crisis of the 1980s that allowed aid to be linked to structural adjustment, increasingly placing the burden of reform on the poor countries themselves. She shows how the countries of the Third World are now divided into two groups: those who demonstrate qualities conducive to market-led development, and those perceived to be beyond reform and in need of a firmer hand. In this way Rojas is able to highlight the specific ways in which aid has served as an instrument of global governmentality across time and space.

Lui adopts a similar approach but her focus is the refugee. Few identities have served as icons of international disorder quite like this troubled figure. Against those who would see the refugee as a nomadic figure transgressing the state system, or a site of potential cosmopolitanism, Lui insists that this figure speaks to the persistence of the state system and its particular territorialization of citizenship. Similarly, she insists that refugees are far from being the forgotten or ignored subjects of the state system. They are certainly excluded, but they are also intensively disciplined and governed. This point is developed through her concept of 'regime', which she gives a somewhat different understanding to that of international relations theory. For Lui a regime is an ensemble of practices and knowledges. But this regime is far from self-contained or unitary. Taking the case of the refugee question in Africa, she shows how it has been constituted through articulation to another international 'machine' – development. Some of the earliest and most important work in governmentality followed Foucault's lead in exploring the constitution of the outsiders – the mad, the poor, the criminal, the insane (Dean 1991; Procacci 1991). In the obscure margins populated by these subjects, at these social extremities, it sought out the 'capillary' operations of power. In tracing the emergence of 'the refugee' as a subject of power, Lui's chapter suggests ways in which this line of analysis might be projected onto the plane of international life. Reading her compelling study we are left wondering what further lessons we might learn about global power from similar genealogies of identities such as the asylum-seeker, the mercenary or the cosmopolitan.

Gearóid Ó Tuathail and Carl Dahlman (Chapter 7) take up the themes of security and conflict resolution in a specific context – that of Bosnia-Herzegovina. Like Dillon, they draw on critical geopolitics as well as governmentality studies in their efforts to develop an account of the piecemeal assemblage of a specific exercise of security by the 'international community'. In his chapter (see below), Andrew Barry notes the failure of governmentality studies to address the irreducible moment of politics. This is not a charge that can be applied here. On the contrary, Ó Tuathail and Dahlman emphasize that global governmentalities are always entangled in the specific complexities of place. Nor is this complexity reducible to the 'global/local' dichotomy that inhabits many accounts of contemporary rule. This is a conflict which plays out along multiple lines; it is between the adversaries for certain. But it also provides us with a glimpse of the apparatus of modern peace, the enactment of Schmittian *nomos* identified by Dean. In the process of describing the multiple modalities of power found in Bosnia-Herzegovina, Ó Tuathail and Dahlman illustrate how the political world is re-territorialized, albeit in ways that are always contested. They trace how the significance of Bosnia-Herzegovina undergoes a shift – from being a civil war which calls for humanitarian responses, to a new sovereign state involving the disposition and alignment of territory, population and security. In this way we see clearly that governmentalities are constitutive of spaces. The question remains, however, as to what kind of space Bosnia-Herzegovina is? Is it a nation-state or is a new kind of political space, perhaps a space of emergency?

The re-territorialization of political space is underlined, in different ways, by William Walters (Chapter 8) and Roger Dale (Chapter 9) in their efforts to make sense of the European Union (EU). Academic analysis of the EU has been dominated by the specialist literature of European integration theory. Due to its preoccupation with identifying the *causes* and the *processes* of European integration, this body of work has often overlooked some of its other aspects. Taking governmentality as his point of departure, Walters argues we can analyse European integration in terms of its political rationalities and technologies. The EU may lack many of the formal attributes of statehood. Nevertheless, like the state, its capacity to govern has depended upon the adoption of particular arts of government. New histories of European integration are possible, he argues, if we think about the different games and machines which have been employed to assemble a space of European governance. He exemplifies this point with a discussion of the modernization game which, closely associated with the name of Jean Monnet, came to provide a certain diagram for European governance in the early years of the European Community.

With his focus on the rise of the Open Method of Coordination (OMC), Dale considers a more recent art of European governance. Focusing especially on newer fields of European integration, such as education and social policy, the OMC deploys various technologies of performance indicators, benchmarks and policy review, so as to promote a regime of policy evaluation and mutual learning amongst EU member-states. As such, OMC might be seen as the application of the rationalities of advanced liberalism to the space of European governance. For this reason one could certainly read Dale's chapter as a contribution to a genealogy of European integration. But it also makes other important points. For instance, he asks how governmentality might be compared with the concept of 'governance' as this has come to be understood by the policy literature. Though the governance literature and governmentality say similar things about the pervasiveness of governance, they have differing understandings concerning political scale. Governance theorists tend to see different political scales as pre-existing, and argue that governance has involved a re-allocation of power to multiple agencies operating at these different levels. Governmentality encourages a sensitivity to the complex geographies of power that give rise to 'scales', and indeed space more generally. Dale's analysis also encourages governmentality analysts to consider more carefully questions of agency. Like Barry and Ó Tuathail and Dahlman, he is concerned to identify how particular forms of knowledge are embodied in particular actors, not least because this helps explain why the techniques highlighted by governmentality may have different meanings in different contexts.

Two of the most significant developments within the recent study of international relations are the growing concern for the field of ethics, especially human rights and a much greater recognition of the role and significance of non-state actors within international politics. Understanding global governmentality as a realm in which business is increasingly expected to govern at a distance, Andrew Barry (Chapter 10) offers a strikingly original treatment of both these themes. Taking the case of British Petroleum and its bid to build an oil pipeline from Baku in Azerbaijan to Ceyhan on Turkey's Mediterranean coast, Barry explores what he calls the 'ethical assemblage'. This concept allows us to think about ethics as a practical rather than a philosophical activity, one that combines the political activities of non-governmental organizations (NGOs) with various techniques of audit and transparency. It is at the level of the ethical assemblage that 'human rights' have entered into circulation with 'the environment' and 'corruption', as though they naturally belong together. It is in terms of this assemblage that we can pose such questions as: How do corporations become ethical? How is ethics practised, contested and operationalized? But Barry's intervention is important not just for emphasizing the practical dimension of ethics, but also for placing the singularity and irreducibility of political events and political actions at the heart of governmentality analysis. Political events, he stresses, should be at the centre, not the margins, of our histories of government.

If ethics is one way in which business is being governed at a distance, benchmarking is another. In their contribution Wendy Larner and Richard Le Heron (Chapter 11) focus explicitly on the comparative quantitative techniques through which globalizing economic spaces are now known. In developing their genealogy of benchmarking and then focusing on the example of global supply chains, they engage with the broader Foucauldian claim about the extension of the ethos of the market into other realms. They show that international comparisons now extend beyond the firm into economic and social life more generally. If ethics is moving into the commercial realm, benchmarking is moving out. Increasingly organizations and individuals are expected to rate themselves and their activities against the rigours of a wider sphere of reference. In turn, this is giving rise to new economic spaces and subjects. Benchmarking sustains the accelerating momentum that underpins the relentless pursuit for international competitiveness, producing differentiated hierarchies based on an abiding concern with 'best practice'. As with Barry, the case study that grounds this chapter emphasizes the point that global governmentalities are not simply the expression of underlying realms such as 'society' or 'economy', nor do they originate in the deliberate thoughts and actions of particular institutions or actors. In contrast, the task of governmentality is to explore how these realms, institutions and actors come to be known, and to know themselves, in particular ways.

Reflecting on their own field of law and society studies, in our final chapter (Chapter 12) Mariana Valverde and Michael Mopas take global governmentality into yet another terrain. Bigo (2002) has recently thematized a 'governmentality of unease' which frames the securitization of many erstwhile 'domestic' issues such as the treatment of immigrants and the policing of narcotics. Like him, Valverde and Mopas show how ideas taken from Foucauldian-inspired work in this area might assist international relations and political science scholars as they grapple with changing configurations of policing and security. While there is now considerable scholarly interest in the transnationalization of policing practices (Sheptycki 2000), Valverde and Mopas (in Chapter 12 of this volume) insist on the 'persistently, unfashionably *non-global* character of much policing, even of supposedly *international* policing'. As such, they caution against the view of globalization as a force that sweeps evenly across all political and administrative fields.

It is with what we might call the epistemology of security that Valverde and Mopas see some of the most interesting changes in the domain of policing. Here they consider some of the ways that policing has shifted from a logic of discipline to one of risk. In the recent past policing was organized, like social policy and many other sectors of governance under the welfare state, according to a logic of universalism. Today we are witnessing what they call 'targeted governance', which operates along several axes of policing, most notably the information-mediated targeting of problem spaces, populations and particular risk activities. The great merit of this concept is to suggest that developments in very different social domains – think of smart bombs, smart drugs, and smart borders – reveal striking similarities in their governmental logic. As such the idea of targeted governance illustrates what we take to be one of the great strengths of governmentality analysis more generally. By understanding governance as something artful and practical, as a question of style and technique, this approach allows us to peer across different specialist fields and subject areas and identify patterns and logics that might otherwise be missed.

Conclusion

We are conscious that the contributions collected here do not work with, nor add up to, a common definition of global governmentality. This was not our intention when commissioning these chapters. Rather, we saw global governmentality as a provocation, and a relatively open space for dialogue between a series of disparate research projects. The conversation initiated by this book encourages the prospect of a genuinely interdisciplinary research agenda, drawing contributors from such diverse fields as political studies, sociology, economic geography, geopolitics, criminology, international relations, international affairs and education. Moreover, it affirms that governmentality can be fruitfully combined with a variety of other approaches. Collectively, our contributors identify a range of cognate literatures, including actor-network theory, critical geopolitics and poststructuralism. Notable by its absence is feminist theorizing, but elsewhere there is evidence of the important contribution this work also makes to a research agenda focused on the constitutive power of 'global' concepts, practices and subjectivities (Franklin *et al.* 2000; Gibson-Graham 1996).

The diverse positions taken by our contributors should not prevent us from concluding by sketching some possible lines of departure suggested by their arguments. Most immediately, studies of global governmentality can be clearly distinguished from globalization. Much of the globalization discussion is characterized by its realism, that is, by an aspiration to account for the processes, agents, policies and particular events which give rise to a world in which global flows, mobilities and networks disrupt a pre-configured world of nation-states. What we have called global governmentality entails a move of 'bracketing' the world of underlying forces and causes, and instead examining the different ways in which the real has been inscribed in thought. In this context, globalization becomes one particular political imagination amongst many, rather than the underlying logic of an epoch or the outcome of global pressures such as international competitiveness. Indeed, we are struck by how few of our contributors even explicitly engage with the term globalization. Global governmentality encourages us to move past accounts of globalization as grand theory, to be much more nominalistic about the diversity of global spaces, and to focus on the irreducible acts of naming that individuate particular sets of forces, institutions, desires and fears and constitute them as specific territorializations. This approach would do a great deal to 'de-inevitabilize' existing accounts of our (global?) present. Global governmentality invites us to interrogate the political rationality of 'the global', and to place it within a wider space of territorializations, comparing it, for example, to 'the international' or 'the colonial'.

If a distinction can be drawn between globalization and global governmentality, one can also be made between the latter and 'global governance'. Global governance is typically taken to imply a shift in how world affairs are regulated (Held and McGrew 2002). While there is considerable variation in its use, there is some consensus amongst scholars and practitioners that global governance refers to particular trends within the international system since the end of World War Two. These include the increasing significance and institutional density of supra-state regulation, particularly with regard to the governance of transborder or 'global' issues such as trade or the environment; a greater emphasis on international rule-making and political coordination amongst states; but also a greater role for non-state actors and emerging 'global civil society' interests within world affairs.

As an analytical perspective global governance shares with governmentality a recognition that governance does not necessarily issue from a single centre or source (Rosenau and Czempiel 1992). Both emphasize that governance can be pervasive and dispersed. However, governmentality can offer a particular kind of historical perspective that is often lacking in the global governance literature. This would involve seeing global governance as a particular technology of rule and placing it within the much longer trajectory of liberal political reason. Global governance would then appear continuous with the earlier liberal political practices which Foucault (1991) describes. These sought to govern not in the totalizing fashion of police, but by securing processes of population, economy and society that were assumed to possess their own immanent forms of self-regulation. The difference is, as Dean observes in Chapter 2, that with global governance, these apparatuses of security are now generalized across the planet.

The chapters collected here are but early indications of the diverse intellectual projects that might come under the rubric 'global governmentality'. The approach remains provisional and experimental; we have not sought to invest the idea of global governmentality with too much theoretical content. Rather, we have presented it as an injunction to explore the potential of governmentality concepts for thinking about various aspects of international affairs. As such, each chapter tries to move the debate beyond the conventional view of power as something that is possessed by given actors (individual, capital, state) towards an examination of the heterogeneous discourses and practices in terms of which power is exercised. Their commonality is that they disrupt and disturb accepted understandings and open up questions that may not otherwise be asked. In doing so, they show how global governmentality might give rise to new ways of understanding contemporary forms of power.

Notes

1 We can also identify something akin to 'globalized governmentality' in Hardt and Negri (2000). Like Fraser, theirs is a narrative in which one system of power replaces another.
2 See for example Cruikshank (1999); Dean (1995); and Rose (1999).
3 This criticism cannot be levelled at poststructuralists working in international relations such as Campbell (1992), Walker (1993) and Weber (1995). In a similar vein, we note the work of scholars who have developed a programme of critical security studies (Lipschutz 1995).

References

Barry, A (1993) 'The European community and European government: harmonization, mobility and space', *Economy and Society*, 22(3): 314–326.
——(1996) 'Lines of communication and space of rule', in A. Barry, T. Osborne and N.S. Rose (eds) *Foucault and Political Reason: liberalism, neo-liberalism, and rationalities of government*, Chicago: University of Chicago Press.
Barry, A., Osborne, T. and Rose, N. (eds) (1996) *Foucault and Political Reason: liberalism, neo-liberalism, and rationalities of government*, Chicago: University of Chicago Press.
Bartelson, J. (1995) *A Genealogy of Sovereignty*, Cambridge and New York: Cambridge University Press.

Bigo, D. (2000) 'When two become one: internal and external securitisations in Europe', in M. Kelstrup and M.C. Williams (eds) *International Relations Theory and the Politics of European Integration*, London: Routledge.

——(2002) 'Security and immigration: toward a critique of the governmentality of unease', *Alternatives*, 27(1) (supplement).

Burchell, G., Gordon, C. and Miller, P. (eds) (1991) *The Foucault Effect: studies in governmentality*, Chicago: University of Chicago Press.

Campbell, D. (1992) *Writing Security: United States foreign policy and the politics of identity*, Minneapolis: University of Minnesota Press.

Cruikshank, B. (1999) *The Will to Empower: democratic citizens and other subjects*, Ithaca: Cornell University Press.

Crush, J. (1995) *The Power of Development*, London: Routledge.

Dean, M. (1991) *The Constitution of Poverty: toward a genealogy of liberal governance*, New York: Routledge.

——(1995) 'Governing the unemployed self in an active society', *Economy and Society*, 24(4): 559–583.

——(1999) *Governmentality: power and rule in modern society*, London: Sage.

Dillon, Michael (1995) 'Sovereignty and governmentality: from the problematics of the "New World Order" to the ethical problematic of the world order', *Alternatives* 20(3): 323–368.

Escobar, A. (1995) *Encountering Development*, Princeton: Princeton University Press.

Foucault, M. (1991) 'Governmentality', in G. Burchell, C. Gordon and P. Miller (eds) *The Foucault Effect: studies in governmentality*, Chicago: University of Chicago Press.

——(1997) 'Society must be defended', in P. Rabinow (ed.) *Michel Foucault. Ethics: subjectivity and truth. The essential works of Foucault 1954–1984, vol. 1*, trans. Robert Hurley *et al.*, New York: New Press.

Franklin, S., Lury, C., and Stacey, J. (2000) *Global Nature, Global Culture*, London: Sage.

Fraser, N. (2003) 'From discipline to flexibilization? Rereading Foucault in the shadow of globalization', *Constellations*, 10(2): 160–171.

Garland, D. (1997) ' "Governmentality" and the problem of crime: Foucault, criminology, sociology', *Theoretical Criminology*, 1(2): 173–214.

Gibson-Graham, J.-K. (1996) *The End of Capitalism (as we knew it): a feminist critique of political economy*, London: Blackwell.

Gordon, C. (ed.) (1980) *Power/Knowledge: selected interviews and other writings 1972–1977, by Michel Foucault*, New York: Pantheon.

——(1991) 'Governmental rationality: an introduction', in G. Burchell, C. Gordon and P. Miller (eds) *The Foucault Effect: studies in governmentality*, Chicago: University of Chicago Press.

Hardt, M. and Negri, A. (2000) *Empire*, Cambridge, MA: Harvard University Press.

Held, D. and McGrew, A. (2002) 'Introduction', in D. Held and A. McGrew (eds) *Governing Globalization: power, authority and global governance*, Cambridge: Polity.

Hindess, B. (1997) 'Politics and governmentality', *Economy and Society*, 26(2)(May): 257–272.

——(1998) 'Neo-liberalism and the national economy', in M. Dean and B. Hindess (eds) *Governing Australia: studies in contemporary rationalities of government*, Cambridge: Cambridge University Press.

——(2000a) 'Citizenship in the international management of populations', *American Behavioral Scientist*, 43(9): 1486–1497.

——(2000b) 'Divide and govern', in R. Ericson and N. Stehr (eds) *Governing Modern Societies*, Toronto: University of Toronto Press.

——(2002) 'Neo-Liberal citizenship', *Citizenship Studies*, 6(2): 127–143.

Kalpagam, U. (2000) 'Colonial governmentality and the "economy"', *Economy and Society*, 29(3): 418–438.

Katzenstein, P.J., Keohane, R.O. and Krasner, S.D. (1999) 'International organization and the study of world politics', in P.J. Katzenstein, R.O. Keohane and S.D. Krasner (eds) *Exploration and Contestation in the Study of World Politics*, Cambridge, MA.: MIT Press.

Kendall, G. (1997) 'Governing at a distance: Anglo-Australian relations 1840–1870', *Australian Journal of Political Science* 32(2): 223–235.

Kerr, D. (1999) 'Beheading the king and enthroning the market', *Science and Society*, 63(2): 173–203.

Larner, W. and Walters, W. (2002) 'The political rationality of the "new regionalism": toward a genealogy of the region', *Theory and Society*, 31: 391–432.

——(forthcoming) 'Globalization as governmentality', *Alternatives* (forthcoming).

Lipschutz, R.D. (ed.) (1995) *On Security*, New York: Columbia University Press.

Lui-Bright, R. (1997) 'International/national: sovereignty, governmentality and international relations', in G. Crowder, H. Manning, D.S. Matheison, A. Parkin and L. Seabrooke (eds) *Australasian Political Studies 1997: proceedings of the 1997 APSA Conference*, vol. 2, Department of Politics, Flinders University of South Australia.

Marks, J. (2000) 'Foucault, Franks, Gauls', *Theory, Culture and Society*, 17(5): 127–147.

Mitchell, T. (1988) *Colonising Egypt*. New York: Cambridge University Press.

Montaigne, Michel de (1965) *Montaigne's Essays*, Book I, Chapter XXXI, trans. John Florio, London: Dent

O'Malley, P. (1996) 'Indigenous governance', *Economy and Society*, 25(3): 310–326.

O'Malley, P., Weir, L. and Shearing, C. (1997) 'Governmentality, criticism, politics', *Economy and Society*, 26(4): 501–517.

Ong, A. and Collier, S. (eds) (2003) *Global Anthropology: technology, governmentality, ethics*, Oxford: Blackwell.

Pasquino, P. (1993) 'Political theory of war and peace: Foucault and the history of modern political theory', *Economy and Society*, 22(1): 77–88.

Peck, J. and Tickell, A. (2002) 'Neo-liberalizing space', *Antipode*, 34(3): 380–404.

Procacci, G. (1991) 'Social economy and the government of poverty', in G. Burchell, C. Gordon and P. Miller (eds) *The Foucault Effect: studies in governmentality*, Chicago: University of Chicago Press.

Rabinow, P. (1989) *French Modern: norms and forms of the social environment*, Cambridge, MA: MIT Press.

Rose, N. (1999) *Powers of Freedom: reframing political thought*, Cambridge: Cambridge University Press.

Rose, N. and Miller, P. (1992) 'Political power beyond the state: problematics of government', *British Journal of Sociology*, 43(2): 172–205.

Rosenau, J. and Czempiel, E.-O. (eds) (1992) *Governance Without Government: order and change in world politics*, Cambridge: Cambridge University Press.

Salskov-Iverson, D., Hansen, H.K. and Bislev, S. (2000) 'Governmentality, globalization and local practice, *Alternatives*, 25(2): 183–222.

Scott, D. (1995) 'Colonial governmentality', *Social Text*, 43: 191–220.

Sheptycki, J. (ed.) (2000) *Issues in Transnational Policing*, London: Routledge.

Stoler, A. (1995) *Race and the Education of Desire*, Durham: Duke University Press.

Thrift, N. (2001) '"It's the romance, not the finance, that makes business worth pursuing": disclosing a new market culture', *Economy and Society*, 30(4): 412–432.

Walker, R.B.J. (1993) *Inside/outside: international relations as political theory*, Cambridge and New York: Cambridge University Press.

Weber, C. (1995) *Simulating Sovereignty: intervention, the state, and symbolic exchange*, Cambridge and New York: Cambridge University Press.

Part I

Rethinking key concepts

1 Liberalism – what's in a name?[1]

Barry Hindess

What's in a Name? That which we call a Rose
By any other name would smell as sweet.
(*Romeo and Juliet*, Act 2, Scene 2, l. 43)

My title recalls the moment from the balcony scene in *Romeo and Juliet* when Juliet briefly imagines that Romeo could be separated from his name, that he could be appreciated for what he is rather than for what he is called: 'Tis but thy name', she laments, 'that is my enemy; Thou art thyself, though not a Montague'. The audience, of course, knows better – as does Juliet herself, although she would prefer to believe otherwise. Thus, while Juliet's immediate answer to the question suggests that what matters is not the name but the qualities of the thing to which the name is attached, the unfolding tragedy of Shakespeare's play presents a very different view, showing that some names have substantial social and political significance.

Like the play, this paper disputes the answer given by Juliet's fantasy, in this case by showing that the use of the name 'liberalism' can have significant implications for political and historical analysis. Standard academic accounts of liberalism tend to present it, on the one hand, as concerned with relations between the state and its subjects and, on the other, as committed to the promotion and defence of individual liberty and/or private property. Even specialists in international relations and international political economy, who have no truck with the first of these elements, tend to endorse some version of the second. This chapter disputes both. Accounts of liberalism in these terms have been advanced in more or less sophisticated forms, sometimes by supporters of liberalism and sometimes by its critics, and there can be no denying that liberals frequently have strong views about these issues. My claim, then, is not that such accounts are entirely false, but rather that they are all seriously incomplete.

My discussion is particularly concerned to stress, along with international relations and international political economy, the cosmopolitan, supra-state aspects of the liberal tradition. However, if we are to grasp fully the character of this cosmopolitanism, it is also necessary to focus on liberalism's governmental character, that is, on its concern with mundane problems involved in the government of populations. We shall see that this focus undermines the second element of the standard accounts noted above: the view that liberalism is committed to the promotion and defence of individual liberty and/or private property.

I suggest not only that the adoption of this broader view of liberalism fosters a better understanding of the work of central figures in the liberal tradition, but also, more importantly, that it provides a fuller and more powerful account of liberal governmental practice at both national and supra-national levels – and especially of many recent developments which, for want of a better name, tend to be grouped together under the label of neo-liberalism. The first section qualifies the view of liberalism as concerned with relations between the state and its subjects while the second and third focus on liberalism's supposed commitment to the defence of liberty and private property. These are followed by a discussion of what is distinctive about neo-liberalism and a short conclusion.

States and their subjects

International relations specialists will hardly need persuading that liberal thought has always been concerned with the regulation and reorganisation of the international sphere (Richardson 2001). Michael Doyle (1983a, 1983b) has identified a tradition of liberal political thought going back at least to Kant, which sees the development of constitutional government within states as a means of securing peaceful relations between them, while Albert Hirschman (1977) and Michael Howard (1978) have both argued that liberals have been concerned to promote commerce within and between states, in part because this was seen as a means of pacifying states and their rulers. John MacMillan (1998) adopts a broader canvass for his account of liberal internationalism, arguing that early liberal thinkers saw absolutist and feudal relations within states and the Westphalian system of relations between them as mutually supportive components of an overarching illiberal order, with the result that their critiques tended to focus on both the domestic and the international aspects of this overarching order. (I will argue that the intimate connection between liberalism and Western imperialism suggests the need for a broader canvass still). Alternatively, drawing on the Marxist tradition in international political economy, one could argue that liberalism has always been committed to the promotion of capitalism – and this too is to say that it has always had significant international as well as domestic concerns.

The great majority of political theorists today, however, are not international relations specialists, and their accounts of liberalism focus primarily on relations between the state and its subjects and on relations among the subjects themselves. Many ignore the international sphere altogether – Pierre Manent's incisive *An Intellectual History of Liberalism* (1994) is a striking case in point– while those who do not tend to treat it simply as a realm in which to apply and adapt liberal principles initially developed in relation to the domestic sphere. These comments should hardly be controversial, and the example of John Rawls' *The Law of Peoples* will serve here to illustrate my point. Rawls insists that the Law of Peoples 'is developed within political liberalism' and that it must therefore be seen as 'an extension of a liberal conception of justice for a domestic regime to a *Society of Peoples*' (1999: 55).[2] His discussion proceeds, first, by adapting the conventional idea of a social contract to a 'society' whose members are not human individuals but 'liberal democratic peoples', and then by extending the idea of such a society further to include 'decent nonliberal peoples' among its members. He uses the example of 'Kazanistan', an imaginary Muslim people, which 'is not aggressive against other peoples...; honors and respects human rights; ...contains a decent consultation hierarchy' (1999: 5) to illustrate this last category.[3] Finally, Rawls acknowledges that there are peoples in the world who are neither liberal nor decent, but they would not be admitted to membership of his society of peoples and they may well be targets of military or humanitarian intervention by the society of peoples or some of its members.

Rawls' analysis serves to illustrate two striking features of what the academic discipline of political theory normally understands by liberalism. First, liberalism focuses primarily on normative issues, giving little serious consideration to the question of what techniques and mechanisms of regulation and control are or could in fact be used in the government of the populations of contemporary states. Second, and more important for the argument of this section, these normative issues are seen, at least in the first instance, as arising primarily in the domestic sphere – in the relations between a state and its subjects and between the subjects themselves – with the result that the international sphere (Rawls' Society of Peoples) and the treatment to be accorded to non-liberal peoples or states within it are considered entirely on the basis of normative principles which are thought to have been established in the domestic sphere. Liberalism is thus seen as treating the existence of numerous such domestic spheres as given, as an unproblematic starting point for analysis. According to this account, then, the question of how states have come to assume such a prominent role in the government of populations has no bearing on our understanding of liberalism itself.

I return to the significance of this question below, but first we should consider another influential account which describes liberalism as focused on the sphere of intra-state relations. This derives from Michel Foucault's later writings on government. Foucault identifies a certain continuity between the government of oneself, the government of one or a few others, and the government of a state, seeing them all as aiming 'to structure the possible field of action of others' (2001b: 341) or, indeed, of oneself. But he also pays particular attention to the modern revival of the classical view of politics which saw the state as 'by nature clearly prior to the family and to the individual, since the whole is of necessity prior to the part' (Aristotle 1988, 1253a: 19–20). This view of the state implies that a special significance should be attached to 'the particular form of governing which can be applied to the state as a whole' (Foucault 2001a: 206). Foucault proposes to analyse liberalism as concerned with government in precisely this sense: that is, as focusing on:

the welfare of the population, the improvement of its condition, the increase of its wealth, longevity, health, and so on; and the means that the government uses to attain those ends are themselves all in some sense immanent to the population.

(2001a: 217)

What particularly distinguishes liberalism, in Foucault's view, from other approaches to the government of the state is its commitment to governing as far as possible through the promotion of certain kinds of free activity and the cultivation among the governed of suitable habits of self-regulation. He suggests, in particular, that the image of the market plays an exemplary role in liberal political thought: it plays 'the role of a "test", a locus of privileged experience where one can identify the effects of excessive governmentality' (Foucault 1997: 76). The market is thus seen as a decentralised mechanism of government operating at two rather different levels. At the first and most immediate level, individuals are assumed to be governed, at least in part, by the reactions of others with whom they interact. Accordingly, the civilised inhabitants of well-ordered states are normally expected to interact in peaceful and orderly fashion – the market itself providing the most obvious example. We might add, although this point plays no part in Foucault's own discussion, that while the promotion of suitable forms of free interaction may thus be seen as an effective way of dealing with the government of civilised populations, it is likely to be regarded as less appropriate in other cases.

Secondly, over the longer term, interaction with others is thought to influence the internal standards that individuals use to regulate their own behaviour – by affecting, for example, their sense of good and bad conduct, of what is acceptable or unacceptable in particular contexts, and so on. At this level, market interaction itself is seen as a powerful instrument of civilisation, inculcating such virtues as prudence, diligence, punctuality, self-control, etc. (cf. Hirschman 1977; Holmes 1995). Here, too, we can go beyond Foucault's discussion to note the implications of this view for the government of what are perceived as being less civilised populations. It suggests that, if only suitable forms of property can be set securely in place and non-market forms of economic activity reduced to a minimum, then market interaction itself may function as a means of improving the character of less civilised peoples. In this case, authoritarian state intervention to reform property relations and impose conditions that would enable widespread market interaction to take off may be seen as a liberal move towards a situation in which individuals may be governed through their free interactions.

I will argue, in the following section, that this Foucauldian view of liberalism as committed to governing through freedom is far too restricted. What should be noted at this point is simply that Foucault's own account of liberalism and most of the governmentality accounts which have followed his lead[4] have focused on the rationality of the government of the state – that is, on the government of state agencies and of the population and territory over which the state claims authority. Thus, while eschewing political theory's normative pretensions, the governmentality approach has nevertheless tended to share its view that liberalism is concerned primarily with the field of intra-state relations (Hindess 2000). I noted earlier that this view treats the division of the world into the populations of states as given.

Consideration of the manner in which states have come to assume such an important place in the government of populations suggests a more complex view of the governmental problems that liberalism seeks to address. There can be no question here of canvassing the substantial literature on the emergence of the modern system of states and its consequences for modern understandings of politics and government.[5] For our purposes, it is sufficient to observe that the modern system of states has its origins in attempts to bring religious conflicts in seventeenth-century Europe under control, and especially in the 1648 Treaty of Westphalia which, together with a number of related agreements, finally put an end to the Thirty Years War. These agreements effectively transformed the condition of the Western part of Europe, assigning populations that had been subject to overlapping sources of authority to sovereign rulers who were acknowledged as having primary responsibility for the government of populations within their territories.

One of the most important consequences of this transformation is that, where the classical view of politics treats the state as 'the highest of all' communities (Aristotle 1988, 1252a: 5), the creation of the modern system of states signals the emergence of a more complex field of political reason. The state retains its super-ordinate position with respect to its own population but there are now important contexts in which the system of states is itself regarded as 'highest of all'. Modern political reason is certainly concerned with the government of states, much in the manner that Foucault suggests, but it is no less concerned with regulating the conduct of states themselves and the larger population encompassed by the system of states. If we understand government, in its broadest sense, as aiming 'to structure the possible field of action of others' (Foucault 2001b: 341), then this latter concern can also be seen as a matter of government. Thus, adapting MacMillan's (1998) argument that early liberal thinkers saw relations within states and relations between them as mutually supportive components of an overarching order which was in need of political reform, we can suggest that liberalism should be seen as a governmental project concerned not simply with the particular populations of individual states, but also with the larger aggregate population which the system of states encompasses. It addresses this governmental task on two levels: first, by promoting the rule of territorial states over populations; and secondly, by promoting treaties, commerce and other devices to civilise and to regulate the conduct both of states themselves and of those within the particular populations under their authority.

Governing liberty

Liberalism is most commonly regarded as a normative political doctrine or ideology which treats the maintenance of individual liberty as an end in itself and accordingly views liberty as setting limits of principle both to the proper objectives of government and to the manner in which those objectives might legitimately be pursued. Critics have sometimes endorsed this account of liberalism while adding that the liberty it is so concerned to promote is not what it seems (for example, Marcuse 1972). I noted above that, while not perceiving the issue in normative terms, Foucault's account of liberalism as a rationality of government also accords central place to individual liberty: the significance which liberalism attaches to individual liberty, he suggests, is intimately related to a prudential concern that the state might be governing too much, that the attempt to regulate directly certain kinds of behaviour might in fact be counter-productive. According to this account, liberal political reason sees individual liberty as a limit, if not to the legitimate reach of government then certainly to its effectiveness. Governmentality scholars (for example, Dean 1999; Rose 1999) have adapted and extended this account of liberalism to produce a powerful and innovative analysis of contemporary neo- or advanced liberalism's uses of market or auditing regimes and the more general promotion of individual choice and empowerment in the government of domains previously subject to more direct forms of regulation.

Nevertheless, in spite of its productivity in this respect, such an account of liberalism as a rationality of government must be regarded as seriously incomplete. Even if we set the international sphere to one side and treat liberalism as concerned primarily with 'the particular form of governing which can be applied to the state as a whole' (Foucault 2001a: 206), then it will always have to deal with individuals and areas of conduct which seem not to be governable solely through available techniques of governing through freedom (Hindess 2001a). In contemporary Western states, for example, we might note the governmental use of both liberal and 'illiberal' techniques in the criminal justice system, the policing of immigrant communities, the urban poor and indigenous peoples, the provision of social services and the management of public sector organisations. Or again, since even the most liberal of states commonly hold in reserve powers for dealing with conditions of war and states of emergency, it is clear that a developed capacity for coercive rule is regarded as a condition of government through freedom in pacified populations. Finally if, as Foucault suggests, the market plays 'the role of a "test"', then it is surely a test which cuts both ways, suggesting not only that some people and some fields of activity can best be governed through the promotion of suitable forms of free behaviour, but also that there are other cases for which alternative forms of rule will be required.

This suggests not only that liberal government will sometimes decide to make use of 'illiberal' methods but also, more seriously, that the need to make such decisions should itself be seen as a central feature of liberal political reason. What is required for the liberal government of populations, then, is a capacity to distinguish between what can be governed through the promotion of liberty and what must be governed in other ways. The line itself has been drawn in many different ways, but it has been made most commonly in historicist, developmental and gendered terms. Such terms have provided tempting rationales for the authoritarian government of populations, and of households within them, by suggesting that the capacity to be governed as a free agent will be most fully developed among the more cultivated inhabitants of civilised communities, and that, even then, it is likely to be exhibited by men more than by women. My point is simply that liberalism is not necessarily committed to such a gendered or developmental view of human capacities. The governmental promotion of a limited sphere of religious freedom in parts of seventeenth- and eighteenth-century Europe, for example, had no need to draw on historicist views of the differential development of human capacities in the religious communities concerned (Hunter 2001). This suggests that the historicist and developmental view of humanity which played such an important role in the practices of liberal imperialism should not be seen as an indispensable feature of liberal political reason. It was, however, an influential liberal response to the problems of governing, and of understanding, populations not encompassed within the original Westphalian system of states. We should not be surprised if, in addressing these problems, liberals have been tempted to draw upon and elaborate further historicist accounts of the development of human capacities initially derived from the experience of Hispanic rule in the Americas (Pagden 1991). Nor should we be surprised if, by the end of the twentieth century, many liberals had begun to question central features of this historicist vision.

This is not to say that historicist accounts of the development of human capacities should be seen as merely an ideological support for Western imperialism. They provided J.S. Mill with an important part of his argument for increased public participation in politics and, in the hands of the new liberalism of late nineteenth century Britain, served to support a powerful case for the promotion of liberty by the state – through intervention in labour market contracts and working conditions, as well as in housing, education and other areas of social policy (Clarke 1978; Collini 1979). Liberal imperialists, of whom there were many among the new liberals, have commonly seen such historicist views as justifying what they liked to think of as a civilising mission, but many liberal opponents of imperialism – from Adam Smith to J.A. Hobson – held equally historicist views. In any event, my comments on the place of historicist and developmental arguments in the history of liberal political thought are concerned less with questions of justification (the legitimacy of the state or the defence of imperialism) than with the mundane governmental question of how to rule the population of a state or an occupied territory. This is one of the areas in which liberal political thought has often drawn on the expertise of social scientists or colonial administrators.

These last points return us to my earlier suggestion that the adoption of a different view of liberalism can provide us with a better understanding of central figures in the liberal tradition. If we treat liberalism as committed to the maintenance and defence of individual liberty then the active involvement of prominent liberals in the practice of imperial rule must appear incomprehensible, at least in terms of their liberal commitments.[6] Pierre Manent's (1994) discussion of Alexis de Tocqueville's liberalism, for example, completely ignores his defence of and practical involvement in French rule in Algeria, while Jennifer Pitts (2000) and Melvin Richter (1963) insist that the latter can only be regarded as an aberration, as something to be explained away by reference to Tocqueville's nationalism and other non-liberal factors. However, if we take a broader view of liberalism, if we treat the need to distinguish between what can be governed through the promotion of liberty and what must be governed in other ways as central to any serious liberal reflection on the government of states and populations, then the fact of liberal complicity in the practice of imperial rule appears in a very different light. Thus, while Tocqueville's nationalism may help to account for his enthusiastic defence of the French take-over of Algeria, it tells us nothing about his proposals for the government of the subject population, which recommend the promotion of commerce in some contexts and the use of force in others (Tocqueville 2001). To understand these recommendations we must turn to the liberal perception, noted earlier, of the uses of commerce as an instrument of government and, more generally, to the historicist and developmental foundations of Tocqueville's view that the promotion of individual liberty had only a limited place in the government of the people of Algeria.

Nevertheless, while liberal politicians and administrators have clearly acknowledged the necessity of employing authoritarian forms of rule, in many cases it is equally clear that the 'liberalism' elaborated within academic political theory has preferred, at least for the most part, to focus on the defence and promotion of individual liberty, paying little attention to the mundane deployment of authoritarian practices of government and often ignoring the issue altogether. If, as I have suggested, liberalism can hardly avoid the question of what to do about individuals and areas of conduct which seem not to be governable solely through the promotion of suitable forms of individual liberty, how should we account for such a striking disjunction between liberal practice and the 'liberalism' of political theory? An important part of the answer, I suspect, lies in the twentieth-century development of political theory as an academic specialism, closely allied to philosophy, and of 'liberalism' as the dominant school within it. The focus of liberal political theory on matters of principle could then be seen as reflecting the broadly Kantian view that, on the one hand, the realm of pure research (political theory in this case) should be clearly separated from the more applied disciplines to which its subject matter is closely related (law, public administration, public policy) and that, on the other, it should subject the latter disciplines to a critical intellectual oversight (Kant 1979). On this view, the task of liberal theory is precisely to work at the level of normative principles, not to get caught up in the mundane governmental concerns that preoccupy the applied disciplines and their political masters.[7]

While there is much to be said for such a response, we shall see that the disjunction between liberal theory and liberal governmental practice could be observed well before political theory became established as a distinct academic specialism. The argument from the division of academic labour must therefore be supplemented by another kind of answer – to which I turn after considering an alternative account which is far less flattering to the ethical pretensions of liberal theory. I refer, of course, to the charge, frequently levied by critics of liberal imperialism (for example, Césaire 1972; Guha 1997; Said 1992), that this disjunction is a straightforward case of hypocrisy and special pleading.

Like so many smart weapons, this charge seems to me slightly off-target: hypocrisy and special pleading have clearly played an important part in liberal imperialism, as they have in other human endeavours, but there need be no inconsistency in insisting on the value of individual liberty in the metropolitan context and the necessity of authoritarian rule elsewhere. What brings metropolitan liberalism to consort with colonial autocracy is the historicist and developmental view of human capacities noted earlier, which provided politicians and administrators with a means of identifying cases in which the governmental promotion of liberty would not be appropriate at present (Helliwell and Hindess 2002). However, while it served to promote a belief in the necessity for authoritarian rule, this historicist view tended also to generate among imperial administrators and politicians a civilised distaste for the work involved in governing those whose capacities for autonomous action were thought to be relatively undeveloped (Hindess 2001a). Colonial administrators in London or Paris commonly took care to distance themselves from the more unsavoury practices of their subordinates in the field, as did many of those lower down the chain of command.

The writings of John Stuart Mill – who, like his father, spent much of his adult life as a senior officer of the British East India Company – provides some interesting examples of this manoeuvre. In his remarks on the people of British India towards the end of his *Considerations on Representative Government*, Mill observes that, in marked contrast to the enlightened views of the colonial government itself, administrators on the ground will often be tempted to 'think the people of the country mere dirt under their feet' (1977: 571) and to treat them accordingly – and he adds that it will always be extremely difficult for the colonial government itself to eradicate such feelings. This observation, and the more general discussion of imperial rule in which it is located, is revealing in a number of respects: first and most obviously it displays Mill's recognition that distinctly unsavoury practices were an inescapable part of the Company's rule over its Indian subjects; but secondly, in the suggestion that he and his colleagues in London would not themselves have condoned such practices, it also serves to convey a corresponding sense of Mill's own degree of civilisation. Without the help of such distancing manoeuvres, Mill's liberalism would not smell half as sweet.[8]

Promoting markets and commercial property rights

Finally, liberalism has often been seen as particularly committed to the promotion of markets and property rights, at least of the kind that are thought to be necessary to their efficient functioning. I have already noted, for example, that in Foucault's view, the image of the market plays an exemplary part in liberal political thought: it plays 'the role of a "test", a locus of privileged experience where one can identify the effects of excessive governmentality' (Foucault 1997: 76). Liberal commentators have generally attached particular importance to economic freedom (that is, to the legal protection of free markets and private property), seeing it not only as a fundamental source of economic growth but also as a precondition for the emergence of civil society and a politically significant middle class. Economic freedom has thus been seen as securing the political foundations on which other forms of liberty must rest – with some commentators going so far as to suggest that these other forms of liberty may sometimes have to be suppressed in order to ensure the fullest development of economic freedom (for example, Friedman and Friedman 1980). Critics of liberalism, too, have often emphasised the centrality of markets and private property to liberal political thought (Polanyi 1957). They have seen it as an ideology of the bourgeoisie and of international capitalism, aiming to insulate economic power from political control and even, according to one account, giving 'privileged rights of citizenship and representation to corporate capital and large investors' (Gill 1998: 23).

For our purposes, this perspective on liberalism can be seen as a particular case of the more general view of liberalism as committed to the promotion and defence of individual liberty, and it therefore calls for much the same response. Key liberal thinkers and organisations have certainly insisted on the defence and promotion of markets and property rights, but many of them have also taken the view that there are important contexts in which the unconstrained development of market relations would be a threat to the liberty of many individuals – the 'new liberalism' noted earlier (for example, Ritchie 1891) providing a striking case in point. Similarly, many liberals have supported the restrictions placed on commercial relations by the legal, medical and other professions. Or again, during the colonial period liberals generally favoured the reform of property relations among subject peoples but they were also concerned to limit the exposure of certain sectors to what they saw as the destructive impact of markets. More recently, some liberal supporters of free trade (for example, Bhagwati 2002) have argued against the proposed Multilateral Agreement on Investment (MAI), suggesting that states may well be justified in imposing social or environmental obligations on corporate investors.

Here, as in the more general case discussed above, an insistence on maintaining limits to markets and the rights of property should be seen, not as evidence of liberal inconsistency, but rather as reflecting its fundamental *governmental* concern – its concern, that is, with the question of what can sensibly be governed through the promotion of appropriate forms of freedom and what must be governed in other ways. In this case too, liberals have disagreed about where best to draw the line. This is another area in which liberal political thought has often called on the expertise of social scientists and experienced administrators.

Post-imperial liberalism, or what is new about neo-liberalism?

The argument of this chapter has been directed against accounts of liberalism which present it as concerned primarily either with the sphere of relations between a state and its subjects or with the promotion and defence of individual liberty and/or private property. Against the first, I have argued that liberalism has been concerned with regulating the conduct of the aggregate population encompassed within the system of states, and that it addresses this task by allocating responsibility for the government of specific populations to individual states, using treaties, trade and other devices to regulate the conduct of states themselves, and promoting within states appropriate means of governing the populations under their control. Against the second, I have suggested that while liberals have certainly been concerned to promote some kinds of liberty and private property, they have generally located these concerns within the broader task of governing populations. Indeed, it is hardly possible to understand the ways in which liberals have actively participated in the government both of free peoples and of various subject populations unless we acknowledge the significance they have attached to this latter task.

In the course of the imperial era, the greater part of humanity was brought within the remit of the modern system of states either directly through imperial rule or indirectly through the complementary and interdependent deployment of a standard of civilisation, elaborate systems of capitulations which required independent states to acknowledge the extra-territorial jurisdiction of Western states, and what Gallagher and Robinson (1953) call 'the imperialism of free trade' (see also Gong 1984; Fidler 2000). The governmental ambitions of liberalism expanded accordingly. I have suggested that the historicist view of the development of human capacities that one finds in the work of so many liberals throughout the nineteenth century and the first half of the twentieth should be seen as perhaps the most influential – but certainly not the only – liberal response to the problem of governing and understanding populations which were seen as being quite unlike those inhabiting the original Westphalian system of states.

If there is any truth in this last suggestion, then we should expect to find that the need to address the novel governmental problems brought about by the end of colonial rule and the widespread disruption of established systems of capitulations by war or revolution has led to some striking new developments in post-imperial liberalism. Before I bring this chapter to a close, let me suggest that a focus on the supra-national, governmental character of liberalism can help to clarify at least two of these developments: the displacement, which is still far from complete, of the most influential rationale for the civilising pretensions of liberal imperialism, and the emergence of neo-liberalism in both the international and the domestic spheres.

The first of these developments is easily understood. While the historicist view of the development of human capacities flourished in the context of restricted electoral franchise in the constitutional states of Europe and the Americas and direct or indirect imperial rule elsewhere, its utility in the post-imperial context is distinctly limited: it can hardly be invoked without offence, for example, in referring either to the leaders of independent states or, if those states have any pretension to majority rule, to the majority of their populations. Governmental projects of improvement or development remain influential in the post-colonial world but, within those projects, intellectual resources have shifted away from older theories and conceptual frameworks which focused on a supposed incapacity for self-government that could only be removed over a period of generations. They have moved instead towards more politically congenial discourses, those which focus on the less obviously offensive problem of dealing with troublesome structural factors: transforming cultures and values, creating infrastructures, promoting civil society, removing political obstacles to development, combating corruption and so on. In the academy, one striking consequence of this shift has been that, where liberal theory once openly acknowledged that the greater part of humanity was not yet able to cope with the demands of self-government, it now tends to insist that the most substantial obstacles to autonomous conduct are to be found in external conditions: if only these can be brought into line, it suggests, then we are all of us capable of a significant degree of autonomy.

As for the second development – the rise of neo-liberalism – we can begin by noting that the historicist vision of a hierarchy of social conditions and a corresponding need to bring about the improvement of the less advanced remains in place but, following the end of empire, the civilising mission can no longer be pursued in its earlier imperial guise. The discourse of improvement has taken a different form, in part for the political reasons just noted, and liberalism's civilising mission is now pursued both by significant minorities in the ex-imperial domains themselves – as it was, in fact, during the colonial period – and by the liberal West itself. But, where it could once rely on the decentralised despotism (Mamdani 1996) of indirect rule over colonial subjects, the Western version of liberalism's civilising mission now has to work through an even less direct form of decentralised rule, reminiscent in many respects of the older system of capitulations (Fidler 2000), in which the inhabitants of post-colonial successor states are governed through sovereign states of their own.

Indirect rule now operates through national and international aid programmes that assist, advise and constrain the conduct of post-colonial states, through international financial institutions and also, of course, through that fundamental liberal instrument of civilisation, the market – including the internal markets of multinational corporations. In the immediate post-colonial period, many of these programs sought to promote development through state planning, with a consequent emphasis on bureaucratic control and technical expertise. However, as we move further away from the decolonisations of the mid-twentieth century, the use of markets to regulate the conduct of states and of governments within them has become increasingly prominent. As a result, the good governance programs promoted by international development agencies seem designed to ensure that the freedom of action of governments is severely constrained by both internal and international markets.

Good governance is also seen as involving the implementation of basic human rights and democracy – in the sense that the governments of states are expected to be at least minimally responsive to the wishes of their citizens and the citizens in turn are expected to own, or at least to go along with, the policies of their government. Indeed, the language of 'ownership' now plays an important part in development discourse. Joseph Stiglitz, while Vice-President of the World Bank, described the Bank's proposed Comprehensive Development Framework as involving 'a new set of relationships, not only between the Bank and the country, but within the country itself.... Central is the notion that the country (*not just the government*) must be in the driver's seat' (1999: 22–3, emphasis added; see also Wolfensohn 1999).

This stress on ownership and participation reminds us of the importance in the development field of an aspect of neo-liberalism which has been a particular focus of governmentality analysis: namely, the governmental use of empowerment, responsibility and self-control as instruments of regulation (cf. Cooke 2003). Thus, far from being a fundamentally disciplinary enterprise, as Stephen Gill (1995) insists, contemporary neo-liberalism combines its disciplinary focus with an emphasis on empowerment and self-government: the promotion of reforms designed to limit the freedom of action of governments, and therefore the ability of citizens to influence those actions, goes hand in hand with the promotion of democracy. While modern democracy allows citizens only a limited role in the government of the state to which they belong, it is often thought to secure a degree of legitimacy for the activities of the state which other regimes are simply unable to match (Hindess 2002). It is this, rather than the expansion of popular control itself, that particularly appeals to the development agencies and financial institutions which promote democracy as a fundamental component of good governance.

This last point bring us, finally, to the late twentieth-century growth of neo-liberalism. If there is a common thread linking the many late twentieth century projects of neo-liberal reform, both within particular states and in the international arena, it lies in the attempt to introduce not only market and quasi-market arrangements but also empowerment, self-government and responsibility into areas of social life which had hitherto been organised in other ways – the corporatisation and privatisation of state agencies, the use of financial markets (and credit-rating agencies) to regulate the conduct of states, the promotion of competition and individual choice in health, education and other areas of what Western states once regarded as the proper sphere of social policy, etc. The image of liberalism as concerned primarily with relations between the state and its subjects invites us to treat neo-liberalism in similar terms: that is, as something which emerges first in response to domestic conditions in, say, the UK, USA and New Zealand, and only later spreads to other states and the international arena. The argument that liberalism has always had a significant cosmopolitan and governmental character suggests a very different view. It tempts us to place the development of neo-liberalism together with the emergence of the new regime of indirect rule just noted: to speculate, in fact, that the problem of governing the post-colonial system of states may be one of the more important sources of this vastly increased emphasis on the governmental uses of the market.

Conclusion

What, then, does the name liberalism bring to mind? In the names of Romeo and Juliet we see death at an early age, while liberalism, in contrast, appears to go from strength to strength: what we see in it is a long and productive life. But, since I began by transposing Juliet's question into the specialised context of academic debate, another kind of answer is called for here. I have argued, first, that liberalism should be seen as focusing both on the field of intra-state relations and on the larger field of international relations in which the internal affairs of individual states are located. It should be seen, secondly, as concerned not only, and certainly not always, with the promotion and defence of individual liberty or private property, but also with the government of populations – both within the territories of individual states and more generally. I have suggested, finally, that there is no singular unity to which the name 'liberalism' refers: rather, there are as many liberalisms as there are procedures for identifying contexts in which the governmental promotion of free interaction is to be preferred.

This last point suggests that there may be little of value to be said for or against, or even simply about, liberalism in general. In practice, however, while they differ, sometimes vehemently, over points of detail, it is not difficult to group the many different liberalisms into a number of distinctive streams which divide and recombine as they meander through the infested marshlands of modern history. By far the most influential of these streams have passed over the fertile soils of enlightenment rationalism and remain coloured by the historicist and developmental view that the greater part of humanity remained in considerable need of improvement. It is here that we find the laissez-faire liberalism of the market; the new or social liberalism of the late nineteenth century and its welfarist progeny; the various national liberalisms, all of which favoured state intervention to control the effects of market relations; and the imperial and anti-imperial liberalisms of the colonial era.

Many of these streams continue, but the main flow has been diverted into other channels, in part by the decolonisations of the mid-twentieth century and the consequent reorganisation of the international system of states. The liberal mainstream has abandoned the historicist and developmental vision of humanity, at least in public, and taken up a less directly offensive perspective on the obstacles to social and economic development. There remains, of course, an influential liberal literature on contemporary 'quasi-', 'rogue' or 'pre-modern' states (Cooper 1996; Jackson 1990) which, in suggesting that such states may be a threat to the international community or to their own inhabitants, implies that the principle of non-intervention may sometimes need to be relaxed. But even this literature is careful to avoid the claim, which many nineteenth-century liberals took for granted, that the problem in such cases is that the inhabitants of these states are not sufficiently advanced to govern themselves. Likewise, the old imperial instruments of direct and indirect rule have been replaced by a greatly expanded use of markets, empowerment and self-government as regulatory devices, albeit still with military intervention remaining in play as a last resort.

This international neo-liberalism is the most powerful, and consequently also the most dangerous, liberalism of our time.

Notes

1   This paper appears as part of a collaborative project, 'Government, Social Science and the Concept of Society', which is supported by the Australian Research Council, and it draws on numerous discussions with my collaborators, Bruce Buchan and Christine Helliwell. This final version has also benefited from seminar discussions at Adelaide and Newcastle universities and the ANU, and the advice of Carol Johnson, Marian Sawer and the editors of this volume.

2   Some of Rawls' liberal critics go further, suggesting that the international sphere should itself be seen as a society not of peoples or of states, as Rawls proposes, but ultimately of individuals (for example, Beitz 2000; Caney 2002; Pogge 2001). On this view, too, principles of justice that are thought to hold within liberal states should in fact be applied more widely.

3   The fact that this example is imaginary suggests that Rawls sees the Islamic world as containing neither liberal democratic peoples nor decent non-liberal peoples. The geopolitical implications of this view play directly to an influential American paranoia about a looming clash of civilisations.

4   Some of the exceptions have been noted in the Introduction to this volume.

5   See the different accounts in Held (1995); Hirst (1998); Schmitt (1950); and Walker (1993).

6   Various aspects of this involvement have been documented in the British case by Mehta (1999); Stokes (1959); van der Veer (2001); and Zastoupil (1994).

7   In a closely related argument Osborne and Rose (1997) note that histories of sociological thought tend to focus on developments in theory, thereby neglecting the work of practitioners in establishing new ways of knowing the social.

8   Perhaps the most striking illustration of this point is to be found in Mill's *Autobiography*, which carries the image of a division of labour between liberal theory and liberal governmental practice to the extreme of suggesting that his direct involvement with the latter had no real influence on his understanding of the former. Zastoupil (1994) shows just how misleading the *Autobiography* is in this respect.

References

Aristotle (1988) *The Politics*, Cambridge: Cambridge University Press.

Beitz, C. (2000) 'Rawls's Law of Peoples', *Ethics*, 110: 669–696.

Bhagwati, J.N. (2002) *Free Trade Today*, Princeton: Princeton University Press.

Caney, S. (2002) 'Cosmopolitanism and the law of peoples', *The Journal of Political Philosophy*, 10(1): 95–123.

Césaire, A. (1972) *Discours sur la Colonialisme*, Paris: Présence Africain.

Clarke, P. (1978) *Liberals and Social Democrats*, Cambridge: Cambridge University Press.

Collini, S. (1979) *Liberalism and Sociology: L. T. Hobhouse and political argument in Britain 1880–1915*, Cambridge: Cambridge University Press.

Cooke, B. (2003) 'A new continuity with colonial administration: participation in development management', *Third World Quarterly*, 24(1): 47–61.

Cooper, R. (1996) *The Post-modern State and the World Order*, London: Demos.

Dean, M. (1999) *Governmentality: power and rule in modern society*, London: Sage.

Doyle, M. (1983a) 'Kant, liberal legacies, and foreign affairs, part one', *Philosophy and Public Affairs*, 12(3): 205–235.

——(1983b) 'Kant, liberal legacies, and foreign affairs, part two', *Philosophy and Public Affairs*, 12(4): 323–353.

Fidler, D.P. (2000) 'A kinder, gentler system of capitulations? International law, structural adjustment policies, and the standard of liberal, globalized civilization', *Texas International Law Journal*, 35: 387–413.

Foucault, M. (1997) 'The birth of biopolitics', in P. Rabinow (ed.) *Michel Foucault. Ethics: subjectivity and truth. The essential works of Foucault 1954–1984, vol. 1*, trans. Robert Hurley et al., New York: New Press.

——(2001a) 'Governmentality', in J.D. Faubion (ed.) *Power. The essential works of Foucault, vol. 3*, London: Allen Lane.

——(2001b) 'The subject and power', in J.D. Faubion (ed.) *Power. The essential works of Michel Foucault, vol. 3*, London, Allen Lane: The Penguin Press.

Friedman, M. and Friedman, R. (1980) *Free to Choose*, Harmondsworth: Penguin.

Gallagher, J. and Robinson, R. (1953) 'The imperialism of free trade', *The Economic History Review*, VI (Second Series) (1): 1–15.

Gill, S. (1995) 'Globalization, market civilization, and disciplinary neoliberalism', *Millennium*, 24: 399–423.

——(1998) 'New constitutionalism, democratisation and global political economy', *Pacifica Review*, 10(1): 23–38.

Gong, G.W. (1984) *'The Standard of Civilization in International Society*, Oxford: Oxford University Press.

Guha, R. (1997) 'Not at home in empire', *Critical Inquiry*, 23(Spring): 482–493.

Held, D. (1995) *Democracy and the Global Order: from the modern state to cosmopolitan governance*, Cambridge: Polity.

Helliwell, C. and Hindess, B. (2002) 'The "empire of uniformity" and the government of subject peoples', *Cultural Values*, 6(1): 137–150.

Hindess, B. (2000) 'Divide and govern: governmental aspects of the modern states system', in R. Ericson and N. Stehr (eds) *Governing Modern Societies*, Toronto: University of Toronto Press.

——(2001a) 'The liberal government of unfreedom', *Alternatives*, 26(2): 93–111.

——(2001b) 'Not at home in the empire', *Social Identities*, 7(3): 363–377.

——(2002) 'Neo-liberal citizenship', *Citizenship Studies*, 6(2): 127–143.

Hirschman, A.O. (1977) *The Passions and the Interests*, Princeton: Princeton University Press.

Hirst, P. (1998) 'The international origins of national sovereignty', in *From Statism to Pluralism*, University College London: London Press.

Holmes, S. (1995) *Passions and Constraints: on the theory of liberal democracy*, Chicago: University of Chicago Press.

Howard, M. (1978) *War and the Liberal Conscience*, London: Temple Smith.

Hunter, I. (2001) *Rival Enlightenments: civil and metaphysical philosophy in early modern Germany*, Cambridge: Cambridge University Press.

Jackson, R.H. (1990) *Quasi-states: sovereignty, international relations and the Third World*, Cambridge: Cambridge University Press.

Kant, I. (1970) 'Idea for a universal history'and 'Perpetual peace', both in H. Reiss (ed.) *Political Writings*, Cambridge: Cambridge University Press.

——(1979) *The Conflict of the Faculties*, Lincoln, NE and London: University of Nebraska Press.

MacMillan, J. (1998) *On Liberal Peace: democracy, war and the international order*, London and New York: I.B. Tauris.

Mamdani, M. (1996) *Citizen and Subject: contemporary Africa and the legacy of late colonialism*, Princeton: Princeton University Press.

Manent, P. (1994) *An Intellectual History of Liberalism*, Princeton: Princeton University Press.

Marcuse, H. (1972) *One Dimensional Man*, London: Abacus.

Mehta, U.S. (1999) *Liberalism and Empire: a study in nineteenth-century British liberal thought*, Chicago: University of Chicago Press.

Mill, J.S. (1977[1865]) 'Considerations on representative government', in J.M. Robson (ed.) *Collected Works of John Stuart Mill*, Toronto: University of Toronto Press.

Osborne, T. and Rose, N. (1997) 'In the name of society, or three theses in the history of social thought', *History of the Human Sciences*, 10(3): 77–104.

Pagden, A. (1991) *European Encounters with the New World*, New Haven: Yale University Press.

Pitts, J. (2000) Empire and democracy: Tocqueville and the Algeria Question', *Journal of Political Philosophy*, 8(3): 295–318.

Pogge, T. (2001) 'Rawls on international justice', *The Philosophical Quarterly*, 51: 246–253.

Polanyi, K. (1957) *The Great Transformation*, Boston: Beacon.

Rawls, J. (1999) *The Law of Peoples*, Cambridge, MA: Harvard University Press.

Richardson, J. (2001) *Contending Liberalisms in World Politics*, Boulder: Lynne Reiner.

Richter, M. (1963) 'Tocqueville on Algeria', *Review of Politics*, 25: 362–398.

Ritchie, D. (1891) *The Principles of State Interference*, London: Swan Sonnenshein.

Rose, N. (1999) *Powers of Freedom: reframing political thought*, Cambridge: Cambridge University Press.

Said, E.W. (1992) 'Nationalism, human rights, and interpretation', in B. Johnson (ed.) *Freedom and Interpretation: the Oxford Amnesty Lectures, 1992*, New York: Basic Books.

Schmitt, C. (1950) *Der Nomos der Erde, im Volkerrecht des Jus Publicum Europaeum*, Cologne: Greven.

Stiglitz, J. (1999) *Participation and Development: perspectives from the Comprehensive Development Paradigm*, Seoul: World Bank.

Stokes, E.T. (1959) *The English Utilitarians and India*, Oxford: Clarendon Press.

Tocqueville, A. de (2001) *Writings on Empire and Slavery*, ed. Jennifer Pitts, Baltimore: Johns Hopkins University Press.

van der Veer, P. (2001) *Imperial Encounters: religion and modernity in India and Britain*, Princeton: Princeton University Press.

Vincent, A. (1995) *Modern Political Ideologies*, Oxford: Blackwell.

Walker, R.B.J. (1993) *Inside/Outside: international relations as political theory*, Cambridge: Cambridge University Press.

Wolfensohn, J.D. (1999) *A Proposal for a Comprehensive Development Framework*, Washington, World Bank.

Zastoupil, L. (1994) *John Stuart Mill and India*, Stanford: Stanford University Press.

2 *Nomos* and the politics of world order[1]

Mitchell Dean

Whether for conservatives, liberals or radicals, the question of world order has once again become fashionable. In an empirical sense it is our apparent inability to answer such a question which presses us most. It is now some time since the end of the Cold War, the 'balance of terror that provided the functional equivalent to a stable world order' (Ulmen 1996b: 4). We stand today at the official conclusion of the most recent Iraq war and at yet another phase of the War on Terror initiated by George W. Bush after the attacks of September 11, 2001. Security has once again become a key political concept and has formed the principle rationale for the reorganization of United States federal government agencies and the establishment of the Department of Homeland Security. One senior British diplomat proposes that a pacific post-modern world must confront zones of pre-modern chaos and a modernist world of states, nationalism, and power plays (Cooper 2000). This results in a kind of liberal imperialism in which we need to '...get used to the idea of double standards':

> Among ourselves, we operate on the basis of laws and open cooperative security. But when dealing with more old-fashioned kinds of state, we need to revert to the rougher methods of an earlier era – force, pre-emptive attack, deception, whatever is necessary.
>
> (2000: 37)

There are also discussions of the widening and fundamental differences between the United States and Europe rooted in relative strength and weakness and historical experiences which gives rise to different political psychologies: one Hobbesian, unilateralist and focused on security; the other Kantian, diplomatic and modulated through international law (Kagan 2002). There are continuing discussions of globalization and, most importantly, the claim that *it* has become the new world order (Friedman 2000). The treatment of refugees by many nation-states would seem to at least present limits to such a thesis. More pessimistically, the events of September 11 appear to confirm those new maps of international relations in which a 'clash of civilizations' replaces Cold War divisions (Huntington 1996). On cue, the fall of the Berlin Wall meets a terrible symmetry in the erection of the security fence or wall around and in the West

Bank to secure Israelis against suicide bombers. What amounts to international law, articulated through the United Nations and its Security Council regulations, has been recently called into question by the behaviour of the US-led 'coalition of the willing' in making a 'pre-emptive strike' upon a member nation, Iraq, on the suspicion that it might possess 'weapons of mass destruction' and before a UN weapons inspection process had been able to run its course. So we are left to wonder where we might stand in relation to questions of international law and order and notions of sovereignty and security. Can what we have amount to some kind of global law and order which, whatever the costs, at least has the benefit of providing a collective framework for security and peace? Or is the world one in which security can be provided for only by the interventionist might of the 'lonely superpower' (and its regional deputies) and in which there is no real rule of international law? The point of this chapter is not so much to answer the question of what *is* the current world order but how is it possible to think about such questions in the first place. What do we mean when we talk about world order, what are the conditions and consequences of such a notion? Here I suggest that the notion of world order can be approached from any number of perspectives: from that of the spatiality and materiality of power relations; from philology and conceptual history; from what I call, following Connery (2001), 'geo-mythography'; and from the interconnected genealogies of international law and war and peace. I shall also offer some connections with the genealogy of the arts of government as conceived by Foucault. Because I want to argue that the spatiality of power relations cannot be divorced from elemental mythologies of the Earth, and of land, sea and air, I shall start the discussion with two emblems of the problem: a drawing and a legend from Plato.

Two emblems of world order

I have been fascinated by two emblems of this problem of world order. The first is a pen drawing, a caricature.[2] The face is of an old man with large ears, sagging neck and tired eyes. The hands of the man are wrapped around a ball, again marked with vertical and horizontal lines. Facing us are the familiar outlines of the Atlantic and the contours which suggest the continents of the Americas to one side and Europe and Africa to the other. These features mean that we understand that the ball is the globe, and its lines are the latitudinal and longitudinal meridians of the Earth. The man's head is at least twice as large as the globe. His eyes neither look at the globe nor at the viewer. They have seen much and the head tilts slightly with a silent but fraught wisdom. He seems asleep or perhaps in a trance, a kind of profound meditation. We might say he's 'got the whole world in his hands' – in the words of an old spiritual – but he doesn't seem very happy about it.

Now we can imagine that this old man might spin the globe on its axis first in one direction and then the next. As he spins it, he asks himself, does the world have the neat order that is represented by the lines on this globe? As it spins on its own axis and follows its rotation around the sun, is it moving from disorder to order or from order to disorder? He asks himself about the globe's portents and promises. He has given answers to these questions. His weariness suggests that he knows that it is a place of much less order, much more chaos, anarchy and danger than the tidy meridians of the globe suggest, and that those meridians indicate only a *project* for the spatial and political ordering of the planet and hence a system of imposition of order and a form of domination. From the perspective of knowledge he is like God. He knows how this world might be rotated to produce order. But from the perspective of action, he is merely the impotent old man who, even if he once sought to make a difference to this world, can only contemplate its degeneration into chaos and catastrophe.

Something of this same problem is found in a discussion in Plato's *Statesman* in which the question at issue is the nature of the politician and his relation to the figure of the shepherd. In order to show that the politician is not a shepherd, the Stranger takes young Socrates though a legend of the reversal of the spinning of the universe around an infinitely small axis. In the first motion, God (Cronus) moves the universe in one direction; in the second, he lets go, and the universe moves in the opposite direction. During the first movement, God was in charge. He was the shepherd of the life of mankind. It is an age of innocence and abundance, one without states and families, because humans did not need such institutions. God cared and provided for them. It was a time when humans lived in the open air without clothing or bedding '...for the climate was tempered for their comfort, and the abundant grass that grew out of the earth furnished them with soft couches' (Plato 1952: 59). The creatures of the Earth, from our present perspective, aged backwards. Because they started in their graves in the ground, and developed backward to become scattered seed, they were an 'earth-born race'. Thus the movement of the universe engenders a temporal sequence. After this movement had fulfilled its allotted cycles, the Great Helmsman threw down his tiller and withdrew to a place of observation as 'fate and innate desire made the earth turn backwards'. As beginning and end collided in an earthquake, an episode of disturbance and confusion reigned. Humans could only pull themselves out of this fix with the gifts of the gods and with the wise activity of their leaders.

This is clearly a story about 'the order of the world', although the image is of the turning of the universe rather than that of a globe. Like the picture of the man, it presupposes a place from which such a story can be told, a position which is similar to that of God, at least in terms of knowledge. We might say it is a position of epistemological sovereignty. The story suggests that without that guidance there is an order of the world which is intrinsic to itself. But it is one in which we are never sure whether we are moving in the right direction. For the initial movement to disorder in the present rotation must be combated not only by the skill and cultivation of human labour but also by the proper role of the politician and legislator. As we know from *The Statesman*, that role is not that of the shepherd. Human rulers are much closer to their subjects than the Divine Shepherd is to his flock. The metaphor of the shepherd is inappropriate for all sorts of reasons – the politician does not feed his flock, or educate them, or heal them. This is left to the farmer, the teacher or the physician. They all have greater claims to be shepherds than the politician. The role of the politician is better described by the art of weaving: of the interweaving of the different characters of humans by common beliefs, honours, interchanges and pledges. That role is to draw them together 'by friendship and community of sentiment into a common life ... omitting nothing which ought to belong to a happy state...' (Plato 1952: 195).

For Plato, then, the question of political activity is connected to a universe which has its own laws, but which requires the politician and the legislator to bind citizens, slaves, women and children together into a 'well-woven fabric', 'the most glorious and best of all textures' (1952: 195). In this legend the world has an order. Yet bereft of the pastoral care of God, that order tends to barbarity and evil and it is the politician or the king who needs to establish the interweaving that binds humans into a happy state and then rule and watch over them.

Michel Foucault (2001) once made much of the impugning of the metaphor of the shepherd in Plato and in Greek thought generally and held that the forcing together of the 'shepherd-flock' game and the 'city-citizen game' in modern welfare states had 'demonic' potentiality. His is a strange voice to enlist in a discussion of world order given the priority he gave to a 'micro-politics' against global accounts of power and state, and how little he had to say about the stuff of world-order discussion: diplomacy, war, conquest, colonialism, and so on. His later work on 'governmentality' is concerned mainly with the arts of government deployed in domestic as opposed to foreign affairs. Yet his analysis of the emergence of these domestic arts of government is at least implicitly framed within a narrative about the European state system which has for its symbol the international order if not inaugurated at least consolidated by the Peace of Westphalia of 1648 (Foucault 1991).

The other man who rejected the image of the shepherd-ruler and predicted a similar crisis of the transformation of political community into an administrative and managerial state concerned with providing for everyone was the one drawn in the picture we first described (Ulmen 1993: 45). That man is Carl Schmitt. A constitutional jurist, a Roman Catholic national conservative in the Weimar republic whose rapprochement with Nazism is intensely troubling. A flawed character. But, nonetheless, often a brilliantly clear author of extraordinary, changing and jagged insight (Balakrishnan 2000). In his weariness, after his interrogations at Nuremberg,[3] however, he was still able to summon up the strength to make what a recent author has called '...the last serious attempt to think through the materiality and spatiality of the earth as a whole in philosophical terms...' (Connery 2001: 176). He did so in a book called *The Nomos of the Earth* and in associated writings (Schmitt 1950, 1993, 1996b). He might be hailed by some as 'the Hobbes of the twentieth century' (Schmitt 1985: xiv), and perhaps as the Hugo Grotius also, but when he died in 1985, *Time* magazine's obituary was short and ended with the claim that Schmitt 'avoided prosecution as a war criminal at Nuremberg and later largely kept his vow to retreat "into the security of silence"'.

Given the immensity and imaginative force of his post-war work on international affairs, particularly relevant to what today passes as discussion of world order, this sentence seems like a classic case of wish-fulfilment on behalf of a quasi-official organ of the American order he relentlessly analysed. Schmitt names and provides a genealogy of the international order which frames Foucault's lineage of domestic arts of government. For him, it is an order which lasts from the seventeenth to early twentieth century and which regulates the relations among European states and their colonial empires – the *ius publicum Europæum* or European international public law. This system, according to Schmitt, is the first and perhaps the only coherent system of global international law ever seen across the face of our planet. Its demise starts with the Versailles Treaty and the formation of the League of Nations, and continues through the cataclysms of the first half of the twentieth century and the system of mutual terror of the Cold War that follows. Schmitt's genealogy of world order – or rather of the *nomos* of the Earth – thus takes the form of an elegy to this system of international law and order. But while we might present Schmitt as the last conscious representative of the *ius publicum Europæum*, we could perhaps consider Foucault's genealogy of the arts of government as tracing the active forgetting within European political consciousness of the dependence of those arts on a *nomos* which logically precedes them and an order of law and sovereignty that historically frames them. One might conjecture that Foucault in this regard is simply exhibiting a trait characteristic of contemporary European thought and consciousness in general. And the revival of cosmopolitanism, stories of individualization, the diagnosis of the decline of sovereignty and the nation, and the themes of governance and networks, new economies, regions and globalization itself, appear everywhere in contemporary European thought as testimonies to the massive effort of the forgetting of *nomos*.[4] With certain exceptions noted later, where the *nomos* returns in contemporary European thought it appears only as chaos, complexity, disorder, as a new *imperium* which refuses the responsibility of actually ruling (Joxe 2002).

If one moves to the other side of the old man's globe, from Europe to the Western hemisphere and the Americas, one finds a different story. From the United States, there is no shortage of attempts to discuss world order. For here History has ended, the Last Man cometh, civilizations clash, global forces crash the Lexus car into the olive tree in a new political order. And America and Europe go their separate ways, at least in thought (Kagan 2002). One wonders whether there is not something to this last idea. From the position of the hegemon, American thought takes up something like the posture of the old man toward the globe, or the retiring God of Plato, at times optimistically (Fukuyama 1992; Friedman 2000), at times pessimistically (Huntington 1996; Mearsheimer 2001). But it does so in order to advise the statesman on the best course of action. It adopts a posture of policy making.

Without doubt these texts are part of a much longer 'genealogy of globalization' which traces the path from which the world is appropriated first in the form of a representation as a globe and then as a project of globalization, that is, a project to integrate the world into a single world order (Karnooh 2002). But is not this genre, if we could call it that, one characterized by a kind of arrogance, by hubris? Perhaps Plato's form of story telling is better than, say, the liberal metaphysics of Fukuyama. Maybe a concern for the political and spatial order of the Earth as a whole better falls within the province of legend rather than science, and when science pretends to do so, it ends up making and mapping myth.[5] Perhaps these works are those of the 'geo-mythographer' and thus operate best through journalistic metaphor like that found in the work of Friedman (2000). And maybe the question of order itself is a symptom of a conservative style of political thought which is concerned with authority, hierarchy and command and its imposition and not the active networks of individuals and groups engaged in either ethical or economic conduct, as contemporary social and political thought would have it. The one attempt to take the vantage point of the active doings of 'the multitude' who provoke authority, power and sovereignty to take new forms across the face of the planet is Hardt and Negri's (2000) *Empire* which, for all its shortcomings and undoubted hubris, at least links the 'old world' of American reason of state to the 'new world' of European civil society. It is of course purely coincidental that it was written by a convicted Italian terrorist and an American literary critic.

And yet, in this vast literature across continents, an historical sociology of knowledge might like to discuss the absence of a concept, of an attempt to conceptualize what we might mean by a world order, what its preconditions might be, how we might separate its analytic from its normative content.[6] Schmitt, who lived through – and has an undeniable moral complicity in – the last catastrophic attempt to constitute a European-based terrestrial order against the twin faces of Atlanticism and Soviet Communism, emerges after the war tired and pessimistic. He is not triumphant like contemporary American thinkers. Yet he is the only one to have thought about the necessity of addressing the basic question: how do we think about world order, and given that we can begin to understand what it is we are talking about, what is its genealogy? For Schmitt the genealogy of the *nomos* of the Earth is also a genealogy of war and of peace. We do not have to adopt Schmitt's posture as the last representative of a grand European tradition, weary at its passing and fearful of what is replacing it, to begin again to address such questions.

Perspectives on *nomos*

According to Schmitt (1993: 53), *nomos* is usually translated by jurists and historians as law in the sense of tradition or custom. Rather than a simple noun, the word is a *nomina actionis* which indicates an action as a process whose content is given in the verb. The primary sense of the word, following his argument, is given by the Greek verb *nemein*, meaning to take, to allot and to assign. Schmitt himself uses the term 'appropriation' to capture this primary sense of the term:

> The history of peoples with their migrations, colonizations, and conquests is the history of land appropriation. Either this is an appropriation of free

land, with no claim to ownership, or the conquest of alien land which has been appropriated under the legal title of foreign-political warfare or by domestic political means such as the proscription, deprivation and forfeiture of newly divided land.

(1993 [1953]: 56)

His primary point, then, is that until the Industrial Revolution, land appropriation is the precondition of all subsequent economics and law.

However, *nomos* has two other meanings, given by other verbs. One is *teilen* (German), meaning to divide or to distribute. For Hobbes, for instance, *nomos* is that act of the sovereign power that introduces and then distributes property. 'And this they well knew of old, who called that *Nomos* (that is to say, *Distribution*,) which we call Law; and defined Justice, by *distributing* to every man *his own*' (Hobbes 1996, emphasis in original, in Schmitt 1993: 55). The distributional question is a social question and thus a question of justice. It presupposes a community that has formed itself into an entity that has appropriated land and other resources for itself and now seeks to resolve the question of justice within that community. To those who might have been excluded from appropriation, this question of justice does not apply. As Schmitt acerbically put its:

> Concretely speaking, *Nomos* is, for example, the chicken every peasant living under a good king has in his pot every Sunday; the piece of land he cultivates in front of his property; the car every worker in the US has parked in front of his house.[7]

As the last example suggests, *nomos* in this sense is linked to the settled communal order and to a conception of economy still linked to the household, to the Aristotelian *oikonomia*. In this respect the model of economy in early modern political thought as concerning the relationship between the settled households of the kingdom presupposes such a notion of *nomos*. When economy was first applied to the policy of states, it retained this earlier sense. Sir James Steuart (1966: 15–16) opened his *Political Œconomy* of 1767 by noting that 'œconomy ... is the art of providing for all the wants of a family, with prudence and frugality', but that what 'œconomy is in a family, political œconomy is in a state...'. Further, early modern forms of political thought such as mercantilism or cameralist *Polizeiwissenschaft* (police science) are based on a kind of 'distributional model' of a kingdom composed of such households. It is precisely this model of settlement, order, household and distribution that underlies the sixteenth-century definitions of government favoured by Michel Foucault, such as that of De la Perrière: 'the right disposition of things as are committed to the charge of any man, to bring them to a meet end' (1599: 23).

Finally, the content of *nomos* is given by the verb *weiden* (German), meaning to pasture, to run a household or to produce. A part of the settled community and its law is the existence of households, agriculture and systems of production. A massive shift in *nomos* occurs in the movement of nomads to settled existence. In a footnote, Schmitt (1993: 54) claims 'nomad' is derived from the Greek *nome*, meaning capturing or grazing or wandering in search of pasture. The nomadic search is then one of appropriation of land for pasture rather than, for example, a movement through and beyond a specific area in a cyclical sense. It is for Schmitt a movement of the *nomos* toward settled community, family and household, toward the *oikos*, which then becomes the primary site of production. He thus agrees with Foucault that the discovery of production as an independent aspect of *nomos* follows rather than proceeds distribution. In Foucault's case, the discovery of the quasi-necessary and natural laws of production occasions a rupture in the arts of government and the emergence of a liberal art of government. For Schmitt, liberalism is concerned to privilege production as the solution to all questions of distribution, to the *social* question.

Schmitt's thesis, then, is stated with all the simplicity and insight he is capable of, as 'Prior to every legal, economic and social order, prior to every legal, economic or social theory, there is this simple question: *Where and how was it appropriated? Where and how was it divided? Where and how was it produced?*' (Schmitt 1993: 56, emphasis in original).

Schmitt's concept of *nomos* can be viewed in part as an attempt to capture not only the appropriation and subsequent division of land but the social and political organization which constitutes a concrete spatial unity and a community in relation to such a division and with its own conceptions of justice. We can see that he is taking aim at positivist conceptions of law which reduce *nomos* to empty and formalistic legislation, and which reduce legitimacy to a mere legality. Indeed the rot sets in quite early. When the Sophists opposed *nomos* and *physis*, they thereby reduced *nomos* from a fact of life to a prescribed ought (Ulmen 1993: 43). Similarly, Schmitt accuses Plato of reducing *nomos* to mere rule (*schedon*). In contrast, Aristotle's distinction between various *nomoi* (laws) and the concrete order as a whole (*nomos*) retains the original conception of *nomos* as spatial unity.

If we take Schmitt's concept of *nomos* to capture a basic understanding of the power relations which traverse the Earth, then we can say that for Schmitt the 'where' of power relations remains fundamental. If Foucault's approach can be characterized as focusing on the 'how' of power in the sense of what happens in any power relation, Schmitt focuses on where power draws lines and boundaries, marks territories, includes and excludes. It creates places and spaces such as villages, cities, states, regions, spheres of influence, and the globe itself. Every act or process of appropriation, distribution and production has a specific locality and constitutes a definite kind of geography. In the history of human civilizations, then, every legal and economic order has depended upon a prior land appropriation, at least until industrial modernity (Schmitt 1993: 56).

During modern times, however, one might say that every *nomos* – or conception of *nomos* – makes problematic the sequence which gives this historical and logical primacy to appropriation. Thus, for Fukuyama (1992), appropriation – and indeed problems of distribution – scarcely exist. Human conflict concerns the struggle for recognition and the sublation of the master–slave dialectic in a liberal-democratic generalization of the need for self-recognition. The preconditions for the development of liberal democracy across the globe are to be found in the liberalization of economic policy and the expansion of production driven by science and technology. The solution to a human universal is thus provided by the liberal expansion of production, which is hardly a new solution to problems, however conceived. Schmitt noted that the 'core of liberalism', like socialism, is concerned with the:

> sequence of production and distribution. Progress and economic freedom consist in freeing productive powers, whereby such an increase in production and in the mass of consumer goods brings about an end to appropriation so that even distribution is no longer an independent problem.
>
> (Schmitt 1993: 59)

Huntington (1996), by contrast, reinstates significant conflict in his account of international order but appears to displace that conflict entirely on to the question of identity – ethnic, cultural and civilizational. While such identity conflicts recall the 'friend–enemy' character of the political noted in 1932 by Schmitt (1996a), the latter gave friend–enemy relations a territorial and geopolitical rather than an ethnic and cultural basis. Schmitt's definition of the political is not intended to be exhaustive or have any substantive content, that is, there is no fundamental basis to the political relationship of friend and enemy and any grouping can become political in this sense. Huntington's friends and enemies have at their core religious and linguistic commonality.

Moreover, there is almost a complete repression of the question of *nomos* in Schmitt's sense in this clash of civilizations. If Schmitt's *nomos* forces us to consider the history of land appropriations, territorial expansions, war and colonialism, the clash thesis alerts us merely to the fundamental differences between religion and civilizations. Thus Huntington views recent conflicts in the Middle East as simply an episode in the conflicts along the 'fault lines' between civilizations that have been 'going on for 1,300 years', a 'centuries old military action between the West and Islam [which is] unlikely to decline' and which has been exacerbated by the dependence of the West upon oil (1993, also 1996: 209–218).

Thus far we have discussed the philological and conceptual aspects of *nomos*. But what makes the *nomos* of the Earth possible? How do we come to consider the Earth as a whole? What might we begin to consider? There are three ways of approaching this: the first is terrestrial, the second, what we might call 'geomythographical', and the third, genealogical.

The *nomos* of the Earth has an elemental character and the primary element is land. The first corollary to the idea of *nomos* is the original land-based character of law. Law is defined as the unity of order and orientation, of order and perhaps what Deleuzians would call 'territorializations'. In this sense, we might want to argue that human beings are terrestrial creatures. Even when we access the Internet to make the financial transactions that in their totality are often said to be key evidence of globalization, we do so from a specific space and locality. While this is sometimes done from the business-class seat of an airplane crossing airspace between continents, it is most often done in an office or a home, which are part of buildings that, together with their land, are owned through a system of land titles guaranteed by an administrative and legal order itself established through the kind of appropriations that Schmitt so well summarizes: war, conquests, appropriation of free space, colonizations, etc. In a famous extension of this notion of *nomos*, Giorgio Agamben (1998, 2000) has recently added 'nativity', with its etymological affinity with the notion of nation, as a third term in the modern *nomos* of nation-state: order, territory, birth. For Agamben, it is along the axis of birth, citizenship and life that the nation-state is today being thrown into crisis. The consequence, according to his thesis, is that 'the camp', as the site of the inclusive exclusion of bare life, is the 'new biopolitical *nomos* of the planet'. While there is much that can be said in relation to this provocative thesis, we can note it here as an example of the revival, extension and critique of *nomos* thinking in contemporary European thought.

Agamben also illustrates the proposition that *nomos* is land-based does not foreclose investigation of other elemental relations such as that of life and death. If we stay with spatial terms, however, we might want to concentrate on land and sea, and, beyond that, the sky and space – and even perhaps cyberspace – as new frontiers of appropriation, distribution and production. In his deeply disturbing book on Hobbes' political symbol of the Leviathan (Agamben 1996c) published in 1938,[8] Schmitt reveals the multiple and symbolic character of the Leviathan image in Hobbes – at once 'mortal god', machine, monster and huge man. The Leviathan as State also becomes a kind of geo-mythography of power relations: a territory, with its capital, and with definite borders or boundaries, and with the different activities of the country taking placing within that territory.

Drawing on the Hebraic bible, Schmitt also shows Leviathan to be a symbol in another kind of geo-mythography. Here Leviathan can be a sea monster, serpent, dragon or whale, who confronts and defeats the land monster, Behemoth. 'The latter tries to tear the leviathan apart with his horns, while the leviathan covers the behemoth's mouth and nostrils with his fins and kills him in that way' (Schmitt 1996c: 9). This image, Schmitt observes, is a 'fine depiction' of a blockade. More broadly, the history of the state and of empires can thus be interpreted in terms of battles between land and sea powers and the role of sea power in the establishment of the British and, later, American hegemonies. In this sense it is interesting that an English political thinker would seek to describe a settled land-based geography of the state using the symbol of a sea monster just at a time when Britain was about to establish the most extensive empire on Earth by means of its maritime superiority. From the Odyssey to the discovery of the New World and the voyages of Columbus and company, from Hugo Grotius' doctrine of the *mare liberum* and the law of the seas to the desire for 'oceanic consciousness' of idealist philosophy and mysticism, from twentieth-century Atlanticism and the North Atlantic Treaty Organization to the deployment of American military power in the Persian Gulf, the symbols of land and sea, and often the domination of the latter by the former, have been powerful ways of imagining the Earth (cf. Connery 2001). Indeed, for Schmitt, the Cold War could be characterized as a dialectical opposition between a continental and maritime power, a power at the heart of the Earth's greatest land mass and the decisive force on the world's oceans (Ulmen 1987: 44).

Today, the 'theory of offensive realism' of Mearsheimer (2001) views the 'stopping power of water' as presenting an exception to the hegemonic ambitions of states in the case of insular powers such as Great Britain and the USA. Moreover, this relationship of sea and land also helps constitute 'regions' and their associations such as the Mediterranean, the Baltic States, Oceania and Asia-Pacific Economic Cooperation (APEC). The struggle of refugees to arrive by boat at Australia or to cross the Mediterranean from North Africa – whether viewed as heroic or criminal – entails far more potent narrative imagery than those many more who would arrive through the airport on a temporary visa and abscond later. The Earth is no longer waiting to be discovered and settled in the heroic manner of the forefathers of the New World, and punishment and prevention await those who try such acts of discovery (whatever one might make of the trajectory linking penal colony and detention camp in Australia). Even with the addition of birth, our account of *nomos* would be seriously incomplete without a consideration of the open sea and of territorial waters, the role of the coastguards and navy patrols, and its relation to the 'bare life', as Agamben puts it, and the plight of the refugee.

The *nomos* of the Earth is an historical formation. It has a genealogy. In Schmitt's account there are three major steps. The first concerns the pre-global international law of the *respublica Christiana*. The second is the formation of the *ius publicum Europæum*. The third is the history of the twentieth century and the decline of the *ius publicum Europæum*. A key point is the similarity between aspects of pre-global international law and the sense of relative international lawlessness present today, especially in relation to the justification of the conduct of the war and the revival of doctrines of just war.

According to Schmitt, European public law emerged as a transformation of medieval notions of just war, derived from St Augustine and Thomas Aquinas and embodied in the twelfth-century Gratian Decree, and of notions of the medieval *respublica Christiana* under the Pope's authority (Schmitt 1996b: 47–50; Kervégan 1999: 59).[9] Even as late as the discovery of the New World, this Christian international law required Christian princes and peoples to fulfil the Pope's missionary mandate as their duty. Thus secular rulers were subject to a higher spiritual authority which require them to ensure the safety of 'free missions', as well as of passage, and of commerce.

Over the next several centuries, this notion of just war would be substantially altered with the development of a Law of Nations. In the first systematic work on this discipline, *De jure belli ac pacis* of 1625, Hugo Grotius maintains the idea of a 'just war', but identifies it with 'solemn public law' or war 'declared formally' by one state on another (Schmitt 1996b: 76–78; Kervégan 1999: 59–60). By the eighteenth century Vattel argues that each state is ultimately judge of the justice of its own causes, and thus effectively displaces the material justification of war with the idea of formal regularity. According to his *Le Droit des Gens* of 1758, both sides in war can be thought of as equally legitimate if they conduct war formally. To put it briefly, there is a shift in European thought beginning in the sixteenth century from the notion of a just war to that of a 'just enemy', which parallels the decline of notions of a unified Christian empire under the unified authority of the Pope (Ulmen 1996a).

It is to the formation of the *ius publicum Europæum* that we must look for an explanation of the changes of outlook. The post-medieval international law displaces the idea of a just war grounded in ecclesiastical law and replaces it with the notion of a just enemy defined by inter-state law (Ulmen 1996a: 103). The intention here is to limit war by bracketing moral evaluations of those who make war. It is, according to Schmitt (1996b: 68), a law between European states or sovereigns which eliminates notions of the Holy Empire or of the Pope's sovereignty as a spiritual power. It is thus a 'de-theologized' law that effects a definitive separation of theological and juridical arguments. Linked to this is 'a non-discriminatory concept of the enemy' as a formal equal to be treated according to rules of war rather than as a perpetual foe (*hostis perpetui*), as medieval Christianity had treated Jews and Saracens.

The establishment of a European system of states and international public law has implications for the *nomos* of the rest of the Earth and gave rise to what Schmitt calls 'global linear thinking' (1996b: 33). The establishment of this European legal order had among its conditions the discovery of the New World and the beginning of the European land appropriations of the Americas. Schmitt demonstrates how the cartography of the Earth had specific political conditions. This is most notable in the secretly concluded 'amity lines' between European states such as England and France which ran along certain lines of the Earth, for example, the Equator or Tropic of Cancer (1996b: 35–42). The most important was the meridian in the mid-Atlantic that marked the spaces within which European inter-state law was active and the spaces for which it became inactive. A condition for these land appropriations and the later colonial empires was the idea of 'free spaces' in which the rules of engagement of European states ceased to exist:

> The general concept was then necessarily that everything which occurred 'beyond the line' remained outside the legal, moral and political values recognized on this side of the line. This was a tremendous *exoneration* of the internal European problematic. The significance of the famous and notorious expression 'beyond the line' in terms of international law lies precisely in this exoneration.
>
> (1996b: 37, emphasis in original)

The primary challenge to the *ius publicum Europæum* is marked by the Monroe doctrine and the consequent emergence of the space of the Western hemisphere. According to President Monroe's proclamation of 2 December 1823, the

Americas were to be excised from the space of European colonization and the USA would exercise its right to defend them (Ulmen 1987: 52–53). As Schmitt points out, the spatiality of US interests was imagined and acted upon in far-reaching excess of its own borders – the origins of a new large space or *Grossraum*. 'This is the core of the great original Monroe Doctrine, a genuine *Grossraum* principle, namely the union of a politically-awakened people, a political idea and, on this basis of this idea, a politically-dominant *Grossraum* excluding foreign intervention' (Schmitt, in Ulmen 1987: 53). This was a decisive moment of decolonization which would initiate a complex set of linkages and tensions between anti-colonialism, anti-Europeanism and American imperialism. With this doctrine, America drew a new set of lines across the planet and established a reversal of the axis of war and peace: the Americas and the New World would henceforth be a zone of peace defined against the zone of war of the Old World. The world had entered no less than a new rotation, to recall Plato. Within less than a century, after the Spanish-American war and the Treaty of 1898 (which gave the US sovereignty over Cuba, and possession of the Philippines, Puerto Rico and Guam), the USA emerged as a bi-oceanic maritime imperial power. For Schmitt, the character of US imperialism would rest upon two factors: the separation of the economic from the political in a dialectic of presence and absence; and the exercise of what President Theodore Roosevelt called an 'international police power' in order to defend universal democratic rights (Ulmen 1987: 58–59).

It is to the Versailles Treaty, with its broad Anglo-Saxon-derived concept of war and its 'war guilt' clause (Article 231), and to the formation of the League of Nations, with the characteristic absent presence of the USA and tacit recognition of the Monroe Doctrine, that Schmitt looks to find the beginning of the end of the *ius publicum Europæum*. This marks the beginning of the outlawing of war as an instrument of *national* policy, but not of *international* policy in which 'just wars' could serve imperialist causes (Ulmen 1987: 62–63). Rather than the just enemy, there is the criminalization of the enemy in the form of a state or its agents who commit crimes against peace and crimes against humanity. War undergoes a new moralization with such notions and ideas as 'humanitarian intervention'. The difference in the modern case is that it is now not a question of finding causes for which it is possible to fight just wars, but the criminalization of aggression itself. By criminalizing acts of war, war ceases to be a public contest between recognized political entities. Instead of a legally governed undertaking with specific rules of engagement, it becomes a kind of international civil war. The just enemy becomes new kinds of *perfidus hostis*: President Reagan's Evil Empire and G.W. Bush's Axis of Evil; the sponsors and perpetrators of international terrorism; rogue states; criminal regimes; warlords; mafias; and narco-business cartels. It is a matter of simple consistency that the USA would be viewed as the Great Satan by its radical Islamic opponents. A key point to note is how the enemy becomes not only an evil foe but also is no longer restricted to states.

Schmitt's genealogy thus places the emergence of the modern arts of domestic government within the context of the techniques of international government of the relations between sovereign states. These techniques are themselves contingent upon the discovery, appropriation and conquest of the New World, the formation of European colonial empires and ideas of war and peace, and the twentieth-century decline of the international law which emerged with the European state system. The Monroe Doctrine, the emergence of the Western Hemisphere, and the manifest destiny of the USA are the cataclysmic events that send the Earth into a different rotation.

The narrative about the formation of modern forms of governmentality should then be re-situated in a narrative about the formation of the European state *system* and the capacity of that system to define the operation of normal sovereignty – the norms of public order and security which frame the relations between recognized sovereign states – and what Schmitt elsewhere called the 'state of exception', the free seas and oceans that could not be appropriated, and the New World and its lands which were 'beyond the line'.[10] This normal sovereignty enframes the emergence of domestic arts of government and the formation of liberalism and its relation to political economy. Rather than an act or decision on the part of the sovereign, governing – within such spaces – is about the subtle manipulation of the laws of production, consumption and distribution. But this liberal *nomos*, if one likes, suppresses the question of appropriation within domestic government. It is in this sense that Foucault's claim that we need to shift attention from 'the theory of sovereignty which refers to the displacement and appropriation on the part of power' (1980: 104) to positive and productive forms of power and government is located within this liberal *nomos*. But once the question of international law and the '*nomos* of the Earth' is posed, the often violent or at least repressive systems of domination, and processes and acts of appropriation that create and secure these spaces of domestic government come into view. The liberal *nomos* thus has another, imperialist side today recognized by those who argue the need to distinguish between the conduct of 'post-modern' liberal states among themselves and their conduct toward a world of failing states or states with aggressive, modernist, attitudes (Cooper 2000, 2002).

If a 'global governmentality' is today propounded by multiple agencies (for example, WTO, IMF, OECD), it operates through both the existing arts of domestic government within nation-states and as an attempted extension and generalization of them across the planet. It thus seeks to move from a liberal art of government to a liberal planetary *nomos* or world order. From a perspective informed by Schmitt, however, the establishment of such a *nomos* of the planet would depend on a prior set of actions and processes which appropriate, establish and secure the spaces in which market forces could operate globally and decide when such a normal market situation prevails. This is why issues of border controls, immigration and refugees, and general issues of security – from energy supplies to the Internet – come to the fore. In present circumstances there are two problematics of this planetary order. The first seeks to establish an understanding of international law based on the defence of human rights and focuses on the use of existing and developing institutions such as the UN and its

Security Council. The second asserts exceptionalism for the lonely superpower, rights to decide illegitimate claims of sovereignty (Iraq but not Pakistan) and to broker international agreements (the 'road map' in the Middle East), and to conduct new forms of just wars against newly criminalized enemies, whether states or terrorist networks. It acts in the name of democracy and freedom. It is the conflict, overlap, and rapprochement between these two geopolitical imaginaries that defines the precarious balance of forces that stand as a substitute for a coherent international order today.

Conclusion

Let me conclude in relation to three points. The first is the question of European thought. In this respect, one does not have to agree completely with Robert Kagan's thesis that the relative strength and weakness of America and Europe has given rise to different psychologies of power, one modernist and Hobbesian, the other post-modernist and Kantian, to allow that the problem of *nomos* can scarcely be posed by many contemporary European intellectuals.[11] But radical thought across the social and political sciences has focused on the decline or deconstruction of sovereignty and the emergence of cosmopolitanism, and on the need for a model of power which is no longer centred on the nation-state. It forgoes the analysis of appropriation and associated violence and domination, and imagines the world in terms of communicative, social and technological networks, exchanges, flows and regions. The recovery of the idea and concept of the *nomos* of the Earth is thus a useful antidote to the active forgetting of violence, coercion, obligation, reason of state and appropriation. It is also an antidote to the kind of views and debates which take up the position of the contemporary hegemon but without any consideration of what is meant by world order.

My second point is the problem of the relation of politics to economics and ethics. Many of the contemporary views on world order, with the exception of those of Huntington and 'realists' such as Mearsheimer (2001), make economics the key to world order and turn politics into a second-order phenomenon. Politics might simply be an obstacle to the new order rooted in a human need for security – the olive tree, however necessary, getting in the way of the Lexus. It might be a matter of achieving 'good governance', meaning certain kinds of public sector, financial and institutional reforms, to best take advantage of global financial flows. Or it might simply be a universal system that oversees the transcendence of the master–slave relation by the rational, calculating and status-seeking *homo œconomicus* as consumer and producer (the 'last man'). My suggestion here is that, on the contrary, to think and describe world in terms of economies, technologies and networks is to imagine different geographies and spatialities – whether of localities, regions, globes, of 'flows' and patterns of interconnections, and of cyberspace. Such imaginations of space are connected to forms of power and particular politics. The protests which now occur regularly, and are fiercely secured against, at international economic forums since the

WTO meeting in Seattle in 1999, reveal the political nature of the policies adopted by international economic organizations. The protests are about recovering the political character of policies so often presented as technical, inevitable and necessary.

The flipside to the language of the economic is the metaphysics of the subject, expressed in terms of identity and recognition, that is, the language of ethics. Whether we talk in terms of the Lexus and the olive tree, or liberal capitalism and mutual self-recognition, the discourse of globalization and contemporary world order continues the oscillation between economic and ethics already noted by Schmitt in 1932:

> The world will not be depoliticalized with the aid of definitions and constructions, all of which circle the polarity of ethics and economics. The often quoted phrase by Walter Rathenau, namely that destiny today is not politics but economics, originated in this context. It would be more exact to say that politics continues to remain the destiny, but what has occurred is that economics has become political and thereby the destiny.
>
> (1996a: 78)

The concept of *nomos*, and the exploration of Schmitt's genealogy of the *nomos* of the Earth, then, provides us with a direct route back to understanding the question of world order as a fundamentally political question, that is, as a question of how the friend–enemy relation is reconfigured today, outside the economism of the boosters of globalization and the moralization of the sphere of foreign policy and of narratives of the present. This is only a starting point but one which nonetheless forms an indispensable resource despite Schmitt's dubious actions and statements during the period of National Socialism.

My final point concerns the ethos of danger. Certainly, Schmitt is not a man one would readily want to have on one's side. His accommodation with Nazism and his anti-Jewish references during the 1930s mean that his work cannot be appropriated without extreme caution. There is coldness and hubris in the relation of this thinker to the globe as well as bold imagination and insight. Our ambivalence regarding Schmitt will always be a part of Schmittian scholarship. But there are also secretive and seductive dangers in this literature of world order. In order to enter into the American literature on world order, we have to come to terms with a kind of subject which can declare such things as 'Greece is not a part of Western civilization' or that Australians 'are the most direct, blunt, outspoken, some would say insensitive, people in the English speaking world' (Huntington 1996: 162, 153). Or try to imagine how a book which claims that globalization is the new post-Cold War world order can end with an anecdote about the wonders of American multiculturalism and with 'God bless America' (Friedman 2000: 475). This is a literature which can divide the world into clashing civilizations, historical and post-historical parts and populations (and one presumes pre-historical), or post-modern zones of safety and pre-modern and modern zones of threat. To take up the question of the *nomos* of the Earth today, one must be prepared to confront the detailed cartography of our own faces as much as the paltry imaginaries we project towards this globe we claim not only to inhabit but to understand.

Notes

1 Presented at the International Humanities Conference, University of the Aegean, Rhodes, July 2–5, 2003.
2 It is by Osvaldo Perez d'Elias. See cover of Mouffe (1999), or *Telos*, 72: 89.
3 See the dossier of Schmitt's interrogation published in *Telos*, 72: 97–130.
4 An exemplar is the work of Beck (1998, 2000a, 2000b).
5 And often ends up producing so much nonsense from a geographical point of view, on which see Lewis (2000).
6 A notable exception is found in what is called 'critical geopolitics'. See, for example, Agnew (1998) and Ó Tuathail (1996).
7 If the car is a Lexus, and every yard has its olive tree – next to a flagpole with the Stars and Stripes – one might imagine the *nomos* according to Thomas Friedman (2000).
8 While Schmitt did not share the racial ideology of the Nazis, this text is clearly and disturbingly anti-Jewish. For example, he retells cabbalistic interpretations of the battle between Leviathan and Behemoth and the ensuing cannibalism of the Jews 'who eat of the flesh of the slaughtered people and are sustained by it' (Schmitt 1996c: 9). The fact that Schmitt broadens his attack to also include the Roman Catholic Church, freemasons, Goethe and Kant does nothing to diminish the impression of a thinker who, notwithstanding his own capacity for brilliant and clear insight, could veer towards paranoid fascist conspiracy theory and anti-Semitism, however opportunistically (1996c: 60; see Turner 1998).
9 This and the next few paragraphs are drawn from Dean (2003).
10 See Agamben (1998: 36–37) on Schmitt's 'obscurity' on the relation between *nomos* and the exception he attributed to the sovereign decision in the latter's *Political Theology* (1985).
11 One of the problems with Kagan's thesis is that it can only be observed in the breach. There are of course Americans who are far from immune to such an outlook. See, for example, James Rosenau (2000). Europeans can also have a less than sanguine view of the world outside their own zone (Cooper 2000, 2002). And Agamben is obviously a major exception.

References

Agamben, G. (1998) *Homo Sacer: sovereign power and bare life*, trans. D. Heller-Roazen, Stanford: Stanford University Press.
Agamben, G. (2000) *Means without Ends: notes on politics*, trans. V. Binetti and C. Casarino, Minneapolis: University of Minnesota Press.
Agnew, J.A. (1998) *Geopolitics: re-visiting world politics*, London: Routledge.
Balakrishnan, G. (2000) *The Enemy: an intellectual portrait of Carl Schmitt*, London: Verso.
Beck, U. (1998) 'The cosmopolitan manifesto', *New Statesman*, 20 March, 1998.
——(2000a) 'The cosmopolitan perspective: sociology of the second age of modernity', *British Journal of Sociology*, 51(1): 79–105.
——(2000b) *What is Globalization?*, trans. P. Camiller, Cambridge: Polity.
Connery, C.L. (2001) 'Ideologies of land and sea: Alfred Thayer Mahan, Carl Schmitt, and the shaping of global myth elements', *Boundary 2*, 28(2): 173–201.
Cooper, R. (2000) *The Post-modern State and the World Order*, 2nd edn, London: Demos.

——(2002) 'The new liberal imperialism', *Observer*, April 7, 2002. Online. Available at: http://observer.guardian.co.uk/worldview/ (accessed July 16, 2003).

Dean, M. (2003) 'Prologue for a genealogy of war and peace', in G. Delanty and E. Isin (eds) *Handbook of Historical Sociology*, Sage: London.

De la Perrière, G. (1599 [1567]) *The Mirror of Policie*, London.

Foucault, M. (1980) in C. Gordon (ed.) *Power/Knowledge*, Brighton: Harvester.

——(1991) 'Governmentality', in G. Burchell, C. Gordon and P. Miller (eds) *The Foucault Effect: studies in governmentality*, London: Harvester Wheatsheaf.

——(2001) '*Omnes et singulatum*': toward a critique of political reason', in J.D. Faubion (ed.) *Power. The essential works of Foucault 1954–1984, vol. 3*, London: Allen Lane, The Penguin Press.

Friedman, T.L. (2000) *The Lexus and the Olive Tree*, London: HarperCollins.

Fukuyama, F. (1992) *The End of History and the Last Man*, London: Hamish Hamilton.

Hardt, M. and Negri, A. (2000) *Empire*, Cambridge, MA: Harvard University Press.

Hobbes, T. (1996 [1651]) *Leviathan*, Cambridge: Cambridge University Press.

Joxe, A. (2002) *Empire of Disorder*, trans. A. Hodges, New York: Semiotext(e).

Huntington, S.P. (1993) 'The clash of civilizations?', *Foreign Affairs*, 72(3): 22–49.

——(1996) *The Clash of Civilizations and the Remaking of World Order*, New York: Simon & Schuster.

Kagan, R. (2002) 'Power and weakness', *Policy Review*, June–July, 2002.

Karnoouh, C. (2002) 'On the genealogy of globalization', *Telos*, 124: 183–192.

Kervégan, J.-F. (1999) 'Carl Schmitt and "world unity"', in C. Mouffe (ed.) *The Challenge of Carl Schmitt*, London: Verso.

Lewis, M.W. (2000) 'Global ignorance (geographical errors by scholars, journalists, intellectuals writing on globalization and world history)', *Geographical Review*, 90(4): 603–628.

Mearsheimer, J.J. (2001) *The Tragedy of Great Power Politics*, New York: W.W. Norton.

Mouffe, C. (ed.) (1999) *The Challenge of Carl Schmitt*, London: Verso.

Ó Tuathail, G. (1996) *Critical Geopolitics: the politics of writing global space*, Minneapolis: University of Minnesota Press.

Plato (1952) *The Statesman*, Loeb Classical Library, London: Heinemann.

Rosenau, J. (2000) 'Governance in a globalising world', in D. Held and A. McGrew (eds) *The Global Transformations Reader*, Cambridge: Polity.

Schmitt, C. (1950) *Der Nomos der Erde, im Völkerrecht des Jus Publicum Europaeum*, Cologne: Greven.

——1985 [1922]) *Political Theology: four chapters on the concept of sovereignty*, trans. G. Schwab, Cambridge, MA: MIT Press.

——(1993 [1953]) 'Appropriation/distribution/production: toward a proper formulation of any social and economic order', *Telos*, 95: 52–64.

——(1996a [1932]) *The Concept of the Political*, trans. J.H. Lomas, Chicago: University of Chicago Press.

——(1996b [1950]) 'The land appropriation of a New World', *Telos*, 109: 29–80.

——(1996c [1938]) *The Leviathan in the State Theory of Thomas Hobbes: meaning and failure of a political symbol*, Westport, CN.: Greenwood Press.

Steuart, J. (1966 [1767]) *An Inquiry into the Principles of Political Œconomy*, 2 vols, Edinburgh: Oliver & Boyd.

Time (1985) 'Obituary', *Time*, April 22, p. 66.

Turner, C. (1998) 'The strange anti-liberalism of Carl Schmitt', *Economy and Society*, 27(4): 434–457.

——(1987) 'American imperialism and international law: Carl Schmitt on the US in world affairs', *Telos*, 72: 43–71.

——(1993) 'The concept of nomos: introduction to Schmitt's "appropriation/distribution/production"', *Telos*, 95: 39–51.

——(1996a) 'Just wars of just enemies?', *Telos*, 109: 99–112.

——(1996b) 'Toward a new world order: introduction to Schmitt', *Telos*, 109: 3–27.

3 Global networks, international networks, actor networks

Gavin Kendall[1]

In the globalization literature, much has been made of the origins of global power and domination in Western imperialism and colonialism. For example, Giddens (1990) argues that modernity – which is characterized by an increasingly global character – has to be understood along four dimensions, each of which has become increasingly global and less local, and all of these four dimensions have developed from an immature form in imperialist and colonialist practice. These dimensions are the system of nation-states, the world capitalist economy, the international division of labour, and the world military order. For Giddens, all four have been transformed in modernity, and it is the concatenation of them all that defines the modern period. Giddens' work can usefully be read in conjunction with the work of Immanuel Wallerstein (1974, 1980, 1989), who has similarly laid out a 'developmental' pattern of globalization that stretches back to the European colonisation ventures of the sixteenth century.

The globalization literature, while it usefully draws attention to trends in increasing internationalization in our era, often confuses cause and effect. It is sometimes unclear whether 'globalization' refers to a *description* of a new series of political, economic and cultural arrangements, and which may be explained by other factors and theories – such as those dealing with liberalization or capitalist development for example – or whether globalization should be understood as an explanatory *process*, a number of strategies which, whether consciously designed by human agents or not, *drives* these new international relations. Globalization, I suggest, should not be imagined to have a life of its own. A better approach, rather, is to describe how global networks are constructed – from the ground up. In this chapter, then, I try to generate a theory of how international networks are constituted and how they survive and prosper. I promote the idea of 'network' as used by Bruno Latour as having utility for this task.

To a certain extent, I run the risk of making these arguments against a straw person, since I argue against a rather one-dimensional composite of globalization and social network theorists, which may not be found exactly in any one work. Nonetheless, I hope that there will be something useful in this argument both as a ground-clearing exercise and as a pointer to future research agendas. I also want to add to Foucault's (1978, 1981) work on governmentality. While I have an appreciation for Foucault's work, and the insights it offers into well-worn themes in political sociology, it does not really foreground the 'technical/techno-logical' aspects of government in general (and global government in particular), nor does it give enough space to the role played by other actors apart from the human, in maintaining the networks of global government. Finally, I explore the idea that ordering is an ontological necessity, and that when thinking about the government of international social spaces there might be something of a 'will to govern' at work. These various ideas are pursued with differing degrees of detail, but I hope that a unifying theme is a concern to inject what John Law and Kevin Hetherington (2001) have termed a 'material semiotics' into governmentality studies. By this, Law and Hetherington urge us not to forget the role of knowledges in the constitution of systems of government and domination (this is the 'semiotic' component), nor to overlook the various material structures that keep such systems functioning.

Before I proceed, I think it is worth a word of caution, which might dispel some possible confusion in the material I discuss. In a number of literatures, the concept of network is currently being used to understand *two* sorts of societies or collectivities – those that self-consciously understand themselves as networks, and those that do not. For example, management gurus and planners make free use of the term 'network'; international empires rarely if ever understand themselves in this way. Consequently, 'network' has recently attained a metatheoretical (or deuterotheoretical) status, especially when it is used as a conceptual term to describe those entities that think of themselves as 'networked'. The point here is simply that we should not take the term 'network' to be unproblematic, or to assume a family resemblance where one may not exist.

Towards a critique of the concept of network

First we need to consider the character of networks in general, and global networks more specifically. The term 'network' has been used rather freely in the recent social sciences, and especially in work that attempts to analyse issues of international or global flows of people, materials, money, animals, wastes, and so forth. Manuel Castells, for example, strongly argues for the coming of a 'network society' – a new type of social arrangement whereby (global) society is interconnected (Castells 1996, 1998, 2000a). Castells is clear that the new global network is singular: 'the vast majority of societies … together … constitute a new type of social structure that I call the network society' (Castells 2000b: 9). The unity of this global enterprise is reinforced later in the same article where Castells asserts: '[the] core, strategic activities [sc. of this new economy] have the capacity to work as a unit on a planetary scale' (2000b: 10). Castells is, moreover, explicit that the network is technological in nature: an automaton. Similarly, in the work of Gary Gereffi (see, for example, Gereffi 1996), the concept of global commodity chains is organized along the lines of a technical network. Indeed, given that this notion arose from the research tradition of Wallerstein's world-system theory, it is not surprising that it has concentrated on the spread of global capitalism through the developing mechanisms of production, distribution and consumption. In general, the term 'network' has had some currency in the field of economic sociology, but it is important to note that this use of the term is very different from its use in fields such as cultural and economic geography, as should become clearer as we move through the chapter.

But what job does the word 'network' do here, in this economic sociology tradition? Is it a description of a new reality: a set of processes which link up distant places and people? Is it, rather, merely a convenient metaphor? Or even the wrong metaphor? Ultimately, we shall turn to Actor-Network Theory (ANT) to answer these questions, since it is there, we think, that the character and reality of networks has been given some proper attention.

The first question we might ask about the character of networks is one which can be approached without thinking too much about the networks *per se*: are networks in this 'new economy' international or global? This is a question that has been considered by Hirst and Thompson (1996: 8–13) in their critique of 'hyperglobalization'. Hirst and Thompson ask whether the new world economy (which they take to underlie, or at least be a good representative of, the new world order of governance, of occupational mobility and of tourism) is primarily based around a series of truly global actors (corporations and the like) whose core activity stretches beyond any single nation-state, and for whom national economic processes are secondary to international ones; or whether the new world economy is still dominated by national economies, whose core activity is at a national level, but who nonetheless engage in a significant element of international trade. The question, then, is whether the national has been subsumed into the global, or whether nowadays we merely see aggregates of primarily national trading processes. Hirst and Thompson's detailed arguments in favour of the second alternative may be regarded as a welcome relief for those who still believe in the possibility and desirability of the national regulation of international transactions and transnational corporations.

Hirst and Thompson's arguments allow us to make some schematic remarks about networks. Let us be agnostic for these purposes as to whether our networks are global or international, or whether they in fact exist at all, and consider whether they exist in the singular or the plural. A 'global network', should it exist, could perhaps be understood in the singular, since the field it traverses is solitary. In this characterisation, nation-states have become increasingly irrelevant, as a leviathan spans the globe: the nodes of this network are not so much nation-states, but the post/transnational corporations (McDonalds, Coca-Cola, Ford, and similar) that can interconnect instantaneously. In this version of the network society, which owes much to Wallerstein, we are faced with an increasingly singularised capitalist world system that can be 'surfed' by a variety of primarily post-national actors.

On the other hand, 'global networks' might be understood in the plural: our post-national corporations would still typically be the building blocks here, but they are understood as much more autonomous, independent and contingently linked; and there is less emphasis on an overarching system. McDonalds, for example, constructs a network of money, humans, machines, animals, waste disposal, and so forth, which is no great respecter of national borders. The other post-national corporations operate their own networks. They often meet up in the 'global economy' (some of McDonalds' soft drink needs can be answered by connecting up to the Coca-Cola network, some of McDonalds' transportation needs are solved by hooking up with the Ford network, and so on).

The second alternative seems the more plausible: it does not take much empirical investigation to work out that these actors can be remarkably different in terms of management structure, orientation outside their home base, reliance upon modes of transportation and dissemination of people, materials, and information. It seems, then, *prima facie* implausible to suggest that a singular network now spans the globe. In essence, there is too much difference, and too many local solutions that every global actor needs to construct.[2] If we put these two lines of thought together – the implausibility of a singular network and the preference for the international over the global – it seems, then, that we are dealing with 'international networks': networks that must be thought of in the plural; networks that are a series of autonomous capillary structures; networks that primarily stretch across a bounded geographical zone, but which may also become more or less 'international'; networks that are freely able to interconnect with one another, but which will not necessarily do so. We may be witnessing a growth in these interconnections between networks,[3] but the connections *between* the networks are weaker than those *within* the networks. Finally, we must remember that networks can be of different *orders*: nation-states can be thought of as networks, as can non-national societies (for example, diasporic groupings), as can corporations, and so on.

Problems with the network metaphor[4]

We can be sceptical, therefore, about the claim that there is a single global network: what we may see instead is a series of plural networks, many of which are primarily based and do most of their business in a nation-state (for example, 'England' – as an 'imagined community' – is based in England, Ford is head-quartered in the USA, and the National University of Singapore operates in Singapore). If we stop to think about the character of these networks we may first of all follow Castells (1996, 1998, 2000a, 2000b), who conceptualises the network as a technical device. This would be a mistake. A technical network is only one possible outcome or description – one possible state – of a network. For example, something like a computer network[5] is precisely bounded, and has a series of compulsory nodes through which all communication must pass. If I, who live in Brisbane, Australia, want to email my mother (Kate), who lives in Essex, just outside of London, I have to sit myself in front of a computer in Brisbane; the email is then routed via a series of compulsory nodes (servers), perhaps by way of Sydney, across the oceans by satellite communication, reaching Kate's ISP in London and eventually getting to her computer in Essex. If there is a breakdown in the system, the message cannot be delivered: the network is not able to reroute by way of the USA, for example, nor can the email make its way to a server on another Queensland University of Technology campus (my work location) if the server at Carseldine, my home campus, is down. Such networks, then, are actually quite weak, in that they can be easily disrupted by any one problem with the compulsory channels through which the message must travel (see Latour 1997). We are all painfully aware of this weakness when we cannot print to a networked printer which may be right next to us physically – close in geographical terms, but far away in network terms – when there is a blockage somewhere in the massively long lines of communication.

However, international networks of government – whether we are talking about nation-states or transnational corporations – do not have the character of such overtly 'technical' networks in the way that Castells assumes. At Ford, if a manager is away sick, another manager will cover the decisions that are required urgently. If one supplier for the spring water fountains goes bust, another will quickly be found to replace it. If shock absorbers cannot be sourced from the usual company, another will step in to fill the breach. International networks, then, may have intensely structured and strategic network elements that they make use of (the phone, the Internet), but they themselves are extremely flexible, and are nothing like the technical network in character. Technical networks tend to be like trees – they can be easily killed off if one gets rid of the compulsory nodes (roots, trunk, and so on) through which nourishment flows. International networks – nations and corporations – are much more like Deleuze and Guattari's (1981) rhizomes.[6] The connections are extremely complex, and the blocking off of one route simply means that the entity or actor will have to find another connection. There are no compulsory nodes, merely a series of possible routes that can be quickly and easily refigured.[7]

The second problem with the technical metaphor of the network as favoured by Castells is that it is merely a *social* network. 'But, who programmes the network? Who decides the rules that the automaton will follow? Social actors, naturally' (Castells 2000b: 16). On the other hand, ANT has avidly insisted upon including non-humans in its descriptions and analyses, and the omission of the non-human is, no doubt, part of the problem with social networks. But there is more to the problem than just this. The concept of social networks is a way for Castells to add microsocial analysis to the macrosocial analysis of states, institutions and corporations. As Latour (1997) puts it, it enables Castells to make the analysis seem more 'realistic' – to fill in the gaps beneath the grand theories of the new global world order. The difference between the two approaches is stark: Castells aims to add social networks to social theory; Latour aims to 'rebuild social theory out of networks' (Latour 1997: 2). As Latour has described it, this entails something of a change of topology, but it is also something that is evident in Foucault's attempt to understand the social by first giving our attention to the microphysical level – that which is local and mobile. The contrast between Castells and Latour is this: the former generates a macrosocial theory and then fills in the gaps with the nodes of a network; the latter suggests that networks are all that exist and that the occasional, laborious formation of something bigger (social order, or what looks like a macrosocial formation) is the exception rather than the rule. So, in Latour's topology, we see that everything is networks, and everything is built from the ground up.

When thinking about global government, then, we have to interpret successfully governed space, not as a self-evident object, but as the result of the associations of networks, which are composed of humans and non-humans, and which are painstakingly built from the ground up. The 'government of space' – even 'globalization' itself – is simply a description of one actor's ability (or perhaps many actors' abilities) to produce some sort of connectability between networks. Understanding international governance can only be done empirically from the ground up, not theoretically from the top down. Additionally, every instance of a network will have its own spatial specificity; it is impossible to have a generalisable 'network analysis'. For example, in the 2003 war between Iraq and the USA and its allies, the leaders of the USA had to put together, with great difficulty, an alliance of human and non-human actors. Part of the work lay in the generation of links between allies at the political level (would it be possible to make France and Germany allies of the USA?); part of the work lay in the coordination of different networks of armies, navies and airforces (how could soldiers from different armies, for example, coordinate their activities?); part of the work lay in the coordination of spaces from which attacks could be launched (would Turkey allow itself to be used as a base by the USA?), or the negotiation of access to airspace, refuelling stations or seaports (which nations would allow the USA to use their 'network space'?). This connectability – this piling of network upon network – is what is needed to govern successfully; yet every example is specific. Future USA military action will have to begin again to generate networks and make connections.

It is also important to recognise that the lines of argument I develop here intersect with other cognate literatures. Recent work in human geography (see especially Amin and Thrift 2002; Harvey 2001) and economic sociology (see, for example, Dicken *et al.* 2001) have also made use of the notion of 'network', especially as inherited from ANT. Just as I try to do in this chapter, these authors have tried to generate a notion of network that is more than simply 'technical'.

Producing a one-way system

The metaphor I use to describe the successful attainment of the government of space is one derived from traffic regulation. If networks are composed of nodes which have multiple dimensions, and which are only occasionally put together into something we can recognize as social order, then how is this achieved? How is the rarity of social order or governance accomplished, especially in an international or global context? To my mind, this is rather akin to that which is done to avoid the potential chaos of a road system in constructing a one-way street: it becomes only possible to move in one direction, and traffic that is shunted in at one end will necessarily move through the network as the engineers desire (what Waddington 1977, in a biological context, has called a 'chreod'). This is where we can stitch some of Foucault's work on knowledge on to the actor-network approach. 'Knowledges' can be understood as the devices or the packages that enable a certain space to be connected up with another space, or for a certain obligatory point of passage (Callon 1986) – a node through which all actors must pass – to be constructed. The flows within a specific network (what Foucault would no doubt call 'power') are only possible, or actualised, because of knowledges.

To take an example from the history of colonialism: in the associations between Britain and Australian colonies during the nineteenth century, the British were able to establish a series of chreods, or one-way streets, that meant flows within the network could only go in one direction. It was impossible, for example, to send orders from Sydney to London; orders could only be conveyed from London to Sydney (Kendall 1997). What holds this one-way traffic conveniently in place is knowledge. Now, by knowledge, I mean something slightly more than what is conventionally thought of by this term (but again, nothing that should surprise the student of Foucault). Knowledge includes all the texts, speeches, materials, institutions, ways of acting and ways of problematising that are associated together in a convenient package. Again, an example should clarify: British colonial knowledge was a mixture of authoritative texts, political speeches, weapons, the telegraph and other (tele)communications devices, attitudes towards subject peoples and so on. Put together, these various elements constitute a 'knowledge' that we might call 'British colonialism'. Although John Law (2001) has recently stressed the importance of the material in making these sorts of arrangements strong, it is not necessarily a good idea to prioritise the material in the construction of what he calls *obduracy*, and what we are calling the one-way street. Knowledges can fall apart even if they are materially strong. There was nothing wrong with the materials used in the asylums of the eighteenth century for example – their durability was never called into question – but the 'knowledge' of madness current in this period was still able to be dismantled, partly because the cures did not work as we might expect, and partly because new authoritative texts came to supplant the old ones (Rose 1985).

What is required, then, for an association to become a one-way street is for a knowledge to be constructed that can be easily and efficiently used in a network. Elsewhere, Latour (1987) has referred to what he terms 'immutable mobiles', which in many ways are similar to knowledges (and a number of other terms, such as 'dispositif' or 'assemblage'). Immutable mobiles are convenient packages that hold together and maintain their coherence even when they are moved, enabling them to be effective in a variety of settings. So, for example, a map is a conveniently packaged-up 'knowledge' which can be transported easily, and which can be used regardless of the war office desk or the battleship where it is spread out. We need to remember that this immutable mobile – the map – is a result of travel, writing, weapons, theories, measurements, tools, and so on. A knowledge, then, is never simply informational, nor is it simply technical, but is a result of the juxtaposition of a number of elements.

For this one-way street to be constructed requires flexibility. As I have suggested above, actors that only have one way of doing things – that are, in this respect, like a *technical* network – are unlikely to be successful in the long run.

What is needed is the construction of a series of associations that are rhizomic, which can reformulate and reroute commands. To return to the example of British colonial practice, the British were never over-dependent on any single aspect of their 'knowledge'. Indeed, a feature of their colonialism was the regular breakdown of communication, disagreement about strategy, disobedience by subject peoples, and similar, but what enabled 'colonialism' to live on was a certain strategic flexibility: one boat might be lost, but another would be sent out; one set of communications would fail to have the desired effect, but a second set sent to a different recipient would enable the breakdown to be bypassed; a governmental failure would generate a new approach (Davidson 1991; Eddy 1969; Kendall 1997; Morrell 1966[1930]).

There is, perhaps, an interesting methodological point here. I do not see any reason to treat modern 'global' networks any differently from older 'colonial' networks. My use of the term 'network' is not linked to any recent technological possibilities, such as computer systems. The network as I understand it is always more than technical, and must include a number of elements – the human and non-human – which are characteristic of pre-modern, modern and post-modern ages (as Latour 1993 argues, even though he is, of course, sceptical of such periodisations). Methodologically, there is also some distance between my own use of the term 'network' and its use in historical sociology (as, for example, in the work of Michael Mann).[8] In historical sociology, there is a tendency first to accept networks as technological – as, for example, when networks are understood as 'information networks'. There is a second tendency to understand them as purely social – as, for example, when networks are understood as 'interaction networks'. It is also the case that much historical sociology tends to work with the 'modern' and the 'pre-modern' sharply distinguished; once again, the approach here suggests that a network analysis can illuminate either, since it attempts to analyse network building without assumptions about the character of the elements that constitute such networks.

In speaking of international governance in another age, John Law (1986) has suggested that three crucial elements are needed for a successful 'one-way street' to be constructed. Law's article dwells on the Portuguese establishment of successful and safe trading routes in the sixteenth century, especially to India. The successful construction of an international network was valuable for commercial, military and political reasons. For Law, the three crucial elements that the Portuguese needed to put in place can be summarised as documents, devices, and drilled people. Documents included such things as the *Regimento do Astrolabio et do Quadrante*, a series of tables and instructions designed to help navigators work out their latitudinal position. Devices included such things as astrolabes and quadrants, technologies for observing stellar and solar positions, but also the specially designed and durable ships or carracks. Drilled people, in this instance, were highly trained Portuguese sailors, who were expert not only in navigation and sailing, but also in battle. Law's account shows us how, with great difficulty, a nascent colonial empire was established. Reliable networks were the key to long-distance control, as Lisbon became an authoritative centre for a number of territories that came under its 'power'.

Law's example is a modest one, but my contention is that 'big' phenomena – such as globalisation – are merely the piling on top of one another of hundreds of specific (international) networks. For example, the global business network, which is taken by some to underlie a global economic system, has to be understood as hundreds of individual companies and other actors (CEOs, business regulators, and so on), every one of which has its own specific 'global' make-up and character. Every one of these companies in turn is constituted by a variety of specific elements – technical, managerial, disciplinary, and so on – which must be put together and maintained. Of course, these companies are often antagonistic towards each other, especially where competition in tightly defined markets takes place (often companies act as if the market is a zero-sum game, and Pepsi and Coca-Cola, Microsoft and Apple sometimes imagine they can only succeed at the expense of their rivals). The 'global business network', then, must be understood as a temporary and unstable phenomenon, always likely to be broken apart, always needing maintenance.

Such networks aim at the diffusion – or better, the generation and regeneration – of power,[9] and the efficient control of peoples, territories and objects that are at a distance. In maintaining this, I suggest that the spaces between the governor and the governed – the spaces of networks of control and domination – must be constructed, as I discuss in the next section, by the management and realignment of Euclidean space.

Bending space

The spatial model of social network theorists such as Castells is too simple. In essence, Castells lays a technical network on top of a simple geographical space.[10] In this way, he is able to shrink the globe, but the relations between the spaces remain fairly constant. This is because the model of the network is one which privileges instantaneous communication, and which does not give sufficient room to the inevitable breakdown and failure of the network. As Law and Hetherington (2001) put it:

> Notwithstanding twentieth-century excitements about the relativity of space-time, in six hundred years of surveying, cartography, nation-building and GIS,[11] the idea that there is (a single) geographical space has been naturalized for Euro-Americans. This means that it is very difficult to imagine space as anything other than some kind of a neutral container, a medium, within which places … may be located. And this in turn means that any attempt to challenge this picture is very hard work and runs against the grain of common sense. As is indeed suggested by the tropes about global space-time compression which, though they index a sense of variability in distance and speed, tend at the same time to re-enact this naturalized geographical view of space.

We can develop Law and Hetherington's point further: spaces are only brought into being by network associations. Space is just as much 'made' as place. What successful (global) governance does is bend space in such a way that distant actors are rendered close. This, of course, is not at all the same as geographical proximity. Latour (1997) has the nice example of the two reindeer in Alaska who are ten metres apart, but separated forever by an above-ground pipeline which means that they would have to travel hundreds of miles to mate. By contrast, the British-made late-eighteenth/early-nineteenth-century Sydney was 'closer' to London than it was to Broken Hill.[12] As Law and Hetherington assert, what we need to understand here is that space is constructed as the result of what they call a 'material semiotics', but what I am calling a 'knowledge'.[13]

What might this mean for global governance? First, we have to reconceptualise our understanding of globalisation to include an engagement with materials. To return once more to our colonial British example, in the middle of the nineteenth century the British struggled to establish efficient telegraphic communication which would make the network they had established that stretched to the Australian colonies more durable (Hirst 1988). The first telegraph link was established from Melbourne to Williamstown in 1854; in New South Wales, the first line went up in 1858, and by 1862 the lines reached to the borders of the colony and every substantial town was connected. A new town joined the telegraph network long before its roads were made and decades before any railway connection (Hirst 1988: 253). Yet there were constant problems, constant oscillations between order and disorder. The achievement of a reasonably stable order only emerged when a heterogeneous network (obedient human actors, efficient technologies, reliable communications, powerful weapons, authoritative texts, acceptable political ideas, commercial imperatives) had been put together. Yet this order constantly oscillated on the verge of disorder. Routinised solutions were occasionally built up, but these were always liable to be disrupted. The network only became strong as a million weak ties were made.

Sociotechnological networks

As I have already suggested, Latour enables us to think a little differently about the character of global networks, in particular providing us with the means to theorise technology and non-human actors. To make this point clearer, we can consider Latour's (1992) paper on the so-called 'missing masses' of sociological theory. Latour begins by alluding to the 'missing mass' in physics, and wonders whether there is something similar that sociology needs to complete itself. He goes on to argue that just as Marxist analysis reinvigorated social research by including the previously overlooked masses, moving us away from social change understood through the lives of 'Great Men', so we can open up some exciting new avenues by expanding sociology to include the non-humans who are so vital in keeping society going. The rest of his article concentrates on a number of vital non-humans – including those who help us with problems such as keeping doors open and closed (fire doors, keys, and so on), and those who help us with traffic regulation (seat-belts, traffic lights, speed bumps). Latour argues that society is a complex mixture of the human and the non-human, and although social science has tended to treat the latter with disdain, they are an irreplaceable part of social order. For Latour, what is characteristic of human society is that it relies on far more than the social – or at least the social as it is usually understood. All of us are continuously embedded in networks in which the human and the non-human are intertwined. He even goes so far as to suggest that non-humans are considerably more 'moral' than the humans with whom they share a network – for example, speed bumps, traffic lights and road signs all enforce, unwaveringly, a morality of road use on (mostly) recalcitrant humans.

When we make use of this perspective to understand global networks, it is clear that we need to analyse them as 'socio-technological' – complex amalgams of humans and non-humans. In the globalisation literature, John Urry has perhaps made the most significant contribution to our attempts to understand networks in this way. While Urry (2000a) is mostly concerned with the emergence of a new form of 'nomadism', it is clear that his concept of the networks across which these nomads move – a concept which stresses fluidity – is profoundly influenced by Latour. Urry also stresses the non-human actors: 'these [sc. global networks and fluids] are inhuman hybrids' (Urry 2000b: 194) – hybrids, of course, of the human and the non-human. For example, consider any international food chain: its networks are both human and non-human. It must have efficient personnel structures (workers, managers, human resource experts and so on), but it must also have efficient non-human structures – it must be able to transport and deliver food supplies, to dispose of waste, to manage its machinery, to maintain computer networks, to communicate, and so forth.

The problem of scale

In general, the globalisation literature has tended to assume that two sets of processes – the local and the global – are at work, with the global broadly displacing the local. But even in those arguments which seek to emphasise the interweaving of a number of different scales – regional, individual, community, national, global – such as Robertson's (1995) notion of the 'glocal', at the very moment of suggesting a dialectical relation between levels, we see their potential separability creeping back in. To return to Castells' vision of the network society, the network is clearly characterised as operating on a double level. By contrast, ANT deliberately eschews scale as a presumption. Networks are composed of many heterogeneous elements, some of which are longer or shorter; as Latour (1993: 122) puts it, 'networks … are by nature neither local nor global but are more or less long and more or less connected'. In this reading, scale is a result of networks, rather than a pre-existing category by which networks might be judged. To the extent that scale is usually understood in terms of relation to geographical space, we can assert once again that space, like scale, is invented by networks, rather than a neutral canvas on to which our networks are laid.

For example, an airline such as Qantas offers the consumer a number of routes. Not all routes are possible; I am unable to fly everywhere I want, for example, and some routes require me to travel 'backwards' in order to go forwards (if I want to go from Brisbane to Bangkok, I have to go to Sydney first, which takes me the wrong way – unless I lose patience with Qantas's routeing and go with Thai Air instead). Qantas also connects up with a number of 'partner' airlines, including British Airways, allowing customers access to other travel possibilities. In this way a network of global air travel is constituted, but the global scale is the result of a number of networks put together, which results in Sydney being nearer to Bangkok than Brisbane is. A further point is that analysis of the Qantas network should proceed methodologically in exactly the same way as analysis of Brisbane Car Hire Ltd. The networks are made up of the same elements (people, machines, fuel, depots, storage facilities and so on). The 'global' network that Qantas gives us access to is no different in kind from the 'local' network that Brisbane Car Hire Ltd gives us access to; it is simply a matter of differing connections and differing lengths.

From disorder to order

Networks are the 'problem spaces' around which various actors[14] – human and non-human – are organised. The ordering of networks is a constant, but this ordering is always contingent and ongoing. Like John Law (1994), I prefer the verbal to the substantive form, because 'order' is quite rare, while 'ordering' is ubiquitous. However, networks can become more and more routinised, more and more stable, in which case they *give the appearance* of being more ordered – they become candidates for descriptions using the substantive 'order'.

Kendall and Wickham (2001) have argued that the tendency to order is some-thing of an ontological necessity, built into social systems. While to a certain extent their argument is influenced by the Nietzschean notion of the 'will to govern', they also make use of the systems theory of such writers as Prigogine and Stengers (1984). Chaotic systems, certainly in some current versions of theo-retical physics, have a tendency to become ordered, or sometimes to oscillate between order and chaos. While Kendall and Wickham argue that these character-istics of physical systems are in principle applicable to any social system, whether termites or humans are under consideration, it is also possible, in less positivist terms, to argue that human society historically has tended towards systems of order – the concern with the over-ordering of society expressed in the work of Weber, Marcuse or Habermas is testimony to such a drift. While such forms of organisation are always likely – that is to say, while we are likely to see networks emerge that can be understood as examples of social ordering – it should be stressed that there is nothing necessary about the particular forms of organised networks that will emerge. These need to be understood as contingent.[15]

But we can say more: networks provide us with the possibility of moving rapidly though time and space, and so networks are the key for those who wish to produce social order and to dominate. But how do we move from a fragile network-in-the-making to a successful, strong and virtually unchallengeable global network?

How did the Portuguese go from an idea in Lisbon to a commercial, territorial and military empire? How did the British make the Australian colonies obedient and responsive? How did Nike become a huge transnational corporation?

One possible answer lies in the ability of actors to delegate to materials (Law 2001). It is important to turn words, ideas and speeches into more durable objects. 'The power of the manager may now be obtained by a long series of telephone calls, record-keeping, walls, clothes and machines' (Latour 1986: 276). What Latour points to here is that only insofar as an actor can embed him- or herself within a durable network, can he or she maintain their position. On their own, human voices, orders and actions do not get very far, but as they are bolstered by non-humans, they take on a new strength – once they are written down as orders, given durability and longevity through effective communications systems, housed in buildings, moved from zone to zone with transportation devices, enforced with weaponry, the wishes and hollow words of humans are given force. As John Law (2001) puts it, the 'obduracy [sc. of a network] is achieved in part by delegating what might have been purely social relations into other materials'. To return to our critique of the social network literature, it seems to us that for Castells, Wallerstein, and Gereffi, global domination is an effect of the will of an individual or a class. While it appears that Castells' emphasis on technological networks is a good example of material delegation, really Castells merely uses the notion of technology to speed up human interactions.[16] Morality and agency are still properties of humans. Castells sees networks as the modern structural form of global capitalism, yet I am urging that networks be seen as fluid, relational processes. I concur with Dicken *et al.* (2001: 91), who argue that networks, rather than firms, individuals or nation-states, are the fundamental units of analysis of the global economy.

Conclusion

In this chapter, I have attempted to produce a workable definition of 'network' that might inform studies of international governance. One of my main tasks was to suggest that the notion of network, which has a long history in globalisation studies, is a problematic descriptive or theoretical device. In particular, I suggested that the networks theorised by Castells, Wallerstein and Gereffi understand the new global economy as composed of a singular network; but the model of network that is used is unhelpful, precisely because it is too technical. In addition, terms such as 'network society' are examples of the misunderstanding of effect for cause. Networks are asked to take on the task of explaining any number of new social arrangements, as well as filling in the microsocial chasm that appears underneath the grand theory superstructure. I propose a very different concept of the network, one which I believe can better describe processes of ordering: in this way, processes that previously we might have been tempted to explain away with the magic word 'globalisation' have now become nothing more or less than networks composed of various longer or shorter connections, but they are also hybrids, mixing freely the human and the non-human, the material and the social, the semiotic and the natural.

Networks must be understood as plural, and always begin from a local, mobile, microphysical point; there is a case for stating that they may better be described as international than global. The technical metaphor of network is misleading; networks may occasionally end up as technical in character, but this is just one possibility, and is a poor description of most networks, which are rhizomic rather than root-like. Technical networks, such as the phone or the Internet, which are heavily strategic, must be understood as the result of previous networks, which included human and non-human actors, and a variety of materials.

Networks are much more than social: they are 'materially semiotic', as Law and Hetherington put it. They are a mixture of human words and ideas, with the material basis that gives the former their durability, their strength and their ability to act at a distance. Networks can and should be used to rebuild social theory from the ground up; however, they cannot be used as a 'filler' to make grand theory more realistic.

Successfully governed space is the result of (material-semiotic) associations; therefore, space is not a given, but is made.[17] One consequence of this view is that there are multiple spaces and multiple times. Again, I stress the difference between this conception of the network and that found elsewhere – the concept of network can sometimes be used to assert the existence of a singular capitalist network, but it seems to us that this is problematic. Analysis of these multiple networks cannot take a general form, but must be done on a case-by-case basis.

It is possible, although difficult, to build networks that endure. Most networks are doomed to failure, or promise much and then collapse. 'Knowledge', understood as an ensemble of practices, texts, materials, ways of acting and problematising, is the key to the production of a durable network. Knowledge – or, if you prefer, 'immutable mobiles' – are the packages that enable networks to cohere and prosper. Strength – reliable durability – comes from building up flexibility in the network, rather than from concentrating on a single route through a network. A strong network is not one that has a single strong pathway – for such a network is easily broken – but one which has multiple, rhizomic connections, and which can reroute and reconfigure when the inevitable problems are encountered.

Network space must be distinguished from geographical space (see also Thrift 1996); networks are about 'bending' space. Those who dominate others have successfully bent space (and time). I suggest that, for a number of reasons, the movement from chaos to order is built into nascent networks. Whether we follow a Nietzschean and Foucaultian line, and understand a 'will to power' as immanent to networks, whether we follow Prigogine and Stengers (1984), and understand the ordering of chaotic systems as guaranteed by the laws of physics, or, indeed, whether we believe in the necessity of complex systems emerging from simple, disordered systems on the basis of probability theory, all of these arguments point to a movement in the direction of increasingly complex networks. No doubt these networks are mostly doomed to fail and collapse, and return to disorder. Although, then, there is an oscillation between ordering and disordering, I suggest an ontological priority for ordering – 'order from chaos'. We start from 'irreducible, incommensurable, unconnected localities, which then, at great price, sometimes end into provisionally commensurable connections' (Latour 1997). Sometimes, with great struggle and over long periods of time, coherent, durable networks will be put together. Understanding these material-semiotic, heterogeneous, human–non-human networks is the key to understanding (global) government.

Notes

1 The author would like to thank the following for comments and discussion: Roger King, Wendy Larner, Mike Michael, William Walters and Gary Wickham.
2 Castells seems to be drawn to the notion of a single network because of: (1) his attachment to a rather unvariegated version of capitalism; and (2) his inability to imagine networks on models other than those of technologies.
3 Interestingly, Hirst and Thompson (1996) suggest that the period 1870–1914 may actually have seen more and stronger interconnections between national actors than the present historical conjuncture.
4 This section depends heavily on some schematic remarks presented in Latour (1997).
5 Here we must understand the computer network as the stabilised state – or result – of a *previous* network which contained engineers, chips, technical problems, silicon and a number of other elements. As should be clear, we are attempting to expand the notion of network beyond the merely technical.
6 A rhizome is a plant that does not have a tree structure, but is a series of roots that interconnect and grow into each other, such as a tuber. This metaphor can be used to understand any network that interconnects unexpectedly and has a rather chaotic series of interlinks. By contrast, tree structures are regular and always grow outward, thus they do not interconnect.
7 This emphasis on the rhizome as the better metaphor for international networks leads to an interesting hypothesis about strength. Networks that are intensively structured – that put all their eggs in one basket, so to speak – are the weakest. The strong network (or corporation) is able to reroute instructions/communications/etc. if there is a temporary breakdown. Strength, then, does not result from building-up one route intensively, but from the ability to flexibly reroute.
8 See King and Kendall (2004).
9 Following Latour (1986), it is better to think of power as something that is continuously generated as it travels along networks and from actor to actor, rather than as a token which loses its strength as it meets with the resistance of others. Power, in this account, is understood as the actions of many, rather than the project of one person.
10 There are exceptions in the social networks literature, especially in the work of geographers such as David Harvey (1989). In addition, we should mention the work of John Urry (2000a, 2000b, 2003), who thinks beyond geographical space precisely because he weds ANT to more traditional theory in globalisation and social network studies.
11 Geographical Information Systems.
12 Broken Hill is a town in New South Wales, Australia.
13 Indeed, it may be possible to think of space as a 'performance': space as the result of a network of many different materials (maps, communications, texts, and so forth) that perform space to bring it into being. That is to say, space is constructed out of all of these various elements, rather than existing a priori.
14 In ANT, it has become more common to use the term 'actant' rather than 'actor', mostly to signify the idea that agency is not the prerogative of humans.

15 Gould (1996) argues that, purely on probabilistic grounds, a number of complex orderings will emerge, even when simplicity is the most likely state of any system. His argument derives not from a Nietzschean 'will to govern', but from the observation that simple orderings (for example, single-celled organisms) are at the left wall of a distribution that runs from simple to complex. Consequently, even random movement is bound to produce increased complexity, because development cannot go in the direction of greater simplicity.

16 Virilio (1986) argues in a similar sort of way to Castells – but speed is not enough. Durability, flexibility, and multiplicity are other characteristics of the successful network.

17 It no doubt follows that time is also 'made', but this is another argument.

References

Amin, A. and Thrift, N. (2002) *Cities: re-imagining the urban*, Cambridge: Polity.

Callon, M. (1986) 'Some elements of a sociology of translation: domestication of the scallops and the fishermen of St Brieuc Bay', in J. Law (ed.) *Power, Action, and Belief*, London: Routledge & Kegan Paul.

Castells, M. (1996) *The Information Age: vol. 1*, Oxford: Blackwell.

——(1998) *The Information Age: vol. 2*, Oxford: Blackwell.

——(2000a) *The Information Age: vol. 3*, Oxford: Blackwell.

——(2000b) 'Materials for an explanatory theory of the network society', *British Journal of Sociology*, 51(1): 5–24.

Davidson, A. (1991) *The Invisible State: the formation of the Australian state 1788–1901*, Cambridge: Cambridge University Press.

Deleuze, G. and Guattari, F. (1981) 'Rhizome', *I&C*, 8(Spring): 49–71.

Dicken, P., Kelly, P.F., Olds, K. and Yeung, H.W.-C. (2001) 'Chains and networks, territories and scales: towards a relational framework for analysing the global economy', *Global Networks*, 1(2): 89–112.

Eddy, J.J. (1969) *Britain and the Australian Colonies 1818–1831: the technique of government*, Oxford: Clarendon Press.

Foucault, M. (1978) 'Governmentality', *I&C*, 6: 5–21.

——(1981) 'Omnes et singulatim: towards a criticism of "political reason"', in S. McMurrin (ed.) *The Tanner Lectures on Human Values, vol. 2*, Salt Lake City: University of Utah Press.

Gereffi, G. (1996) 'Global commodity chains: new forms of coordination and control among nations and firms in international industries', *Competition and Change*, 1: 427–439.

Giddens, A. (1990) *The Consequences of Modernity*, Cambridge: Polity.

Gould, S.J. (1996) *Full House: the spread of excellence from Plato to Darwin*, New York: Harmony Books.

Harvey, D. (1989) *The Condition of Postmodernity: an enquiry into the origins of cultural change*, Oxford: Blackwell.

——(2001) *Spaces of Capital: towards a critical geography*, London, Routledge.

Hirst, J.B. (1988) *The Strange Birth of Colonial Democracy: New South Wales 1848–1884*, Sydney: Allen & Unwin.

Hirst, P. and Thompson, G. (1996) *Globalization in Question*, Cambridge: Polity.

Kendall, G. (1997) 'Governing at a distance: Anglo-Australian relations 1840–1870', *Australian Journal of Political Science*, 32(2): 223–235.

Kendall, G. and Wickham, G. (2001) *Understanding Culture: cultural studies, order, ordering*, London: Sage.

King, R. and Kendall, G. (2004) *The State, Democracy and Globalization*, London: Palgrave Macmillan.

Latour, B. (1986) 'The Powers of Association', in J. Law (ed.) *Power, Belief and Action*, London: Routledge.

——(1987) *Science in Action: how to follow engineers in society*, Milton Keynes: Open University Press.

——(1992) 'Where are the missing masses?', in W. Bijker and J. Law (eds) *Shaping Technology/Building Society*, Cambridge, MA: MIT Press.

——(1993) *We Have Never Been Modern*, Hemel Hempstead: Harvester Wheatsheaf.

——(1997) 'The trouble with actor-network theory'. Online. Available at: http://www.ensmp.fr/~latour/poparticles/poparticle/p067.html

Law, J. (1986) 'On the methods of long-distance control: vessels, navigation and the Portuguese route to India', in J. Law (ed.) *Power, Action and Belief: a new sociology of knowledge?*, London: Routledge.

——(1994) *Organising Modernity*, Oxford: Blackwell.

——(2001) 'Ordering and obduracy', Centre for Science Studies and the Department of Sociology, Lancaster University. Online. Available at: http://www.comp.lancs.ac.uk/sociology/soc068jl.html

Law, J. and Hetherington, K. (2001) 'Materialities, spatialities, globalities', Department of Sociology, Lancaster University. Online. Available at: http://www.comp.lancs.ac.uk/sociology/soc029jl.html

Morrell, W.P. (1966) *British Colonial Policy in the Age of Peel and Russell*, London, Cass (1st edn 1930, Oxford).

Prigogine, I. and Stengers, I. (1984) *Order out of Chaos: man's new dialogue with nature*, New York: Bantam Books.

Robertson, R. (1995) 'Glocalization: time–space and homogeneity–heterogeneity', in M. Featherstone, S. Lash and R. Robertson (eds) *Global Modernities*, London: Sage.

Rose, N. (1985) *The Psychological Complex*, London: Routledge.

Thrift, N. (1996) *Spatial Formations*, London: Sage.

Urry, J. (2000a) *Sociology Beyond Societies: mobilities for the twenty-first century*, London: Routledge.

——(2000b) 'Mobile sociology', *British Journal of Sociology*, 51(1): 185–203.

——(2003) *Global Complexity*, Cambridge: Polity.

Virilio, P. (1986) *Speed and Politics: an essay on dromology*, New York: Columbia University Press.

Waddington, C. (1977) *Tools for Thought*, London: Paladin.

Wallerstein, I. (1974) *The Modern World System, vol. 1*, London, Academic Press.

——(1980) *The Modern World System, vol. 2*, London, Academic Press.

——(1989) *The Modern World System, vol. 3*, London, Academic Press.

4 The security of governance

Michael Dillon

> In a previous lecture on apparatuses of security, I tried to explain the emergence of a set of problems specific to the issue of population, and on closer inspection it turned out that we would also need to take into account the problematic of government. In short one needed to analyse the series: security, population, government.
>
> (Foucault 1991: 87)

How is it that the peace of liberal governance is so suffused with the logics of war? What distinguishing features do those logics of war display? How is it that self-regulating freedoms of governance are so intimately correlated with systems of surveillance? How is it that such freedoms require extensive apparatuses of security? How is it that liberal governance finds itself so comprehensively endangered in the ways that its hyperbolic preoccupation with security indicates that it does? This is a preoccupation that transcends traditional international relations distinctions between inside and outside, especially now that governance has gone global. How are these features related to the biopolitical ways in which liberal regimes of power have come to operate both at home and abroad since the dissolution of the Cold War? How, especially, to explain the ways in which liberal biopolitics, so dedicated to power over life rather than power over death, is simultaneously also such a supremely well-armed geopolitical project globally. Geopolitical, moreover, *as a biopolitical project* in pursuit of the propagation of population welfare, rather than the more traditional geostrategic goals associated with sovereignty, the control of territory and the sequestration of resources.

Are these emergency measures only, fundamentally antipathetic to the real nature of liberal regimes of power, forced upon global liberal governance by agents radically hostile to its civilising-through-rationalising project of global pacification? Do these features somehow contradict the many other aspects of global governmentality that construe individuals and populations as agents in the operation of self-regulating freedoms, denying the depth ontologies that have characterised traditional discourses of national and international security? Are the many ways in which security operates within the political rationalities and technologies of liberal criminology (O'Malley 1998; Valverde 1998), or the diverse ways in which governmental subjectivities are constrained to manage their own securities through insurance, economy and welfare (Valverde and Cirak 2003; Ewald 1991), at odds with global governmentality as a geopoliticised biopolitical project? Must an account of the micro-politics of securitisation – including, for example, the arcane ways in which catastrophe insurance for individual and corporate risk is securitised through the distribution of risk into the capital and bond markets (Bougen 2003) – conflict with the recognition that depth ontologies are also at work in global governmentality? How is the Manichean rhetoric of the 'war on terror' to be reconciled with the ways in which the terrorist threat is rendered governable through the provision of terrorist insurance; a further illustration of the diverse ways in which what was once known as national security has become a complex public/private partnership through which individuals and corporations become agents in the securing of both their own security and public safety?

I think not. On the contrary, governmentality is born of a technological ontology that proceeds through reflexive epistemologies. Here the dialogical interplay of the ontological and the technological is in evidence. If it takes a metaphysic to imagine a technic, it takes a technic to realise a metaphysic. But even that rendition fails to do justice to the co-evolutionary dynamic that exists in the power relations between technology and ontology. This is a mutually disclosive relationship in which each seems propelled by independent dynamics as well: the technologist continuously to interrogate and refine systems, the ontologist to secure the meaning of being.[1] But they have a deep affinity for one another in that each seeks to secure its object of reference.

Are these features integral to liberal governance in general and to global governmentality in particular? Is there something about the operational logics of liberal regimes of power – even as reflexive, epistemically driven, dividing practices concerned to promote diverse forms of agency as the principal means of deploying individuals and populations across fields of power relations governed by self-regulating freedoms – that is deeply complicit with security and war? Could one refer to the liberal way of war and the liberal way of peace as two sides of the same political coin? A political rationality equally at home with exposure to death as it is with promotion of life?

These suspicions run throughout Foucault's exploration of liberal regimes of power, and surface powerfully in global governmentality where the intersection of sovereign and biopower provides a turbulent confluence of the detailed operations of power that preoccupied Foucault throughout his life. Foucault's lecture series *Society Must be Defended* (1997a) and *Security, Territory, Population* (1997b), while addressing many other issues, also project a broader analytic of the relationship between security and biopolitics. It is one that encourages a complexification of Foucault's account of the distinction between sovereign juridical and other forms of disciplinary power/knowledge, anatamo-power and biopower.

This chapter pursues these and other insights I have learned through Foucault's account of power in general, and of the relation between sovereign power, governance and biopower in particular. Three points are worth emphasising in summary fashion. First, power is not a universal or a meta-physical principal that applies to all things across space and time. Both sovereign and governmental power are relational phenomena that have spatially and temporally specific idioms (Dillon 2003b). Second, the many idioms of power are not mutually exclusive. They may co-exist in either tension-filled or mutually supporting ways. Third, and most importantly, the generative principle of formation governing any idiom of power and how we are construed by that idiom must be explored.

It is the third point that especially concerns this chapter. To anticipate the argument, something profoundly important happens to the problematisation of security and war when the referent object of biopower – species life – becomes the material for the strategising of power relations. Since liberalism in its governmental and biopolitical forms is a regime based upon the promotion of species life, liberalism becomes deeply implicated in this re-problematisation of security and war. As I pursue this insight, it becomes evident that global governmentality is an extraordinary complex of power relations in which the ontological is inextricably mixed with the epistemological – no epistemology or technology without ontology we might sloganise[2] – and in which the imperatives to punish and kill are deeply implicated in the political rationalities, technologies and subjectivities favoured by governmentality. Here, the bio of biopower, how human material must be construed to be amenable to different idioms of power, mutates across different racial and cultural, as well as digital and molecular, registers. Above all, it becomes clear there is no power over life that does not simultaneously expose that life to mortal danger and death.

Life exposed to death is, one might say, the human condition. But that truism is not the issue. Different regimes of order expose life to death in ways peculiar to the operation of those regimes (Agamben 1998). If power is idiomatic so too are its cruelties. Exposure of life to mortal danger is instantiated through different discourses of danger and problematisations of security. To put it in the biopolitical terms that concern this chapter, just as there is no single way of recruiting species life into the strategising of power relations – what Foucault called the operation of biopower and biopolitics – there is no single way of exposing life to mortal danger and death. Different problematisations of security and war will depend upon how species life is known and classified, as well as what power/knowledge techniques and political rationalities are employed. This even applies to regimes committed 'in good faith' to the promotion of species life. Nor is this a paradox. It is an effect of the logic of those regimes, a function of their biopolitical generative principles of formation. That said, a further, more threatening, logic is deeply installed in the biopolitics of governance: one that leads to a hyperbolicisation of the governmental preoccupation with security. The primary purpose of this chapter is to explore how that logic operates within and alongside global governmentality, a domain distinguished above all by complex intersections of sovereign and biopolitical idioms of power.

The changing problematisation of security

The epigraph that heads this paper specifies the close tie Foucault detected between security, population and government. What began as an interest in the military as a site of disciplinary organisation (*Discipline and Punish* 1982), burgeoned into a wide-ranging problematic concerning the character of biopower (*The History of Sexuality* 1987; 'The Birth of Biopolitics' 1997c; 'On the Government of the Living' 1997d). That preoccupation soon encompassed liberal regimes of power ('Governmentality' 1991) and eventually the widest possible relation between power, politics and war ('Society Must be Defended' 1997a; 'Security, Territory, Population' 1997b; 'The Tanner Lectures' 1988). In these enquiries, security begins to recur as a pivotal term although it never becomes a sustained focus of analysis in the same way, for example, that 'sex' did. One has therefore to reconstruct a Foucauldian reading of security. It cannot slavishly follow Foucault since he didn't give a direct lead. It must also innovate in a Foucauldian voice to flesh out other concerns and paradoxes of security that do not occur among his reflections.

Viewed through a Foucauldean analytic of power and problematisation, the history of security cannot be construed as the pursuit of a universal value by pre-formed political agents such as the state or subject. That is not the way things work for Foucault. Subjects are always the subjects of power. Security is above all a source for the power relations that constitute human beings as subjects of security. Neither can the history of security be concerned exclusively with the preservation of life and collective ways of living, since security discourses are sutured into other discursive formations, politically economically, socially and scientifically. Securitisation subjectifies and objectifies in manifold ways. The grand narratives of geopolitics, sovereignty, national self-determination, imperial conquest and ideological conflict would also be bracketed-off, replaced with accounts of the micro-practices by which individual and collective bodies are inscribed by power, recruited into self-subjectification through their desiring and freedom, fears and insecurities.

Political conditionality and good governance criteria attached to development aid policies and loans have been one fruitful source of micro-political practices of global governmentality (Rojas 2001; Kapur and Webb 2000). So too are the security-development complexes that emerged during the 1990s, involving governmental, non-governmental and international organisations (Duffield 1997, 1999, 2001). Within contemporary aid discourse, not only is poverty and under-development associated with conflict, conflict itself is regarded as complicating poverty and deepening underdevelopment.

Not only is underdevelopment thus classified as dangerous, violence-laden, endemic conflict amongst impoverished populations appears to deepen that danger. The micro-practices of underdevelopment are both a source of conflict and a result of conflict: the locus of a vicious cycle of violence and human rights abuse. By the 1990s such sentiments provided the rationale for the widespread incorporation of a security problematic committed to conflict prevention and conflict resolution into development aid policy. This represented the securitisation of the politics of development (Duffield 1997, 1999, 2001; Crush 1995; Escobar 1995). Because of the tight correlation of underdevelopment and conflict, the conduct of conduct became a major focus of concern for aid agencies. Thus, according to a World Bank and Carter Centre report on conflict resolution:

> First, *behaviour* must be altered from the application of violence to more peaceful forms of dispute settlement; second, a transition from wartime to a peace *mentality* needs to occur; third, the *system of risks and rewards should* encourage peaceful pursuit of livelihoods, rather than intimidation, violence and rent-seeking; fourth, *adversaries must come to view each other as members of the same society, working toward a common goal a peaceful and prosperous future; and fifth, structures and institutions must be amended to support these new peaceful transformations.*
> (In Rojas 2001: 3–4, emphasis in original)

Whereas political realists tend to treat security as a foundational value to identity and polity alike, the history of security, as these brief references indicate, is clearly a history of changing problematisations. Critical security discourses in international relations, together with human rights discourses, have helped to generate a more variegated account of security over the past twenty years (Cassese 1999; Adler 1998; Kratochwil 1998; Held and McGrew 1998). Here, security is seen to be a function of social construction, integral to successful development and dependent upon the extension of liberal democratic values and respect for human rights, simultaneously a prerequisite for and a product of good governance (Lipschutz 1995; Russett 1993; Rakenerud and Herge 1997; Oneal and Russett 1999; Barbieri and Schneider 1999; Donnelly 1998; Stefek 2003).

In a Foucauldean vein security becomes much more, however, than a problematisation. Such an investigation of security must also examine its regime of truth and its moral economy. That moral economy is formed in part by the way in which discursive formations of biopower invite their subjects to regulate themselves in pursuit of their changing wellbeing. Since the dissolution of the geopolitics of the Cold War the security politics of global liberal governance has come to depend extensively upon risk, insurance, surveillance, criminalisation and the vernacular of street architecture to shape rational behaviour by empowering security-conscious subjectivities (Dillon 2003a, 2003b; Dillon and Reid 2000, 2001). Discourses of security must, in addition, pose the following two questions: How is one to punish? And, who is it permitted to kill? To answer these questions, a Foucauldean analytic of security would investigate a given regime of security, noting how it differs from others. The sources of those differences would most likely be found in changing understandings of truth and power, the redefining of security as an epistemic object, and the changing moral economies concerning the bodies subject to security practices as well as the political rationalities in which all these are bound up.

One of the challenges to a classically micro-political Foucauldian approach is the huge political register at work in security and the way in which war regularly functions as the privileged locus of the real. It is difficult to sustain the privi-leging of the micro over the macro that Foucault usually champions precisely because security provides a powerful point of intersection between the two. With discourses of security, the micro-political regularly becomes the macro-political, for example when minor infringements of codes of normalisation become incite-ments to nationalistic fervour, and when macro-political calls to nation result in the inscription of everyday conduct. This point was noted by Colin Gordon (1991), who refers to security as a 'specific principle of political method and practice' that joins the governing of the social body to the 'proper conduct' of the individual, to the governing of oneself. Foucault also referred to it as the process of internal colonisation.

The very etymology of security betrays ancient links to foundational truths, as well as to identity and survival, and the deployment of the word in political philos-ophy constantly ties it into the essence of social identity as well as to the foundation of political order (Dillon 1996). Foucault's insistence on the specificity of discourses thus has to be reconciled with the imperial temper and universalising impulses of security. Because problematisations of security are simultaneously problematisations of the political subject, security discourses concern foundational claims to truth and politics. Discourses of security effect an intersection rather than a differentiation between micro and the macro practices of power. An apparatus of security must therefore become a *dispositif* or broad grid of political intelligibility that does not so much concentrate forces as lay out a dynamic field of possibilities that is extensive as well as intensive, ontological as well as epistemic.

Just as discourses of security effect an intersection between the micro- and the macro-political, they effect an equally important intersection between geopolitics and biopolitics. In fact there is no geopolitics that does not imply a correlate biopolitics, and no biopolitics without its corresponding geopolitics. Take, for example, the ways in which Malthus' population science was recruited into racial geopolitical projects in the nineteenth century; how racialist doctrines informed European imperialisms, liberal as well as autocratic; and how racial 'science' informed German geopolitics throughout the first part of the twentieth century. Spatiality is directly linked there, for example, to raciality through the resonant terms '*raum*' and '*Lebensraum*', where '*raum*' becomes the very geopolitical project required for species existence (Diner 1999; Ó Tuathail 1996).

Global governmentality, biopolitics and the securing of species life

Since liberal regimes of power are amongst the most historically successful at developing biopolitical forms of power, liberalism is ineluctably incorporated into Foucault's analytic of power. In the process it falls under hermeneutics of suspicion concerning not only relationships between biopower, population and governance, but also the closely allied problematisations of security and war. These take their character from the implications that follow from recruiting species life into the strategisation of power relations.

Species life is not, however, a datum. It is an undecidable. In recruiting species life into power relations biopolitics must therefore first speciate the human. I think this is what Giorgio Agamben (1998) means when he talks about the production of bare life. However much speciated, human life is engaged in its own interpretative transformation via techniques of power that derive from the practices of speciation (the same goes, of course, for the use of the term 'human'). The human has not always and everywhere been a species. Even within the Western tradition, humans were once Children of God: a very different thing. In short, speciation is itself a dividing practice of power/knowledge. Biopolitically, species life may be determined in all sorts of ways, furnishing principles of formation for different kinds of power relations. Indeed, one of the distinguishing features of liberalism is its self-reflexive success in generating new principles for governing species life as the specification of species changes (Dean 1999; Rose 1999; Novas and Rose 2000).

The bios of biopower has shifted significantly since the geopolitics of the nineteenth and twentieth centuries. Once located in blood and soil, bodies or populations have come to be distinguished by cultural markers. Balibar and Wallerstein define the 'new racism' as:

> a racism whose dominant theme is not biological hereditary, but the insurmountability of cultural differences, a racism which, at first sight, does not postulate the superiority of certain groups or peoples in relation to others, but 'only' the harmfulness of abolishing frontiers, the incompatibility of lifestyles and traditions.
>
> (1991: 2)

But the bios of biopower has also been returned to the biological through molecular science and digitalisation. The bios has become code in a biophilosophical strategic discourse that has emerged through the Revolution in Military Affairs (RMA), empowered by the digitalisation of weapons and the championing of a new form of 'network-centric' warfare (Dillon 2002, 2003c, 2003d; Dillon and Reid 2001). One result of this development is that space and species life both go virtual in governmental networks with a corresponding intensive and extensive hyperbolicisation of security. Indeed, in Baudrillardian fashion, a hypersecurity emerges – witness many aspects of the current war on terrorism – in which the referent object of security lacks all significant source outside the network-centric circulation of security itself. The threat is already within the circuits. Viral-like, the danger is already there within the codes. The new strategic discourses of network-centric and strategic information warfare argue as much (Arquilla and Ronfeldt 1993, 1996, 1998, 2001; Libicki 1994, 1999; Alberts and Czerwinski 1994).

As the bios is reinterpreted via molecularisation and digitalisation, biopower and biopolitics follow suit. The biopower of biopolitics has mutated into the recombinant biopower of code. Biopower is developing a deep concern with the science of systemic behaviour not simply of biological bodies, but also of hybrid and cyborg-like assemblages, or complex adaptive systems. Since code is the common denominator of the digital and the molecular revolutions, all material is beginning to be conceived as code, circulating and operating through networks themselves conceived in informational terms (Bogard 1996). Information as code is elevated from a commodity or medium of communication into a new object of knowledge and a new organising principle for ordering social, economic, epistemic, political and military relations of power. Under the ontological and epistemic commonplaces of the mode of code, information is no mere asset. It is *the* constituent element of all matter – conflating the organic and the inorganic. Biopolitics thus acquires a new ontology as it assimilates cybernetic and informational techniques of knowing, and administers individuals and populations in their relations with one another and their material environments recombinantly via code.

These bodies-in-formation are both assemblages of people, for example organisations or populations, and assemblages of people and machines, for example the information systems of cybernetics. Biopower has thus been tracking the evolution of the life sciences in their epistemic shift towards first the molecular, and now the molecular genetic vision of life (Kay 1993). Its interest has progressed from regulating sex and social relations through the specification of norms to the recombinatory regulation of assemblages and networks through the architecture of code (Baudrillard 1998).

The production of these bodies-in-formation also radically subverts security's traditional problematisation of pre-formed bodies operating in processes of exchange classically formulated by Carl Schmitt. According to Schmitt (1995: 26), a political entity comes into being when the distinction between friend and enemy is drawn. The new ensemble of recombinant biopolitical powers, drawing on a new biophilosophical interpretation of life, induces a new problematisation of security. As information or code, the human is no longer a stable referent, the application of which would securely differentiate between friends and enemies. Informational bodies-in-relation are dynamic, adaptive, re-combinatory, mutable and non-linear. Neither friend nor enemy can be given beforehand since the emergence of living assemblages is contingent on the dynamics of the modes, affects and effects of always already being related. In the dissolution of the friend–enemy distinction, the security problematic re-emerges in terms of the becoming-dangerous of recombinant modes of relation. Bodies-in-formation cannot be subject to the security problematic of the friend/enemy distinction, instead they become subject to becoming-dangerous and its allied symptomatologies of pathology, or epidemiologies of danger. Security goes hyperbolic as unlimited knowledge and surveillance of infinitely definable assemblages, populations and networks – as complex adaptive systems – is logically called for (Dillon and Reid 2001).

Risking the species

Pursuing a Foucauldian problematisation of security and war driven by biopolitical imperatives also requires a reformulation of the relationship between sovereign and biopower. It goes to the very heart of Foucault's analytic of power, challenging his sometimes radical overdetermination of the difference between them. Giorgio Agamben's critical reading of Foucault provides an indispensable guide to their conceptual interdependence.

Agamben, too, is concerned with what he calls the hidden point of intersection between juridico-institutional and biopolitical models of power. Noting that such an intersection is, 'logically implicit in Foucault's work', Agamben observes that it remains 'a blind spot'. It is a vanishing point in which the perspectival lines of Foucault's enquiry converge but never meet. In a stunning reinterpretation of sovereign power as a strategic operation of power rather than the expression of a subjective will, Agamben discovers this intersection in the very manoeuvre of sovereign power itself. Without detailing his argument the crux of the matter is this. Sovereign power is continuously reinstituted by a manoeuvre that renders life into raw life in order that the living may be distributed and dispersed across the realms of value and utility (Foucault 1987: 144). When dealing with discourses of security one has to remember that the values and utilities associated with these processes of dispersal are intimately related to the exposure of individuals and populations to mortal danger and death. Value and utility is a topography whose reverse scape is poverty, danger and death, as the correlation of health statistics with social welfare demonstrates. Agamben's formula, following classical texts, is to talk of the excluded-included-as-excluded. In the strategic game instituted by the play of the excluded-included-as-excluded, a power of adjudication is instituted. That power is sovereign power. Its raw material is life reduced to nothing but raw material: species life, life in its bare necessities, the body as biological extremis. Recall that Foucault's biopower thesis concerns the recruitment of species life into the strategic play of power. Thus: 'the inclusion of bare life in the political realm constitutes the original – if concealed – nucleus of sovereign power' (Agamben 1998: 6). Agamben's conclusion is as simple as it is stark: '*It can even be said that the production of the biopolitical body is the original activity of sovereign power*' (1998: 6, emphasis in original). In short, biopolitics is necessarily implicated in the sovereign manoeuvre of the excluded-included-as-excluded because that is what makes species life available politically. Conversely, sovereign power is deeply implicated in biopolitics since without what Agamben calls bare life there is no zone of indistinction between *nomos* and *phusis* invoking the adjudication of the power we call sovereign (Agamben 1998).

Discourses of security therefore operate as powerful points of intersection between the many discursive practices of modern social orders. They help tie these together but also operate as switch points such that the organisational vocabulary and imperatives of security course throughout allied discourses of power, especially in management, economics, industry, education, science and technology. The ways in which organisation for war is systematically reflected in organisation for everything else has long been noted, and not only by Foucault (Pearton 1982). To analyse a regime of security is thus to analyse a regime of politics in which governance and sovereignty intersect.

The issues raised by this analysis are not merely concerned with who is to be governed and how, but with the totality of the stakes to be wagered on the playing out of the problematisation of security and its allied strategies of power. Whereas traditional analysts see security and war as the final locus of the real – the bottom line recourse to which cuts the crap of discourse and its equivocal relation to truth – a Foucauldean analytic would be concerned not only with how we came to understand and practise security as this locus of the real but also with the collateral effect, the price to be paid, for the truth and reality of the securities that govern us. Indeed, Foucault himself was drawn towards the conclusion that one of the distinguishing features of contemporary security discourse is the stakes at issue. Whereas realist and neo-realist analysts invoke those stakes in ways designed to elide the problematising of security, Foucault invokes these stakes as a more powerful incentive to pursue his critical analytic of modern power.

Foucault captures all these points in one of his most pithy and troubling observations: 'What might be called a society's threshold of modernity', he observed, 'has been reached when the life of the species is wagered on its own political strategies' (Foucault 1987: 143). The force of the observation lies in the way in which Foucault is tempted to link issues of security and war to the defining characteristic of the age itself. Ordinarily chiding us against grand theories, Foucault is drawn to associate the ways in which, via the problematic of population, the life of the species has not only been drawn into the ambit of power in the modern age (the biopower thesis) but also how the politics of that age then becomes distinguished as the strategisations to which populations are subject, where the stake involved progressively becomes species survival.

In short, one has to presuppose that security is a discursively constituted problematisation. One has also to understand what Foucault means by discourse and what is entailed in discursive constitution. Above all, one has to understand Foucault's strategical account of power. Generative principles of formation differentiate one discourse of security from another. A Christian such as Luther, preoccupied with the loss of his soul and desperate to achieve salvation, cultivates a soteriological discourse of security. A political philosopher such as Thomas Hobbes, concerned to understand the foundational principles that ground political order, develops a significantly different security discourse. Both discourses rely on, and themselves articulate, a regime of truth. For Luther that regime was founded in faith in the theological absolutism of an increasingly distant God. For Hobbes man could only know with certainty those things he had himself created. Such discourses are regimes of practices that open a space of dispersion in which relationships evolve and successive displacements of principles of formation take place, affecting discontinuities in the play of discourse and exciting the desires that fuel them. In the process the subjects and objects of security acquire definition and specificity while also being subject to transformation and change. Cold war security discourses, for example, mutated from massive retaliation through mutual assured destruction to flexible response. They did so as much via internal transformation of the Cold War's deterrent-based rules of formation as in response to external factors. New security discourses associated with the advent of 'new terrorism' articulate different principles of formation insisting that: 'Deterrence will not be an option against an adversary seeking an apocalyptic confrontation, or one that is "virtual" and simply too difficult to target' (Simon and Benjamin 2001: 14). Yet others directed at rogue states and their leaders, Iraq under Saddam Hussein for example, seemed to adopt a strategy explored by Foucault (2001) in the concept of 'The Dangerous Individual'. No discourse of security is isolated either. Each is inter-articulated with other discourses: of economy, political identity, civilising standards, organisational behaviour and so on.

Every discourse of security also acts as an archive where memories of the dead and the sacrificed mingle with the memory to come of those willing to kill and be killed. Archives, of course, anaesthetise as they mobilise. Forgetting helps enable living. Every security discourse calling to mind some present danger in relation to which we are called to be self-regulating subjects installs its own forms of forgetting as well. Every discourse of security re-produces and refines, often amplifying and extending the danger against which it is invoked. Iconic discourses of security become monuments to the terminal character of a civilisation; even those regimes of global liberal governance that operate through biopolitical mechanisms seeking to enhance the life of populations.

Biopower, security and war

Governance and biopower are therefore intimately linked for Foucault because governance is the generic term covering the problematic of the conduct of conduct that arises when power relations take the properties of individual and collective bodies as their field of strategisation. Biopower denotes the ways in which, from the very early part of the modern period, the properties of individual and collective bodies are brought under the strategising play of power relations. Governance, biopower and the political strategies of liberalism are intimately connected because of the ways in which liberal rationalities rely upon the properties of bodies. What distinguishes them is their critical reflexivity and reliance on what Nikolas Rose (1999) called their powers of freedom, in particular their capacity for self-governance as the condition of possibility for both strategisation and the critique of power. Since liberal rationalities presuppose the autonomous properties of the bodies to be governed, it is possible for them to be governed and secured too little as well as too much. Thus, as Deleuze noted, liberal regimes are constantly concerned with the modulation of government through the strategising of biopower in cybernetic rather than in disciplinary ways. These features have been extensively developed and globally disseminated through the digital revolution in information and communication technologies and the molecular revolution in biology.

The link between biopower, security and war – and thus the insertion of security into regimes of governance – is first broached in the celebrated chapter 'Right of Death and Power over Life' (*Volume 1, The History of Sexuality* 1987) in which Foucault explores the assimilation of populations into the calculus of power relations. This was not simply a matter of greater positivity for power. Neither was it only a matter of power relations strategising to 'incite, reinforce, control, monitor, optimise, and organise the forces under it ... impeding them, making them submit, or destroying them' (Foucault 1987: 136). The very terrain of power mutates. It is one thing for the terrain of power to be circumscribed by the rights and duties of juridically empowered sovereigns. It is another for power to take life, specifically the properties of life speciated, as its terrain of strategic operations, and to do so fuelled by a will to knowledge dedicated to harnessing the truth of the species to its own self-governance and continuous betterment. A new moral and political economy of life with exponentially increased death-dealing powers thereby make its appearance. Ironically, Foucault notes, just as the power that traditional sovereigns deployed never matched the power of contemporary biopower, neither did the death-dealing forces of traditional sovereigns come close to the holocaustal imperatives of modern power regimes:

> Wars are no longer waged in the name of a sovereign who must be defended; they are waged on behalf of the existence of everyone; entire populations are mobilised for the purpose of wholesale slaughter in the name of life necessity; massacres have become vital. It is as managers of life and survival, of bodies and the race, that so many regimes have been able to wage so many wars.
>
> (Foucault 1987: 137)

Foucault does not omit the capacity of military-technical technology to kill on a genocidal scale. But such technology cannot be isolated from the governing technologies in which it is always embedded. Think, for example, of the many technological ways in which it is possible to drink soup – spoon, straw, cup, bowl, chop sticks with ladle – or to make and draw a bow. Composite bows made to be fired from horseback are quite different from those crafted from wood for use on foot: the horseman holds the string and draws the bow; the longbowman holds the bow and draws the string (Ihde 2002). The point for Foucault was ultimately the nature of the social technology through which power strategises species life, and the different outcomes that result from different modes of strategisation:

> The principle underlying the tactics of battle – that one has to be capable of killing in order to go on killing – has become the principle that defines the strategy of states. But the existence in question is no longer the juridical existence of sovereignty; at stake is the biological existence of a population. If genocide is indeed the dream of modern powers, this is not because of a recent return of the ancient right to kill; it is because power is situated and exercised at the level of life, the species, the race, and the large-scale phenomenon of population.
>
> (Foucault 1987: 137)

In general, then, security is a regime of truth expressed as a discourse of danger through which government takes place in the name of fears that are nonetheless functional to the re-production of the political order. In its specificity, that discourse details threats and dangers that in turn are closely allied to the ways in which truth, power and knowledge were formulated and to the dividing practices that constitute social power relations.

The key observation to be extracted from Foucault's reflections on biopower, governance, security and war is this. When truth and power take the whole of species life as their strategic field of operations, the security business goes hyperbolic. For knowledge of a species that is its own undetermined project is without limit and the development of species life is similarly unconstrained. The human genome project does not, for example, circumscribe but rather explodes the horizons of species life. This does not mean that it lacks specificity, it means simply that there is no end to its specification (Beurton *et al.* 2000). Biopolitically driven discourses of security know no bounds since knowledge of the species and its needs is unlimited. The governance of security is hypersecurity.

Society must be defended

In the lecture course *Society Must be Defended* Foucault seeks to re-institute biopower, security and war as part of a broader problematic: that of the modelling of power and politics. Ultimately, this too leads in the direction of liberalism because, by the end of the eighteenth century, 'the terms liberty and security have become almost synonymous. The security of laws and individual liberty presuppose each other' (Gordon 1991: 139). Liberalism is not targeted out of ideological antipathy to it as a normative political philosophy, but because liberal technologies of power are amongst the most historically successful at assimilating species life into the strategising of power relations. Specifically, if your problematic requires understanding the wagering the species life though discourses of security and war, then you must interrogate the power and specificities of liberal regimes. You don't need the additional incentive of noting that the most successful liberal power in history is the most heavily armed historically. But it helps.

As ever, Foucault's starting point is the anteriority of radical relationality: 'the relation is what determines the elements on which it bears' (Foucault 1997a: 59). Strategising power relations is a game of instituting principles of formation that order relationalities in ways that determine their elements and outcomes differently. So, he asks: 'Who first thought that politics was war pursued by other means?' (Foucault 1997a: 60), since the elements of a power network based on war as the generative principle will be constructed quite differently from those organised according to some other principle: honour, duty, potlatch and so on. His answer is not Hobbes but a variety of historical discourses in England and France during the course of the sixteenth and seventeenth centuries that argued historically, and not theoretically, that war derived from racial conflict on behalf, on the one hand, of the Anglo-Saxons and, on the other, of the Franks.

Foucault's concern was threefold. First, was the historical concern. When, to reverse Clausewitz's dictum, did politics become the extension of war?:

> Who imagined that the civil order was an order of battle: who perceived war in the watermark of peace: who has sought the principle of intelligibility of order, of the state, of its institutions and its history in the outcry, in the confusion and in the mud of battles?
>
> (Foucault in Stoler 1999: 64)

Second, was the radically hermeneutical concern. What, he asks shrewdly, must politics and war have been thought to be for Clausewitz to have to tell everybody that war was now the extension of politics by other means. Politics and war must have been understood otherwise, or Clausewitz would not have had to point out they were intimately related. And of course they were. They were a direct reflection of the forms of power characteristic of medieval societies and feudal warrior caste systems. In short, forms of war and forms of life are correlated. They were then, and they remain so now, albeit of course differently. How was it, in a resonant Foucauldean turn of phrase, 'that war became the cipher of peace?' (Foucault in Stoler 1999: 64). Third, was the re-problematisation of security and the emergence of security as an entire socio-political apparatus of geopolitical biopower.

In this notion of history the grid of intelligibility for society is the theme of permanent war. In the process security and war are re-problematised. Posing war as the generative principle of formation instituting the social is a result, Foucault says, of certain racially informed historical discourses, not the political theory of Thomas Hobbes which pivots around the equality of man in the state of nature (Foucault 1997a). According to Foucault, as the Middle Ages waned private wars were cancelled and war progressively became the public prerogative of the state. Paradoxically, as war moved to the legal and territorial margins of society, becoming as it were 'statisised', so force relations came to saturate social relations. As the bourgeoisie appropriated national discourse, it transformed the notion of war from a 'condition of existence' to a 'condition of survival', positing internal war as a defence of society 'against the dangers that are born in its own body' (Foucault in Stoler 1999: 79). Foucault traces this emergent property of biopower through techniques of power centred on the individual body and comprised first of the disciplinary techniques familiar to us from *Discipline and Punish* and later to the biopolitical techniques broached in *The History of Sexuality*. But in the lecture series *Society Must be Defended* he goes on to differentiate a further technology: 'a technology of power that would not exclude the first, but that would encase it, integrate it, partially modify it and that would most of all come to utilize it ...' (Foucault in Stoler 1999: 82).

Addressed not to the individual, but to the life of the species and its 'global mass', this variant of biopolitics presides over the processes of birth and death, production and reproduction. But it is not individualising. Rather, Foucault says, it is 'globalising' or massifying (*massifiante*). Such biopolitics focuses on the 'endemic', those permanent factors that cut into the time for work, that lower energies, that diminish and weaken life itself. Its primary instrument is not the disciplinary technology of individual dressage, but 'regularization', which he calls a 'technology of security'. A 'bio-regulation' by the state of its internal dangers, biopower begins to evolve down the trajectory of threatening life in the name of securing it.

Foucault is of course still working here with the biopower thesis of power over life. A key question arises then for biopolitics as it elaborates the allied apparatuses of security that will positively promote species. The question is: 'How to exercise the power of death in a political system centred on biopower?' (Foucault in Stoler 1999: 84). Foucault must ask: How does biopower, committed to the fructification of life, specify how one is to punish and who it is permitted to kill in the name of life? How does it give the order to kill, to expose to death not only its enemies but even its own citizens?

It does not follow that the only answer biopolitical projects can give to this question are those given in terms of historical discourses of race that Foucault explored in the lecture course. Racial distinction – variously drawn historically – is one means 'of introducing a fundamental distinction between those who must live and those who must die' (Foucault in Stoler 1999: 84). It fragments the biological field by defining a hierarchy of races in which certain races are classified as good, fit or superior. But there are many other ways of doing this. Population and species may be divided up according to different practices and dispersed across grids of utility and value according to many generative principles of formation and differentiation. Global governance is involved in the same process, for example, in the ways it constitutes the global poor, the deserving asylum seeker, the undeserving economic migrant and so on (Ahmed 2001; Cohen *et al.* 2002; Dummett 2001). But governance is not racist in the ways of those early racial discourses in France and England that Foucault analyses. It is nonetheless biopolitical, and war is sutured into the social in as much as both governance and war are concerned with the recruitment of raw life as the base material for the strategising of power relations.

Not obliged to give a single racist answer to the specification of the species life secured via the strategising of power relations, biopolitical governance is, however, committed to evolutionist or developmental answers since the promotion of life is its very *raison d'être*. Of course reference will be made to other aspects of the liberal tradition: just war theory; human rights and so on. But, drawn into the strategisation of power relations, the life and the lives of species existence promoted biopolitically via global liberal governance must continuously be differentiated into the deserving and undeserving, those to be nurtured and fostered and those marked out for correction and punishment. In this process, violent discrimination necessarily follows against population groups that fail to meet the criteria of evolution or development, albeit always in the name of the promotion of life itself.

Enemies here are not political adversaries in the existential sense identified by Schmitt (1995), but those identifiable as antipathetic to the promotion of species development as such. How else, Foucault asked rhetorically, could a biopolitical regime kill 'peoples, a population, civilizations', if not by activating the themes of 'evolutionism' and 'racism?' (Foucault in Stoler 1999; Foucault 1997a). The answer today, via criteria that eschew racialist dogmas of the past but are no less invested with neo-Hegelian and neo-Darwinian evolutionary imperatives, takes the form of new civilising standards historically committed to the general welfare of global populations.

Notes

1 Barry (2001), for example, has recently given another instance of where the genitive works both ways in that it is an account of how technology governs as it is governed.
2 For Martin Heidegger (1977), of course, 'technology' was the final expression of the onto-theology of the West.

References

Adler, E. (1998) 'Conditions of peace', *Review of International Studies*, 24, Special Issue (December).

Agamben, G. (1998) *Homo Sacer: sovereign power and bare life*, trans. D. Heller-Roazen, Stanford: Stanford University Press.

Alberts, D.S. and Czerwinski, T. (1994) *Complexity, Global Politics and National Security*, Washington, DC: INSS and NDU.

Arquilla, J. and Ronfeldt, D. (1993) *Cyberwar is Coming, RAND Report*, New York: Taylor & Francis.

——(1996) 'Information, power and grand strategy: in Athena's camp', in S. Schwartzstein (ed.) *The Information Revolution and National Security: dimensions and directions*, Washington, DC: The Centre for Strategic and International Studies.

——(1998) *In Athena's Camp: preparing for conflict in the information age, RAND Report*, New York: Taylor & Francis.

——(2001) *Swarming and the Future of Conflict*, Santa Monica, CA: RAND.

Balibar, E. and Wallerstein, I. (1991) *Race, Nation, Class: ambiguous identities*. London: Verso.

Barbieri, K. and Schneider, R. (1999) 'Globalization and peace: assessing new directions in the study of trade and conflict', *Journal of Peace Research*, 36(4): 387–404.

Barry, A. (2001) *Political Machines: governing a technological society*, London: Athlone Press.

Baudrillard, J. (1998) *The Consumer Society: myths and structures*, London: Sage.

Beurton, P., Falk, R. and Rheinberger, H.J. (2000) *The Concept of the Gene in the Development of Evolution: historical and epistemological perspectives*, Cambridge: Cambridge University Press.

Bogard, W. (1996) *The Simulation of Surveillance: hypercontrol in telematic societies*, Cambridge: Cambridge University Press.

Bougen, P. (2003) 'Catastrophic risk', *Economy and Society*, 32(2): 253–274.

Burchell, G., Gordon, C. and Miller, P. (1991) *The Foucault Effect: studies in governmentality*, Hemel Hempstead: Harvester Wheatsheaf.

Cassese, A. (1999) '*Ex iniura oritur*: are we moving towards international legitimation of forcible humanitarian countermeasures in the world community?', *European Journal of International Law*, 10(1): 22–30.

Cohen, S., Humphries, B. and Mynott, E. (2002) *From Immigration Controls to Welfare Controls*, New York: Routledge.

Crush, J. (ed.) (1995) *Power of Development*, London: Routledge.

Dean, M. (1999) *Governmentality*, London: Sage.

Dillon, M. (1996) *Politics of Security*, London: Routledge.

——(2002) 'Network society, network-centric warfare and the state of emergency', *Theory, Culture and Society*, 19(4): 71–80.

——(2003a) 'Culture, governance and global biopolitics', in C. Weber and F. Debrix (eds) *Mediating Internationals*, Minneapolis: Minnesota University Press.

——(2003b) 'Correlating sovereign and biopower', in J. Edkins, V. Pin-Fat and M. Shapiro (eds) *Sovereign Lives: grammars of power in an era of globalisation*, New York: Routledge.

——(2003c) 'Global liberal governance, networks, resistance and war', in F. Cocherane, R. Duffy and J. Selby (eds) *Global Governance and Resistance*, London: Routledge.

——(2003d) 'Intelligence incarnate. Martial corporeality in the Digital Age', *Body and Society* 19(4), December.

Dillon, M. and Reid, J. (2000) 'Global governance, liberal peace and complex emergency', *Alternatives*, 25(1): 117–143.

——(2001) 'Biopolitics, security and war', *Millennium: Journal of International Studies*, 30(1): 41–66.

Diner, D. (1999) 'Knowledge of expansion: on the geopolitics of Klaus Haushofer', *Geopolitics*, 4(3): 161–188.

Donnelly, J. (1998) 'Human rights: a new standard of civilization', *International Affairs*, 74(1): 1–23.

Duffield, M. (1997) 'Post-modern conflict: aid policy and humanitarian conditionality', a discussion paper, London: Emergency Aid Department, Department for International Development, London, July 1997.

——(1999) 'Globalization and war economies: promoting order or the return of history', *Fletcher Forum on World Affairs*, 23(2): 21–36.

——(2001) *Global Governance and the New Wars: the merging of development and security*, London: Zed Books.

Dummett, M. (2001) *On Immigration and Refugees*, London: Routledge.

Escobar, A. (1995) *Encountering Development: the making and unmaking of the third world*, Princeton: Princeton University Press.

Ewald, F. (1991) 'Insurance and risk', in G. Burchell, C. Gordon and P. Miller (eds) *The Foucault Effect: studies in governmentality*, Hemel Hempstead: Harvester Wheatsheaf.

Foucault, M. (1982) *Discipline and Punish: the birth of the prison*, Harmondsworth: Peregrine Books.

——(1987) *The History of Sexuality, vol. 1: an introduction*, Harmondsworth: Peregrine Books.

——(1988) 'The Tanner lectures', in L.D. Kritzman (ed.) *Michel Foucault: politics, philosophy, culture. Interviews and other writings*, New York: Routledge.

——(1991) 'Governmentality', in G. Burchell, C. Gordon and P. Miller (eds) *The Foucault Effect: studies in governmentality*, Hemel Hempstead: Harvester Wheatsheaf

——(1997a) 'Society must be defended', in P. Rabinow (ed.) *Michel Foucault. Ethics: subjectivity and truth. The essential works of Foucault 1954–1984, vol. 1*, trans. Robert Hurley *et al.*, New York: New Press.

——(1997b) 'Security, territory, population', in P. Rabinow (ed.) *Michel Foucault. Ethics: subjectivity and truth. The essential works of Foucault 1954–1984, vol. 1*, trans. Robert Hurley *et al.*, New York: New Press.

——(1997c) 'The birth of biopolitics', in P. Rabinow (ed.) *Michel Foucault. Ethics: subjectivity and truth. The essential works of Foucault 1954–1984, vol. 1*, trans. Robert Hurley *et al.*, New York: New Press.

——(1997d) 'On the government of the living', in P. Rabinow (ed.) *Michel Foucault. Ethics: subjectivity and truth. The essential works of Foucault 1954–1984, vol. 1*, trans. Robert Hurley *et al.*, New York: New Press.

——(2001) 'About the concept of the 'dangerous individual' in nineteenth century legal psychiatry', in J.D. Faubion (ed.) *Power. The essential works of Foucault 1954–1984, vol. 3*, London: Allen Lane, The Penguin Press.

Gordon, C. (1991) 'Governmental rationality: an introduction', in G. Burchell, C. Gordon and P. Miller (eds) *The Foucault Effect: studies in governmentality*, Hemel Hempstead: Harvester Wheatsheaf.

Heidegger, M. (1977) 'The question concerning technology', in M. Heidegger, *The Question Concerning Technology and Other Essays*, New York: Harper.

Held, D. and McGrew, A. (1998) 'The end of the old order?: globalization and the prospects for world order', *Review of International Studies*, 24(5): 219–245.

Ihde, D. (2002) *Bodies in Technology*, Minneapolis: Minnesota University Press.

Kapur, D. and Webb, R. (2000) 'Governance-related conditionalities of international financial institutions', Harvard: G-24 Discussion Paper Series, UNCTAD, International Center for Development, August, 2000.

Kay, L.E. (1993) *The Molecular Vision of Life. Caltech, The Rockefeller Foundation and the Rise of the New Biology*, New York: Oxford University Press.

Kratochwil, F. (1998) 'Politics, norms and peaceful change', *Review of International Studies*, 24, Special Issue (December).

Libicki, M. (1994) 'The mesh and the net: speculations on armed conflict in a time of free silicon', McNair Paper 28, Washington, DC: INSS and NDU.

——(1999) 'Illuminating tomorrow's war', McNair Paper 61, Washington, DC: INSS and NDU.

Lipschutz, R. (ed.) (1995) *On Security*, Columbia: Columbia University Press.

Novas, C. and Rose, N. (2000) 'Genetic risk and the birth of the somatic individual', *Economy and Society*, 29(4): 484–513.

O'Malley, P. (ed.) (1998) *Crime and the Risk Society*, Aldershot: Ashgate.

Oneal, J. and Russett, B. (1999) 'Assessing the liberal peace with alternative specifications: trade still reduces conflict', *Journal of Peace Research*, 36(4): 423–442.

Ó Tuathail, G. (1996) *Critical Geopolitics*, London: Routledge.

Pearton, M. (1982) *The Knowledgeable State: diplomacy, war and technology since 1830*, London: Burnett Books.

Rakenerud, A. and Herge, H. (1997) 'The hazards of war: reassessing the evidence for the democratic peace', *Journal of Peace Research*, 34(4): 385–404.

Rojas, C. (2001) 'Governing through the social: the role of international financial institutions in the Third World', paper presented to the International Studies Association, Chicago, 2001.

Rose, N. (1999) *Powers of Freedom*, Cambridge: Cambridge University Press.

Russett, B. (1993) *Grasping the Democratic Peace: principles for a post-Cold War world*, Princeton: Princeton University Press.

Schmitt, C. (1995) *The Concept of the Political*, Chicago: Chicago University Press.

Simon, S. and Benjamin, D. (2001) 'The terror', *Survival*, 43: 5–18.

Stoler, A.L. (1999) *Race and the Education of Desire: Foucault's history of sexuality and the colonial order of things*, Durham: Duke University Press.

Stefek, J. (2003) 'The legitimation of international governance: a discourse approach', *European Journal of International Relations*, 9(3): 249–75.

Valverde, M. (1998) *Diseases of the Will: alcohol and the dilemmas of freedom*, Cambridge: Cambridge University Press.

Valverde, M. and Cirak, M. (2003) 'Governing bodies, creating gay spaces: security in "gay" downtown Toronto', *British Journal of Criminology*, 43(1): 102–121.

Part II

Problems, practices, assemblages, regimes

5 Governing through the social

Representations of poverty and global governmentality[1]

Cristina Rojas

> There are, as we have already seen, conditions of society in which a vigorous despotism is in itself the best mode of government for training people in what is specifically wanting to render them capable of higher civilization.
>
> (J.S. Mill 1859)

> We must embark on a bold new program for ... the improvement and growth of underdeveloped areas. More than half the people of the world are living in conditions approaching misery. Their poverty is a handicap and a threat both to them and to more prosperous areas. For the first time in history, humanity possesses the knowledge and the skill to relieve the suffering of these people.
>
> (Truman 1949)

> By taking the side of liberty and good government, we will liberate millions from poverty's prison.
>
> (G.W. Bush 2002)

Separated by a century and a half, these statements share three commonalities: the authors are economic liberals by conviction, they speak from a hierarchical position and they justify foreign intervention in the name of the poor. I concur with those that see in liberalism an intrinsic impulse to govern stirred up by the perception that certain groups of the population or entire nations are not ready for freedom (Hindess 2002a; Valverde 1996; Mehta 1999). Although a liberal vision assumes that the state rules over autonomous individuals, it also supposes that an important part of the humanity does not possess the same capacities for autonomous action (Hindess 2002a: 133). Aid to the poor is one of liberalism's preferred instruments for governing those declared unfit for self-government.

During the nineteenth century philanthropists aimed to transform the poor in their relations to the economy, to other poor and to themselves (Ewald 1996: 42, 43). In the early twentieth century philanthropists internationalized programmes of assistance to the poor but it was not until the presidency of Truman (1945–1953) that aid became integral to the foreign policy of states.

In this chapter I argue that aid to poor countries is a mechanism of global government. I contend that the power of aid stems from the way it represents the Third World as in need of government, converting recipient countries into subjects of intervention and donors into their natural rulers. Aid establishes a relation between donor and recipient regulated by the promise of transforming the recipient country. Although poverty alleviation is a continuum for justifying aid, representations of who is poor and what causes poverty vary and, therefore, modes of intervention change accordingly.

My aim is to outline a history of the transformation of aid practices in light of their present relationship to the US-led war on terror. Specifically I look at the role of aid in the so-called neo-imperialist phase where the United States has embarked on a new civilizing mission. This history shows how aid plays a crucial role in providing the rationale for putting in place different mentalities of government based on the differentiation and exclusion of states and complementing the use of force. This chapter explores how transformations in aid practices produce differentiated governing subjects, acting as a complement of markets and the state. Where the market homogenizes, aid differentiates. Where security performs a negative task by identifying external enemies, aid performs a positive task – bettering the population.[2] Thus aid oscillates between reinforcing security and the market.

The chapter traces this genealogy of aid, beginning in the early twentieth century when private philanthropists internationalized aid practices. I also consider briefly the statization of aid during the Cold War. The following section traces the changes that took place under the developmentalization of aid, specifically a change in mentality allowing a nationalization of the social in the state apparatus and its multilateralization in international institutions. The debt crisis of the 1980s transformed aid from a national strategy of states towards one where aid sought to integrate national economies into a global liberal order. A neo-developmentalism predominates as the rationale for governing. Unlike the previous development-mentalility, neo-developmentalism relies much more heavily on the market. The final section concentrates on the return of civilization as an interpretive grid for world politics. Particularly in the wake of the events of September 11, 2001, this has reintroduced the old imperial distinction between countries capable of self-reform and those requiring force under the policing of the empire.

The approach

Two main approaches dominate the debate on foreign aid: realism and liberalism. Realists see foreign aid as little different from diplomatic or military policy, since 'all [are] weapons in the political armoury of the nation' (Morgenthau 1962: 309). In their view aid benefits the interest of donor states. On the contrary, liberals firmly believe that aid is a mechanism of economic development benefiting poor countries. In the liberal view foreign aid replaces colonial relations and centres not on power relations but on economic growth (Chenery and Strout 1966: 679). Aid is considered an input that will help to transform poor, stagnant countries to the point that their economies will be comparable to those of industrialized countries.

I use analysis of governmentality as a theoretical point of reference. A central element of this approach is a different understanding of liberalism: as a positive project of government concerned with the practical problems involved in governing states and their populations (Hindess 2002a: 134). Seeing liberalism as a practice supersedes the dichotomy found in the 'liberal' and 'realist' analyses where aid either produces economic development or works as an instrument of realpolitik. Promoting economic development is a way of governing as it is an instrument of political loyalty as proposed by realists.

A governmentality approach has a broader understanding of the concept of government by including state and non-state actors as involved in government relationships (Foucault: 1991: 87). Unlike the realist precept of state as the main actors promoting national interest and foreign aid, this chapter demonstrates that philanthropists, international institutions and market actors all participate in different forms of government through aid practices.

An additional strength of a governmentality approach is that it links forms of representation and forms of rule. Foucault illustrates how the emergence of the concept of population made possible the transformation of the art of government from reason of state to a liberal form of government (Foucault 1997: 73). Thus power is rationalized differently in diverse modalities of government, and specific knowledges are associated with different forms of rule. By governing in the name of the social, liberalism defines as its object specific problems of populations (Foucault 1997: 79).

Governmentality is genealogical, allowing the exploration of historical trajectories and mutations of rule (Larner and Walters 2002: 394). A genealogical analysis does not take rationalities of government for granted. Governmentality asks about the mechanisms making possible the constitution of countries as subjects of government. Specifically, I examine how different representations incorporate the story of the Third World into spatial and temporal categories and how, through these categories, countries are re-presented as in need of reform (Rojas 2001).

The internationalization of aid

Philanthropy

Private philanthropists paved the way for international interventions in Third World affairs in what was considered a 'philanthropic revolution' in the early twentieth century (Smith 1999: 36). Such American philanthropists as Carnegie, Rockefeller and Margaret Sage were considered pioneers in the promotion of international assistance. Their mission was defined on a world basis. It concentrated on the health of population, particularly in terms of programmes to control tropical diseases. A prominent example here was the Rockefeller campaign against yellow fever in Latin America (Packard 1997; Cueto 2001).

In the 1940s the rationale for intervention changed to population control. It was feared that a decrease of mortality without diminishing birth rate could produce a population explosion worldwide. Population became a public matter and moved away from its location in the pre-WWII women rights movement (Whitworth 1994: 81). The centre of attention was planning and the family as reflected in the Planned Parenthood Federation (PPF) inaugurated in 1942.

This concern with population growth resonated with the Cold War climate of containment of Communist doctrines at home. As the PPF put it: 'A nation's strength does not depend upon armaments and man power alone; it depends also upon the containment … of its people' (in Gordon 1976: 350). As the expression 'population explosion' suggests, population acquired a global dimension during this period through its representation as a global threat. Private foundations adopted an international dimension, as was the case with the International Planned Federation (IPF) founded in 1952. As argued by Michael Moore, president of a private foundation, the aim was to shift the image away from an organization 'for the protection of motherhood and the family' to 'the new angle of the preservation of peace' (in Sharpless 1997: 192).

Interventions to control population faced opposition from the church authorities, Catholic nations, Communist regimes and former colonies. Their argument was that the richer nations were using population programmes as way to avoid responsibility for centuries of exploitation (Reed 1978: 286). Such opposition also imposed limits to private interventions, especially regarding the capacity of private donors to transform the recipient country (Reed 1978: 282). To accomplish this more encompassing goal, private donors sought collaboration with the government of the United States. Foundations sponsored 'demographic missions' to Third World countries. In these missions they met with high-level officials and produced reports targeted at policy-making elites in the United States and overseas (Sharpless 1997: 181). Despite this collaboration, the government of the United States was reluctant to adopt population control as a legitimate intervention. For instance, Eisenhower rejected the idea of intervention to alter population dynamics (Sharpless 1997: 195).

The statization of aid

It is during the Cold War period that aid becomes an instrument for governing other states. According to the draft report of the House Foreign Affairs Committee Report (1956), 'foreign aid appears to be the most useful non-military device available to the United States for influencing other nations' (in Hagen and Ruttan 1988: 7). From 1952 to 1961 the agenda is dominated by security concerns (1988: 3). The Mutual Security Act of 1951 stated that economic aid, technical cooperation and military aid would be directed at strengthening the free world's resistance to Communism (Augelli and Murphi 1988: 84). At this time military aid was the largest single component of US bilateral aid (45 per cent), with 99 per cent given in the form of grants (Hattori 2001: 642).

Military assistance was not an easy mechanism for governing other nations. This is suggested by several disagreements between Latin American leaders and the United States.[3] People in the Third World were not happy either. According to Hagen and Ruttan (1988: 7), a turning point in the change of approach was inspired by 'Vice-President Richard Nixon's disastrous South American tour, during which he was assaulted by angry mobs'. As the next section demonstrates, the incorporation of development allowed international institutions to take a more a positive role in the governance of aid.

Developmentalization of aid

The emergence of development as a category of analysis in the early 1960s solved some of the contradictions inherited in the concepts of population and military aid as targets of state intervention. As Escobar (1995: 9) argues, development created an efficient apparatus for producing knowledge, and exercising power over the Third World. Development became a natural ally for foreign assistance, as it was oriented towards population improvement. National governments also encountered a legitimate goal for intervention on behalf of its population.

Aid was 'developmentalized'. Development was represented as a condition of countries. These were portrayed as discrete territorial areas endowed with specific geographical, social and economic characteristics (Larner and Walters 2002: 401–402). Poverty and income per capita were hallmarks to compare nations over time and across space. Developing countries became a belated duplication of industrialized ones whose assistance was needed to achieve maturity (Mallon 1994: 12). Foreign aid would provide the inputs needed to advance in an established category.

Reflecting this new orientation, in 1961 the Mutual Security Act was transformed into the Foreign Assistance Act. Aid was established as a bilateral relation between states. In 1961 the United States created the Agency for International Development (AID). Several countries followed this lead, creating aid agencies across Europe and Canada. The OECD countries created in 1960 the Development Assistance Committee (DAC) – a donor umbrella organization.

Debates between academic and political advisers centred on the most appropriate mechanisms to transform the Third World. In the 1960s, a group of US scholars criticized the 'militaristic' approach to foreign aid and called for a focus on values and culture. Gabriel Almond (Buxton 1985: 203–204) questioned whether the outcome of the 'East–West' struggle would be determined by military competition. In his view cultural change provided the political rationality for foreign intervention (Almond 1960).

A different group of scholars, led by Samuel Huntington, advocated political development as the best road to development. In his statement to Congress he mentioned that, mistakenly, 'the United States has actively attempted to reduce poverty and to promote development of the nations of the world [and] devoted little attention to the problems of promoting political stability and political development in these countries'. As a result of this debate the Title IX amendment of the Foreign Act of 1966 was changed to include *political development*. A crucial criterion for granting aid was the degree of its *effectiveness* in producing stable political order.

The focus of reform split policy makers between those in favour of cultural change and those advocating political stability. Programmes such as the Alliance for Progress covered a wide spectrum of goals, including both political and socio-economic development.

Multilateralization of aid

Multilateral institutions became missionaries of development. The International Bank of Reconstruction added the term 'development' to its brand. In 1961 the World Bank created the International Development Association – a soft-loan window. Regional development banks were also created at this time: the Inter-American Development Bank (1959); African Development Bank (1964); Asian Development Bank (1966).

Multilateral institutions granted a third of Official Development Assistance by 1974 (Hattori 2001: 644). This movement was accompanied by a focus on poverty. Under the presidency of Robert McNamara, the World Bank became a leader in sponsoring anti-poverty programmes. Strategies of intervention were transformed from lending for infrastructure for economic growth to biopolitics; life was made the target and object of government (Dillon and Reid 2001). These concerns are reflected in the favoured projects of this time: basic needs, population, nutrition and health.

Strategies of intervention changed accordingly. First, national governments were made responsible for the eradication of poverty (Streeten and Burki 1978: 412). There was a call for a more substantial role for government in terms of providing public services and changing incentives through the use of indirect taxes and subsidies (1978: 414).

Second, national strategies of development were linked to international organizations whose role extended beyond financing to providing technical assistance. The Food and Nutrition Policy and Planning and Integrated Rural Development programmes followed this model where countries were asked to establish special nutrition planning offices under the planning ministries (Escobar 1995: 102). This approach required further collaboration between international development agencies and governments in the Third World:

> Aid agencies, in addition to formulating an overall policy for the allocation of their own resources, should establish within countries or field missions, coordinating committees to work closely with national ministries in reviewing the spatial implications of potential projects and investments.
>
> (Rondinelli and Ruddle 1978: 492)

Third, the health and nutritional condition of the population was governmentalized, that is, transformed from individual conditions into broader socio-economic and government issues. In the words of Alan Berg, MIT professor and main architect of the nutrition strategy (Berg 1973: 206–207, in Escobar 1995: 205):

In a successful nutrition activity ... the issues move beyond the clinic, the laboratory, and experimental field project. Concerns shift to operations, communications, logistics, administration and economics, and the need shifts to professional planners, programmers and managers.

Nutrition and rural development policies called for a systemic approach coordinated by planning authorities. The methodology asked for the elaboration of detailed nutrition plans including information on food supply (types of crops, conditions of cultivation, food trade balance, commercialization of food); food demand (demographic factors, cultural factors, economic conditions and consumption factors such as diet composition by region); and biological utilization of food considering health and environmental factors (Escobar 1995: 119). Nutrition and population experts displaced political scientists as development experts.

Aid buys economic reforms

The debt crisis of the 1980s transformed mentalities of rule. Economic turmoil added a new rationale for global governance: economic instability. President Reagan's speech during the Caribbean Basin initiative in 1982 perceived the problem as a danger to the North as much as to the South. For it highlighted the linking role of South–North migration of population: 'this economic disaster is consuming our neighbour's money, reserves, and credit, forcing thousands of people to leave for other countries, for the United States, often illegally, and shaking even the most established democracies' (in Schoultz 1987: 97).

One consequence of the debt crisis was the increased power granted to International Financial Institutions (IFIs) due to the drying up of private sources of capital (Stalling and Peres 2000: 38). IFIs saw this situation as an opportunity to push for greater market openness and deregulation. John Williamson (1990) summarized the IFI agenda of economic reform in ten policy instruments known as the Washington Consensus.[4] This new cartography of power has as its centre Washington and its principal form of government economics. Washington includes the political, technocratic Washington and the US economic agencies. Washington is a geographical site from where countries are being observed and constitutes the new site of authority. Sound economic policies depend on how well they reflect Washington's desires. State-owned enterprises are rejected with the argument that '[t]his is again a nationalistic motivation and hence commands little respect in Washington'. Social instruments were discarded because Washington did not believe in them: 'I excluded from the list anything which was primarily distributive ... because I felt the Washington of the 1980s to be a city that was essentially contemptuous of equity concerns' (Williamson 1993: 1329).

The Washington Consensus was made possible by the assumption that economic experts know what works best. A former vice-president of the World Bank, Joseph Stiglitz (2000), describes such experts as 'older men who staff the bank – and they are overwhelmingly older men – [that] act as if they are shouldering Rudyard Kipling's white man's burden'.

The rationale for supporting national development strategies shifted towards strengthening commitments to an international economic order characterized by free markets, private property, economic incentives and a smaller state (Gore 2000: 792). This commitment to liberal order did not diminish the desire for more government on the part of international organizations; instead it increased the power of aid as a governing instrument. This commitment was expressed bluntly as 'aid buys reforms' (Collier 1997: 56). International aid, in the form of grants and loans, became a centrepiece of the structure of governance by international institutions such as the World Bank and the IMF. Conditionality[5] was the instrument linking aid to policy reform under structural adjustment loans. Hattori (2001: 645) equates this mechanism to a 'condition of debt bondage on a world scale': between 1975 and 1990, 338 structural adjustment loans were extended to 71 debt-burdened countries.

Conditionality widened and deepened.[6] The use of conditionality as a governing technology cannot be made comprehensible without the change in representations of development and poverty. In the first place national narratives of development were abandoned. Under the Washington Consensus the attention centres on 'performance assessments' where countries are ranked according to their performance in selected indicators (Gore 2000: 794). Unlike the vision of development where countries move along a historical trajectory, these indicators are applied regardless of a country's position in space or time. Furthermore, they do not rank countries but measure their degree of integration in a global space by for example average level of tariffs, controls on foreign investment, fiscal deficit and ratio of state-owned property to GDP. The goal is not development but international competitiveness (Larner and Walters 2002: 414).

Second, economic reforms did not require the developmental state but its dismantling, ensuring that governments would be kept under the discipline of the market. The main rationale for the so-called 'second-generation reforms' is the perception that economic reforms were endangered if politics was allowed to intervene: 'it is imperative that governments concentrate on the unfinished business of structural reforms. Failure to do so imperils the victories already won against the dysfunctional apparatuses of closed, populist, interventionist policies' (Burki and Edwards 1996: 15). Proposals to discipline the state included the creation of independent central banks, non-partisan budgetary process, reform of the relationship between central and sub-national governments, and a limited state which is 'involved in activities that the private sector does not perform or performs poorly' (1996: 25).

Third, this change in ruling practices was accompanied by a transformation in the representation of poverty. Increasingly it was formulated not as a consequence of economic patterns of growth, but as an obstacle to growth:

> Widespread poverty is a moral outrage, a profound obstacle to sustainable growth, a threat to the consolidation of democracy, and arguably the single

greatest impediment to long-term political and social stability. In recent years, poverty has been a prime factor in the deterioration in the quality of life in many of the region's countries, a deterioration which is marked by the decline in the ability of families and schools to socialize children and adolescents, the increase in crime and violence, the rise in alcohol and drug addiction, and the erosion of social capital.

(Burki and Perry 1997: 87)

The poor, not countries, are divided according to temporal and spatial categories. The World Bank distinguishes (Burki and Perry 1997: 103) the *chronically* from the *transient* poor. The former 'suffer from physical or mental disability, long-term illness, or old age'; they 'are best helped through systems of social insurance'. Transient poor are vulnerable because of temporary events or shocks that produce a decline in their capacity to work or earn. They 'require targeted programmes, which may take different forms according to event-specific and country-specific circumstances, to help them through short-term stress and calamities'. Social Investment Funds (SIF) – previously called 'emergency funds' – were the strategy directed to alleviate transient poverty.

Knowing more about the poor became crucial for designing policies according to these categories. Countries are asked to conduct poverty assessments where they would produce information about 'where the poor live, the size and composition of their households, what they do for a living, what they own and purchase, what risks they face, and how they fit into the society around them' (Burki and Perry 1997: 29).

The focus on the individual and spatial dimensions of poverty conceals the link between poverty and structural conditions and displaces the solution away from social rights. Poverty is about the good government of the family, including women's responsibility as part of the problem. Consider the following observation made by two specialists at a Conference on Poverty: 'Poverty is hereditary. Like a defective gene, it is passed on from generation to generation' (Van der Gaag and Winkler 1996: 200). As poverty is passed from mother to children, the former are provided with an increased share of responsibility for their children's poverty; consequently, strategies against child poverty passed through the female body (1996: 201): 'That children are over-represented in poor households is not surprising. Quite simply, poor families are larger than families that are not poor'. Thus the misfortune of poor children is to be born in poor families (1996: 202).

Neo-developmentalism

By 1995 the use of aid as a mechanism for enforcing economic reform was being called into question. First, international organizations such as the United Nations pictured a world divided into a few wealthy countries and a vast majority of poor ones. The 1999 UN Human Development Report (UNDP 1999) revealed that almost half of the world's population (2.8 billion) live on less than $2 dollars a day. Poverty becomes global.

Second, the crisis of good reformers in the 1990s (Mexico and Southeast Asian countries) undermined the legitimacy of structural adjustment programmes that had concentrated only on economic reforms. In his message to its Board of Governors in 1998 the president of the World Bank reported:

> We talk of financial crisis while in Jakarta, in Moscow, in Sub Saharan Africa, in the Slums of India, and the barrios of Latin America, the human pain of poverty is all around us … We must address this human pain. We must go beyond financial stabilization … We must focus on the social issues.

Third, the infallibility of economic experts came under attack after their proven lack of capacity to solve the crisis in Southeast Asia (Stiglitz 1998). Finally, Third World countries and an internationalized civil society raised their voices against the effects of structural adjustment programmes. Some manifestations of this uneasiness include street demonstrations at the meetings of multilateral economic institutions, such as those in Seattle, the Economic Forum at Davos and the Summit of the Americas in Quebec City. Criticism also came from academic and NGO circles. Policy papers did not hide the effects of structural adjustment loans and stabilization programmes and their relationship to the deterioration of economic conditions and poverty.

After two decades of applying conditionality the verdict arrived: 'conditionality has failed' (Collier 1997: 51). In David Collier's view, 'the purchase of policy reform became little more than a charade' (1997: 59).

At this point we can begin to detect a new mentality which promotes the representation of poverty in a global space. Indicative of this movement is the 1995 Copenhagen Declaration on Social Development in which world leaders committed to the eradication of poverty and the integration of social goals into structural adjustment programmes (World Summit for Social Development 1995). A step forward was taken in 1996 when OECD members established worldwide goals including the reduction of the proportion of people living in extreme poverty by half by the year 2015. UNDP called for globalization with a 'human face' to counterbalance the concentration of the benefits of globalization within a few rich countries (UNDP 1999: 3). The World Bank (2001: 5) claimed that 'a world free of poverty and free of the misery that poverty breeds' is the most compelling of human desires.

The voices for reform coming from social movements and Third World countries increase the pressure for a reform in global governance, including aid practices. As the vice-president of the World Bank, Joseph Stiglitz, recognized, it was increasingly difficult to ignore those voices opposing the imposition of structural adjustment:

> They'll say the IMF is arrogant. They'll say the IMF doesn't really listen to the developing countries it is supposed to help. They'll say the IMF is secretive and insulated from democratic accountability. They'll say the IMF's

economic 'remedies' often make thing worse – turning slowdowns into recessions and recessions into depressions. And they'll have a point.

(Stiglitz 2000)

As a result IFIs initiated a series of reforms. First, we see how the social returns as a legitimate target of aid. This is captured in the words of the president of the World Bank (Wolfensohn 1999):

> In a global economy, it is the *totality* of change in a country that matters. Development is not just about adjustment. Development is not just about sound budgets and fiscal management. Development is not just about education and health. Development is not just about technocratic fixes ... Development is about putting all the component parts in place – together and in harmony.

However, the social is not elevated to a single global space – a sort of global society – but is represented within the boundaries of the nation-state. With the social as a national concern there is a return to a development mentality. But this mentality differs from the development project of the 1960s. The emphasis is now on the transformation of society without the state; the creation of an 'active society' (Walters 1997) where civil society, NGOs and the poor are called to be part of the solution. One expression of this new paradigm is the Comprehensive Development Framework (CDF):

> Development represents a *transformation* of society, a movement from tradi-tional relations, traditional ways of thinking, traditional ways of dealing with health and education, traditional methods of production, to more 'modern' ways. For instance, a characteristic of traditional societies is the acceptance of the world as it is; the modern perspective recognizes change, it recognizes that we, as individuals and societies, can take actions that, for instance, reduce infant mortality, extend lifespan, and increase productivity.

(Stiglitz 1998)

The strategy incorporates the voices of the poor in the planning and implemen-tation of programmes.[7] The new development mentality aims at increasing the feeling of a country's ownership as long as 'governments have the responsibility for putting all together in a comprehensive review of all the elements required for growth and poverty alleviation'. According to the Bank, 'countries must be in the driver's seat and set the course'.

Instead of reducing the Bank/IMF governing role, we find a move to 'govern at a distance'. There is the design of new technologies where countries have the illusion of 'being in the driver seat'. Yet they remain firmly under the guidance of IFIs. This is certainly the case with the Heavily Indebted Poor Countries which were asked for the elaboration of Poverty Reduction Strategy Papers as a condition to qualify for debt reduction. Unlike a regime of enforced conditionality, in the new strategy countries are asked to reform themselves voluntarily (Collier 1997: 70).

Conditionality is translated into *selectivity*, whereby the reforming process is represented 'as a political and ethical choice of nation-states' (Larner and Walters 2002: 419). The governing capacity of selectivity is demonstrated in the increasing number of 'consensual' conditionalities: Tanzania's policy matrix contained a list of 157 policies that the government must implement during the 2000–2002 period. Charles Abugre, director of the Integrated Social Development Centre (ISODEC), an NGO from the south, captures well this increase in government:

> Through the initiative, the IMF and the World Bank assume new powers over low-income countries. It is unprecedented for the IMF and the World Bank to endorse a national strategy, such as PRSP, that has been developed by a government together with its citizens and approved by its parliament. These creditor institutions only underwrite a small, almost insignificant, part of the costs of national strategies, yet they have the final say over national strategies. That is wrong. The function of endorsing or vetoing national strategies is a supra-governmental role that erodes the sovereignty of borrowing governments.
>
> (Abugre 2000)

New imperialism: the return of civilization

Towards the end of the Millennium, a global representation of a world divided along lines of civilization has made its return to the world of international relations, offering to make sense of the new landscape of global politics after the Cold War. Samuel Huntington (1996: 266), architect of the new paradigm known as the 'clash of civilizations', sees a 'hate dynamics' emerging, comparable to the 'security dilemma' in international relations. As Barry Hindess argues (2002a: 133–134), during the nineteenth century narratives of civilization and their corresponding projects of reform through civilizing missions served as an organizing principle of imperial rule. In this representation the world population was divided into three categories. First, there were the 'hopeless cases' who could not be expected to progress and who were seen as an obstacle to the progress of others. Identified with 'inferior races', this category was to be governed by force, or made to disappear, as with programmes of genocide. Second were the 'subjects of improvement' who were considered reformable, either through paternalism or authoritarian rule. The third category is identified as those in need of temporary intervention because they are in the midst of some sort of social or economic crisis. They are comparable to the subjects of welfare in Western countries, for whom social insurance and similar interventions constitute a 'safety net'.[8]

The events of September 11, 2001 and US President Bush's 'War on terror' link the mentality of civilizations with a call for a 'new imperialism'. Robert

Cooper (2001), from the UK-based Foreign Policy Centre, classifies countries along lines that echo the older civilizational paradigm. He identifies *pre-modern* states, which are former colonies where state power has broken down (for example, so-called 'failed states' such as Somalia); *modern* states such as India and Brazil; and, finally, the highly integrated *post-modern* states most typified by the European Union. Cooperation is the most appropriate form of politics amongst these civilized countries. However, this is not necessarily the case for relations between the post- and the pre-modern zones:

> [W]hen dealing with more old-fashioned kind of states outside the post-modern continent of Europe, we need to revert to the rougher methods of an earlier era – force, pre-emptive attack, deception, whatever is necessary to deal with those who still live in the nineteenth century world of every state for itself. Among ourselves, we keep the law but when we are operating in the jungle, we must also use the laws of the jungle.
>
> (Cooper 2001: 3)

Max Boot from the Council of Foreign Relations (2003) elaborates the new rationality:

> As long as evil exists, someone will have to protect peaceful people from predators. The international system is no different in this regard from your own neighbourhood, except that predators abroad are far more dangerous than ordinary robbers, rapists and murderers. They are, if given half a chance, mass robbers, mass rapists and mass murderers.

Aid is called upon to play the role of differentiating and managing these groups by selecting good governments. This is explained by Sebastian Mallaby:

> In countries such as China and India, which have functioning governments broadly committed to development, aid and technical advice have greatly accelerated the escape from poverty … but in countries such as Chad, Haiti, or Angola, aid cannot accomplish much. Such places are beyond the reach of economists who prescribe policies from afar. If outsiders want to make a difference in this kind of environment, they must begin by building the institutions that make development possible. They must engage, in other words, in the maligned business of nation building.
>
> (2002: 4)

The Third World is divided into two groups: (1) those subjects of reform where aid is called to promote the market qualities conducive to development; and (2) hopeless cases which are the countries considered beyond reform. For the latter, donors recommend 'force'. The United States should act as world constable, as Boot argues from the pages of the *Financial Times* (2003):

Since the earliest days of the Republic, American traders, missionaries and soldiers have penetrated the farthest corners of the world. America even has a long history of military action abroad. In 1904, President Theodore Roosevelt declared: 'Chronic wrongdoing, or an impotence which results in a general loosening of the ties of civilised society, may ultimately require intervention by some civilised nation, and in the western hemisphere the adherence of the United States to the Monroe Doctrine may force the United States, however reluctantly, in flagrant cases of such wrongdoing or impotence, to the exercise of an international police power'.

When Roosevelt wrote those words, the Western hemisphere was the only place where the United States exercised military hegemony. In the rest of the world, America could count on the Royal Navy to defend 'civilised society'. Today, America exercises almost as much power everywhere around the world as it once had only in the Caribbean. In fact, it has more power in both relative and absolute terms than any other state in history. Thus, by Roosevelt's logic, the United States is obliged to stop 'chronic wrongdoing' for the simple reason that nobody else will do the job. That is what America has been doing for the past decade in places such as Bosnia, Kosovo, Afghanistan, and now Iraq.

Foreign aid plays a pivotal role in governing the new global divide. This role is registered in the most recent guide to the US aid agency (USAID) (2002) which, in a similar way to the Mutual Security of Act of 1951, links national interest, security and aid. This is reflected in its title: 'Foreign Aid in the National Interest. Promoting Freedom, Security, and Opportunity'. The document takes its inspiration from President Bush's Millennium Challenge Account (MCA), which is seen as a powerful instrument *'to draw whole nations into an expanding circle of opportunity and enterprise'* (see Economic Perspectives 2003). According to the new doctrine foreign assistance will be 'devoted to projects in nations that govern justly, invest in their people and encourage economic freedom'. To accomplish this objective countries are ranked according to criteria measuring government commitment to: (1) good governance, including rooting out corruption and adherence to the rule of law; (2) investment in health, immunizations and schools; and (3) economic freedom or policies that foster private interest, entrepreneurship, open markets and sustainable budget deficits.

In the new cartography of power underdevelopment becomes dangerous (Duffield 2001: 26). Consider the initial statement of USAID:

More than ever, U.S. security is bound up with the outside world. And as the world has become more connected, it has become more hazardous. Weapons, germs, drugs, envy, and hate cross borders at accelerating rates. Just as the tools, ideas, and resources for progress can quickly move from industrial to developing countries, many forms of risk stability can travel in the opposite direction.

(2002: 1)

In this new mentality the global is not only interconnected by its financial and trade circuits but also by the problems of mobility of population and the germs associated with them. Paul Krugman (2003) refers to the current strategy as the 'Martial Plan' not only because of the amount spent on defence as compared to reconstruction, but also for the tendency to turn the foreign aid budget into a tool of war diplomacy. With this tendency small countries receive favourable treatment for aid requests in attempts to influence their vote on the UN Security Council or by allowing its troops to be used in combat.

Current technologies of governance turn aid into private business. This is the case with the MCA and the World Bank strategy for reforming services in poor countries (World Bank 2003). Economic freedom and furthering private interest is a criterion when judging country eligibility for international aid.

Last, but not least important, the new mentality of government calls for a return to bilateral aid and grants as a mechanism to reward the policies put in place by the world constable (the United States). This is reflected in the increase in bilateral aid allocated to the MCA. This is set to increase by more than 50 per cent over the next three years. Full funding of MCA would result in a $5bn annual increase in assistance over current levels by 2006 (Economic Perspectives 2003). It is also reflected in Bush's proposal that the World Bank and other multi-lateral development banks provide their assistance in the form of grants rather than loans, with the condition that the increase in funding be tied to clear and measurable results (Sanford 2002: 741).

Conclusion

Aid is a powerful instrument of global government. Ironically, while Overseas Development Aid contribution has decreased, its power to govern has moved in the opposite direction. Its power increased with the statization of aid during the Cold War. It increased further with the multilateralization of aid, especially after the debt crisis of the 1980s, by linking aid to structural adjustment programmes. The passage from conditionality to selectivity placed the burden of reform on the poor countries while increasing the power of those governing in the name of ethical and moral standards. Recent divisions between good reformers – able to receive aid – and bad performers – to be reformed by force – gives almost incommensurate power for intervention in the name of freedom from poverty in the affairs of an already stigmatized population.

The representation of poverty in terms of spatial and temporal categories is a crucial element in the way aid governs. Where the number of poor constituted a menace to First World security, aid provided the means to control the number of births. Where Third World countries lagged behind in indicators of poverty or economic growth, it was expected that aid would provide the input needed for climbing the ladder of national development. A poor and undernourished popu-lation living in isolated spatial localities provided the ground for collaboration between national planning offices and experts affiliated to multilateral institu-tions. From targets of intervention, the poor became an obstacle to be superseded through economic reforms. Emergency funds became the appropriate response to a situation of transient poverty whose long-term solution would be provided by structural adjustment reforms. It is the dangerousness of poverty that provides the rationale for military intervention: everything in the name of the poor.

But the recipients of aid have refused to be merely passive subjects of the donors' instruments. On the contrary, they have actively resisted subordination. From the early negotiations around foreign assistance to street demonstrations against structural adjustment programmes, the Third World has been a site of resistance to rule. The dismissal of conditionality and debt bondage was the object of concerted action of NGOs and indigenous and women movements. Several transformations in donors' institutions reflect as much the pressure of global social movements as they do internal dissent within these institutions. Recently a coalition of policy analysts (Reality of Aid 2002) have argued that conditionality and imposed policies deepen poverty and inequality. While accusing donor countries of double standards, Oxfam asked for an end to the use of conditions attached to IMF-World Bank programmes, which force poor countries to open their markets without considering the impact on the poor.

Proposals towards global democracy, cosmopolitan politics and global civil society are paving the way for new forms of solidarity. I would argue that the movement towards 'global solidarity' would depend on the constitution of non-hierarchical and de-securitized relationships between countries. But that would be the subject of another paper.

Notes

1 I appreciate the comments of Michael Dillon, Marc Duffield, Barry Hindess, Wendy Larner and William Walters. This research was possible thanks to a grant from Canada's Social Sciences and Humanities Research Council.
2 See Foucault (1988: 82).
3 On this point see the excellent article by Margarita Lopez-Maya (1991).
4 The ten policy instruments are: fiscal discipline; public expenditures in education and health; tax reform; positive but moderate market-determined interest rates; competitive exchange rates; liberal trade policies; openness to foreign direct investment; privatization; deregulation; and protection of property rights (Williamson 1990).
5 The IMF defined conditionality as the link between the approval or continuation of the Fund's financing and the implementation of specific elements of economic policy by the country receiving this financing (IMF 2001).
6 The average number of criteria for conditionality rose from about six in the 1970s to ten in the 1980s. In the Bank's case the average number of conditions rose from 32 in 1980–1983 to 56 by the end of the decade (Kapur and Webb 2000: 7).
7 *World Development Report 2001/2002* (World Bank 2002) asked people in 60 countries to analyse and share their ideas on poverty.
8 See Rojas (2002).

References

Abugre, C. (2000) 'Who governs low-income countries?', *IMF and World Bank, News and Notices*, 2(3), Rethinking Bretton Woods Project, Autumn 2000. Online. Available at: http://attac.org/fra/toil/doc/gci301.htm

Almond, G. (1960 [1950]) *The American People and Foreign Policy*, New York: Frederick A. Praeger, Inc.

Augelli, E. and Murphy, C. (1988) *America's Quest for Supremacy and the Third World: a Gramscian analysis*, London: Pinter Publishers.

Berg, A. (1973) *The Nutrition Factor*, Washington DC: The Brookings Institution.

Boot, M. (2003) 'America's destiny is to police the world', *Financial Times*. Online. Available at: http://news.ft.com/servlet/ContentServer?pagename=FT.com/StoryFT/Full Story &c=StoryFT&cid=1045510812215&p=1012571727088 (accessed 18 February, 2003).

Bush, G.W. (2002) 'Remarks at the International Conference on Financing Development', Monterrey, Mexico, March 22.

Burki, S.J. and Edwards, S. (1996) *Dismantling the Populist State: the unfinished revolution in Latin America and the Caribbean*, World Bank Latin American and Caribbean Studies.

Burki, S.J. and Perry, G. (1997) 'The Long March: a reform agenda for Latin America and the Caribbean in the next decade', Washington DC: The World Bank.

Buxton, W. (1985). *Talcott Parsons and the Capitalist Nation-State*, Toronto: University of Toronto Press.

Chenery, H.B. and Strout, A.M. (1966) 'Foreign assistance and economic development', *The American Economic Review*, 56(4): 679–733.

Collier, P. (1997) 'The failure of conditionality', in C. Gwin and J.M. Nelson (eds) *Perspectives on Aid and Development*, Washington: Overseas Development Council.

Cooper, R. (2001) 'The post modern state', *Re-Ordering the World: the long term implications of September 11th*, United Kingdom: Foreign Policy Centre. Online. Available at: http://fpc.org.uk/hotnews/full?activeid=169&tableid=writes (accessed 11 April, 2002).

Cueto, M. (2001) *The Return of Epidemics: health and society in Peru during the twentieth century*, Aldershot: Ashgate.

Dillon, M. and Reid, J. (2001) 'Global liberal governance: biopolitics, security and war', *Millennium: Journal of International Studies*, 30(1): 41–66.

Duffield, M. (2001) *Global Governance and the New Wars: the merging of development and security*, New York: Zed Books.

Economic Perspectives (2003) *An Electronic Journal of the U.S. Department of State*, 8(2), March 2003. Online. Available at: http://usinfo.state.gov/journals/ites/0303/ijee/toc.htm

Escobar, A. (1995) *Encountering Development: the making and unmaking of the Third World*, Princeton: Princeton University Press.

Ewald, F. (1996) *Histoire de L'État Providence*, Paris: Grasset.

Foucault, M. (1988) 'Politics and reason', in *Politics, Philosophy, Culture: interviews and other writings 1977–1984*, London: Routledge.

——(1991) 'Governmentality', in G. Burchell, C. Gordon and P. Miller (eds) *The Foucault Effect: studies in governmentality*, Chicago: University of Chicago Press.

——(1997) 'The birth of biopolitics', in P. Rabinow (ed.) *Michel Foucault. Ethics: subjectivity and truth. The essential works of Foucault 1954–1984, vol. 1*, trans. Robert Hurley *et al.*, New York: New Press.

Gordon, L. (1976) *Women's Body, Women's Rights: a social history of birth control in America*, New York: Grossman.

Gore, C. (2000) 'The rise and fall of the Washington Consensus as a paradigm for developing countries', *World Development*, 28(5): 789–804.

Hagen, J.M. and Ruttan, V.W. (1988) 'Development policy during Eisenhower and Kennedy', *The Journal of Development Areas*, 23: 1–30.

Hattori, T. (2001) 'Reconceptualizing foreign aid', *Review of International Political Economy*, 8(4): 633–660.

Hindess, B. (2002a) 'Neo-liberal citizenship', *Citizenship Studies*, 6(2): 127–143.

——(2002b) 'The liberal government of unfreedom', unpublished paper, Australian University.

Huntington, S. (1968) *Political Order in Changing Societies*, New Haven: Yale University Press.

——(1996) *The Clash of Civilizations and the Remaking of World Order*, New York: Simon & Schuster.

IMF (2001) 'Conditionality in fund-supported programs – overview', paper prepared by the Policy Development Review Department, 20, February 2001. Online. Available: http://www.imf.org (accessed 20, April 2001).

Kapur, D. and Webb, R. (2000) 'Governance-related conditionalities of international financial institutions', G-24 Discussion Paper Series, UNCTAD, International Center for Development Harvard University, August 2000.

Krugman, P. (2003) 'The Martial Plan', *New York Times*. Online. Available at: http://www.nytimes.com/2003/02/21/opinion/21KRUG.html

Larner, W. and Walters, W. (2002) 'The political rationality of "new regionalism": towards a genealogy of the region', *Theory and Society*, 31: 391–432.

Lopez-Maya M. (1991) 'The change in the discourse of US–Latin American relations from the end of the Second World War to the beginning of the Cold War', *Review of International Political Economy*, 2(1): 135–149.

Mallaby, S. (2002) 'The reluctant imperialist: terrorism, failed states, and the case for American empire', *Foreign Affairs*, 81(2): 2.

Mallon, F. (1994) 'The promise and dilemma of subaltern studies: perspectives from Latin American history', *The American Historical Review*, 99(5): 1491–1515.

Mehta, U.S. (1999) *Liberalism and Empire: a study in nineteenth-century British liberal thought*, Chicago and London: University of Chicago Press.

Mill, J.S. (1972 [1859]) in H.B. Acton (ed.) *'On Liberty', Utilitarianism, Liberty, Representative Government*, London: J.M. Dent & Sons.

Morgenthau, H. (1962) 'A political theory of foreign aid', *The American Political Science Review*, 56(2): 301–309.

Oxfam (2002) 'Rigged rules and double standards. Trade, globalization and the fight against poverty'. Online. Available at: http://www.maketradefair.org-unfairtrade\report

Packard, R. (1997) 'Visions of postwar health and development and their impact on public health interventions in the developing world', in F. Cooper and R.M. Packard (eds) *International Development and the Social Sciences*, Berkeley: University of California Press.

Reed, J. (1978) *From Private Vice to Public Virtue: the birth control movement and American society since 1830*, New York: Basic Books.

Rojas, C. (2001) 'Development: what's in a word? Views from the paradigms', *Canadian Journal of Development Studies* 22(3): 571–596.

——(2002) *Civilization and Violence: regimes of representation in nineteenth century Colombia*, Minnesota: University of Minnesota Press.

Rondinelli, D.A. and Ruddle, K (1978) 'Coping with poverty in international assistance policy: an evaluation of spatially integrated investment strategies', *World Development*, 6(3): 479–497.

Sanford, J.E. (2002) 'World Bank: IDA loans or IDA grants?', *World Development*, 30(5): 741–762.

Schoultz, L. (1987) *National Security and United States Policy Toward Latin America*, Princeton: Princeton University Press.

Sharpless, J. (1997) 'Population science, private foundations, and development aid', in F. Cooper and R.M. Packard (eds) *International Development and the Social Sciences*, Berkeley: University of California Press.

Smith, J.A. (1999) 'The evolving role of American foundations', in C.T. Clotfelter and T. Ehrlich (eds) *Philanthropy and the Nonprofit Sector in a Changing America*, Bloomington and Indianapolis: Indiana University Press.

Stalling, B. and Peres, W. (2000) *Growth, Employment and Equity: the impact of the economic reforms in Latin America and the Caribbean*, Washington, DC: Brookings Institution Press; Santiago, Chile: United Nations, Economic Commission for Latin America and the Caribbean.

Stiglitz, J. (1998) 'Towards a new paradigm for development: strategies, policies, and processes'. Lecture given as the 1998 Prebisch Lecture at UNCTAD.

——(2000) 'The insider: what I learned at the world economic crisis', *The New Republic On Line*. Online. Available at: http://www.tnr.com/041700/stiglitz041700.html

Streeten, P. and Burki, S.J. (1978) 'Basic needs: some issues', *World Development*, 6(3): 411–421.

Truman, H. (1964 [1949]) *Public Papers of the Presidents of the United States: Harry S. Truman*. Washington DC: U.S. Government Printing Office.

UNDP (1999) *Human Development Report 1999*, United Nations Development Program, Oxford University Press.

USAID (2002) *Foreign Aid in the National Interest: promoting freedom, security and opportunity*. Online. Available at: http://www.usaid.gov/fani/overview/index.htm

Valverde, M. (1996) ' "Despotism" and ethical liberal governance', *Economy and Society*, 25(3): 357–372.

Van der Gaag, J. and Winkler, D.R. (1996) 'Children of the poor in Latin America and the Caribbean', in S.J. Burki, S.-R. Niyer and R. Hommes (eds) *Poverty and Inequality*, Bogotá: Annual World Bank Conference.

Walters, W. (1997) 'The "active society": new designs for social policy', in *Policy and Politics*, 25(3): 221–233.

Whitworth, S. (1994) *Feminism and International Relations*, London: Macmillan Press.

Williamson, J. (1990) 'What Washington means by policy reform', in J. Williamson (ed.) *Latin American Adjustment: how much has happened?*, Washington, DC: Institute for International Economics.

——(1993) 'Democracy and the "Washington Consensus"', *World Development*, 21(8): 1329–1336.

Wolfensohn, J.D. (1999) 'A proposal for a comprehensive development framework' (A discussion draft), Memo to the Board of Governors, January 21.

World Bank (2001) *World Development Report 2000/2001. Attacking poverty*, Oxford: Oxford University Press.

World Bank (2002) *World Development Report 2001/2002*, Oxford: Oxford University Press.

World Summit for Social Development (1995) 'The Copenhagen Declaration and Program Action', March 6–12.

6 The international government of refugees

Robyn Lui

On 26 June 2002, the United Nations High Commissioner for Refugees (UNHCR) submitted the findings of its Global Consultations on International Protection to the Executive Committee. The 27-page document titled *Agenda for Protection* was the outcome of an 18-month consultative process conducted across the globe, involving a diversity of actors from states, inter-governmental bodies, UNHCR and other UN agencies, NGOs (non-governmental organizations), to academics and experts in refugee law.[1] Its purpose was to provide a set of strategies for those concerned with the management of refugees, and therefore it contained recommendations on a range of topics from responsibility-sharing arrangements, strengthening partnership with civil society, to improving conditions for voluntary repatriation. The Global Consultations process, with its emphasis on the importance of cooperation among diverse actors and coordination of programmes, networking, information gathering and dissemination, illustrates the wide-ranging strategies adopted to tackle the issue of refugees.

This aggregate of actors and activities makes up what is commonly referred to as the international refugee regime. Some have asserted that the development of a comprehensive international refugee regime reflects the growing recognition of universal human rights norms (Barnett 2002; Bayefsky and Fitzpatrick 2000; Gorlick 2000; Helton 2002); and others emphasize the threat posed by displaced population and cross-border entry to national and regional stability (Barutciski 1999; Weiner 1994; Loescher 1992). And then there are policy-makers whose duty of office requires them to prioritize 'national security', 'national interest' and 'public order' above refugee protection. For them, the international refugee regime is, at best, a foreign policy instrument, and at worst, an infringement on the norm of state sovereignty in domestic and international politics. These positions represent the prevailing twin views of refugees as victims/villains and the purpose of the international refugee regime as humanitarian/political.

This essay aims to resist this trend. Rather than taking the refugee phenomenon as a given, I will consider how concepts and practices, their production and transformation, operate towards the constitution of the 'refugee problem'. I draw upon Foucault's analytics of biopower and government in the modern West in suggesting that the 'refugee problem' is an effect of biopolitics and geopolitics (Foucault 1991, 1997). The former politicizes life and the government of human beings as population. The latter politicizes territory and constructs a relationship between territory and population.

The starting point of the investigation is the global system of sovereign territorial states. In the modern political landscape, refugees occupy the amorphous border that simultaneously divides and joins the national and international. While the national and international are conceptualized as distinctive domains of activities, in practice, they are inextricably linked in that both are the effects of a system of sovereign states.[2] This system of states is the disciplinary tool that produces a key historical condition of possibility for ordering and governing the multitude of human population. The refugee regime with its assemblage of knowledge and practice orders relations between states and between populations of citizens and non-citizens. The proposition is that, at the fundamental level, the problems presented by refugees to international relations cannot be separated from the organization of the world and the human population into national citizens within sovereign territorial states. Like schools, hospitals, and prison, the states system is a governing apparatus – albeit a globalizing one – aimed at the human population. The cartography of sovereign states, with its distinctive territorial character, maps political life according to an inside/outside arrangement, thus distinguishes the community of citizens from the body of non-citizens. Citizenship and refugeehood are two sides of the same coin.

In this context, the various programmes of international refugee regimes, rather than being in opposition to the sovereignty game, play a crucial role in sustaining the order of territorial states. The proposition is that the refugee becomes a subject of government through two tactics of subjectification: first, the arrangement of sovereign states; and second, the international refugee regime with its specific set of knowledges, institutions, legal instruments, and heterogeneous programmes. We need to recognize that 'refugee' is an historical term embracing multiple meanings and issues. We also need to question the oppositional frame of incorporation/inclusion and marginalization/exclusion in thinking about the role of the international refugee regime.

A number of scholars have exposed the 'violence' of the international system. Dillon (1998), Nyers (1998, 1999), Soguk (1999), and Xenos (1996) have remarked on the implications of national state building and the anxiety of sovereignty for the creation of population displacement and the ways in which refugee issues are characterized in politics. These studies, though insightful, locate the refugee problem only within the state/nation/citizen hierarchy of international life. I want to argue that incorporation of non-Europeans into the refugee regime is more complex than the articulation of the state-citizen ideal. We cannot ignore the far-reaching consequences of conceptualizing a world divided into different stages of development. The juxtaposition between the first world of advanced modern peoples and the 'Third World' of traditional peoples is particularly important because as the geography of displacement shifted from Europe to Africa, the 'thick' meaning of and responses to refugees also changed. Whereas European refugees were governed as political subjects, African refugees were governed as subjects of underdevelopment.

The chapter is organized into three parts. The first section considers the connection between the modern system of states, the government of population, and the subject of refugees. The second section presents a broad overview of the refugee regime as an art of government. Conventional theories of regime emphasize the desirability of international coordination and cooperation and the positive outcomes of consensus building. I take a slightly different view of regimes and suggest that the diverse activities of regimes are significant because they construct norms of conduct that normalize a particular view of political reality. The final section presents two schematic examples of the international government of refugees. The first looks at some of the responses to population displacements in Europe between 1921 and 1945. The second briefly examines the 'discovery' of the displacement–development nexus as a way of explaining and resolving the refugee problem in post-colonial Africa. Given the scope of the task, it goes without saying that the following issues under consideration can only be dealt with selectively.

The geopolitical character of life and the refugee problem

The discourse of globalization has brought the state back in the political limelight. Although a highly contested term, globalization is generally used to speak of the effects of economic, socio-cultural and technological processes on human activities and human relations. Whether one is convinced or doubtful about the historical uniqueness of globalization, the point to note is that both 'globalists' and 'global-sceptics' have structured their arguments around the continuing relevance of states and the meaning of sovereignty. In international relations, the debate has focused on the tension between globalization and sovereignty. The Westphalian order, it seems, still sets the limits to what constitutes politics. The state and its attributes of sovereignty, territory and population anchor understandings of modern politics (Jackson 1999: 423). The idioms of territory and sovereignty remain central to our understanding of dilemmas in international affairs, such as humanitarian intervention and mass refugee flows.

'International affairs' as a discreet domain depends upon a territorial arrangement that is global in scope and which defines the relationship between the community and its inhabitants on one hand, and between the community and its neighbours on the other. The etymology of 'territory' provides a clue to the relationship between the territorial state and the government of population. The obvious derivation of territory seems to be the Latin *territorium*, which describes the land surrounding a town that is under the jurisdiction of the town (Baldwin 1992: 209). But the origin of the Latin word is not the obvious *terra* – earth, but rather *terreor* – to frighten. From this, *territorium* suggests that it is a place where people are frightened off, rather than the conventional meaning of land (1992: 209–210). If we take this view, the idea of territorial sovereignty has a regulative effect on the government of population movement. Sovereignty is instrumental in the territorialization of political community, while territory provides a tangible basis for the exercise of sovereign power to divide the human population, and circumscribe relationships.

Political geographers such as Thom Kuehls (1996) and Kennan Ferguson (1996) have suggested that the way we understand territory is a result of acts of territorialization, whereby heterogeneous elements are transformed, regrouped and experienced as a unity. Their writings suggest that the 'mechanics' of making territory impose order and define political and social relations. According to jurists such as Grotius, Pufendorf, Vattel, and Lauterpracht, the purpose of international law is the delimitation of the exercise of sovereign power on a territorial basis. The tenets of modern international law assign to territory an essential role in relations between states. Indeed, the most basic tenet of modern international law is the concept of recognition and a basic rule of interstate relations is the prima facie recognition of territorial integrity.[3] International law functions as a territorializing norm, and becomes an extremely useful and malleable instrument for governing interstate conduct, populations as groups, and individuals.

The links between territory and sovereignty are reinforced by heterogeneous governmental programmes and institutions, which aim, with varying degrees of success, to control populations over vast geographical areas. The recent writings of Barry Hindess (2000, 2002) and Engin Isin (2002) on modern citizenship have prompted an important (re)consideration of the government of populations through relations of citizens and non-citizens. Hindess' work draws attention to the political implications of portioning the human population into sovereign territorial states whereby they become governable subjects. His writing is also a useful corrective to Foucault's internal, or domestic, analytics of government. The viability of governing population constituted as a given political community, namely a state, is dependent upon, among other things, the capacity and programmes to govern populations outside the state. I have argued elsewhere that the formation of a modern state does not occur in isolation; state formation is relational (Lui-Bright 1997: 587). The art of government is an international project that deploys tactics of state sovereignty, territory and citizenship to achieve its diverse goals.

The proper relationship between a state and its citizen is the central concern of modern political theory. According to liberal political thought, state legitimacy rests on, among other things, the state's capacity to satisfy some version of the good life, that is, to contribute to the realization of an individual's liberty and justice. If a state is empowered on the grounds of their capacity to advance claims about peace, justice, and humanity of the population, then, this population should be citizens. Until recently, political theory has ignored the realm of politics outside the domesticated space of the state. The silence, however, is not indicative of the far-reaching effects of the modern 'internalist' characterization of citizenship on international relations and the treatment of those placed outside the boundaries of citizenship. Like sovereignty, citizenship has internal and external aspects.[4] Citizenship entails legal, social, cultural and normative dimensions with important consequences for the treatment of populations inside and outside the state. It is a discriminatory institution in that, as a citizen, one enjoys privileges within one's member-state that are not available to non-citizens.[5] In other words, a person's status vis-à-vis a particular state defines the set of rights that he or she can enjoy and a state's obligation towards that individual's wellbeing. The crossing of territorial boundaries more often than not transforms the legal status of a citizen into an 'alien'. From this perspective, citizenship demarcates the limits of rights, obligations and duties in international relations, and produces the difference as embodied by the figure of the alien. Although 'alienage' can be used to describe the condition experienced by anyone outside his or her citizenship-state, for the limited purpose of this chapter, it refers to the refugee condition.

I am not suggesting that states do not have obligations towards various categories of 'aliens' such as resident foreigners, migrant workers, international students, travellers and other foreign citizens who are found within their territory. They do to various degrees. On the one hand, states have signed on to various international instruments that set out the appropriate treatment of non-citizens. For example: international refugee law outlines the obligations a state has towards asylum seekers. On the other hand, the migrant labourer and the international student represent voluntary forms of population movement. They have exercised their liberty to move. Their citizenship-states have not disregarded their obligations towards them. These people remain under their protection and therefore can make few claims on other states. Refugees, however, are forced to move because of their state's inability or refusal to protect them as citizens. Being a refugee, because and despite of his or her anomalous state, enables the person to make various 'humanitarian' claims on the international community.

What we have today, then, is a complex and hierarchical differentiation of legal status and rights for citizens, foreign residents, migrants, and refugees. If human beings are considered equal, their equality is recognized within the bounds of the state to which they belong. We make appeals for refugees in the name of common humanity but the grounds on which claims about peace, justice, and equality are advanced are not to some global cosmopolis but against a certain state which is the 'contractual guardian' of its citizens. Liisa Malkki (1994) argues that imaginaries of the *national* form and the *national* citizen provide the grid of intelligibility in contemporary discourses of 'international community' and 'humanity'. Cosmopolitanism is not in opposition to the state–nation–citizen order; the cosmopolitan aspirations of 'humanity' are articulated through the discourse of national citizenship. In other words, human rights are protected and enforced only as national rights conferred by a national state. It is beyond the scope of this chapter to discuss the historical relationship between state and nation, their link to sovereignty, and the complex ways in which all three are implicated in the constitution of modern citizenship. Suffice to say that, in *The Origins of Totalitarianism*, Hannah Arendt makes an important point about the emergence of the national state and national citizenship and the corruption of both institutions of politics by nationalism. The conquest of the state by the nation, she argues, has resulted in 'the perversion of the state into an instrument

of the nation and the identification of the citizen with the member of the nation'
(Arendt 1976: 231).

What I am suggesting is that the modern articulation of political legitimacy
and identity has shaped the way we imagine and characterize the foreignness of
refugees and the 'refugee problem'. In *Being Political* (2003), Engin Isin suggests
that we consider citizenship as a potent strategy of otherness and exclusion.
Within the territorial community of the nation-state, citizenship differentiates
some people as virtuous and superior and others, namely outsiders and aliens, as
moral questionable. Modern political rule depends upon a twin strategy of
spatializing and nationalizing political community, states and citizenship. These
forms of provincialism mark the boundaries of belonging and allow for the
possibility of being a refugee.

Yet, some writers have misconstrued the relationship between refugees and
states. They claim that refugees represent the emergence of a different world
order – a deterritorialized politics that challenges state-centrism. Soguk (1996)
argues that by cutting across space, refugees create a new space not subject to
traditional notions of boundaries and boundedness. Skran (1995: 3) also claims
that refugees present a challenge to conventional ways of thinking about international politics because they 'do not fit neatly into the state-centric paradigm
which assumes that each individual belongs to a state'. On the contrary, the issue
of refugees highlights the centrality of the order of states. Refugees is an issue in
international relations because the world is divided into a plurality of states in
which the human population is segmented, ordered, and governed. What will be
our understanding of refugees if states are not the political and spatial foundations of modern life and the ideas of nation and nationality have no value? It is
worth noting that the concept of 'durable solutions' in the international refugee
regime reinforces citizenship as a form of life. A permanent solution to the
refugee problem is one that transforms the refugee into the citizen and re-establishes
the citizen–state regulatory bond. The three accepted durable solutions – repatriation to the country of origin, integration into the country of asylum, and
resettlement to a third-country – all affirm the value of citizenship and states for
experiencing the spectrum of goods that is often equated with human rights.

The international refugee regime and the government
of refugees

In the field of International Relations, a 'regime' is defined as the implicit or
explicit set of 'principles, norms, rules, and decision-making procedures around
which actors' expectations converge in a given area of international relations'
(Krasner 1982: 186). Regimes are concerned primarily with creating the conditions for maximizing cooperation and minimizing conflict and competition
among actors. They are the outcome of deliberation of autonomous rational
actors. For some, international regimes represent the new location of political
community because they transcend the territorial imperatives of statist community and question the assumption that states are unitary actors in international

relations (Samhat 1997). Regimes constitute transnational networks that challenge the 'hard shell' of the state and influence the international agenda beyond confines of state interest. This argument is often accompanied by claims about the emancipatory political potential of regimes and emergent global civil society. For others, regimes are sites of domination and contest disguised under presuppositions of benevolence, legitimacy, and consensus. Susan Strange (1982) argues that a benign view of regimes obscures the unequal economic and power relationships in international politics where the weak are forced to act according to the dictates of the powerful. Her 'forced consumption' argument rejects any significant role for principles, norms, rules, and decision-making procedures in international relations. James Keeley (1990: 84) insists that regimes go beyond agenda setting to include disputes over the 'correct' naming and evaluation of things, over standards of judgement, and over objectives and mechanisms. For him, the core issue is that regimes are not liberal enough; there are non-democratic tendencies.

Much discussion on the international refugee regime has followed similar lines. Claudena Skran (1995) celebrates the invention of the regime as a triumph of internationalism. Others such as Alex de Waal (1997) and B.S. Chimni (1998) criticize the contemporary refugee regime as being a 'humanitarian mode of power' and 'corrupted by geopolitics'. But there is another way to examine the refugee regime. In an attempt to read policy through an anthropological lens, Cris Shore and Susan Wright suggest that policy functions in at least three distinct ways: as a rhetorical narrative that either justifies or condemns the present; as a charter for action; and as discursive formations that empower some people and silence others (1997: 7). They go on to claim that policies not only codify norms and values, they also explicitly contain models of society (1997: 7). This approach is also useful for analysing the self-evident qualities of the refugee regime. Regime describes 'what is' and prescribes 'what should be'. It establishes and orders relationships and interactions with far-reaching implications. The practices and activities of the regime produce effects of the normal and universal in the way we have to think about refugee issues.

The administration of the conduct of refugees requires data and knowledge that distinguish a specific set of regularities of the refugee phenomena. Problems are far from self-evident, they become known, or knowable through grids of evaluation and judgement (Dean and Hindess 1998: 9). In this sense, the production and circulation of knowledge is indispensable in these activities. Statistical analysis is one way to reveal the inner dynamics of populations. But quantitative techniques are not enough. Numbers and graphs need to be situated and supported by abstract theories of social processes (1998: 6). The art of government requires techniques that locate and link definitions, categories and knowledge within a field of meanings. Knowledge is not just ideas, but ideas directed towards a certain goal. It is theoretical and technical. The human sciences, and similarly public and social policy, are deeply involved in the problematization of life. Their representations of reality enable varying modes of governmental intervention.

If the systematic acquisition and circulation of information renders a domain thinkable and translatable into policy, the refugee regime requires an investment in intellectual machinery with the capacity to conceptualize processes and theories (Rose and Miller 1992: 182). Experts and policy-makers are at the forefront of interpreting and transforming the 'reality' of refugees. Expert knowledge explains social and political processes, identifies desirable goals, and allows the creation and application of practices. It articulates the cause-and-effect relationships of complex problems, frames the issues for debate, and proposes specific policies or solutions. The government of refugees requires particular analyses that can project the probability of events occurring, link apparently discrete processes into a chain of events, establish causal-effect relationships, and predict possible consequences. The ethical investment in experts as independent and neutral authorities gives credence to their knowledge as truth. The dissemination of information among experts, agencies, and other actors forges alliances and brings into being a sense of shared interest. The debates between experts, disagreements over methodology and theory, policy enterprise, interests and goals, and even normative beliefs are part of the activities of governing refugees.

In its diagnostic and prescriptive functions, the refugee regime produces norms and principles that are potent regulatory devices for international order. The regime creates a set of shared symbols and references, mutual expectations and visions of the international political order. The appeal to a common good deepens the meaningfulness of a specific vision of order. The concern is with order as both prescription and aspiration. The values and normative principles shape the perimeters for action and agency. In other words, the international refugee regime seeks to achieve international order through a process of ordering, which defines relationships between actors based on certain values and norms and principles. Knowing, naming and defining a normative order is not an act of making transparent what is merely there, a given, that is passively registered by others. Instead, to know and to make claims on behalf of truth and knowledge is a political activity, an exercise of power.

But the regime cannot be understood simply as an exercise of oppressive power. It is also misleading to reduce the invocation of norms and principles to ideology and the development of rules and procedures to manipulation. Such interpretations neglect the affirmative, positive and productive effects of the regime. Although definitions and categories appear self-evident at first, definitional boundaries are tactics that seek to standardize and differentiate individuals. The very category 'refugee' is a historical artefact rather than a necessity. Categorizing and labelling are processes of subjectification. Both are important activities for governing refugees and restoring order. They impact on the formulation of refugee policy and the allocation of assistance. It can also be said that regime practices can create agency and provide the space for the practice of a 'responsible' liberty. They encourage active participation. For example, the publications by UNHCR often refer to the need to create the conditions for the development of enterprising refugees and partnerships with civil society. The organization's refugee programmes are packed with tactics of education, persuasion, inducement, and motivation.

Today the international refugee regime is a composite of inter-state and non-state institutions operating on various levels, national government departments, refugee policies, emergency aid assistance, development programmes, handbooks and code of conduct manuals, experts, research institutions, academic publications, conferences, speeches, briefing notes, information kits, evaluations, camps and transit centres, safe havens, international laws, travel documents, and so forth. It is made up of a set of knowledge, practices and rituals, and belief about the relationship between sovereign territorial states and populations of citizens. It is a set of regulatory technologies that institutionalizes refugee issues, puts them on the international agenda, sanctions conduct, procedures, practices and norms, and socializes those who are participants.

Another important aspect is the appeal of humanitarian ethics, that is, practices of welfare and philanthropy in governing refugees. Humanitarian relief offered to refugees has as one of its strategic goals 'social progress', which includes economic wellbeing and the development of moral character, personal responsibility, and self-sufficiency. Both welfare and philanthropic programmes are strategies to inculcate habits of providence and independence. Thus, the government of displacement is concerned with ends that include the establishment of those negative and positive conditions that 'empower' refugees to cultivate the self-governing attributes of citizenship, that is, autonomy and self-responsibility. As we shall see below, in both historical instances, refugees were governing through, among other things, tactics of welfare and philanthropy.

Governing refugees

Institutionalizing the refugee problem in Europe[6]

Prior to 1921, there were few international legal arrangements that addressed the movement of refugees. Voluntary agencies and non-governmental organizations such as the International Committee of the Red Cross (ICRC) met the needs of the displaced. Russian nationals were the first group of people to receive international assistance from governments in Europe. The League of Nations took tentative steps toward a more coordinated relief effort after an appeal by Gustave Ador, President of the ICRC, who pointed out that close to two million Russians were scattered across Europe, without status or protection (Kulischer 1948: 54).[7] Given the post-war situation in Europe, opinions differed sharply about the implications of involvement in matters concerning population displacement. While some states felt there were more urgent matters than humanitarian assistance, France, Britain and the new states in Eastern Europe all had a stake in advocating a 'burden-sharing' approach. The new eastern European states were particularly eager to adopt measures to control the presence of Russians in their territories.

With an objective of maintaining peace and order in mind, the League of Nations gave attention only to those refugees from regions that were considered most disruptive to the new European order, such as the Russians and, later, refugees from the former Ottoman Empire. Post-WWI Europe was the historical moment when the 'peacemakers' assembled and then essentialized the sovereign territorial state and national citizenship bond to secure peace and order (Lui 2002). The Wilsonian peace plan counselled that stability in the region required the effective government of territory and populations. His solution was a redefinition of the boundaries of political communities based on the principle of nationality and reorganization of territory and population into national states. But the implementation of the principle of national self-determination as the legitimate basis for statehood subsequently endorsed the homogenization of pluralistic community into the national state. The paradox of national state making was that in creating *the* nation, it also created other nations – national minorities or ethnic minorities within a state. The outcome of these events was mass population displacement.

Population exchanges were one way to deal with many displaced persons. While expulsions unilaterally carried out by governments were considered unacceptable, deportations based on agreements between sovereign states were legitimate. Likewise, compulsory exchanges or transfers that sought to unmix populations were uncontroversial. The most notable examples of the transfer of minorities included the Treaty of Lausanne of 1923 between Greece and Turkey, and the Convention on Reciprocal Voluntary Emigration between Greece and Bulgaria signed at the same time as the Treaty of Neuilly.[8] The Treaty of Lausanne involved the compulsory removal of 1.5 million Greeks and 400,000 Turks, while the arrangement between Greece and Bulgaria involved the transfer of 100,000 Bulgarians and 35,000 Greeks (de Zayas 1975: 222–223). Indeed, the Treaty of Lausanne, often cited as an achievement in international law, set the precedent for population cleansing in the form of the 'orderly and humane' transfer of populations during and after World War II.

In terms of legal strategies of governing refugees, between 1922 and 1946 international agreements adopted a group category approach to the definition of refugees. The instruments that determined the status of refugees were based on national origins and not a general definition of the concept or an abstract notion of individual persecution. The Institute of International Law proposed the idea of a universal definition of refugee in 1936. But the idea failed to receive support because the acceptance of a universal definition would require states to allocate further resources to refugees. During this period of high employment and inflation, states were not only reluctant to offer assistance to refugees, they also imposed restrictive entry policies, and expulsion was not an uncommon practice.[9] Under the *1933 Convention relating to the International Status of Refugees* and the *Provisional Agreement* and *Convention concerning the Status of Refugees coming from Germany*, it was recognized that refugees were not to be expelled or sent back across state borders, and especially not sent back to Germany. But in a shrewd move, many European states subverted their non-refoulement obligations by not distinguishing between refugees and other categories of aliens in their national legislation and forcible return became widespread practice.[10]

Immediately after World War II, other categories of displaced persons emerged in an attempt to impose order on the immense wave of displaced population. The main classifications were as follows: evacuees, war or political fugitives, political prisoners, forced labourers, deportees, civilian internees, ex-prisoners of war, and stateless persons. This method of organizing a conglomerate of people into definable categories with specific conditions and experiences enabled the formulation of 'target' solutions to the problem. It was designed also to exclude some people from assistance: *Volksdeutsche* and *Reichdeutsche* who had been living in the occupied territories of Eastern Europe before the war would be denied both refugee and displaced person status and therefore would not qualify for assistance (Salomon 1990: 161). Ethnic Germans expelled from Poland, Hungary, Czechoslovakia, Romania, and Yugoslavia were the responsibility of the German authorities. The suspicion that German nationals, and worse still German spies, were disguising themselves as displaced persons led to tight controls on the movement, reception, and distribution of German nationals across Europe (Schechtman 1947: 262). Nationality screenings and eligibility checks at borders and assembly centres also operated as exclusionary procedures. When the movement became out of control, the Potsdam agreement authorized a programme of compulsory transfer or removal of *Volksdeutsche* remaining in Poland, Czechoslovakia, and Hungary.

International refugee agencies were crucial to the management of population displacement. These organizations generated knowledge about population displacement and institutionalized the phenomenon as an issue of concern. Their mandate set the limits of operation, including who would receive assistance, what forms of assistance were offered, who participated in the decision-making process, and who carried out the programmes. International government agencies coordinated and harmonized the activities of states and various agents, distributed funds, and functioned as a forum for consensus-building and collective action.

An important function of the Office of the High Commission of Refugees was to resolve the problem of Russian refugees by conceptualizing them as human resources. The initial failure of the Russian repatriation programme marked the beginning of the involvement of the International Labour Organization (ILO) in the management of refugees. In 1924, Fridtjof Nansen, the appointed League of Nations High Commissioner for Refugees, persuaded the ILO to assist in the technical problems of employment, settlement, and migration. The Refugee Service of the ILO made inquiries in all European countries as to the conditions of refugees, their occupations, and whether they were employed, or employable (Simpson 1939: 203). It was also responsible for the vocational training of refugees. Finally, the Service conducted investigations about the possibilities of settlement of large numbers of refugees in South America.[11]

Gradually, the activities undertaken by the High Commission for Refugees expanded. The Inter-Governmental Arrangement of 1922–1928 authorized the High Commission to carry out consular functions – 'services' that were normally the tasks of the national governments. Its responsibilities now included:

> [C]ertifying the identity of the position of the refugees; their family position and civil status, …; testifying to the regularity, validity, and conformity with the previous law of their country of origin, of documents issued in such countries; certifying the signature of refugees and copies and translations of documents drawn up in their own language; testifying before the authorities of the country to the good character and conduct of the individual refugee.
>
> (Holborn 1975: 11)

Such 'services' allowed refugees to be documented and to be assimilated or integrated into their countries of refuge. If refugees could not be repatriated to their countries of origin, then it was important for the High Commission to facilitate the creation of a new bond between the refugee and the country of refuge. Since being a refugee was an anomalous condition in the regulatory citizen–state arrangement, the task was to convince the host-state that the refugee had the necessary temperament to become the good citizen.

The scale of population displacement caused by flight, expulsion, and organized population transfers across Europe during World War II saw the expansion of humanitarian activities. The British and American governments funded the operational expenditure of the previously impotent Inter-Governmental Committee on Refugees (IGCR).[12] This was a departure from previous practices under the League when governments expected private, voluntary agencies to finance humanitarian relief for refugees (Holborn 1956: 12). In fact, the IGCR began to subsidise the relief programmes of voluntary agencies. In an effort to coordinate the work of voluntary relief and welfare organizations during and after the war, the British and American governments introduced innovative administrative measures to the organizational structure of the Committee.

As the war continued, the role of the IGCR was enlarged from a diplomatic one of coordinating the efforts of governments to include operational tasks. The Committee's new function was 'to undertake negotiations with neutral or Allied States or with organizations, and take steps as may be necessary to preserve, maintain and transport' refugees within its mandate (Sjöberg 1991: 16). It coordinated its activities with those of the High Commissioner of the League of Nations, the ILO, and later the War Refugee Board of the USA and the United Nations Relief and Rehabilitation Administration (Holborn 1975: 18). It devised an orderly migration programme for the thousands of refugees, and thereby laid the foundation for the massive international migration scheme of the International Refugee Organization (IRO).

Non-governmental organizations were active in administering care to displaced populations and their participation became increasingly important after World War II. Beyond the International Committee of the Red Cross, consultative bodies of voluntary agencies were formed in Britain and America: the

Council of British Societies for Relief Abroad (COBSRA) and the American Council of Voluntary Agencies for Foreign Services (ACVAFS). Governments deployed these humanitarian agencies to carry the distribution of relief to refugees. Empowered by their capacity for compassion, these agencies cooperated with military authorities to carry out rigorous programmes of supervision and revitalization aimed at transforming refugees from states of injury to autonomous bearers of vigour.

Development deficit and the government of refugees

In the post-WWII period, there were two distinct ways to think about refugees. The East–West divide provided the grid of intelligibility for refugees who were mostly Europeans fleeing Communist regimes. This distinction was based on political ideology. The 'reality' of non-European refugees was economic backwardness or 'underdevelopment' rather than political.[13] Thus in addition to the East–West order, another perception of world order had states and the populations within them divided into stages of development, from primitive to advanced.

Development is one of the most powerful assemblages of thought and practice ordering human relations. It creates the 'developed' First World and the 'developing' or 'underdeveloped' Third World, each with its distinct life forms; and governs the mode of interaction between the two spheres. According to Escobar (1995: 213), development can be seen as a mechanism 'that links forms of knowledge about the Third World with the deployment of forms of power and intervention, resulting in the mapping and production of Third World societies', where 'individuals, governments and communities are seen as "underdeveloped" and treated as such'. What this means is that under the rubric of development, enormous and dispersed territory and population are made governable at a distance. As a metaphor for transformation towards growth and maturation, the development trajectory not only makes the idea of a 'Third World' possible, it also locates the populations of this world as the 'not-yet' objects of constant improvement. As 'underdevelopment' becomes a domain of experience, strategies for dealing with the 'problem' resulted in the subjection of people who in turn subjected themselves to systematic and comprehensive intervention.

The 1950s saw the beginning of a development knowledge industry. 'Development economics' became a distinct field of knowledge and policy pursuit. Most economists believed that, with significant investment, developing countries could 'take-off' (Rostow 1960). The United Nations organized a series of expert groups to study the problems of underdevelopment and created a number of short-lived economic development funds before setting up the United Nations Commission on Trade and Development (UNCTAD) in 1964 and the United Nations Development Program (UNDP) in 1966. Regional development banks were created for Africa in 1964 and for Asia in 1966. The strategic plan was simple: the means of development were macroeconomic policies, the agent of development was the state, and the goal of development was growth. But macroeconomic policies yielded uneven results. Signs of industrialization and growth could be seen in some countries in Asia but not in many parts of Africa and South America. This success and failure of development planning raised the question of conditions for development and growth. 'Modernization theory' was an attempt to unravel this puzzle. The path to development corresponded with the path to being modern. According to Myron Weiner (1966) and Samuel Huntington (1968), development and modernization depended on the complex interplay between forms of political and social organization, the dynamics of social and political change, and the conditions for order and institutional design. By analysing the features of traditional and transitional societies, the mechanisms of change, and the sequences of political development, industrialization, and urbanization, traditional societies could follow the historical trajectory of the West and become modern. Western policy-makers and social scientists, along with the political leaders of Africa and Asia, believed that with meticulous planning they could reshape society.

The link between refugees and development emerged from a predicament of practice. Once considered as largely separate and distinct activities, refugee assistance and development policy merged to address 'refugee-related development issues' or 'development-related objectives in refugee-impacted areas' when two decades of refugee relief and humanitarian programmes failed to solve the refugee problem in post-colonial Africa. At first, the assumption was that the displacement was a temporary condition and people would return to their homes after the conflict, and after gaining independent statehood. But by the mid-1960s there were a large number of 'long-stayers' – for example, Ethiopian refugees in Somalia, Mozambicans in Malawi and other neighbouring countries, Saharawis in Algeria, and Angolans in Zambia and Zaire – who could not be repatriated. Western governments stressed the importance of alleviating the refugee burden placed on neighbouring countries of asylum while at the same time dismissed resettling these people to their countries as an unworkable solution.

By the time population displacement became an economic and political problem Africa was already a laboratory for theories and practices of development. Thus, not surprisingly, development provided a framework of analysis and a guide to activity on the refugee problem. Accordingly, the appropriate response to governing refugees in Africa, beyond the initial disaster relief activity, is to provide development assistance that supports both countries of origin and countries of first asylum. Policy-makers hoped that development programmes could secure the conditions for repatriation and integration as well as prevent future flows. In the 1960s, UNHCR, UNDP, and the World Bank were encouraged to collaborate on activities that linked refugee programmes with development plans.

The 'development' needs of neighbouring countries of asylum were major concerns, as it was believed that the presence of refugees could hinder the development of the host countries. In this context, refugee resettlement schemes arose out of the twin concern to reduce the burden on host governments and to foster among refugees as high a level of self-reliance and self-sufficiency as possible. Tanzania, Botswana, and Sudan experimented with rural refugee settlement schemes during the 1960s before these spread throughout Africa. The UNHCR, ILO, and national governments carried out the strategy of 'zonal development' in Burundi and Zaire in 1963 (Pitterman 1985: 75). The schemes expanded to other regions when the UNDP was established in 1966. The UNDP planned full-scale zonal development projects that incorporated refugee settlements. International voluntary agencies also gave their support to these schemes. The aim was to integrate rural schemes into broader national rural development strategies (Loescher 1993: 82). Such schemes were also considered an effective way to integrate refugees into the country of asylum. In other words, the purpose of zonal development was to build and strengthen the economic and social infrastructure of a region, which would lead to improvements in the local living conditions and contribute to the economic potential of the country as a whole (Holborn 1975: 912). Proposals for the World Bank to fund large-scale, income-generating development projects were also among the recommendations to strengthen and stabilize the economies of host-states with large refugee populations.

Another concern was to create refugee programmes that would empower the refugee as a participant in the development of the host-state. The Third World refugee was a subject of intervention who had experienced the double disruption of displacement and underdevelopment. S/he was someone whose survival depends, first, on the goodwill of others and secondly, on the opportunity to cultivate the self-determination to be a productive and autonomous subject. Thus, a vital aim of the refugee-development strategy was to reinvigorate the capacity of refugees to become self-sufficient agents who could contribute to the overall economic development of 'developing' host countries or countries of origin.

The connection between refugee movement and development was consistently affirmed in the many international conferences attended by donor countries and their development assistance agencies, host countries, representatives of international organization, NGOs, UN agencies, and experts. The concept of burden sharing was introduced at the Pan-African Conference on the Situation of Refugees in Africa, convened in Arusha, Tanzania to encourage cooperation in dealing with mass refugee movements. The 'root cause' debate expanded the field of refugee administration to include states that generated refugee flows and established a consensus on the problem of refugees and development as an appropriate strategy for African refugees. The unfailing belief that underdevelopment was the self-evident condition of Africa led refugee agencies to concentrate their efforts on domestic problems of economic underdevelopment and poverty, which neutralized the effects of the kinds of international political and economic interactions African states were caught up in.

Conclusion

This chapter has explored some aspects of the subjectification and problematization of a population group categorized as refugees and the arts of governing them. It has challenged a common mischaracterization of responses to refugees;

namely, that the politics of indifference has led the neglect of some of the most vulnerable people in the world. But refugees are not forgotten people. One should not confuse the effects of exclusion with indifference. Within the modern global political arrangement states, as the sovereign power in domestic and international politics, have exclusive control over the entry of people into its territory of jurisdiction. Thus the movement of people is a highly regulated affair and the refugee regime is one system among many that is concerned with regulating inter-state movement.

Being a refugee refers to population movement of a very particular kind. Refugees are distinct from migrants because of their inability to actualize either the formal or substantive expressions of modern citizenship. The failure of their 'protector' states to provide the minimal conditions for political life force them to seek protection elsewhere. The refugee regime offers 'international protection', but this protection is conceivable and feasible because states have agreed to treat non-citizens in a particular way. Yet the forms of protection offered voluntarily by states are circumscribed by the state–citizen regulatory norm, which creates an international hierarchy of duties and obligations. In other words, the relationship between the boundaries of citizenship and the system of states has profound effects for claims of equality. Each state is accountable, first and foremost, for the welfare and protection of its own citizens. This hierarchy as an outcome of locating political communities constituted as sovereign states becomes the fertile ground for a vision of politics centring on us/them or friend/enemy interactions.

Refugees thus are subjected to myriad forms of disciplinary and regulatory practices. The international refugee regime, with its multifarious practices and pedagogical and transformative programmes, is key to the government of refugees. The regime legitimatizes certain kinds of political interactions and solutions. Nowhere is this more apparent than in the twin discoveries of the Third World and the connection between being a refugee and the condition of underdevelopment.

In no way is the argument presented here meant to discount the ways in which refugee programmes and agencies have contributed to the alleviation of human misery. Rather, it is an appeal to be attentive to the potential and subtle forms of violence embedded in governance practices. The first challenge is to lay bare the relations of power that produce sites of governance. If there is a political project in the governmentality approach, it is in the contestation of thought and practice. The second challenge is to avoid false necessities. A world of territorial sovereign states and a humanity of national citizens have come about due to specific historical conditions; there is nothing necessary about either institution. Historical contingency compels critical investigations into the histories of refugees, and such positioning, in a way, permits refugees to be other than anomalous beings.

Notes

1 UN Doc. AC.96/965/Add.1
2 See Lui-Bright (1997).

3 See Brownlie (1966).
4 Political theory and sociology tend to focus on the 'domestic' view of citizenship, without considering its political purpose in the division of the world's population.
5 The general perception of citizens is as members of a culturally nationalized population with attributes that make them governable. Non-citizens, however, are characterized as less governable because they do not possess the historical memory and cultural etiquette of the 'host' state.
6 For a more in-depth look at the history of the institutionalization of refugee problem see Lui (2002).
7 After 1922 very few refugees came from the Soviet Union because the authorities prohibited emigration. Meanwhile, mass deportations took place within the country. Populations from the mountains, steppes, peninsula and Volga (the southwestern border region of the Soviet Union) were transferred to eastern and central Siberia.
8 See Ladas (1932).
9 This was a time when many European countries were asked by the League to accept Jewish refugees.
10 The meaning of the principle of *non-refoulement* is found in Article 33 of the 1951 Refugee Convention. It states that states, parties to the Convention, have an obligation not to return individuals back to their countries of origin or to any other country where they would be at risk of persecution and where their life and freedom would be threatened. The exception applies if the refugee presents a danger to national security and public order, and if he or she has committed a serious crime.
11 The ILO's efforts to expand employment arrangements for refugees were met with unwillingness on the part of governments and the situation became even more difficult with the onset of the economic crisis.
12 Based on an American initiative, the IGCR was set up in 1938 as an independent intergovernmental refugee organization outside the League of Nations framework.
13 The 1951 Convention and the Statute of UNHCR were designed to address political refugees from Eastern Europe and not refugees outside of Europe. The General Assembly authorized the UNHCR to assist refugees who did not fall within the statutory definition for the first time in 1957 for Chinese refugees in Hong Kong.

References

Arendt, H. (1976) *The Origins of Totalitarianism*, San Diego, New York and London: Harcourt Brace.

Baldwin, T. (1992) 'The territorial state', in H. Gross and R. Harrison (eds) *Jurisprudence: Cambridge essays*, Oxford: Clarendon Press.

Barnett, L. (2002) 'Global governance and the evolution of the international refugee regime', *International Journal of Refugee Law*, 14(2,3): 238–262.

Barutciski, M. (1999) 'Western diplomacy and the Kosovo refugee crisis', *Forced Migration Review*, 5: 8–11.

Bayefsky, A. and Fitzpatrick, J. (eds) (2000) *Human Rights and Forced Displacement*, The Hague: Martinus Nijhoff Publishers/Kluwer Law International.

Brownlie, I. (1966) *Principles of Public International Law*, Oxford: Oxford University Press.

Chimni, B.S. (1998) 'The geopolitics of refugee studies: a view from the south', *Journal of Refugee Studies*, 11(4): 350–374.

de Waal, A. (1997) *Famine Crimes: politics and the disaster relief industry in Africa*, Bloomington, IN: Indiana University Press.

de Zayas, A.M. (1975) 'International law and mass population transfer', *Harvard International Law Journal*, 16(2): 207–258.

Dean, M. and Hindess, B. (1998) 'Introduction: government, liberalism, society', in M. Dean and B. Hindess (eds) *Governing Australia: studies in contemporary rationalities of government*, Cambridge, New York and Melbourne: Cambridge University Press.

Dillon, M. (1998) 'Epilogue: the scandal of refugee: some reflections on the "inter" of international relations', *Refuge*, 17(6): 30–39.

Escobar, A. (1995) 'Imagining a post-development era', in J. Crush (ed.) *Power of Development*, London: Routledge.

Ferguson, K. (1996) 'Unmapping and remapping the world: foreign policy as aesthetic practice', in M. Shapiro and H.R. Alker (eds) *Challenging Boundaries: global flows, territorial identities*, Minneapolis: University of Minnesota Press.

Foucault, M. (1991) 'Governmentality', in G. Burchell, C. Gordon and P. Miller (eds) *The Foucault Effect: studies in governmentality*, Hemel Hempstead: Harvester Wheatsheaf.

——(1997) 'Security, territory and population', in P. Rabinow (ed.) *Michel Foucault. Ethics: subjectivity and truth. The essential works of Foucault 1954–1984, vol. 1*, trans. Robert Hurley et al., New York: New Press.

Gorlick, B. (2000) 'Human rights and refugees: enhancing protection through international human rights law', UNHCR New Issues in Refugee Research, Working Paper No.30.

Helton, A. (2002) *The Price of Indifference: refugees and humanitarian action in the new century*, Oxford: Oxford University Press.

Hindess, B. (1997) 'Divide and govern', Paper presented in the Lecture series on Governing Modern Societies, University of Victoria, Canada. Published as (1998) 'Divide and Rule: the international character of modern citizenship', *European Journal of Social Theory*, 1(1): 57–70.

——(2000) 'Citizenship in the international management of populations', *American Behavioural Scientist*, 43(9): 1486–1497.

——(2002) 'Neo-liberal citizenship', *Citizenship Studies*, 6(2): 127–143.

Holborn, L. (1956) *The International Refugee Organization: a specialized agency of the United Nations: its history and work 1946–1952*, London: Oxford University Press.

——(1975) *Refugees: A Problem of Our Times: the work of the United Nations High Commissioner for Refugees, 1951–1972 vols 1 and 2*, Metuchen, NJ: Scarecrow Press.

Huntington, S. (1968) *Political Order in Changing Societies*, New Haven: Yale University Press.

Isin, E. (2002) *Being Political: genealogies of citizenship*, Minneapolis and London: University of Minnesota Press.

Jackson, R. (1999) 'Introduction: sovereignty at the millennium', *Political Studies*, XLVII: 423–430.

Keeley, J. (1990) 'Towards a Foucauldian analysis of international regimes', *International Organization*, 44(1): 83–105.

Krasner, S. (1982) 'Structural causes and regime consequences: regime as intervening variables', *International Organization*, 36(2): 185–205.

Kuehls, T. (1996) *Beyond Sovereign Territory: the spaces of ecopolitics*, Minneapolis: University of Minnesota Press.

Kulischer, E.M. (1948) *Europe on the Move: war and population changes 1917–1947*, New York: Columbia University Press.

Ladas, S. (1932) *The Exchanges of Minorities: Bulgaria, Greece and Turkey*, New York: Macmillan.

Loescher, G. (1992) *Refugee Movement and International Security*, Adelphi Paper No.268, London: International Institute of Strategic Studies.

——(1993) *Beyond Charity: international cooperation and the global refugee crisis*, Oxford: Oxford University Press.

Lui, R. (2002) 'Governing refugees: 1919–1945', *Borderlands*, 1(1). Online. Available at: http://www.borderlandsejournal.adelaide.edu.au/vol1no1_2002/lui_governing.html

Lui-Bright, R. (1997) 'International/National: sovereignty, governmentality and international relations', in G. Crowder, H. Manning, D.S. Mathieson, A. Parkin and L. Seabrooke (eds) *Australasian Political Studies 1997: proceedings of the 1997 APSA Conference, vol. 2*, Department of Politics: Flinders University of South Australia.

Malkki, L. (1994) 'Citizens of humanity: internationalism and the imagined community of nations', *Diaspora*, 3(1): 41–68.

Nyers, P. (1998) 'Refugees, humanitarian emergencies, and the politicization of life', *Refuge*, 17(6): 16–21.

——(1999) 'Emergency or emerging identities? Refugees and transformations in world order', *Millennium: Journal of International Studies*, 28(1): 1–26.

Pitterman, S. (1985) 'International responses to refugee situations: the United Nations High Commissioner for Refugees', in E. Ferris (ed.) *Refugees and World Politics*, New York: Praeger.

——(ed.) (1987) *Refugees: a Third World dilemma*, Totowa, New Jersey: Rowman & Littlefield.

Rose, N. and Miller, P. (1992) 'Political power beyond the State: problematics of government', *British Journal of Sociology*, 43(2): 173–205.

Rostow, W.W. (1960) *The Stages of Economic Growth: a non-communist manifesto*, Cambridge: Cambridge University Press.

Salomon, K. (1990) 'The Cold War heritage: UNRRA and the IRO as predecessors of UNHCR', in G. Rystad (ed.) *The Uprooted: forced migration as an international problem in the post-war era*, Lund: Lund University Press.

Samhat, N.H. (1997) 'International regimes as political community', *Millennium: Journal of International Studies*, 36(2): 349–378.

Schechtman, J. (1947) 'Resettlement of transferred *Volksdeutsche* in Germany', *Journal of Central European Affairs*, 7(3): 262–284.

Shore, C. and S. Wright (1997) 'Policy: a new field of anthropology', in C. Shore and S. Wright (eds) *Anthropology of Policy: critical perspectives on governance and power*, London and New York: Routledge.

Skran, C. (1995) *Refugees in Inter-War Europe: the emergence of a regime*, Oxford: Clarendon Press.

Simpson, J.H. (1939) *The Refugee Problem: report of a survey*, London and New York: Oxford University Press.

Sjöberg, T. (1991) *The Powers and the Persecuted: the refugee problem and the Inter-Governmental Committee on Refugees (IGCR), 1938–1947*, Lund: Lund University Press.

Soguk, N. (1996) 'Transnational/Transborder bodies: resistance, accommodation, and exile in refugee and migration movement on the U.S.–Mexican border', in M.J. Shapiro and H.R. Alker (eds) *Challenging Boundaries: global flows, territorial identities*, Minneapolis: University of Minnesota Press.

——(1999) *States and Strangers: refugees and displacement of statecraft*, Minneapolis: University of Minnesota Press.

Strange, S. (1982) '*Cave! hic dragones*: a critique of regime analysis', *International Organization*, 36(2): 479–496.

Weiner, M. (1966) *Modernization: the dynamics of growth*, New York: Basic Books.

——(1994) 'Security, stability and migration', in R. Betts (ed.) *Conflict After the Cold War: arguments on causes of war and peace*, New York: Macmillan.

Xenos, N. (1996) 'Refugee: the modern political condition', in M. Shapiro and H.R. Alker (eds) *Challenging Boundaries: global flows, territorial identities*, Minneapolis: University of Minnesota Press.

7 The clash of governmentalities

Displacement and return in Bosnia-Herzegovina

Gearóid Ó Tuathail and Carl Dahlman

On 10 April 1992 Jose Maria Mendiluce, the UNHCR's most senior official in the former Yugoslavia, left Belgrade for Sarajevo after a meeting with Serbian president, Slobodan Milosevic. Mendiluce was traveling through a region where the nexus of population, territory and security was in crisis and violently coming apart. A month previously, the Yugoslav Republic of Bosnia-Herzegovina had conducted a referendum on independence that Bosnian Serbs largely boycotted yet which the majority endorsed. Four days earlier, European Union foreign ministers recognized the independence of Bosnia-Herzegovina, followed a day later by the United States government. As he crossed the Drina, now an international recognized border, into the northeast Bosnian town of Zvornik, Mendiluce stumbled upon a scene of terror, murder and displacement, what the world would soon recognize and later prosecute as the war crime of 'ethnic cleansing'.

Though on the border with Serbia, Zvornik was a typical Bosnian place. The census the year before showed the population of the Zvornik region (a 500-square-kilometre *opstina* or county) at 81,111, 59 per cent registering as Muslim and 39 per cent as Serb. Most of these people lived in villages to the north and south of the main town or in the more remote mountain villages surrounding it. Like many non-urban Bosnian regions, these settlements were largely but not exclusively monoethnic, a product of decades of people living together but mostly in separate settlements. The town was different, a multiethnic place where Muslims were more numerous than Serbs but all interacted as neighbours and acquaintances in a town small enough for everyone to know each other.

In the power struggle to re-constitute and re-arrange Yugoslav space, administrative identities and census demographics were to terrorize everyday multiethnic life in Bosnia. Slobodan Milosevic's drive to accumulate enough power to become the 'new Tito' of Yugoslavia had started a process of polarization that led to the secession of Slovenia and Croatia from the Federal Republic of Yugoslavia (Sell 2002). Governmentality was revisioned along ethnonationalist lines with the slogans 'all Serbs in one state' and 'Croatia for the Croatians' replacing the Tito-era slogan of 'brotherhood and unity'. As Yugoslavia came apart Milosevic switched to a more explicit 'greater Serbia' strategy, fomenting the proclamation of 'autonomous Serb regions' in Croatia and Bosnia. A war to produce discrete ethnonationalist homelands was unleashed against the quotidian sociality of multiethnic regions and towns.

The instruments of that war for the Milosevic regime in Belgrade was a Serbianized Yugoslav National Army (JNA), special paramilitary units of the Ministry of the Interior (the Red Berets) and a nexus of Serbian militias under the loose control of the Ministry of the Interior (Cigar 1995). These forces worked together to initiate the process of ethnic cleansing that began in eastern Slavonia in 1991. A town would be surrounded by the JNA and its defenders subjected to artillery fire. Irregular Serb militia forces, in coordination with the JNA, would then enter the town and terrorize its inhabitants, murdering some, raping others, and plundering all. A concerted effort would be made to round up as many non-Serb residents of the town as possible. Some would be transported out, others placed in concentration camps, and others murdered *en masse*. Though it appeared to be the antithesis of governance, 'ethnic cleansing' is a technique of governmentality, a public–private partnership of violence that mixes professional military force and organizational logistics with freelance plunder, criminality, and lawlessness. Institutionally, it represented the emergent structure of power in Serbia under Milosevic: an alliance of Communist bureaucracy with parochial religious nationalism and criminal mafia economics (Thomas 1999).

The Zvornik town center that Jose Maria Mendiluce entered in April 1992 was in the throes of ethnic cleansing. The attack on the city had begun April 8 with artillery and mortar shelling from positions in Karakaj, in the north, and in Mali Zvornik, across the river in Serbia. Tanks, snipers and infantry soon crushed the city's defenders and Serbian-based militias assumed the leading role in the conquest of the city (Ludwig Boltzmann Institute of Human Rights 1994). Accompanied by local Serbs, most of whom were founding members of the Serb Democratic Party (SDS), they systematically engaged in house searches, killings, rape and looting. Mendiluce described the scene:

> I could see trucks full of dead bodies. I could see militiamen taking more corpses of children, women and old people from their houses and putting them on trucks. I saw at least four or five trucks full of corpses. When I arrived the cleansing had been done. There were no more people, no one on the streets. It was all finished. They were looting, cleaning up the city after the massacre.
>
> (Silber and Little 1995: 246)

With the destruction of the local Muslim population, the Serb separatists established the 'Provisional Government' of the 'Serbian Community of Zvornik', issuing new proclamations while cooperating with paramilitary units seeking to remove the remaining Muslim population from the countryside surrounding the town. A proclamation broadcast on Radio Zvornik called on residents to return to their workplaces. A nightly curfew was declared and a pass was required to move around the city during the day. This could only be obtained at the Zvornik police department, now run by a founding SDS member (ICG 2000b). Muslim men who showed up for work or tried to obtain a pass were rounded up and sent to special detention buildings in Karakaj, the worst of which was located on the grounds of a former agricultural cooperative called *Ekonomija*. According to an authoritative human rights report on the ethnic cleansing of Zvornik, in 'the secluded buildings, numerous tortures and murders were committed ... In one slaughter-house room, a virtual butchering of the victims took place' (Ludwig Boltzmann Institute of Human Rights 1994: 52). While many managed to flee Zvornik that April, others were forced to work for what became the Bosnian Serb army, digging trenches and supplying soldiers fighting forces loyal to the Bosnian government in Sarajevo. The town emptied out but its abandoned and looted buildings were soon occupied by Serbs fleeing 'Muslim regions' of Bosnia such as the nearby town of Tuzla. A violent and bloody ethnic engineering of Bosnian space had begun.

The clash of governmentalties

In his discussion of the emergence of the art of government in the early modern era, Foucault seizes upon a quote from Guillaume de la Perrière's which specifies government as 'the right disposition of things, arranged so as to lead to a convenient end' (Foucault 1991: 94). Constituting, arranging and legitimizing government as the management of population, territory and security over the subsequent centuries took many different forms and gave rise to competing systems of political thought. Liberalism, nationalism and communism are all idealizations of how population, territory and political forms ought to be organized. As laws and codes for the arrangement of political space and the disciplining of subjects, these are global governmentalities in aspiration and inspiration. But, besides competing with each other, such modern governmentalities of state formation, territorial arrangement and population administration have long clashed with the messiness of actually existing places, with localized power structures, accumulated historical legacies, and pluralities of peoples and identities.

The war in Bosnia-Herzegovina has long been explained by some as a 'clash of civilizations' (Huntington 1996: 126–128). But rather than a clash between essentialized antagonistic identities, the war in Bosnia and its aftermath was a complex and multi-scalar clash of governmentalities. This chapter reviews some of the violence, pragmatics and contradictions of this antagonism of governmentalities, a contest that sometimes appeared as 'local' versus 'global', and 'fascist ethnonationalism' versus 'liberal internationalism', but which, more often than not, was a dense entanglement of multiple actors – international diplomats, local leaders, regional mafia, the United Nations, a war crimes tribunal and non-governmental organizations from the international press to Mercy Corp and the International Crisis Group – asserting their governance mentalities in conditions of war and negative peace. Briefly noted are a few of the modalities of power characterizing this collision of governmentalities: tactics of ethnic engineering, map making at peace conferences, implementation and conditionality strategies after the war, check points and crime, the imposition of uniform laws upon a dysfunctional state, and the shadow of war crimes accountability. Grounded in an examination of local displacement and return under the gaze of multiple global governmentalities, it illustrates how governmentality is never singular and smooth but always entangled in the complexities of places and scalar dynamics.

Globe-spanning governmentalities of states, media and international institutions were all deeply implicated in the crisis of Bosnia's emergence as a sovereign state. Encouraged by the European Union and the international community, the Bosnian parliament had forced through an independence referendum that did not have the support of the majority of Bosnian Serbs, one of the republic's three 'constituent nations'. For the international community of states 'the right disposition of things arranged so as to lead to a convenient end' was the establishment of Bosnia as an independent state where each of these constituent nations would be represented and secure. For Serbian and Croatian nationalists, this was manifestly the 'wrong disposition of things' as they sought to organize post-Yugoslavian spaces around the 'rationality' of ethnoterritorialism, namely one ethnos – one territory – one government. What unfolded was a concerted effort by Serb and Croatian ethnonationalists to dismember Bosnia in the name of 'self-determination'. The practical result was the spectacle of 'ethnic cleansing,' a euphemism represented as a necessary phase in the establishment of the 'right disposition of things' by ethnonationalists but a morally abhorrent 'wrong disposition of things' for many networks of the international community.

Though a commonly evoked identity formation, the 'international community' was never a unified community but a heterogeneous group of actors asserting and generating 'global governmentalities' that were varied, overlapping, cross-cutting and contradictory. On the one hand, one had the society of international states whose leaders and institutions set the prevailing legal standards for recognition, aid and connectivity to the global economy. They pronounced on the legal status of Yugoslavia – a federal state in the process of 'self-dissolution' in the words of the Badinter Commission – and initially interpreted 'self-determination' to mean the sentiment of the majority of the residents within the pre-established borders of the territorial republics of the Yugoslav Federation. Yet by this same logic they failed to recognize the autonomous territory of Kosovo, whose Albanian majority had enjoyed nearly the same status as the republics since 1974 and who clearly wished to quit Serbia. Further still, many also implicitly endorsed the congruence of territory, nation and government, for their own states represented this to varying degrees and had bloody histories of violence and exclusion to prove it. On the other hand, one had international institutions, like Mendiluce's UNHCR, the International Red Cross and freelance media reporters on the ground in Zvornik and elsewhere in Bosnia as it came under systematic assault. Their reports, dispatches and images constituted a form of 'videocameralistics' that brought the horror of ethnic cleansing to the world's attention and generated strong moral and institutional imperatives to 'do something' to address the violent dismemberment of a new sovereign European state under attack (Luke and Ó Tuathail 1997). But while these globe-spanning governmentalities enframed a 'global Bosnia', on the ground the realities of 'local Bosnia' from April 1992 until December 1995 were shaped by the violent governmentality of ethnic cleansing.

The conflict in Bosnia was a war between two clashing geopolitical visions of that state, competing governmentalities with very different notions of how its territory, population and political life should be ordered (see Table 7.1). One vision represents Bosnia as an 'organic' place, a historically unique and enduring region of diversity and tolerance that occasionally succumbed to violent episodes but only when instigated and provoked by outside forces. For the historian John Fine, 'toleration has marked Bosnia's entire history, except when foreigners or locals stirred up by foreign governments or foreign movement have incited the Bosnians to other paths' (Fine 2002: 7). The advocates of 'organic Bosnia' recognize its history as an independent territory in the Balkans and embrace its particular patterns of human settlements, politics and history as irreducible and indivisible (Bringa 1995).

The other vision regards Bosnia as an 'artificial' creation, an unnatural and unstable territory characterized by ancient ethnic hatred and irresolvable differences (Mahmutcehajic 2000). States, in this vision, are best organized as homogeneous national spaces which reflect a defining moment of 'primary acquisition' of that territory by an imagined ethnos (Geary 2002). Bosnian territory is claimed by both Serbian and Croatian nationalists who refuse to concede its own independent history and right to be a state. Bosnia is a 'land of hatred' because it is contested between different nationalities; its diversity is held to be an explanation for its violence. Both Serbian and Croatian nationalism have particular historiographies and genealogies of territorial governance in the region, and presented themselves as (re)emergent cartographic rationalities to domestic and foreign observers as Yugoslavia collapsed. The greater Serbia slogan of 'all Serbs in one state' is a governmentality that presents itself as modern and rational. It emerged within the context of an 'anti-bureaucratic revolution' in Yugoslavia in the late 1980s that was the discursive legitimation of Milosevic's drive to become the new Tito. But Milosevic's tactical use of Serbian nationalism stimulated the rise of Croatian nationalism and Franjo Tudjman, who envisioned a 'greater Croatia' at Bosnia's expense. Not only was Bosnia an 'artificial state' in Tudjman's eyes but he claimed that Croatia's 'current pretzel-shape is unnatural' without western Herzegovina (Mahmutcehajic 2000: 31). Squeezed by these two revisionist nation-state building projects was the Bosnian President and Muslim leader Alija Izetbegovic who nominally resisted the division of Bosnia into 'national territories' yet was forced to concede to its logic on a number of occasions.

The capture of the media in Belgrade and Zagreb by ethnonationalist ideologists ensured that the notion of Bosnia as artificial was widely proclaimed and circulated. For greater Serbia advocates, the rationality of partition rested on the numerical superiority of Serbs within many of the counties of Croatia and Bosnia. These regions, it was claimed, had the local right to 'self-determination' in uniting with Serbia. In Bosnia, the Serb leadership claimed over 60 per cent of the state based on county majorities or ownership of private land (Magaš 1993: 169–170). Meanwhile, Croats in Bosnia saw their own interests reflected in the rising Serb separatism in Bosnia. But unlike Bosnian Serb claims to demographic dominance and self-determination, Croat nationalists sought to gain territory on a largely historic claim to western Herzegovina, a territory that would enlarge Croatia's southern region by incorporating most of southern Bosnia.

Table 7.1: 'Clashing geopolitical visions of Bosnia'

Geopolitical Vision	ARTIFICIAL BOSNIA	ORGANIC BOSNIA
Local Advocates	Radovan Karadzic. Mate Boban.	Haris Silajdzic, Rusmir Mahmutcehajic (2000).
Regional Advocates	Slobodan Milosevic, Franjo Tudjman.	Stipe Mesic, Branka Magaš.
Country Definition	Bosnia is an unnatural nonviable construct.	Bosnia has a unique identity as a country unified by its diverse traditions.
Geopolitical Description	An unstable in-between territory characterized by 'ancient hatreds'.	An historical crossroads characterized by centuries of coexistence.
History	Tradition of enmity and violence.	Tradition of tolerance and diversity.
'Common Rhetorical Articulation'	'We cannot and will not live together any longer'.	'We have lived together in the past and can continue to do so'.
Borders	As artificial as those in Africa.	Traditional and relatively stable.
'Proper Bosnian Spatial Order'	Partition into three ethnonationalist territories: *Republika Srpska, Herzeg-Bosna* and an Islamic state'.	A unified state made up of multiethnic regions and three constituent nations'.
Conception of Identity	Essentialist, primordial, exclusivist and antagonistic.	Essentialist for some but not others, historically fluid, inclusivist and accommodating.
Presumed Solution	Peace will come when all nations have their respective homelands.	Peace comes out of mutual toleration for other traditions and religions.
Geopolitical Expression	Karadordevo Agreement between Milosevic and Tudjman to divide Bosnia	A unified and centralized Bosnia recognized by its neighbours.
Geopolitical Methods	Ethnic cleansing, ethnic engineering, and genocide.	Resistance against secessionism. De-centralization of power.
Geopolitical Metanarrative of the War	A clash of civilizations.	Denial of Bosnia. Outside aggression against a multiethnic sovereign state.
Story of Muslim Identity	Muslims are really Serbs or Croatians who converted.	All people are Bosnian, even Serbs and Croats despite themselves.
Bosnia as Metaphor	Symptomatic of Hobbesian world of international politics.	Model for European progress.
'Place of Muslims'	In an 'Islamic state' enclave or back in 'Turkey'.	One of three traditions in a unified state.
Metaphorical Symbol	Borders. Destroyed religious monuments.	Bridges. *Stari Most* of Mostar.
'Moment of Primary Acquisition' (Geary 2002)	Medieval kingdoms of Croat' Tomislav (910–928) or Serb' Stefan Dusan (1331–1355).	Medieval Bosnia kingdom of Tvrtko (1353–1391).

These plans were discussed in 1991 by Milosevic and Tudjman at Karadordevo and an apparent partition of Bosnia was agreed (Silber and Little 1995: 131–132). For his part, Milosevic wanted most of eastern and western Bosnia, and Tudjman was willing to give up the Croat areas of northern Bosnia for his interests. Between these territories, they would leave a buffer Muslim state. Indeed, when Bosnian Serb and Croat nationalists finally claimed autonomous regions on the eve of the war, the exclusive Serb claims covered 63 per cent of Bosnia's territory and those of the Croats 21 per cent, while jointly claiming over 12 per cent, leaving less than 4 per cent for an 'Islamic state'. These claims flew in the face of the actually existing Bosnia which had always had a multiethnic character and territoriality. In 1991 Muslims and Serbs were distributed across 94 per cent of Bosnia's territory, and Croats across 70 per cent (Mahmutcehajic 2001: 144). Since Bosnia's population did not fit idealized nationalists maps, nor necessarily share its politics, a war of cartographic redesign was unleashed and directed against civilians living in real places rather than on a map.

The map before returns, 1992–1995

The international community's response to the ethnic cleansing in Bosnia was an ambivalent one. As the murder, disappearances, population displacement and forced imprisonment that accompanied the process became visible to the international public in the summer of 1992, there was widespread moral condemnation and calls for forceful Western intervention. The coercive displacement of people from their homes and notions of population transfers appeared anachronistic in a late twentieth-century Europe marked by self-confidence, re-emergent unification, and economic prosperity. This, after all, was the supposed 'hour of Europe' according to Jacques Poos, the chair of the European Community's Council of Foreign Ministers (Gow 1997: 48). The London Principles of August 1992, developed at a meeting of the International Conference on the Former Yugoslavia (ICFY), were released soon after the existence of the Bosnian-Serb-run Omarska concentration camp came to light and Holocaust-like pictures of emaciated inmates behind barbed wire were broadcast across the world. The principles represent the zenith of a moral liberal internationalist governmentality toward the Bosnian war. They called for a cease fire, for 'non-recognition of all advantages gained by force', for respect for the highest standards of individual human rights, for the implementation of constitutional guarantees of fundamental freedoms and the right to self-determination, and for compliance by all parties with obligations under humanitarian law such as the Geneva Convention. One principle totally condemned 'forceful expulsions, illegal detentions and attempts to change the ethnic composition of populations, and effective promotion of the closure of detention camps, and of the safe return to their houses of all persons displaced by the hostilities who wish this'. Another principle stressed the 'vital need for humanitarian aid to be provided and, under appropriate protection and with the full cooperation of the local authorities, to reach the populations in need, with special consideration to the needs of children' (in Campbell 1998: 131–133).

Already in the articulation of these principles, however, was evidence of how international political leaders preferred to conceptualize the situation in Bosnia in ways that avoided any analysis of the power struggle driving the conflict. By August the United States and the European Community had come to a consensus that the situation in Bosnia was a 'humanitarian nightmare' but did not rise to the standard of international aggression. In making policy, political leaders in Britain, France and the United States were refusing to analogize the situation in Bosnia to that of the invasion of Kuwait in 1990 (Ó Tuathail 2002). Rather, Bosnia was conceptualized as a 'civil war', a potential quagmire such as Vietnam or Northern Ireland. The humanitarization of the conflict allowed policy-makers to respond to the symptoms of the crisis but avoid confronting its causes, namely Milosevic and Tudjman's plans to carve it up. The international community thus identified 'the vital need for humanitarian aid' but not the vital need to aid a newly independent state resist invasion and a pincer movement of ethnoterritorialism designed to dismember and partition it. Policy-makers consciously adopted and fiercely promoted this script against alternatives for they had concluded that Bosnia was not sufficiently in their individual or collective interest to intervene militarily to bring the fighting to a stop. Thus, while there were some military leaders who presented viable plans for intervention by the West and NATO, their position was marginalized by a dominant policy line that declared intervention was too risky, would not work, and would leave Western forces in a quagmire.

The result was that the large powers confined their intervention to a humanitarian mission of providing food and aid for those in the war zone. Sanctioned by the United Nations, the UN Protection Force (UNPROFOR) had a mandate that rendered it neutral in a country where crimes against humanity were being perpetrated. Refusing analysis of the larger dynamics of the conflict as a case of invasion aiding secessionism, its commanders tended to become absorbed in the daily routine of broken cease-fire management and aid logistics. Given their position, the parties were morally equivalent, distinctions between aggressors and victims dissolved into the generic discourse of 'warring factions' (Simms 2001).

Diplomatically, since the large powers had concluded that it had no overwhelming interest in the outcome of the conflict and was not going to use force to impose a settlement, the search for a peace settlement was dependent upon the correlation of force on the battlefield and the will of the antagonists. In effect, this left the leaders of the 'international community' in the hypocritical position of condemning ethnic cleansing and the use of force to seize territory, and asserting the rights of the displaced to return to their homes, while being pragmatically disposed to a settlement that rewarded ethnic cleansing, the forceful displacement of people from their homes and the apartheid thinking of partitionists. The so-called 'realist' position of the international peace negotiators – Jose Cutiliero, Lord Carrington, Cyrus Vance, David Owen, Thorvald Stoltenberg and others – prioritized the development of the best map to 'solve' the conflict rather than the rights of the displaced to return to their homes and seek justice for the crimes committed against them and their murdered fellow citizens. This pragmatic search for a cartographic fix revealed the degree to which the international community's peace negotiators conceded to the governmentality of the paramilitaries dismembering Bosnia (Campbell 1998: 141). In effect, the cartographers of peace became more interested in creating the fictional 'racist' vision of a Bosnia divided into distinct ethnoterritories – the fantasy of those that started the war – than in the process of recovering a Bosnia that always existed, namely a multiethnic state where people of different ethnicities lived together. They participated in the 'denial of Bosnia' (Mahmutcehajic 2000). The drawing and establishment of borders, in other words, took precedence over the possibility of returns.

The 'humanitarian' scripting of the Bosnian war, and the search for a peace settlement based on the good will of the warring parties was unsustainable policy. Bosnia's meaning exceeded the 'humanitarian nightmare' script and the creation of a weak dismembered apartheid state built on ethnic cleansing was not a recipe for stability in South East Europe. The persistent videocameralistics from the region began to have an impact on the wider strategic agenda in Europe, particularly plans for the expansion of NATO eastwards through the incorporation of Poland, Hungary and the Czech Republic as new members. The ongoing failure to stop the fighting and the siege of Sarajevo was punctured by regular media spectacles such as the airlift rescue of a wounded Muslim baby in August 1993 (who subsequently died in April 1995), the destruction of Mostar's *Stari Most* in November 1993 or the murder of 68 in a Sarajevo marketplace in February 1994. Of no material strategic value in itself, Bosnia was becoming a 'strategic sign' because it was coming to represent the failure of the United Nations and NATO as institutions of security (Ó Tuathail 1999). Once described as a local problem, then a European problem, foreign policy decision-makers were eventually forced to recognize Bosnia as a 'test' of global governmentalities after the Cold War.

There were three distinct moments in this process of strategic inflation by videocameralistics in 1995. The first was the failure of selective NATO bombing – widely derided in the press as 'pin-prick attacks' – to halt Bosnian Serb shelling of Sarajevo and UN-designated 'safe areas' in May 1995. The Bosnian Serbs retaliated by taking more than 350 UN peacekeepers captive. The images of these peacekeepers humiliatingly handcuffed to trees and telephone poles underscored the international community's policy failure. The second was the failure of the United Nations and NATO to prevent the Bosnian Serb army from capturing the so-called UN 'safe areas' of Zepa and Srebrenica. As is well known, what followed were massacres the horrific dimensions of which generated front-page headlines across the world in subsequent weeks. The third spectacle was yet another marketplace massacre in Sarajevo brought on by the launching of mortars against civilians going about their daily activities in that city. The resultant carnage, a repeat of similar scenes over the previous three years, finally triggered sustained NATO military intervention – the very name, Operation Deliberate Force, signalled a conscious change in policy that created the conditions for Anthony Lake's 'endgame strategy' to succeed (Daalder 2000).

Security before returns, 1996–1999

The Dayton Peace Accords (DPA) brought the violence in Bosnia to an end but the peace it created was a negative one. It was claimed that the accords did not reward ethnic cleansing by, first, nominally refusing to partition the state of Bosnia into three ethnic territories as hard-line nationalists wanted and, second, by establishing provisions for all refugees and displaced persons to return home (Holbrooke 1998). Nevertheless, in practice the DPA legitimated a *de facto* political geography of ethnic territorialism in Bosnia by creating a state of three constituent peoples composed of two territorial entities, one a Serb Republic and the other a Bosniak-Croat Federation, which was itself strongly divided between Bosnian Croat dominated cantons and the rest of the Federation. The entities were divided by an 'inter-ethnic boundary line' (IEBL), consciously described as a 'boundary' and not a 'border'. The continuity of the DPA with previous partitionist peace plans and the earlier discussions of Tudjman and Milosevic is evident in the centrality of the 49:51 territorial percentage deal to the Accords. The Report of the International Commission on the Balkans suggests the DPA left Bosnia's political geographic future undecided, foreclosing neither reintegration nor partition. The agreement 'did in theory create a window of opportunity for new political forces' in Bosnia-Herzegovina to reverse the displacement and destruction of ethnic cleansing, and to support the reintegration of the country. But this opportunity, the report notes, 'depends upon rigorous implementation' by the most powerful of these new political forces, the institutions created by the international community itself, most prominently the Peace Implementation Council (PIC), the military implementation force (IFOR and later SFOR), the Organization for Security and Cooperation in Europe (OSCE), and the Office of the High Representative (OHR) (Tindemans *et al.* 1996: 77).

The DPA launched a complex and multilayered governance over Bosnia, with 'implementation' the key organizing mandate and concept. Beyond ensuring that war would not re-start, a fundamental challenge for the governance of Bosnia after the war was addressing the massive population displacement caused by ethnic cleansing and the war. Out of a pre-war population of 4.4 million, over half of the population (2.3 million) were displaced: 1.3 million left Bosnia, though only half secured official refugee status, while about 1 million more were internally displaced within Bosnia itself.[1] Annex 7 of the DPA explicitly addresses the return of refugees and displaced persons to their homes. It declares:

> All refugees and displaced persons have the right freely to return to their homes of origin. They shall have the right to have restored to them property of which they were deprived in the course of hostilities since 1991 and to be compensated for any property that cannot be restored to them.

This statement also forms Article II: 5 of the Bosnia-Herzegovina Constitution. The Annex also enshrines the right of refugees *not* to return, though this is represented as a commitment to the principle of non-refoulment which protects a refugee from being returned to an unsafe situation, and a commitment to dignified returns, which forms a key element in UNHCR policy governing the right for individuals to choose the time and manner of their return. This dual commitment to the implementation of Annex 7 and to the protection of the displaced was articulated by the High Commissioner for Refugees before the PIC on 9, December 1995: 'Whereas ethnic cleansing was an objective, of some parties, during the war, ethnic repopulation should not become an objective during peace' (Ogata 1995). Yet, while the war fighting was at an end, Bosnia was not a post-conflict situation and this dual commitment became highly political. For those looking to re-establish the organic Bosnia torn asunder by the war, the promotion of return was central. For those looking to maintain what they considered to be their hard-won ethnonationalist homelands, return was deeply threatening, whether it be Bosniaks returning to the *Republika Srpska* or Serbs returning from *Republika Srpska* to their former homes in the Federation. After some time, the PIC and international donors decided to give funding priority to so-called 'minority returns', displaced persons who had to enter a hostile ethnoterritorial space to return home. This committed part of the international community to 'reverse ethnic cleansing', but it was to prove a challenge to maintain a commitment to safe and dignified returns while also challenging the ethnonationalist forces who held power at the county and entity level, a power awarded democratic legitimacy when many triumphed in elections.

Since Dayton, the implementation of Annex 7 has been fraught with political, institutional, financial, and legal difficulties. First, the international community has been divided within itself between those institutions with a narrow security mandate and those institutions, governmental and non-governmental, with a much broader mandate to promote reconstruction and return. Historically, security institutions such as the Stabilization Force (SFOR) have not considered implementation of Annex 7 a priority. Growing donor fatigue over the years and a consistent reluctance of military and political leaders to risk personnel in duties with the potential for violence have hampered the efforts of the UNHCR and the OHR to assist refugee and displaced persons in returning to their pre-war places of residence. Second, the efforts of international governmental institutions and partner non-governmental organizations to create the administrative and legal basis for returns have been hampered by the ethnoterritoriality legitimated at Dayton. Implementation of Annex 7 is at the heart of a contradiction in the DPA that, on the one hand, rhetorically promises to reverse ethnic cleansing while, on the other hand, legitimizes ethnopolitical entities and assemblies constructed from the results of ethnic cleansing. Among the obstacles to returns was the continuing 'security gap' that left local paramilitary organizations free to harass and intimidate returning persons. Likewise, wartime laws created by provisional local governments, as in Zvornik, had 'legally' redistributed the property of displaced Muslims to Serbs who had fled the Federation. Double occupancy was a major problem, with local power brokers using housing as part of their patronage system. The numerous 'legal' obstacles to property recovery forced the OHR to confront the need for uniform standardized laws across the country. But initially the OHR had neither the staff nor the political power to take on the ethnonationalists that dominated localities like Zvornik.

In the first year after the war, Bosnia did witness about 250,000 returns, largely refugees returning from Europe, where they had been granted only temporary asylum, and internally displaced persons returning within friendly ethnoterritorial space. This represented only about 10 per cent of the total refugee and displaced population. Of these returns, only 45,523 were minority returns (see Figure 7.1).[2] The next two years witnessed even slower rates of returns. During this period, the Bosnian Serbs treated the IEBL as an international border and erected a series of signs demarcating it – some mined so they could not be removed easily – as well as deploying roadblock patrols. Nevertheless, a number of returns, spontaneous and organized, did take place during the first three years after the war. These returns were generally of two forms, returns to rural villages within the 'zone of separation' and returns to 'open cities'. The former returns were typically self-organized community returns to their former, now unoccupied, villages within a 4-km buffer zone of the IEBL. In some cases, returns were undertaken with IFOR protection and UNHCR assistance though they were more typically spontaneous. In many cases, the level of destruction of villages, the pervasive and unmarked threat of landmines, and the presence of hostile mobs organized by local ethnonationalists made such returns difficult and daunting. Urban returns were daunting also since if homes were not destroyed they were invariably occupied by squatting majority nationals. The Open City Initiative was an attempt by the UNHCR in 1997 to use the promise of international assistance to municipalities that cooperated in efforts to re-open urban spaces to minority returns. Though partially successful in promoting returns, the programme had uneven and weakly communicated criteria and was relatively ineffective in overcoming entrenched obstacles to return.

In sum, the period from the peace accords to 1999 was marked by a high degree of obstructionism by ethnonationalists to all initiatives that could roll-back the de facto partition of Bosnia. At the same time, it was a period of experimentation and capacity building within the international community as it sought to come to grips with the challenges facing it and the obstacles that needed to be surmounted in order to rebuild Bosnia. While the implementation of a sustainable peace focused at first on security and Bosnian institution building, the international community eventually closed the security gap as Bosnia's ethnonationalists were becoming more isolated by changing political winds in Zagreb, Belgrade and, to some extent, Sarajevo.

Returns and ethnic engineering, 1999–2003

The possibility that the international community might be able to reverse some of the most egregious aspects of ethnic cleansing and allow those desiring to return to their pre-war domicile improved considerably from 1999 onwards. A number of factors were at work. First, the civilian side of the international community's

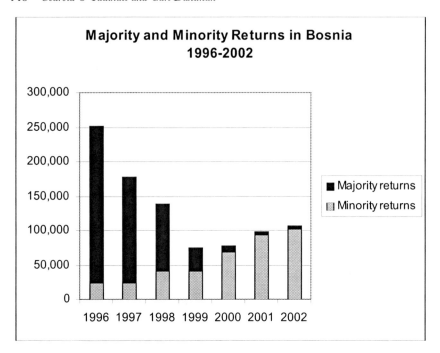

Figure 7.1 Total (majority and minority) returns in Bosnia, 1996–2002

Note: These statistics do not distinguish between Bosniak returns to their pre-war residences in
             Republika Srpska and Bosnian Serb returns to Sarajevo and other places of pre-war residence
             in the Federation entity

Source: UNHCR

mission in Bosnia-Herzegovina began to build sufficient organizational capacity
and coordination to make an impact in particular localities. The lessons learned
during the first four years spurred the creation of new organizational forms, the
most important of which was the Reconstruction and Return Task Force
(RRTF), an inter-agency coordinating committee composed of representatives
from the OHR, OSCE, UNHCR, SFOR, IPTF and various non-governmental
organizations involved in reconstruction and return projects. RRTFs were organized at the regional level and usually met monthly to organize and plan the
whole process of return. This process promoted considerable policy innovation
in helping to secure return sites, provide for infrastructure and housing reconstruction and promote conditions for sustainable returns.

Second, the Office of the High Representative acquired augmented powers
which gave him the capacity to remove obstructionist local officials even if they
were democratically elected. Carlos Westendorp (1997–1999) first exercised
these powers to impose a uniform law on citizenship and travel throughout the
country. His replacement, Wolfgang Petrisch, showed a willingness to use this
power to remove politicians from office. In March 1999, for example, Petrisch
dismissed Nikolas Poplasen, the recently elected president of *Republika Srpska*, for

obstructionism and hampering the 'smooth implementation of the Dayton process'. [3] Poplasen's party, the Serbian Radical Party founded by Vojislav Seselj, was banned from politics the next year.[4] Obstructionist mayors, council members, assembly representatives and even housing office officials were removed from office and usually banned from political life. During his tenure (1999–2002) Petrisch sacked 64 local hard liners and passed 246 laws including those designed to protect ethnic minority groups and advance democratic governance at state and entity level. The OHR broke the log-jam on a number of key issues hindering movement in Bosnia, decreeing a standardized car license plate for the whole country which made it easier for people from one entity to travel to the other without being an overt target of intimidation and violence.

Third, the OHR drafted and eventually imposed a series of laws which streamlined the returns process. Central to this effort was the Property Law Implementation Process (PLIP) which created a uniform legal procedure for the displaced to reclaim their pre-war property. These efforts had a combined effect as the OHR and OSCE representatives to a local RRTF, for example, could formally recommend to the OHR removal of obstructionist local officials who were failing to implement the PLIP. The PLIP itself was designed and functioned as a statistical index of compliance with the DPA with OHR or UNHCR officers serving as PLIP focal points reporting rates of compliance to Sarajevo. Property law implementation rates were calculated on the basis of number of claims filed with the housing offices in the various counties and the percentage of those claims formally resolved. Obstructionist counties were quickly identified and conditionality placed on access to funding dependent upon PLIP implementation levels, and evictions of double occupants.

Finally, the shifting power relationship between the OHR and the country's entities and local authorities helped facilitate a degree of cooperative behavior from certain 'moderate' nationalist politicians. Particularly significant in this process was the ascension of Milorad Dodik as Prime Minister of *Republika Srpska* in January 1998. Dodik was leader of the small Serb Independent Social Democrats (SNSD) but was able to form a cabinet of non-SDS members after considerable backroom manoeuvres by the international community. Dodik's cabinet was hardly less nationalistic that the SDS – his Minister of Justice was one of those responsible for notorious ethnic cleansing of Foca, for example – but he did show a degree of willingness to cooperate with the International Criminal Tribunal for the former Yugoslavia by surrendering two suspects to the Hague in February 1998. He also was nominally open to the process of 'minority returns' and willing to trade staying in power for cooperation in implementing Dayton's Annex 7.

The result of these developments was a dramatic increase in the number of minority returns in the period 1999–2002 (see Figure 7.1) (ICG 2000a). PLIP monitoring by the international community and monthly RRTF meetings established a process that developed momentum and, over time, a degree of inevitability. This is not to say, however, that obstructionism and resistance disappeared. Rather, its form changed and tended to become less violent and more bureaucratic. This is also not to say that returnees were necessarily going back to stay in their former homes. Returns statistics to date suggest that approximately one-half of those displaced by the war have found durable solutions. In many instances, the displaced participated in the PLIP in order to acquire their former property. If the property was destroyed and it was possible to secure some international funds to aid in its reconstruction, they might pursue this option. And, if the local conditions were sufficiently benign then they might consider staying, thus making the return a genuine one. This was not always the case, however. Uncontested space returns to property that was not occupied and generally in a rural area presented a lot less problems than contested space returns to urban areas where those who participated in ethnic cleansing still lived and retained considerable local power and sway. Rates of rural return, however, were impacted by the fact that ethnic cleansing was a form of forced urbanization for those peasant populations that survived it. Ten years later, with embedded networks of work, education and social support formed in towns and cities, the prospect of return was appealing only to an older demographic cohort. In some instances, returnees acquired their property and simply sold it to the displaced family squatting there. In other cases, returnees sought to return only to suffer discrimination in access to health care, pensions, and education. Throughout Bosnia the picture was a very mixed one.

One feature of the tenure of Milorad Dodik as *Republika Srpska* Prime Minister was the practice of 'land allocations'. In theory, this was an immanently reasonable process of reform in which land previously socially owned under the communist Yugoslav system was privatized and distributed to displaced and marginalized Bosnians in need of housing, shelter and services. In practice, the process of land allocations by local counties – for the ownership of the land was controlled by Bosnia's *opstina* – was a discriminatory system of patronage and political favouritism designed to 'lock in' ethnic majorities in the entities and counties of *Republika Srpska*. Bosnian Serbs who had fled or been violently displaced from the Federation were ideologically encouraged not to return to their place of origin but to build a new house in 'their' ethnic homeland. Further, material assistance in the form of cement, bricks and tiles to land recipients drained the *Republika Srpska* budget of funds that otherwise should have assisted minority returnees (ICG 2002). The process was a systematic response to the inevitability of 'minority returns' and a second wave of ethnic engineering after the brutalities of the initial ethnic cleansing. The practice, which came to be widely adopted and implemented across *Republika Srpska* from 2000 onwards, was identified by the OHR as illegal and largely banned. But this law proved to be a major headache for the OHR and an enforcement gap developed between what the OHR ruled and what local authorities did in practice. Ethnic engineering through land allocation was not exclusive to the Serbs. Similar practices on a smaller scale are evident in ethnonationalist strongholds for both Croats and Bosniaks. The practice was pioneered by Bosnian Croats in the Neretva valley south of Mostar during the war with material aid provided by a Tudjman government eyeing the region as a new part of Croatia and eager to establish 'facts on the ground'. Bosniaks have more typically used new apartment construction in cities to consolidate ethnically dominant majorities, providing housing for those unwilling to return to their pre-war home but no longer able to illegally occupy the property of returning minorities.

The development of the practice of discriminatory land allocations for the purpose of ethnic engineering marked a transition in the attitudes and coping practices of the ethnonationalists that dominated *Republika Srpska* as they adjusted to scrutiny by the international authorities in Bosnia. The governmentality of those that ran *Republika Srpska* during and immediately after the war was 'fascist ethnosupremacy', proudly defiant of the international community (while nevertheless craving their approval and recognition) and obstructionist towards the DPA (Watch 1996). Identity was conceptualized in a primordial and racist way, territoriality was governed by apartheid logics (with border maintenance anxieties, and visions of a Bantustan-like 'Islamic state' for the 'Muslims'), and political power rested in the hands of extreme nationalists and mafia criminals (often both one and the same) (ICG 2000b; Watch 1998). As it adjusted to monitoring and conditionality from the international authorities empowered by the DPA, the governmentality of the *Republika Srpska* adjusted to a neoliberal discursive climate by transitioned to a 'neoliberal ethnosupremacy'. Primordial, essentialist and racist notions of identity largely persisted but they were muted by demonstrations of tolerance for 'minorities' (as long as they remained minorities), a selective yet trumpeted commitment to the DPA – because this recognized, institutionalized, and guaranteed the ethnonationalist homeland – and a tactical use of the language of neoliberalism – emphasizing 'reform', 'privatization', 'incentives' and 'choice' – in order to present a soft face to the persistent pursuit of ethnic engineering.[5] Corruption was not as overt but nevertheless entrenched with the financial structure of political parties dependent upon a few major companies and benefactors with sources of revenue that were not always transparent (ICG 2002; Pugh 2002).

Zvornik today: building on genocide

Ethnonationalist governmentality in Bosnia has transitioned from violent wartime ethnic cleansing to the politically directed privatized ethnic engineering of today. Despite the international community's efforts to reverse ethnic cleansing and restore 'Bosnia 1991' (for 1991 census demographics are the foundation of many laws and policies in contemporary Bosnia), Bosnia cannot and will not be put back together again. Yet the international community has had some success in reversing the legacy of ethnic cleansing as the numbers of minority returns indicate. And from the experience of engaging post-war ethnonationalist forces and structures, new standards and practices of state-building governmentality are being generated, asserted and proclaimed. In a speech to the International Rescue Committee in June 2003, for example, Paddy Ashdown claimed that the international community:

have made a reality, in Bosnia, of a fundamental human right that elsewhere, tragically, only existed on paper – the right of refugees to return
home. We have set a standard and established a precedent. War will never
be the same again. Some good has come out of evil.

The picture in Bosnia's localities is a good deal more complex. While Bosnia's
civil institutions, including a Bosnian judiciary, are slowly being reformed, the
struggle over the 'right disposition of things' continues in places such as Zvornik.
The war in Bosnia left the county of Zvornik partially divided by the IEBL. The
portion that remained in the *Republika Srpska* went from a 1991 population of
about 65,000 to a 1997 population estimated at just over 30,000, with an additional almost 19,000 Serbs displaced from elsewhere. What was a majority
Muslim region became almost wholly Serb. While Zvornik recorded some of the
earliest minority returns in 1996 to the unoccupied zone of separation, minority
returns have been slow. Since 1996, only 10,000 Bosniaks have returned to
Zvornik from a prewar population of 48,000, largely to the rural hinterland
rather than the main city, though small numbers of minority returns are now
being recorded in the city also.

In response to the prospect of an increasing number of minority returns, the
local Serb authorities have sought to consolidate their wartime ethnic supremacy.
Land allocations have proceeded despite OHR objections. In remote, rural parts
of the county, enormous socially owned farms have been subdivided and given
to displaced Serbs, particularly to veterans and their families, as well as to loyal
Serb nationalist party members. One of these communities is a vast settlement of
500 homes near Karakaj. It is named after the former agricultural cooperative
Ekonomija, the very site where Bosniaks were tortured and murdered in 1992.

While the International Criminal Tribunal for the former Yugoslavia has
pursued top-level instigators of ethnic cleansing and genocide in Bosnia,
numerous mid- and lower-level officials who participated in these practices are
still powerful in Bosnian localities. In Zvornik, for example, the richest man in
town and reputedly one of the richest in *Republika Srpska* is a former police chief
and founding member of the SDS. He made a fortune in petroleum smuggling
during the war and switched, after the fighting ended, to the construction business, resigning from the SDS but still serving as an elected official on Zvornik's
county council. He has a wide variety of business interests including gas stations
and a mineral water factory. His construction company is building a number of
high-rise apartment complexes in downtown Zvornik on land previously owned
by Bosniaks and adjacent to the destroyed mosques in the town. He claims this
property was voluntarily sold to him by former residents and that he sold the first
apartment in his high-rise complex to a returning Muslim resident.[6]

There is little doubt that there is considerable demand for the new accommodation among displaced Serbs who are being forced to give up the Bosniak
property they once thought was theirs forever. For many Serbs in the town, the
dream of building their own ethnonationalist homeland lives on. But their right
disposition of territory, population and security, 'arranged so as to lead to a

convenient end', keeps bumping up against international norms and inconvenient facts from the past. On 9 July 2003 the internationally funded Bosnian Commission on Missing Persons announced that they had exhumed nearly 100 bodies of Bosnian Muslims, most of them in the black plastic body bags of the former Yugoslav army, from six mass graves just outside Zvornik. The victims were executed between April and June 1992. Commission officials indicated that they expected to find more bodies at the same location.[7]

Notes

1   By 1998, 500,000 of the 1.3 million that left Bosnia during the war had secured 'durable solutions' outside Bosnia and were not likely to return (Bose 2002: 36).
2   The total minority returns for 1996 and 1997 was only 45,523. All statistics on returns are derived from estimates and counts made by the UNHCR in Bosnia-Herzegovina, available at www.unhcr.ba.
3   Office of the High Representative, 'Decision Removing Nikola Poplasen from his position as RS President, March 5, 1999.' Online. Available at: http://www.ohr.int/decisions/removalssdec/
4   Seselj was indicted by the International Criminal Tribunal for the former Yugoslavia in February 2003 and is currently awaiting trial.
5   Perhaps the most absurdist expression of this governmental mimicry was the plan to 'incentivize' cooperation with the International War Crimes Tribunal by paying suspected war criminals to turn themselves over to the Hague. Indicted suspects could collect a lifelong stipend of 200 euros a month, with their families entitled to free tickets to the Netherlands three times a year to visit them as well as 250 euros every two months for other expenses. The programme had no takers (Katana 2003).
6   Interview, Zvornik, 24, June 2003.
7   *Washington Post*, 'News in brief,' 9, July 2003: 23.

References

Ashdown, P. (2003) 'Broken communities, shattered lives: winning the savage war of peace'. Speech by the Right Honourable Paddy Ashdown, High Representative in Bosnia and Herzegovina, to the International Rescue Committee, London.

Bose, S. (2002) *Bosnia After Dayton: nationalist partition and international intervention*, New York: Oxford University Press.

Bringa, T. (1995) *Being Bosnian the Muslim Way*, Princeton: Princeton University Press.

Campbell, D. (1998) *National Deconstruction: violence, identity, and justice in Bosnia*, Minneapolis: University of Minnesota Press.

Cigar, N. (1995) *Genocide in Bosnia: the politics of 'ethnic cleansing'*, College Station, TX: Texas A&M University Press.

Daalder, I. (2000) *Getting to Dayton: the making of America's Bosnia policy*, Washington DC: Brookings Institution Press.

Fine, J. (2002) 'The various faiths in the history of Bosnia: Middle Ages to the present', in M. Shatzmiller (ed.) *Islam and Bosnia: conflict resolution and foreign policy in multi-ethnic states*, Montreal: McGill-Queen's University Press.

Foucault, M. (1991) 'Governmentality', in G. Burchell, C. Gordon and P. Miller (eds) *The Foucault Effect: studies in governmentality*, Chicago: University of Chicago Press.

Geary, P.J. (2002) *The Myth of Nations: the medieval origins of Europe*, Princeton: Princeton University Press.

Gow, J. (1997) *Triumph of a Lack of Will: international diplomacy and the Yugoslav War*, New York: Columbia University Press.

Holbrooke, R. (1998) *To End a War*, New York: Random House.

Huntington, S. (1996) *The Clash of Civilizations*, New York: Simon & Schuster.

ICG (2000a) 'Bosnia's refugee logjam breaks: is the international community ready?', Sarajevo: International Crisis Group.

——(2000b) 'War criminals in Bosnia's Republika Srpska', Sarajevo/Brussels/Washington: International Crisis Group.

——(2002) 'The continuing challenge of refugee return in Bosnia and Herzegovina', Sarajevo/Brussels: International Crisis Group.

Katana, G. (2003) 'Bosnia: "cash for crimes" scheme slammed', *Balkan Crisis Report No. 449*, 1 August.

Ludwig Boltzmann Institute of Human Rights (1994) *'Ethnic cleansing operations' in the Northeast City of Zvornik*, Vienna: Ludwig Boltzmann Institute of Human Rights. Available at: *http://www.univie.ac.at/bim/download/zvornike.pdf* (last accessed 7, January 2004)

Luke, T. and Ó Tuathail, G. (1997) 'On videocameralistics: the geopolitics of failed states, the CNN International, and UN Governmentality', *Review of International Political Economy*, 4: 709–733.

Magaš, B. (1993) *The Destruction of Yugoslavia: tracking the break-up 1980–92*, New York: Verso.

Mahmutcehajic, R. (2000) *The Denial of Bosnia*, Philadelphia: University of Pennsylvania.

——(2001) 'The road to war', in B. Magas and I. Zanic (ed.) *The War in Croatia and Bosnia-Herzegovina, 1991–1995*, London: Frank Cass.

Ó Tuathail, G. (1999) 'A strategic sign: the geopolitical significance of "Bosnia" in U.S. foreign policy', *Environment and Planning D: society and space*, 17: 515–533.

——(2002) 'Theorizing practical geopolitical reasoning: the case of US Bosnia policy in 1992', *Political Geography*, 21(5): 601–628.

Ogata, S. (1995) Statement by Mrs. Sadako Ogata, United Nations High Commissioner for Refugees. Peace Implementation Conference for Bosnia and Herzegovina, London.

Pugh, M. (2002) 'Postwar political economy in Bosnia Herzegovina: the spoils of peace', *Global Governance* 8(4): 467–482.

Sell, L. (2002) *Slobodan Milosevic and the Destruction of Yugoslavia*, Durham: Duke University Press.

Silber, L. and Little, A. (1995) *The Death of Yugoslavia*, London: Penguin.

Simms, B. (2001) *Unfinest Hour: Britain and the destruction of Bosnia*, London: Penguin.

Thomas, R. (1999) *Serbia Under Milosevic: politics in the 1990s*, London: Hirst & Company.

Tindemans, L., Cuffer, L., Geremek, B., Roper, J., Sommer, T., Veil, S., and Anderson, D. (1996) *Unfinished Peace: Report of the International Commission on the Balkans*. Washington DC: Carneagie Endowment for International Peace.

Washington Post (2003) 'News in brief,' 9, July p. 23.

Watch, Human Rights (1996) *Bosnia Herzegovina: the continuing influence of Bosnia's warlords*, New York: Human Rights Watch.

——(1998) *'A Closed, Dark Place': past and present human rights abuses in Foca*, New York: Human Rights Watch.

8 The political rationality of European integration[1]

William Walters

In his influential lecture on 'governmentality', Foucault suggests that what is really interesting about our present is not the '*étatisation* of society', but rather the 'governmentalization of the state' (Foucault 1991: 103). It is now more than twenty-five years since Foucault delivered this lecture at the Collège de France. In the meantime our political culture has found other preoccupations besides the statization of society – most notably, perhaps, 'globalization'. Nevertheless, as a result of the many studies that have taken up, developed and sometimes challenged Foucault's work in this area, there now exists a significant body of work exploring this governmentalization of the state and its profound implications for our political subjectivity. But what of the governmentalization of other social and political spaces? At a time when political debate concerns regional and global as much as national economies, when political movements speak not only in the name of a national but also a global civil society, or when international migration, transnational crime and global warming are pressing policy issues, then perhaps it is appropriate to investigate more closely the governmentalization of the space between, above or across the system of states?

It is with this question in mind that I take up the theme of European integration. More specifically, I want to explore the governmentality of the political project that is most closely associated with the 'integration' of Europe – formerly the European Community, now the European Union (EU). The study of European integration has been the subject of notable theoretical innovation in recent years (Rosamond 2000). What was for some time a topic dominated by the main currents of American political science has now emerged as a site of investigation and theoretical development for a range of perspectives, including social constructivism (Christiansen *et al.* 2001), and 'multilevel governance' (Marks *et al.* 1996). But with a few notable exceptions, the possibility of investigating European integration as a field of governmentality has not been canvassed.[2]

This is unfortunate for several reasons. First, governmentality would seem particularly well equipped to study what the former President of the European Commission famously called '*un objet politique non-identifié*' (Schmitter 1996: 1). One of the advantages of governmentality analysis is that it does not require us to define things like The State, Society, or The Individual in advance. Instead, research in this area has typically practiced a kind of nominalism. Central to its research process has been the task of identifying just how it is that these and other entities come to be defined and operationalized in particular ways within particular regimes of discourse and practice. Hence governmentality encourages us to analyse unique political formations such as the EU not by projecting them against a given field of political-economic forces (for example, globalization), nor slotting them into conventional categories of political forms (federalism, confederalism, etc.), but by interrogating the particular subjects, objects, arts and spaces that they bring into existence. Governmentality prompts us to ask such questions as: What does it mean to govern Europe as a 'common market'? What kinds of political subjectification are at stake with the advent of practices of EU citizenship? In these ways it seeks to grapple with the specificity of governing Europe, and the historical mutability of identities.

There is a second reason to regret this lack of connection between governmentality and EU studies. Governmentality studies would also benefit from greater engagement with the field of European integration. This could be a mutually beneficial encounter. As a subject area European integration is rich in possibilities for pursuing such questions as the internationalization of biopolitics, the transformation of sovereign power, and changing modes of geopolitics and security. In short, it offers a promising area for exploring governmentality 'above' as well as 'beyond' the state.

This chapter is oriented by a very general question: how might we think about the EU as a site of governmentality? In the first part I suggest that it might be useful to interrogate European governance at the level of its rationalities and mentalities. This is to raise questions about the different ways in which 'Europe' has been posed as a 'problem'. It requires that we consider the grids of intelligibility which have underpinned political thinking and policies of European integration. The second section suggests that we can also interrogate European governance at the level of its changing practices.[3]

I should emphasize that what follows does not claim the status of an exhaustive discussion of the governmentalities, techniques or tactics which have enframed the European integration project, but something more modest. My purpose is to sketch some possibilities for future research, and to exemplify some potentially useful analytics for such work. It is not to set out some kind of governmentality 'theory' of European integration. I employ the headings of 'mentalities' and 'technologies', but one could also fruitfully explore European governance under many other headings, such as its tactics and strategies or its subjectifications.

Mentalities of European government

Scholars of the EU have been not been particularly interested in the discursive aspect of European integration. Whether European integration is analysed in terms of a dynamic interplay of geopolitical and economic 'interests', as an unfolding 'process' driven forward by increasing socioeconomic and political 'interdependence', or as a shift from a system of 'state-centric' to 'multilevel governance', one thing is quite constant. It is that questions of the discursive framing of 'Europe' have been relatively marginal to these endeavours. With the exception of the growing number of researchers interested in the social construction of European integration, far too little attention has been paid to the historically changing ways in which Europe has been discursively framed.[4] Instead, studies of the EU have been overwhelmingly 'realist' in their ontologies, searching for the underlying processes and structures which might 'explain' integration.

Here I want to argue the case for shifting our attention away from questions of deep structures and institutional processes, and toward an understanding of European integration at the level of mentalities and rationalities of government. This involves what Nikolas Rose has nicely termed an 'empiricism of the surface', a much greater concern with the identification of 'the differences in what is said, how it is said, and what allows it to be said and to have an effectivity' (Rose 1999: 57). Exploring the changing ways in which European integration has been 'said', I want to argue, can tell us much about the 'how' of European governance. That is, it can answer questions about the possibility of governing regional and international spaces above and across the system of states.

The moment of modernization

How might our accounts of European integration change if we approached this subject in terms of changing mentalities of government? What might we learn about the rationalities of European governance if we interrogate more closely the actual ways in which leading authorities, practitioners and commentators on the EU have themselves sought to understand their task? Obviously, this chapter is not the place to attempt any kind of comprehensive overview of the changing rationalities of European integration. Instead, as a way of illustrating the promise of this angle of inquiry, I want to examine one particular text. Published in 1964, Ernst Haas' essay 'Technocracy, pluralism and the New Europe' offers some key insights as to how leading academic authorities understood European integration during its early years (Haas 1968). Haas is an important source because of his status as a leading theorist of European integration. But he is also interesting because the theory of 'neofunctionalism' that often bears his name has come to be regarded as 'a systematic academic elaboration' of the strategy that was embodied in the Treaty of Rome, a founding moment of the European project (Harrison 1974: 75, in Bellamy and Warleigh 1998: 451n). In other words, neofunctionalism has close affinities with the 'method' employed by Jean Monnet and his associates as they sought to 'unite' Europe in the aftermath of World War II.

Scholars of European integration generally read Ernst Haas as a leading exponent of neofunctionalism. As such, he has been placed squarely within a literature of 'European integration theory' in which neofunctionalism has as its principal theoretical rival 'intergovernmentalism' (Moravcsik 1998). A typical interpretation of neofunctionalism would go something as follows (Strøby Jensen 2003). Whereas intergovernmentalism tends to view European integration as the outcome of strategic bargains struck by the major European powers and then codified in treaties, neofunctionalism regards European integration as a gradual and cumulative process. At its core is the mechanism of 'spillover', the process whereby cooperation between states in one policy area will inevitably create pressure for coordination in neighbouring areas. Policy cooperation becomes embedded in regional and/or supranational institutional arrangements. With time these institutions tend to become more important because they become focal points for pluralist pressures emanating from a diverse array of experts, business groups and other 'societal actors'.

The problem with the integration theory reading of Haas is that it's rather selective. Its principal referents are often other integration theories, past and present. But reading Haas from the perspective of governmentality involves a somewhat different emphasis. Instead of situating him within an evolving theory of European integration, governmentality would draw attention to the specific ways in which he produces a particular knowledge of Europe. What should strike the reader of 'Technocracy, pluralism and the New Europe' is the way in which it is shot through with the progressivist language and assumptions of what James Scott has called 'high modernism'.[5] What is so interesting is the extent to which Haas imagines the governance of Europe through the kinds of discourse that were prevalent within societies in the 1950s and 1960s. Haas heralds a 'New Europe' emerging out of the shadows of nationalism, poverty, class conflict and war. It is a Europe of 'adaptative interest groups, bureaucracies, technocrats and other units with modest but pragmatic interests resembling the traditional nationalisms of *Grosspolitik* only very remotely...' (Haas 1968: 155). Within this New Europe 'the technocrat has become the *éminence grise* of all government, local, national and regional' (p. 158, emphasis in original). But most significant for our purposes is the way in which Haas identifies a new form of governance – 'supranationality' – as the political form of this 'New Europe':

> Supranationality, not federation, confederation or intergovernmental organization, seems to be the appropriate regional counterpart to the national state which no longer feels capable of realizing welfare aims within its narrow borders, which has made its peace with the fact of interdependence in an industrial and egalitarian age. It represents the method adopted to secure maximum welfare, including military security, for a post-capitalist state which no longer conceives of its interests in starkly political and nationalistic terms. The advent of supranationality symbolizes the victory of economies over polities, over the familiar ethnocentric nationalism which used to subordinate butter to guns, reason to passion, statistical bargaining to excited demands.
>
> (1968: 159)

Here we see how ideas of planning and technocracy, and assumptions about the inevitability of modernization, serve to make possible a particular style and ethos of governance for Europe. The governance of Europe is cast as a game of enhancing the welfare of the combined populations by expert-led interventions into markets and societies. Like the political rationality of welfare, the supranational governance which Haas describes seems to occupy a space somewhere between classical liberalism and state socialism. It imagines a political game in which the freedoms of individuals and firms are to be circuited into a framework of planning which harnesses their energies to the improvement of the whole. It was the desire of modernization and welfarism at the domestic level to make the old structures and centres of politics, of parliaments and militaries, if not redundant then certainly subordinate to the new centres of expertise and corporatist representation. With Haas we see how this dream is translated at a regional-European level. The old alternatives of federalism or intergovernmentalism can be displaced by the proliferating systems of supranationalism. Supranationalism is not a competing *political* structure; strictly speaking it does not appear to belong to a series of governmental forms which includes alliances, republics, and confederations. For it abandons such games in favour of governing through emerging socioeconomic spaces in which 'non-state actors' have a prominent place alongside the state.

Obviously this reading of Haas is just an example of how we might explore the political rationality of European integration. Any extensive investigation of the mentalities of European government during the 1960s would need to examine the competing ways in which a space of governance was marked out, for instance through the idea of a European 'free trade area', but also through the revival of more 'classical' geopolitical discourses. In addition, it would be important for a governmentality study of European integration to investigate the tactics and techniques by which this neofunctionalist-welfarist mentality of governance was operationalized – a theme I pick up below. Nevertheless, even on the limited basis of this reading, it is still possible to make a number of observations.

First, there is a point about the rarity of discourse. Clearly there are generative principles and rules governing what can be said about Europe and when. The concepts and language of European integration do not just appear out of the blue. Rather, it is a case of borrowing and adapting languages and idioms from adjacent political fields. In the above case, the language of modernization and the 'end of ideology' trope serve as preconditions for a certain concept (and telos) of integrated Europe.

Second, it is worth noting the flexible and labile nature of political rationalities. We tend to think of welfarism as a game of domestic governance, a way of thinking and managing questions of social and economic life *within* the nation. However, the case of European integration suggests that welfarism was much more flexible and could be applied to spaces across and above the system of states. It was not just 'society' that was to be planned, managed and guided according to the confident predictions and calculations of the technocrat, but 'Europe' and, no doubt, many other political spaces as well.

From modernization to globalization?

There is a final point we can take from this brief reading of Haas, one that concerns its implications for any history of the present. This reading of Haas is more than just about exemplifying how we might study mentalities of European governance. One advantage of choosing a text such as this is that its tropes and narratives stand out more clearly than when we read contemporary arguments. Its idiom strikes the reader as slightly obsolete and dated. More than anything one is struck by its investment in the teleological discourse of *modernization*, the way in which it imagines political change in Europe as an almost inexorable, linear process from old to new. For Haas, as for his contemporaries, the idea of modernization was almost second nature. Today this kind of faith in modernization has largely dissipated. One should certainly not ignore the way that various aspects of modernization theory have been recoded and still operate within political discourse (e.g., Cooper 2000). But from the vantage point of the present, where we seem to be much more sceptical about the idea of progress, it is hard to believe that so much faith, so much political passion, could have been invested in the linear scheme of modernization.

But rather than congratulate ourselves on the superiority of our wisdom, perhaps this should prompt us to be more reflexive about some of the core propositions of our own time. What if globalization functions within contemporary discourses about European integration much as modernization did for Haas? Is globalization the new modernization? Won't observers in twenty years' time also look back and ask: 'How did they come to take "globalization" so seriously?' Scholars of European integration, and other 'new regionalisms' (Larner and Walters 2002) generally regard globalization as a force or a process which, in its economic, political and social aspects, 'challenges' states and other actors. For some the EU is understood then as a 'response' to globalization. For others it is regarded as a catalyst or cause of globalization. Whatever their differences, both views tend to take globalization at face value. But my point is this: what if globalization is, like modernization (or, for that matter, the nineteenth-century idea of civilization), less a real process rooted in the substrate of human societies, and instead a historically specific way of imagining, spatializing and temporalizing the present? Perhaps we are faced with another instance where the EU fixes its identity and legitimates its mission by invoking an 'exterior' of intractable forces and processes.[6]

Technologies of European government

Besides examining its changing mentalities, a second level at which a Foucauldian account of European integration might operate is that of political technologies. That is, it would want to consider what Dean calls the '*techne* of government', posing the question 'by what means, mechanisms, procedures, instruments, tactics, techniques, technologies and vocabularies is authority constituted and rule accomplished?' (Dean 1999: 31). However, the use of the term 'technologies of government' has been quite varied within the governmentality literature. For the purposes of the following discussion I want to suggest at least three levels at which it might be employed to advance our understanding of EU governance.

Inscribing European governance

The first level is the most microphysical. In the case of the EU there is certainly plenty of scope for studies which examine the 'humble and mundane mechanisms by which authorities seek to instantiate government' (Rose and Miller 1992: 183). What new understandings of the constitution of Europe as a territory of rule might be attained if, for a moment, we turned our attention away from the great episodes of treaty-making, or the endless debates as to the essential political character of the Union (intergovernmental, quasi-federal, multilevel?), or even the process of European policy-making, and focused on what Thrift (2000) calls 'the little things'. Consider some of the ways this might be done.

First, this focus might include some of the ways in which European integration is materially inscribed, included in charts and tables, or 'scoreboards', and made calculable. Second, it could consider the particular prominence of techniques of temporalization (Ekengren 2002) within European integration, such as the salience of timetables and deadlines. From the early reports of The High Authority of the ECSC where the 'development of the common market' constitutes an official heading,[7] to various bulletins on the readiness of the accession countries for membership, one sees that the governance of Europe is something always in progress. Its development has never been spontaneous but rather is the subject of constant scrutiny and surveillance. Third, a focus on the inscription of European integration could reflect on some of the ways in which Europe has been mapped and *geo-graphed*:[8] for instance, as a unitary space of coal and steel production, or more recently as a space of regions and cities with their different levels of social development. Nowhere do these three grids of intelligiblity – tabulations, temporalizations and geo-spatializations – come together more conspicuously than in the country reports which the EU regularly prepares for its present as well as prospective members. Here one finds a veritable inscription of nations.

But a concern with mundane techniques of inscription and depiction need not confine itself to the study of texts in isolation. It might also consider some of the sites where such inscriptions intersect with other technologies of training, surveillance, assessment, and so forth, to form assemblages within which human conduct is governed. I have already mentioned the social constructivist current within EU studies. One of its arguments is that extended participation in European institutions can 'socialize' actors into a more European identity by exposing them to new ideas, norms, beliefs, etc. (Checkel 2001). What this emphasis on the power of ideas, norms, values and intersubjective beliefs tends to overlook are the ways in which conduct is often shaped by *sociotechnical* – as opposed to purely social – mechanisms. Elsewhere I have argued at some length that a more nuanced account of power and identity in the EU is possible if we examine certain sociotechnical encounters.[9] One example concerns banal arte-facts such as standardized forms and other reporting tools. Take the case of document inspection advisers whose job it is to monitor customs and immigra-tion officials at the EU's 'external' frontiers. Whatever their adherence to certain norms may be, their work is also subtly shaped by durable, tangible little things like checklists and report cards. It is on the basis of these and countless other minor objects that European authorities seek to shape the conduct of agents in distant places.

Another seemingly trivial example of what I have in mind is the use of signs in international airports. In recent years there has been a concerted effort to standardize the design and placement of the EU logo in the passport and immi-gration control areas of international airports across Europe. This move is connected to a sort of quotidian pedagogy which seeks to school passengers in the habit of quietly and patiently sorting themselves into EU and non-EU queues. The aim is to speed up passport checks. What is interesting is how this use of signs, coupled with the reorganization of the airport space, subtly enrols the passenger in a strategy which seeks to produce European mobility at a very local level.

These are seemingly insignificant and admittedly rather scattered examples of the power of inscription. But the point is that a whole history of European integration remains to be written from the perspective of such micropractices, and the hitherto unnoticed way they construct objects and subjects of European power

Machines

There is a second sense in which we might investigate the *techne* of European government. For want of a better term, I want to call this the perspective of the machine. Machines are relatively durable arrangements of bodies, technologies, practices, instruments, spaces (Deleuze and Guattari 1987; Barry 2001). They do not have economic or biological life as their material substrate. For machines are productive. It is through these machines, these regimes of knowledge and practice, that seemingly natural subjects and objects are produced, but always in a specific form – 'the economy', 'society', 'the public', 'the unemployed', etc.

Machines are not reducible to the state. Nor are they its property or instru-ment. Rather, we need to recognize how, and under what conditions, the state reconfigures itself in a relationship with these machines. Hence, there is the question of how the state becomes a sort of welfare machine at the start of the twentieth century; how it connects itself to innumerable practices – each with their own history, their own material density – of knowing, moulding, disci-plining, securing individual and collective subjects. Or the question of how the state becomes a war machine which, by the middle of the same century, will operate in a fateful conjunction with this welfare machine.

Perhaps it might be useful to think about the governance of Europe in these terms as well. That is, we might envisage accounts of European integration not in terms of political bargains between states, nor as a singular process that unfolds, but in terms of different machines and how these have traversed and configured an historically changing space of European governance. It is a case of how these machines come to provide the conditions of possibility by which a series of decision-making centres, whether located formally within the EU or within national governments, can both see and act on 'Europe'.

We have already observed how it is possible to read neofunctionalism not just as an academic theory of European integration, but as a particular, quasi-welfarist mentality of European governance. Here we might pursue this idea further, but now at the level of the planning machine. Let us take the example of Jean Monnet, who is generally regarded as one of the 'founding fathers' of the European project. His pivotal role in the launching of the European Coal and Steel Community is well documented, as is his particular philosophy of European integration. But we might also see Monnet as a biographical figure, a passage that connects 'Europe' to, and makes it governable in terms of, a certain planning machine. In his capacity as a planner of Allied war supplies during both World Wars, and as the architect of France's post-war modernization plan, it seems Monnet improvised certain novel methods of planning economic affairs (Duchêne 1994; Featherstone 1994; Mazey 1992; Monnet 1978). Equally significantly, he saw the very activity of planning as a site for concatenating a diverse field of public and private agents. Though tasked with the modernization of France, Monnet did not occupy an office that could simply plan economic life in a top-down, totalizing fashion. Instead, he was compelled to improvise a form of planning almost from the margins. He developed a method which did not supplant the established centres of power, but worked around them, weaving them into its scheme.

With the creation of the European Coal and Steel Community in the early 1950s (in retrospect, the institutional prototype for the European Community) Monnet would transpose many of these practices and tactics to a 'European' level. Here the task would be one of implicating not just government ministries and departments, but national governments in a new regime of governance. My point is that by following these little lines of development we can emphasize the rarity and mobility of governance, the way in which methods and practices are first invented in confrontations with particular political and technical exigencies, but prove transportable and adaptable to other locales.

Of course, governance is a complex and multifaceted phenomenon. We should not analyse it on the basis of a single machine but rather as an interconnection as well as the opposition amongst several. A fuller account of European governance in the 1950s and 1960s would have to recognize the ways in which Monnet's ambitions were significantly compromised. For instance, the High Authority (and later the European Commission) he envisaged as the future centre of European governance would not achieve the planning powers he wanted. Hence, this fuller account would observe how European governance was configured in part through practices of planning, but perhaps much more through the technology of a social-market machine first assembled to address the problems of reconstructing post-war West Germany. Finding its intellectual rationalization in the reflections of German ordoliberal thinkers such as von Rüstow and Röpke (Peacock *et al.* 1989; Tribe 1995), this was a machine which combined the instrument of a powerful pro-competition policy and the juridico-legal device of an economic 'constitution' in order to implicate society in a game of governance through competitive markets. As Foucault noted in his governmentality lectures, whereas classical liberalism understood the market as a spontaneous order, for ordoliberalism it was an artificial creation (Gordon 1991: 42). There is surely a line, perhaps a crooked line, which runs from West Germany's reconstruction as a 'social market economy' to the rebuilding of Western Europe in the image of a 'common market'.[10]

The promise of this notion of the machine is to rethink European integration in a highly contextualized, historicized way, one that pays close attention to regimes of practices and the spaces they configure. In principle one could examine any particular moment of European integration in terms of the constitutive power of the machine – from the creation of the Coal and Steel Community to the current program to recast Europe as an 'area of freedom, security and justice'. Scholars of the EU often note that it is a 'composite polity' (Tarrow), a *sui generis* political phenomenon' (Sbragia 2000: 219). But inasmuch as the EU can only govern by adopting, combining and borrowing technologies that were often first invented elsewhere, and often intended to serve other ends, the point surely is that it is in certain respects not unlike the modern, governmental state.

Political creation

There is a third and final path I want to sketch for investigating the *techne* of European governance. This is to think about the EU as a site of political creation, to ask what novel ways of governing does it bring into being? What new political styles and techniques does it make available to the wider field of governance? The last section emphasized how the governance of Europe has to be seen in relation to the adoption and appropriation of existing practices, the borrowing of techniques from elsewhere. But here I want to stress the flipside: the creation of techniques that did not previously exist.

In seeing the EU as a moment of political creation I am following the lead of the historian Keith Michael Baker. Baker poses the rhetorical question: 'What would a Foucauldian account of the French Revolution look like?' (Baker 1994). In his answer he suggests that one of its chief characteristics would be to examine the 'technologies of power' which the Revolution has bequeathed to our modern political culture. These include its particular ways of individualizing political subjects as citizens while universalizing their social relations within the political body of the nation. They also include a 'tactics of denunciation'. This is the method of identifying and eliminating particular individuals and groups whose corrupt or immoral ways obstruct the fulfilment of national citizenship.

The scandalous treatment of those labelled 'bogus asylum-seekers' or 'welfare cheats' suggests that these tactics of denunciation remain firmly embedded in our political culture.

A case could certainly be made for regarding certain institutional innovations associated with the EU as political creations. For instance, there is the fact of its capacity for supranational law-making, an attribute which sets it apart from all other international organizations (Geddes 2003: 129). Or there is 'comitology' – the complex and unique system of scrutinizing European administrative and technical decisions through committees of national representatives, one of the mechanisms which has been improvised to mediate the tension between supranational and intergovernmental political logics. These and similar institutional aspects have been well documented within the political science literature as unique features of the EU. However, with the two examples I offer below I want to discuss political creation in a somewhat different sense. In what follows I want to suggest that it can be useful to place the EU within wider trajectories of governmental development.

Harmonization as an art of European government

If one were to query the significance of the EU for the history of arts and styles of government, a strong case could surely be made for harmonization. Harmonization is often regarded as a relatively minor and technical aspect of the EU, one that hardly rates as a defining characteristic. Otherwise, it is seen as the technical component of the implementation of a 'neoliberal' project during the 1980s. In one of the few explorations of the governmentality of the EU, Andrew Barry has argued that harmonization deserves to be taken more seriously (Barry 1994, 2001). It should be seen, he suggests, as nothing less than an 'art of European government'. Here I want to briefly summarize Barry's analysis since it offers an excellent example of how we might think of the EU as a sort of laboratory of governmental arts and techniques.

Barry advances our understanding of harmonization by setting it within a genealogy of arts of governing extended social and economic spaces. As such, harmonization can be compared to the technique of standardization. Whether it was the capacity of Britain to constitute itself as a global trading machine, or of large corporations to master the art of mass production, what lay behind these accomplishments were certain techniques of standardization. The standardization of weights and measures was nothing new. But this was joined by many other standards by the end of the nineteenth century. One of the most notable was the standardization of electrical technologies such as the telegraph. This was to make possible long-distance communication, a practice crucial for modern empires. In this and many other ways, standardization functioned as a relatively flexible technology, serving to constitute state and non-state domains as relatively homogenous spaces of communication, knowledge and governance.

It is not standardization but harmonization that has, beginning with the single market project in the 1980s, become central to the possibility and practice of

European governance. In some cases, this entails the creation of common European standards or even, as in the case of the single currency, common units. But more generally, harmonization involves the 'mutual recognition' of national standards (Barry 1994: 49). This particular art does not, for the most part, aim to reproduce state power at a higher level. Instead, it seeks to 'align the capacities of already existing technologies that hitherto had operated within the restricted territorial boundaries of individual nation states' (1994: 49–50). Through the harmonization of national standards Europe is to be constituted as a relatively smooth space, open to the free movement of professions, goods, services and much else. Standardization accompanied the idea of a strong state that could 'contain' social and economic life. Mindful of the capacity of flows to escape organizational domains, the policy of harmonization is founded precisely upon a growing recognition of the limits of this mentality. It is, as Barry recognizes, 'a project that aims to work within the context of global inter-dependencies, insta-bilities and risks' (1994: 52).

For Foucault, the essence of liberal government is 'the introduction of economy into political practice'. 'To govern a state', he observes, 'will therefore mean to apply an economy at the entire level of the state' (Foucault 1991: 92). Perhaps we can say that the real significance of harmonization is that it enhances the possibility of a liberal governance of greatly extended social and economic spaces, of areas comprising many states. Harmonization is 'economic' in the classical sense because it seeks as far as possible to utilize existing govern-mental capacities rather than create a new superstate. It is perhaps this characteristic that Pascal Lamy, the EU's Trade Commissioner, has in mind when he heralds the EU as 'the most innovatory approach to governance that we can find in today's world', and nothing less than 'a laboratory of global gover-nance' (Lamy 2001).

A partially denationalized citizenship?

For a second example of the EU as a moment of creativity within the history of government we might consider its contribution to the practice of citizenship. Much attention has been focused on the possibility of a European citizenship, the prospects for a European demos or public sphere, and the extent to which individuals are acquiring, perhaps in addition to their national affiliations, a sense of European identity (Linklater 1998; Weiler 1999). Despite their different lines of analysis, many of these studies are linked in at least one respect. They tend to assume what Barry Hindess has called an 'internalist' view of citizenship, albeit now at a European level. That is, they tend to see citizenship as 'a complex package of rights and responsibilities accruing to individuals by virtue of their membership of an appropriate polity' (Hindess 2000: 1487).

But Hindess has shown that, when seen from a governmental perspective, there is a second dimension to citizenship. This is how it operates as 'a marker of identification, advising state and nonstate agencies of the particular state to which an individual belongs' (Hindess 2000: 1487). The internalist view of citizenship construes it as a practice of membership and even solidarity, an identity whose promise is a certain kind of equality. The second view foregrounds its implications as a principle for dividing and distributing the world's population to states and territories. Hence, while citizenship may offer various valuable benefits to those who are citizens of the state in which they live, it has a variety of less benign consequences. Not the least of these is to sanction certain forms of movement and mobility amongst its members, while discouraging or suppressing others. 'The culture of citizenship ... provides all modern states with good reasons for discriminating against noncitizens who cross or live within their borders' (Hindess 2000: 1495).

If the EU represents an innovation in citizenship, the nature of that innovation can be best appreciated in this second sense. The novelty of EU citizenship is to be found less in the founding of a pan-European identity or demos, but rather in the manner in which it places the relationship between the state and foreigners on a new basis. Ulrich Preuß (1998) has summarized this quite nicely. He argues that citizenship of the Union is not primarily a relation of the individual to Community institutions. Rather, it is a novel kind of sociolegal status which means that member states have to cope with the fact the individuals who are not their nationals are nevertheless, by virtue of their EU citizenship, acquiring a legal citizenship within their territories and their institutions (Preuß 1998: 147). Drawing an analogy with a particular ruling of the US Supreme Court (1869), Preuß presents this move as one of removing 'from the citizens of each state the disabilities of alienage in the other States' (1998: 146). It is a question of making persons feel 'at home' in a foreign country (1998: 146).

To put the matter in more governmental terms, this is a system of population management in which states commit themselves to affording the same rights to foreigners as to their own citizens. Here there is a parallel with the art of harmonization. It does not imply a move of standardization: the content of these rights is not made uniform across the EU. But there is a principle that in many areas of social and economic life within a given state, all EU nationals should be treated the same. Italians living in Germany are to have the same access to jobs and social benefits as Germans, and so on. What is so interesting is that it is not primarily the system of European institutions from which citizens enjoy rights and services; the EU is not a welfare *state*. Instead, this mostly remains the task of the national systems. The unique character of the EU is that while the rights and duties of EU citizenship are with regard to the Community, the principal addressee and guarantors are national member states (Preuß 1998: 141).

How might we name this transformation of citizenship in a way that captures its novelty? Does it signal the *Europeanization* of citizenship? 'Europeanization' is a misleading term since, as I have argued, the advent of EU citizenship does not appear to correspond with a shift of subjective identification with Europe as a political or cultural community, at least not in the way that the 'nationalization' of citizenship has done. But it is an unhelpful term for another, possibly more important, reason: it makes the EU and the extension of its institutions synonymous with 'Europe'.[11] But it bears emphasizing that the EU is not Europe, as such, but rather a political project which seeks *to speak in the name of Europe*. As the history of the idea of Europe reveals (Pagden 2002; Wilson and Van der Dussen 1993), there have been many enterprises that have, for different reasons and with various consequences, claimed or asserted the right to speak for Europe – the Catholic Church, Napoleonic France and Nazi Germany to name but three. From this perspective the EU is a particularly well-institutionalized attempt to represent Europe, but it is not the first, and perhaps not the last. Concepts such as 'Europeanization' serve only to naturalize what is in fact a political relationship. Europe is a contested concept not a process.

My preference is to regard this movement in more modest terms – as one entailing a partial denationalization of citizenship (Bosniak 2000). Unlike concepts such as 'postnational' citizenship, this does not imply a move beyond nationality as a regulative principle. Citizenship of the EU is, after all, restricted to nationals of the member countries. But the EU does imply a governance of population in which the nationals of a given state are, in many areas (e.g., social rights) but by no means all, no longer the privileged subjects of governance. Through the EU, states become implicated in a sort of mutual governance of one another's populations. Put differently, the EU does represent the most sustained attempt to move beyond what Aristide Zolberg calls 'the hypernationalist version of citizenship' (Zolberg 2000). That is, it seems to point beyond a world in which citizenship is located within a complex of rival nationalisms and exclusive political loyalties, a world in which citizens are friends and foreigners are always potential enemies.

However, this notion of denationalization should be carefully qualified. It is only a *partial* denationalization. The EU involves a commitment to end discrimination amongst EU nationals, not among all foreigners. This is nonetheless quite an accomplishment, and can be compared favourably with other trading regimes such as NAFTA which make no provision for the free movement or non-discriminatory treatment of persons. As such, it is not to be belittled or dismissed. But it is perhaps not a coincidence that the advancement of the idea and status of EU citizenship has come at the same time as a range of measures in the field of 'internal' security, immigration and asylum policy – both at a national and European level – the overall objective of which is to emphasize and strengthen, both literally and figuratively, the external borders of the EU. The development of the EU as an 'area of freedom, security and justice', has been profoundly influenced by a fear of certain kinds of foreigners, such as refugees, asylum-seekers and migrant workers (Bigo 2002). These figures have become signifiers within populist political appeals and much media commentary for a range of erstwhile 'social' problems like drugs, unemployment, and crime. European cooperation has been amplified with regard to surveillance, migration, policing and asylum measures, not for the purposes of extending human rights, but largely for the protection of European citizens from these unwanted and uninvited 'others'.

The EU's ongoing 'enlargement' would seem to suggest that its model of citizenship is capable of being extended beyond the current club of member states.

In other words, like some of the other arts of governance we have discussed, it too is mobile and flexible. Yet its articulation with these political and legal logics of population division and discrimination suggests that this is only a partial denationalization of citizenship. The geographical extension of this game of denationalized citizenship should not be confused with the transcendence of the modern, territorial norms of modern citizenship which Hindess and others describe.

Conclusion

Implicit in what I have presented here is the possibility of writing a different kind of history of European integration. This would be a history that was not centred on the evolution of European institutions, though these cannot be ignored. Nor would it privilege the great moments of political bargaining and diplomacy which have punctuated the course of the EU's development; those episodes of frenzied negotiation and treaty-making. Instead, it would be an account of European integration in terms of its changing political rationalities. It would be a history that investigated the discourses within which the aims, means and ends of European integration have come to be posed. Likewise, it would examine the particular arts and techniques which have been identified as critical to the pursuit of those ends.

In this short chapter I have only been able to hint at some of the possible features of such a history. Taking the example of neofunctionalism, I argued that rather than see it as a predictive theory about European integration we could read it as a discourse. To do so reveals how the possibility of governing Europe, at least during the early years of the European Community, was framed in relation to the characteristic terms and assumptions of modernization discourse. While the European Community was not envisaged as a welfare state, European governance was nevertheless to be conducted on the basis of many of the same techniques, including the creation of administrative agencies of expert planners, and the machinery of managed markets.

What lines might we follow if we wanted to take such a project further? What lines should we identify if we are to better understand the way in which these rationalities and techniques have shifted? One possibility would be to contrast the rationality of neofunctionalism with the kinds of political assumptions embedded in the present enthusiasm for the 'Open Method of Coordination' (OMC). The OMC is discussed at length by Roger Dale in Chapter 9 of this volume (but see also Haahr 2004), so I will be brief here. Neofunctionalism spoke the language of technocracy; its political dream was an integration process orchestrated and overseen by an elite body of European experts. With OMC we see how many of the techniques associated with advanced liberal rule – the performance indicator, the peer review, etc. – have come to reconfigure the space of European governance. If the OMC can be said to have a dream of European governance, it is no longer one where an institutional centre possesses a superior knowledge and uses this to direct the integration process. Instead, we can identify a new game in which governance is associated with institutionalized processes of mutual learning, peer review and policy learning within a community of states. Perhaps with OMC one sees a decentring of the space of European governance.

Of course, there are countless other lines such a project could trace. The important point to make is that any genealogy of European integration would need to be a plural and aggregative endeavour carried out on many fronts. It would need to consider diverse facets of the EU. As I hinted in my discussion of the partial denationalization of citizenship, what we make of European governance and European citizenship is highly context-dependent. From the perspective of the EU national, this is a liberal or neoliberal project which focuses on enhancing mobility and freedom across an extended European space. But from the perspective of those now named and shunned as 'asylum-seekers', European governance might invoke the renewal of a much older art of government – that of police – but now on a transnational basis. In sum, any genealogy of European integration would surely reveal that there is no singular 'system' or 'logic' of governance, but rather a tense combination or hybrid of quite different governmental projects.

Notes

1   This chapter has benefited from the input and comments of Wendy Larner and Jens Henrik Haahr, and the financial support of Canada's Social Sciences and Humanties Research Council (#410–2000–1415). Many of its themes are pursued at greater length in my forthcoming text, co-written with Jens Henrik Haahr – *Governing Europe: Discourse, Governmentality and European Integration.*
2   These exceptions include the work of Andrew Barry which I take up below, Beeson and Jayasuriya (1998) and Haahr (2004)
3   Here I use 'European governance' as a shorthand for the whole system of policies, rules, regulations, and institutions that centres upon the EU, but which implicates national and other systems of rule in complex ways. It is important to note that the EU does not exhaust the field of European governance; many other actors and agencies have, with varying degrees of success, governed cultural, political, economic, geographical and other aspects of Europe.
4   See Christiansen *et al.* (2001) and Joergensen (1997). For an impressive attempt to push social constructivist studies of Europe in a more post-structuralist direction, see Diez (1999).
5   Scott develops the idea of high modernism from David Harvey. At its centre is 'a supreme self-confidence about continued linear progress, the development of scientific and technical knowledge, the expansion of production, the rational design of social order.... High modernism is thus a particularly sweeping vision of how the benefits of technical and scientific progress might be applied – usually through the state – in every field of human activity' (Scott 1998: 89–90). Scott includes Jean Monnet alongside the likes of Le Corbusier, Rathenau and Lenin within his pantheon of high modernist thinkers and planners.
6   For a different way of developing this point see Hay and Rosamond (2002).
7   European Coal and Steel Community. The High Authority. *Report on the Situation of the Community*, Luxembourg, 1954.

8 I borrow this term from Ó Tuathail (1996: 2). He uses it to emphasize how map-making and other geographical knowledges are historically bound up with political aspirations to seize and control territory.
9 The following examples are discussed at greater length in Walters (2002).
10 On the place of ordoliberalism within the political-economic thought of the common market see Gerber (1998) and Sauter (1998).
11 I am grateful to Barry Hindess for pointing out the dangers of equating Europe with the EU.

References

Baker, K.M. (1994) 'A Foucauldian French revolution?', in J. Goldstein (ed.) *Foucault and the Writing of History*, Oxford: Blackwell.

Barry, A. (1994) 'Harmonization and the art of European government', in C. Rootes and H. Davis (eds) *Social change and Political Transformation*, London: UCL Press.

——(2001) *Political Machines: governing a technological society*, London: Athlone.

Beeson, M. and Jayasuriya, K. (1998) 'The political rationalities of regionalism: APEC and the EU in comparative perspective', *Pacific Review*, 11(3): 311–336.

Bellamy, R. and Warleigh, A. (1998) 'From an ethics of integration to an ethics of participation: citizenship and the future of the European Union', *Millennium: Journal of International Studies*, 27(3): 447–468.

Bigo, D. (2002) 'Security and immigration: toward a critique of the governmentality of unease', *Alternatives*, 27(supplement): 63–92.

Bosniak, L. (2000) 'Citizenship denationalized', *Journal of Global Legal Studies*, 7(2): 447–509.

Checkel, J. (2001) 'Social construction and European integration', in T. Christiansen, K.E. Jorgensen and A. Wiener (eds) *Social Construction of Europe*, London: Sage.

Christiansen, T., Jorgensen, K.E. and Wiener, A. (eds) (2001) *Social Construction of Europe*, London: Sage.

Cooper, R. (2000) *The Postmodern State and the World Order*, London: Demos/The Foreign Policy Centre.

Dean, M. (1999) *Governmentality: power and rule in modern society*, London: Sage.

Deleuze, G. and Guattari, F. (1987) *A Thousand Plateaus: capitalism and schizophrenia*, London: Athlone.

Diez, T. (1999) 'Speaking "Europe": the politics of integration discourse', *Journal of European Public Policy*, 6(4): 598–613.

Duchêne, F. (1994) *Jean Monnet: the first statesman of interdependence*, New York: Norton.

Ekengren, M. (2002) *The Time of European Governance*, Manchester: Manchester University Press.

Featherstone, K. (1994) 'Jean Monnet and the "democratic deficit" in the European Union', *Journal of Common Market Studies*, 32(2): 149–70.

Foucault, M. (1991) 'Governmentality', in G. Burchell, C. Gordon and P. Miller (eds) *The Foucault Effect: studies in governmentality*, Chicago: University of Chicago Press.

Geddes, A. (2003) *The Politics of Migration and Immigration in Europe*, London: Sage.

Gerber, D.J. (1998) *Law and Competition in Twentieth Century Europe: protecting Prometheus*, Oxford: Clarendon Press.

Gordon, C. (1991) 'Governmental rationality: an introduction', in G. Burchell, C. Gordon and P. Miller (eds) *The Foucault Effect: studies in governmentality*, Chicago: University of Chicago Press.

Haahr, J.H. (2004) 'Open coordination as advanced liberal government', Special Issue on OMC, *Journal of European Public Policy* 11(2).

Haas, E. (1968) 'Technocracy, pluralism and the New Europe', in J. Nye (ed.) *International Regionalism*, Boston: Little Brown.

Harrison, R. (1974) *Europe in Question: theories of regional international integration*, London: Allen & Unwin.

Hay, C. and Rosamond, B. (2002) 'Globalization, European integration and the discursive construction of economic imperatives', *Journal of European Public Policy*, 9(2): 147–167.

Hindess, B. (2000) 'Citizenship in the international management of populations', *American Behavioral Scientist*, 43(9): 1486–1497.

Joergensen, K. (ed.) (1997) *Reflective Approaches to European Governance*, Basingstoke: Macmillan.

Lamy, P. (2001) 'Between globalisation and enlargement', speech delivered at the Free University, Berlin, February 8, 2001. Online. Available at: http://europa.eu.int/comm/enlargement/speeches/arch_2001.htm

Larner, W. and Walters, W. (2002) 'The political rationality of the "new regionalism": toward a genealogy of the region', *Theory & Society*, 31: 391–432.

Linklater, A. (1998) 'Citizenship and sovereignty in the post-Westphalian European state', in D. Archibugi, D. Held and M. Köhler (eds) *Re-imagining Political Community*, Cambridge: Polity.

Marks, G., Scharpf, F., Schmitter, P. and Streeck, W. (1996) *Governance in the European Union*, London: Sage.

Mazey, S. (1992) 'Conception and evolution of the High Authority's administrative services (1952–1956): from supranational principles to multinational practices', in E.V. Heyen (ed.) *Yearbook of European Administrative History*, Baden-Baden: Nomos Verlagsgesellschaft.

Monnet, J. (1978) *Memoirs*, trans. R. Mayne, Garden City, NJ: Doubleday.

Moravcsik, A. (1998) *The Choice for Europe: social purpose and state power from Messina to Maastricht*, Ithaca, NY: Cornell University Press.

Ó Tuathail, G. (1996) *Critical Geopolitics: the politics of writing global space*, Minneapolis: University of Minnesota Press.

Pagden, A. (2002) *The Idea of Europe: from antiquity to the European Union*, Cambridge: Cambridge University Press.

Peacock, A.T., Willgerodt, H. and Johnson, D. (1989) *German Neo-Liberals and the Social Market Economy*, New York: St. Martin's Press.

Preuß, U. (1998) 'Citizenship in the European Union: a paradigm for transnational democracy?', in D. Archibugi, D. Held and M. Köhler (eds) *Re-imagining Political Community*, Cambridge: Polity.

Rosamond, B. (2000) *Theories of European Integration*, New York: Macmillan.

Rose, N. (1999) *Powers of Freedom: reforming political thought*, Cambridge: Cambridge University Press.

Rose, N. and Miller, P. (1992) 'Political power beyond the state: problematics of government', *British Journal of Sociology*, 43(2): 172–205.

Sauter, W. (1998) 'The economic constitution of the European Union', *Columbia Journal of European Law*, 4(1): 27–68.

Sbragia, A. (2000) 'The European Union as Coxswain: governance by steering', in J. Pierre (ed.) *Debating Governance*, Oxford: Oxford University Press.

Schmitter, P. (1996) 'Examining the present Euro-polity with the help of past theories', in G. Marks *et al.* (eds) *Governance in the European Union*, London: Sage.

Scott, J. (1998) *Seeing Like a State: how certain schemes to improve the human condition have failed*, New Haven: Yale University Press.

Strøby Jensen, C. (2003) 'Neo-functionalism', in M. Cini (ed.) *European Union Politics*, Oxford: Oxford University Press.

Thrift, N. (2000) 'It's the little things', in K. Dodds and D. Atkinson (eds) *Geopolitical Traditions: a century of geopolitical thought*, London: Routledge.

Tribe, K. (1995) *Strategies of Economic Order: German economic discourse 1750–1950*, Cambridge: Cambridge University Press.

Walters, W. (2002) 'The power of inscription: beyond social construction and deconstruction in European Union studies', *Millennium: Journal of International Studies*, 31: 83–108.

Weiler, J. (1999) 'To be a European citizen – eros and civilization', in J. Weiler (ed.) *The Transformation of Europe*, Cambridge: Cambridge University Press.

Wilson, K. and Van der Dussen, J. (eds) (1993) *The History of the Idea of Europe*, London: Routledge.

Zolberg, A.R. (2000) 'The dawn of cosmopolitan denizenship', *Indiana Journal of Global Legal Studies*, 7(2): 511–518.

9   Forms of governance, governmentality and the EU's Open Method of Coordination

Roger Dale

The continuing expansion and deepening of the European Union (EU) has generated a range of questions about the nature of governing. It has both introduced intriguing new questions about the EU's own nature and characterization, and added piquancy to debates about the nature of the nation-state. The main focus of this paper will be the Open Method of Coordination (OMC), introduced at the EU's Lisbon Summit in 2000 alongside an agenda that set out to charter the Union's trajectory for the next decade. More broadly, the OMC can be seen as an alternative method of supranational governance to be brought about through such means as benchmarking, peer review and so on. The reasons for its introduction, its possible consequences, and not least its own character, frame in new, theoretically and substantively interesting ways, important questions around government at national and supranational levels and the relationships between them in the current era.

The OMC is of interest on three specific grounds. First, it is explicitly presented as a new form of governance that has been made necessary by the limitations of other available means at EU level. Second, it is sponsored by, and to be put into effect by, the EU, acting as a body that has some but not all characteristics of a state. And third, it was explicitly brought into being as the key means of bringing about the substantive developments, particularly in social areas, promulgated at the Lisbon Summit in 2000, through which Europe was to become the 'most competitive, dynamic, knowledge based economy in the world, capable of sustainable economic development, with more and better jobs and social cohesion' (European Council 2000). The details of these innovative features make the OMC an especially attractive topic in the context of this volume. In particular, it provides an outstanding opportunity (that has not, surprisingly, been widely taken up) to investigate governmentality at a supranational level.

The remainder of the chapter will be organized as follows. I will first outline very briefly the major formal features of the OMC. I will then consider two different perspectives from which it has been interpreted, 'governance' and governmentality; it is important to note that these perspectives are not regarded either as homogeneous or as offering zero-sum or mutually exclusive options. The major focus will be governmentality, and what we might learn about both the OMC and governmentality from applying it to the OMC. I will then briefly compare these perspectives in their appropriation of the concepts of 'benchmarking' and 'learning', both of which are central mechanisms of the OMC.

The Open Method of Coordination

As stated in the Bulletin on the Conclusions of the Portuguese Presidency, 'the open method of coordination, which is designed to help the Member States to progressively develop their own policies, involves:

- fixing guidelines for the Union combined with specific timetables for achieving the goals which they set in the short, medium and long terms;
- establishing, where appropriate, quantitative and qualitative indicators and benchmarks against the best in the world and tailored to the needs of different Member States and sectors as a means of comparing best practice;
- translating these European guidelines into national and regional policies by setting specific targets and adopting measures, taking into account national and regional differences;
- periodic monitoring, evaluation and peer review as mutual learning processes.
  (European Presidency 2000, paragraph 37)

The OMC was introduced as the means of implementing the very far reaching and ambitious Lisbon agenda, and it is crucial to make three points about that agenda itself and their implications for our understanding of the OMC:

- it contains at least five distinct, potentially contradictory, discourses ('competitiveness', 'knowledge based-economy', 'sustainable growth', 'more and better jobs' and 'social cohesion');
- it is clear that 'competitiveness' is seen as the dominant discourse (see, for example, Rosamund 2002; Radaelli 2003; Dale 2003b);
- any contradictions between the 'economic' and 'social' discourses are to be overcome through the development of 'productive social policy' (see Scharpf 2002; Jenson and Pochet 2002).

What these elements of the Lisbon agenda make clear is that in making the OMC the appropriate means through which to secure them, the Portuguese presidency regarded the OMC as more than a merely technical device (see Rodrigues 2002). Its introduction also assumes and reinforces the idea that: (a) that 'Europe' is an entity that has authority over these areas; (b) that it is able to act effectively in the absence of the existing 'Community method' (that 'creates uniform rules that member states must adopt, provides sanctions if they fail to do so, and allows challenges for non-compliance to be brought in court'); and (c) that in doing so it can 'act on itself'. The key point for this chapter is that these assumed competences are quite differently incorporated into the two perspectives to be discussed, with different consequences for conceptions of 'Europe'.

There is now a voluminous literature on the OMC (there are around 90 papers in the main database held at the European Center at the University of Wisconsin, and I estimate that my searches have revealed at least twice as many elsewhere). However, it would be neither possible logistically nor appropriate in terms of the aims of this chapter, to attempt to survey it comprehensively. Instead, I will try to context the introduction of the OMC (though, as will be argued below, 'introduction' is not quite the appropriate term for what was essentially an amalgam of existing methods) through setting out five challenges, which might be seen collectively as constituting its rationale, to which it was seen to offer at least a new approach, if not a solution:

- The challenge of 'politically sensitive areas' (see de la Porte 2002), where the use of the existing method would be impossible (and where 'the OMC has rapidly become a virtual template for EU policy making' (Zeitlin 2002)). These include pensions, social inclusion and employment.
- These are also areas where national interests are very strong, and where 'Europe' would be resisted powerfully if it sought to intervene in the traditional ways. As Jacobsson (2001: 2) puts it: 'the European integration project has now reached a phase where the core areas of the welfare state are directly affected … In these areas supranational decision making has not met support'.
- The challenge of areas where there is no Treaty mandate for European-level action, but where coordinated action is seen to be required. As the former Director General of Employment in the European Commission puts it: 'the introduction in the Maastricht Treaty of the subsidiarity principle in combination with the traditional Community method of legislation left the EU to manage an unbalanced agenda, an agenda focused on the promotion of change in the form of a single Market and a Single Currency, but very little room for initiatives to manage change in a socially responsible way' (Larsson 2002: 16).
- The challenge of the diversity of welfare state models; it is recognized that it would not be possible to devise a single model that would be acceptable to all of the welfare state 'families' found in the EU (see Scharpf 2002).
- Combining all these, the challenge of creating a 'social Europe', to find a means of market-taming to match the market-making actions that have dominated the EU to date, as well as responding to the 'productive social policy' elements of the Lisbon agenda, which has been seen as representing 'a true watershed in the Europeanisation of employment and social policy' (Esping-Andersen *et al.* 2002), a 'turning point' in European social policy (Ferrara *et al.* 2002) and a 'Maastricht for Welfare' (Rhodes 2000).

However, it is important to keep in mind the wider context into which the OMC was introduced. One key aspect of this has been pointed out by Fritz Scharpf:

> the selection of policy goals confirms the expectation that, under the constitutional priority of European law, policies promoted through the open method of coordination must avoid all challenges to the acquis of the

internal market and monetary union. Even when responding to OMC guidelines, therefore, member states continue to operate under the same legal and economic constraints of economic coordination which limit their policy choice when they are acting individually.

(Scharpf 2002: 165)

This effectively indicates the limitations of the OMC, which sometimes tend to get lost in more detailed discussions.

Perspectives on the OMC

As I suggested above, I will distinguish two main perspectives on the OMC. The first, and much the most common in the literature, might be referred to as the 'OMC as governance', since it takes the OMC as essentially a means of redressing the shortfall in the governance capacity of the EU in the face of the five challenges listed above.

The second, 'governmentality', focuses more closely on the wider 'Europeanising' consequences of the processes through which the OMC operates than on their intended outcomes.

OMC as 'governance'

The overall literature on the OMC reflects the centrality of a governance discourse in approaching the topic, and whether the OMC represents a new, and for some, normatively preferable, form of supranational or transnational governance (see, for example, de la Porte and Pochet 2002; Hodson and Maher 2002; Trubek and Mosher 2003; Zeitlin 2002).

However, the frequency with which the term is used does little to remove the conceptual ambiguities around it. While there is no space to go into those differences in detail, there appears to be some broad agreement that governance became prominent in the 'post-Keynesian welfare state' literature as one part of the response to the changing role and nature of the state.[1]

However, one useful point that emerges from the discussions of governance is that they reveal that it is mistaken to assume that there was no 'governance' before 1989 or whenever. Rather, certainly in public sector areas such as education, the (state-dominated) forms taken by the activities and their coordination that we have begun to refer to as governance became so familiar as to disguise what lay beneath/behind them. With the recognition that the state had never 'done it all', and that at least the great majority of the activities of governing were not dependent on the state doing them, the question becomes, as it essentially always should have been, what forms of governance (as 'the coordination of coordination') are in place where, and why; in a sense, the state moved from being *explanans* to *explandum*, though it is crucial to note that it is still largely the state, through its role as 'coordinator in chief', that determines by whom and under what conditions government will be accomplished. To put it another way, one of the benefits to be gained from looking closely at governance is that it reveals the degree to which we have tended to, in a sense, fetishize the post-war social democratic state and to see departures from it as pathological rather than trying to theorize them.

In terms of the OMC as a form of governance, Radaelli (2003: 24–26) has recently produced an 'ideal typical format' that rests on six characteristics: a new, and more limited, role of law; a new approach to problem-solving, based on iteration, mutual cooperation and standard-setting; participation; diversity and subsidiarity; new ways to produce usable knowledge; and policy learning. The main focus of this approach is 'problem-solving'. It is essentially concerned with whether and how effectively 'Europe' can become an effective policy actor in a range of areas where the existing method cannot be used, but where its future development depends on it being able to act. In particular, the crucial question about the OMC is whether it will prove an effective means of implementing the Lisbon agenda. Its component parts – benchmarking, indicators, best practice, monitoring and so on – are judged on the basis of their effectiveness as mechanisms for achieving the goals set at Lisbon.

The OMC and 'Europe as an entity'

In this case, the theoretical basis of the governmentality approach, which is the focus of this volume, as well as its understanding of the OMC, will be of central interest.

One important reason for looking at the contribution of a governmentality approach is the surprising (given the centrality to the OMC of mechanisms that have been central to it) absence from analyses of the OMC. Though there are one or two passing references to governmentality, the only substantial piece I have been able to find was a conference paper (now transformed into an article for the forthcoming special issue on the OMC of the *European Journal of Public Policy*) by Jens Henrik Haahr (Haahr 2004), and this will form the basis of the substantive discussion of governmentality and the OMC below.

Governmentality

Given its basis, largely in records of lectures and rather fragmentary sources, it is inevitable that there has developed a very wide and rich range of different understandings and different applications of Foucault's concept of governmentality. Rather than attempting to summarize, let alone adjudicate on, that literature, I shall use the account of the development of the idea provided in recent work by Thomas Lemke (2001, 2003a, 2003b), which both 'embeds' it well and benefits from material by Foucault that has not been easily accessible or widely known and commented upon. As a basis for an adequate assessment of the potential of governmentality, Lemke stresses two points. The first is the relatively familiar one about the hybrid nature of the concept, with its combination of 'gouverner' and 'mentalité' – governing and modes of thought, or technologies of power and political rationality (which 'constitutes the intellectual processing of the reality which political technologies can then tackle' (2001: 191)). The second is the scope of 'government' for Foucault, which historically sees government as covering, for instance, household management and self-control as well as a more narrowly conceived political realm; it is for this reason that he (Foucault) defines government as the conduct of conduct, not only of individual, but of collective 'bodies'. This is an especially important point when we are involved in an analysis of governmentality as an approach to understanding how a supranational body attempts to shape and change the practices and activities of its member states; the member states are here the bodies to be 'worked on'. Lemke refers to the 'neo-liberal harmony in which not only the individual body but also collective bodies and institutions ... corporations and *states* have to be 'lean', 'fit', 'flexible' and 'autonomous' (2001: 203; emphasis added).

It is useful to consider why and how the concept of governmentality entered Foucault's – and later, the world's – conceptual armamentarium, since it can be seen as a response to changes that were becoming quite evident in the nature of the state and political rationalities in the second half of the 1970s. As Lemke puts it:

> Foucault was sensitive to the growing fragility of the old formation ... (and) from the middle of the seventies ... we can observe a growing theoretical distancing from the disciplinary model. Complementing this ... there arises a new problematic that centers on the concept of government,
>
> (2003a: 176)

and he goes on to quote Foucault:

> It seems to me that through the current economic crisis ... it may be clearly seen how in the more developed nations a crisis of government has begun. And by 'government' I mean the set of institutions and practices by which people are 'led', from administration to education etc. It is this set of procedures, techniques and methods that guarantee the 'government' of the people, which seems to me to be in crisis today ... We are, I believe, at the beginning of a huge crisis of a wide-ranging reevaluation of the problem of 'government'.
>
> (Foucault 1991: 75–77)

One key point for the argument of this chapter is that it is possible to recognize a parallel trajectory for 'governmentality' to that sketched out above for 'governance'. There I suggested that the implicit assumption that there was no 'governance' until the crisis of the 1980s was misleading, that it was necessary for the institutional and practical coordination implied by 'governance' to be made explicit, and that the work of governance always has to be carried out, even when the role of the state in its execution seems so dominant as to obscure the contribution of other agencies. In a similar way, it might be suggested that not only did governmentality not begin with neo-liberalism, but it has always been an element of governing,[2] is not reducible, as Foucault makes clear, to either sovereignty or 'discipline'. The very common use of the pair 'neo-liberal governmentality' sometimes threatens to suggest that, on the one hand, there is nothing more to neo-liberal government than governmentality, and on the other that governmentality only emerged with the rise of neo-liberalism. Both these propositions are faulty, and both have quite serious consequences. And this argument also undermines the attractive but misleading suggestion of a 'post war' chronology of government–governance-governmentality.

Two elements of this account of governmentality make it especially promising as a means of understanding more clearly the OMC. The first is that governmentality, and the technologies through which it operates, is not be seen as exclusive of other types of power, but as always present as a mode of government. And this is, of course, extremely relevant in the case of the OMC, which is explicitly introduced in areas where it is not possible to govern through law.

The second is that it makes clear not only that there is no zero-sum relationship between the state and governmentality; the state has not 'disappeared' or been sidelined under neo-liberalism but, on the contrary,

> the state in the neo-liberal model not only retains its traditional functions, but on the contrary takes on new tasks and functions [though it should be noted that it has also in many cases ceded some of those tasks and functions, such as the control of public utilities RD]. The neo-liberal forms of government feature not only direct intervention by means of empowered and specialized state apparatuses, but also characteristically develop indirect techniques for leading and controlling individuals without at the same time being responsible for them.
>
> (Lemke 2001: 201)

Governmentality and the OMC

In his discussion of the OMC as 'advanced liberal government', Haahr (2004) advances three elements of what he calls 'the analytics of government' that are of particular significance, not least because he does draw very productive comparisons with the prior 'welfare state' mode of government, catching the nature of the changes very nicely as the shift from 'society as a domain of needs, calling for regulation and insurance' (p. 9) to 'society as a pool of resources, the energies of which can be released through partnership' (p. 11).

He discusses first, 'technologies of agency', which include technologies of contract and technologies of involvement. In terms of contract, he suggests that the Lisbon agenda itself may be seen as a 'quasi-contract', and that a 'mentality of contract' can be perceived in the European Employment strategy. Rather more interestingly, he suggests that 'technologies of citizenship' might be more effectively reformulated as technologies of involvement in the context of the EU, since 'when we shift focus from citizens and state, individuals and authority, to …

forms of governance transcending state boundaries, subjects more frequently appear as associations, agencies or institutions rather than as individuals' (2004: 12); these technologies share 'the presupposition that government is the employment of techniques for the release of resources found in a domain outside itself' (p. 12). He suggests, however, drawing on research into Danish government agencies and (echoing Jacobsson's (2003) concept of 'elite socialisation') that the most prominent technology of involvement is:

> the systematization of knowledges, the comprehensive possibilities it establishes for deliberation, consultation and negotiation, both within each member state and between states ... (which) means the active involvement of whole new groups of primarily civil servants at a national level in the processes of European 'opinion formation'.
>
> (Haahr 2004: 13)

The next discussion, of 'technologies of performance', essentially rehearses some ways in which the 'traditional' concepts of governmentality might be applied in the case of the OMC. However, importantly it goes further in developing the possibility that we may be witnessing the establishment of:

> a specific system of indirect 'government at a distance' ... with the objective of penetrating the knowledge domains and national frame of reference of MS bureaucracies ... which transforms its participants into 'calculative individuals' within a specific 'calculative space', namely the notion of a European economy.
>
> (p. 14)

This crucial idea is then developed further in the most important section of Haahr's paper. Having discussed the ways in which the presentation of community-wide data makes member states visible and (deliberately) comparable, he suggests that not only does this present a 'narrative of self-improvement via purposeful self-control and conscious self-management' (where, of course, the 'self' referred to is an individual member state of the EU), but that it also constructs a 'set of *identities* which are being continuously reproduced in the framework of the Lisbon process' (2004: 20, emphasis in original). These identities include that of the EC as an institution that can legitimately grade and compare member states, and member states as involved in competitive self-improvement. But most importantly, Haahr argues that they:

> reproduce and reinforce one further identity ... the notion of Europe as some entity ... All these indicators ... presuppose that it is meaningful and natural to conceive of problems (such as economic reform and social cohesion) as common EU problems and of their solutions as common EU solutions.
>
> (p. 20)

And he concludes the section: 'It may be that the notion of a European identity has not gained foothold among the European populations at large. At the level of EU policy development, the OMC serves to illustrate its significance' (p. 22).

The importance of this point is reinforced if we examine the history of the OMC a little more closely. Rather than its being 'introduced' at the Lisbon summit as a freshly minted initiative, it would be more accurate to see what happened there as the ex-post 'naming' of a series of similar existing processes, such as those introduced in the Amsterdam Treaty, the Monetary Union strategy and the Employment strategy (see Pochet 2002: 8). This 'naming' is in itself a highly significant move; it gives a substance, authority and degree of legitimation to the process that its multiple predecessors individually could not aspire to. Indeed, Claudio Radaelli sees the OMC as eminently a 'legitimising discourse':

> that provides a community of policy makers with a common vocabulary and a legitimising project ... with the result that practices that ... a few years ago would have been simply labeled 'soft law', new policy instruments and benchmarking are now presented as 'applications' if not 'prototypes' of 'the' method'.
>
> (2003: 7)

One other point that may be added here is that the OMC does not help construct only different (and far from homogeneous) scales (nation, subnational, Europe) but also different *sectors*. It is something of a commonplace (though nevertheless a valuable one) in the main body of writing on the OMC that it applies to multiple sectors, and operates in different ways in each of them. The response to this is to warn that the OMC is to be seen as 'a cookbook rather than as a recipe' (Vandenbroucke 2002: 9). However, it should not be overlooked that whatever the different forms it takes within them, the OMC is simultaneously *constructing* both the scope and the content of those sectors; one vivid example of this is the shift from 'Poverty' to 'Social Exclusion' as the sector label). In all these instances the introduction of the OMC is offered as a unique European method for addressing unique European problems; its introduction thus assumes and reinforces a supranational rather than intergovernmental mode of European governance. It might, then, be argued that without the naming, the consequences of the activities undertaken under the aegis of the OMC would have been quite different. The establishment of a Community method that crosses not only national but institutional/sectoral boundaries is what makes possible the wider elements of significance that Haahr sees the OMC as producing.

Thus, for Haahr, it is the *significance* of the OMC, especially in the construction of an idea of a distinctive European space, that is crucial for the analytics of government. His argument, in essence, is that the significance lies in the following:

> The OMC ... confirms a specific European identity, namely as some 'community of destiny': both the formulation of overall objectives for the Union and

the systematic comparisons of performances in relation to a comprehensive range of indicators presuppose that the Method of Coordination is there to contribute to the realisation of some common destiny'.

(2004: 24)

– though we may wish to go further on the basis of the discussion of the emergence of the OMC and suggest that its contribution is to the construction of the idea of a common destiny as well as to its realization. The importance of this argument is that to a degree it trumps arguments about differential national commitments and rates and depth of implementation and commitment. In a sense, it recapitulates Power's (1997) argument that the preparedness to submit to audit is of as great a significance as the outcomes of the process, and in doing so it contributes very effectively to our understanding of the European project.

There are three main areas where we might see Haahr's work alongside others contributing to an enhanced understanding of the OMC.

(1) *The conception of the discursive construction of Europe.* This is, of course, not a new or uncommon idea, and it has been particularly well articulated by Ben Rosamund. He argues that:

[it] is integral to discussions about the extent to which integration should proceed and the form that it should take ... Advocacy proposing European-level policy responses to exogenous challenges ... requires the imagination of 'Europe' as a policy space ... and this requires more than statistical aggregation of attributes of member state economies ... acts of discursive construction are part and parcel of the behaviour of policy actors.

(2002: 172)

Beyond this, a number of cognate ideas have been specifically developed around the OMC, such as Radaelli's (2003) conceptions of it as a 'legitimating discourse', or as enabling 'ideational convergence', and Ferrara *et al.*'s (2002) allusion to its 'conditioning' of states. However, Haahr's explicitly 'governmentalist' argument about the significance of the OMC does add something to the other notions of the discursive construction of Europe, namely that it describes elements of what Rosamund would call 'banal' activities (as opposed to 'heroic' acts) of regional construction, especially through the creation of what might be called a 'consciousness of the European dimension' among member states in their policy-making; though their responses to it may vary, the OMC means that they cannot escape responses of some kind.

(2) *Studying states as objects of government.* Following from the last issue, the idea that the OMC 'works on' states may offer potential for considerable development from a governmentality standpoint, particularly as more empirical evidence of the kind collected by Jacobsson (2003) on the 'subtle transformation of states', becomes available. In particular, the ideas she advances (following

Ekengren) on the effects of the management of time as well as knowledge at the European-level and the consequences of a European administrative timetable that is effectively disruptive of national timetables seem to merit much greater development, particularly perhaps from a comparative perspective (both synchronic and diachronic).

(3) *The 'problematic' of the OMC.* Here, Haahr makes clear both the differences between the prevailing 'governance' approaches to the OMC, and the specific contribution of the governmentality approach. The main way in which this is approached is through the 'outcome versus significance' debate, and in the way that it enables a comparison of approaches based on the idea of 'architecture', on the one hand, and 'construction' on the other. Chris Rumford has recently discussed on the basis of 'the concept of reflexive governance' what he sees as shortcomings of sociological accounts of the relationship between globalization and European governance, arguing that the issues are about 'focussing attention on forms of rule rather than looking for evidence of state building' (Rumford, 2003: 14), and that 'the problem of constructing an integrated polity has caused the EU to focus more and more on securing the mechanisms of government – the govern-mentalization of government, in Foucault's terms' (p. 19). And he goes on:

> the strength of the concept of reflexive governance … is that it draws atten-tion to the multiplicity of forms of rule currently *coexisting* in the EU … and sees the EU involved … in a project to establish pragmatic forms of govern-ment in an environment in which EU governance is increasingly problematic and uncertain.
>
> (p. 19, emphasis added)

All that said, and welcoming the novelty and boldness of Haahr's contribution, there are three main points of critique I would like to raise, as much for the fact that they are relatively common in the governmentality literature. These relate to the tendency for questions of agency, politics and of the 'telos' of the project to be somewhat neglected in favour of its processes and techniques, the somewhat uncertain handling of issues of scale, and the identification of the mechanisms through which technologies of power operate.

Critique of governmentality and OMC

Questions of agency

The first set of comments to be made relate to the tendency for governmentality as a process to be somewhat 'isolated'. It often seems to come over as a process without agency, contexts, conditions, or contradictions. In terms of the lack of agency, there is a rather common tendency in the governmentality literature for abstract nouns, rather than individual or collective agents, to be the subjects of sentences. Haahr provides one clear example: 'advanced liberal practices … contract, consult, negotiate, create partnerships, empower and activate forms of agency, liberty, and the choice of individuals in their different capacities' (2004: 20). This is not just a carping point (nor is it confined to governmentality theorists, as a perusal of a high proportion of papers on 'globalization' would confirm). It may be associated with a tendency to see technologies of power as all pervasive and universal in their effects and to focus on them at the expense of what, or who, is driving them. An illustrative contrast may be drawn with an article by Nancy Fraser on 'rereading Foucault' (Fraser 2003). Here the agents are clearly apparent; '*Henry Ford's* managers sought to rationalize … the family and community life of their workers' (p. 163); 'disciplinary apparatuses subsisted side-by-side in the space of the national-social, *their agents* cooperating and competing on a par' (p. 164, emphasis added). In each of these cases, the identification of agency enables us to understand more clearly the status and operation of the technologies. In the first case, the fact that it is 'Henry Ford's managers' that were seeking to rationalize workers' home lives surely carries a different significance from what would be implied by 'social security officials' or 'priests', while all of these carry quite different connotations from 'technologies of power'. In the second case, our understanding of the disciplinary apparatuses is surely enriched by the knowledge not just that they had agents, but that their agents might cooperate or compete, and that the outcome was consequently uncertain. In the case of the OMC, it would be helpful to know which national, international or subnational agents were associated with which technologies of power, and how and when they used them (because, as will be argued below, the 'same' technology – benchmarking, for instance – can have very different meanings in different contexts).

Contexts, too, seem to be 'flattened' in Haahr's account of the OMC. While, quite appropriately, he seeks to redress the balance currently tipped in favour of 'governance' approaches and assumptions through an emphasis on the *practices* of the OMC, in order to 'make explicit the thought that is largely tacit in the way we govern and are governed and in the languages, practices and techniques by which we do so' (forthcoming: 21), his emphasis is on making explicit the tacit features of the *technologies*, at the expense of making explicit the tacit features of the other half of the governmentality hybrid, *political rationalities*. Here, it seems essential to an understanding of the OMC, even conceived of as a set of technologies, to ask what limits, if any, on possible technologies are contained within the dominant political rationality. This would involve taking into account the dominance of the competitiveness discourse, and of supply-side social policy, for instance, as reflected in Scharpf's comment quoted above on the intrinsic limits to the OMC.

Finally, the OMC is implicitly regarded as a straightforward process in Haahr's account. Certainly, there is little evidence of any of the kinds of contradiction pointed to by Radaelli (2003: 8), who specifies 'endemic tensions' between cooperation and imitation on the one hand, and diversity and competition on the other, and between the pursuit of competitiveness and the development of a European social model, or by Wincott (2003) between the substantive agenda for welfare and the logic of the European regulatory order.

The outcome of all these silences is an essentially apolitical account of what is very clearly a political initiative, and a depoliticized account of a set of processes and practices that are clearly pregnant with political tensions, within and between states, sectors and scales of government.

Questions of scale

Haahr also has relatively little to say about issues of scale. While he very effectively identifies the ways that the OMC might construct the idea of Europe as a community of destiny, it is not clear exactly what is the significance of government taking place at different scales. Indeed, it seems that this is not merely an omission, for he is quite clear that 'regardless of whether the situation is one of the active involvement of citizens in community development or the engagement of ministerial bureaucracies or 'social partners' from different states in common processes of deliberation, the technologies employed share certain characteristics' (2004: 12). This may be accurate at a literal level, but it surely misses significant differences between the two scales. The implicitly national focus of much governmentality work has been noted before (for example, Hindess 2000; Fraser 2003), and it seems to emerge here in the form of an equation for all relevant purposes of the regional and national levels. Nancy Fraser's commentary makes conceptualizing the transnational character of contemporary governmentality a high priority, arguing that it is not just a matter of displacement from the national state, but that 'the locus of governmentality is being unbundled, broken up into several distinct functions, and assigned to several distinct agencies which operate at several distinct levels, some global, some regional, some local and subnational' (2003: 167).[3] It is important to note, too, the point made by Fritz Scharpf, that:

> the responsibility for those policy choices [made under the OMC] that cannot or should not be made directly by the 'political' institutions of the Union (Council and Parliament) would be left to Member States where they would become the responsibility of politically accountable national and subnational governments. These policy choices, however, would not be those of sovereign, 'Westphalian' nation states. They would be taken in an institutional setting in which 'common concerns' are integrated into the preference function of national and subnational actors, and in which the effectiveness of nationally divergent solutions needs to be demonstrated in comparative analyses under conditions of peer review.
>
> (Scharpf 2001)

This offers a somewhat more nuanced account than is made available in Haahr's paper, and one that could increase and extend its existing richness and value without doing any violence to the existing body of concepts.

Questions of mechanisms

Finally, I want to consider the mechanisms through which the OMC operates. It is useful to do this because the nature and consequences of the mechanisms used are a major point of difference between the governance (in the form often deployed in analyses of the OMC) and governmentality approaches. For the former, the issue is largely whether the OMC, being both voluntary and non-enforceable, can ever be effective as a method of EU governance. For the latter, the EU's use of the OMC provides an interesting opportunity to examine how mechanisms previously taken as national operate as means of pluri-scalar government. I will consider here two major mechanisms called on in the OMC: learning and benchmarking. I shall suggest that in neither approach is the nature and operation of the mechanism always articulated in sufficient detail to enable adequate analyses to be made.

Benchmarking

The example of benchmarks is useful, both because of their ubiquity within the OMC and because their application appears frequently to be taken somewhat unproblematically. However, benchmarking is neither a single nor a simple technology. Benchmarks can be used – and have been used – in distinctly different ways. For instance, Sissons *et al.* distinguish:

> performance benchmarking, which involves quantitative comparisons of input and/or output measures; process benchmarking, applied to the efficiency and quality standards of business processes and activities; and strategic benchmarking, which involves comparing the driving forces behind successful organizations.
>
> (2002: 2)

However, they go on to argue that because of the technical and practical difficulties of benchmarking, including defining 'best practice', 'performance benchmarking rarely becomes process benchmarking, let alone strategic benchmarking. Instead of being about learning and continuous improvement ... benchmarking tends to be concerned exclusively with quantitative measures' (p. 16); and far from encouraging learning, this may lead to ' "catch up benchmarking", [which] can put a stop to serious analysis of problems and/or experimentation with their solutions' (p. 16).

From a different angle, Colin Scott has suggested that benchmarks can be used to enhance quality and performance (the original sense in which the concept was used in industry), or applied to adherence to policies as opposed to operational standards (which he suggest is how benchmarking has been used in some domains of EU governance), where:

> the target of the intervention is to align policies rather than performance *per se*. In this manner (benchmarking) is likely to come to resemble the OMC ...

in the sense that it is likely to have to address divergence not only or mainly of performance, but rather divergence in policy views.

(Scott 2002: 72–73)

This is a very significant element of flexibility. It means, for instance, that *performance* benchmarks (or 'good practice') could be used internationally to lay down proscriptive/exclusive limits within which member states may operate, and *benchmarks as policy tools* could be used to align member states' policy supranationally.

These two examples show the complexity of benchmarking and the significance of the different meanings attached to it. And yet there is not a great deal of evidence that this is recognized in either approach. For the governance approach, the value of benchmarking might be limited to quantitative assessment of member states' progress towards targets. In terms of governmentality, the (different) kinds of distinction made by Sissons *et al.* and Scott seem rarely to be taken up, possibly because mechanisms often appear to be consistent in their effects, irrespective of the level of, for instance, self-government that is involved.

However, the importance of the distinctions is theoretical as well as pragmatic. It is not merely a matter of the difficulties of using different kinds of benchmark, or of different purposes for them, as might be assumed from a governance perspective, nor, from the governmentality approach, of the limits to which they are self-explanatory. Rather, we might identify a non-recognition of their status as mechanisms. The point I want to make here draws on an argument developed by Ray Pawson (2002) as a means of refining understanding of the effects of social intervention programmes. Briefly Pawson's argument is that in attempting to find a basis for the generalization of successful (or rejection of unsuccessful) social interventions and innovations, such as anti-crime initiatives, it is crucial to distinguish between what he calls the 'Programme' and the 'Programme Ontology'. Basically, the Programme is the intervention, or policy, or innovation that is being introduced or implemented with a view to bringing about beneficial changes in some social phenomenon. The 'Programme Ontology', by contrast, accounts for *how* programmes, policies, etc., actually work. It is essentially the 'theory' of the programme as opposed to its content (and 'the theory' is typically quite likely to be implicit). As Pawson puts it: 'It is not "programmes" that work; rather it is the underlying reasons or resources that they offer subjects that generate change' (2002: 343). The point, I hope, is clear – that failure to distinguish between benchmarks as programmes and programme ontologies, increases the difficulty both of accounting for their success or failure, and of specifying their effects on self-government.

Learning as a mechanism

'Learning' has been a major focus of analyses of the OMC. Indeed, Paul Teague has argued that:

Europe learning from Europe could be the new motif of EU social policy. Benchmarking is the main policy tool behind such learning activities, an approach that holds out much promise ... as a policy mechanism it is virtually tailor-made for EU social policy with the heavy emphasis on obtaining policy convergence in the context of institutional diversity'.

(Teague 2001: 23)

The problem is that 'learning' in this context is an innocently potent term – as may be inferred from Teague's association of learning and benchmarking.

One feature of much of the governance literature is that it views 'learning' almost exclusively as *cognitive* learning. So, for instance, Radaelli (2003), in the course of the development of the list set out above (p. 4) (in all but the first of which 'learning' is a key element), points out that there is some debate about whether the learning stimulated by the OMC is 'top-down' or 'bottom up'. The former sees learning as deriving from following European-level guidelines; the latter sense includes the OMC acting as a radar that searches for solutions, and as a diffuser of 'knowledge that creates the condition for bottom up learning' (p. 8), as well as being based on mechanisms such as benchmarking that may be seen to be intrinsically linked to learning. The key point is that all these examples are essentially examples of *cognitive* learning. The importance of this is captured by Frank Vandenbroucke, who argues that:

The open method of coordination is both a cognitive and a normative tool. It is a 'cognitive' tool because it enables us to learn from each other ... (it) is a normative tool because, necessarily, common objectives embody substantive views on social justice.

(Vandenbroucke 2002: 9)

The restriction of learning to the cognitive domain is implicit in most discussions of its place in the OMC, but it is the element above all that restricts its value in analysing the method, because it contains a strong tendency to tie it to the achievement of particular ends. To a degree, it assumes/implies an exchange among and between equals, and that all those involved share similar aims, targets and objectives. Indeed, the construal of 'learning' as an element of rational problem-solving, following the logic of rationality rather than the logic of appropriateness, is where we see the distinction between the governance and other perspectives on the OMC most clearly. (A similar point is very well developed by Radaelli (2000), in the context of a discussion of 'policy transfer' within the EU, but it is interesting that he does not extend its logic to his (2003) discussion of learning in the OMC, referred to above).

The alternative 'logic of appropriateness' approach is based on that developed in institutional theory, particularly by DiMaggio and Powell (1983) (see also Radaelli 2000; Dale 2003b). The central issue for DiMaggio and Powell is explaining what they call organizational isomorphism, by which they mean a process that leads organizations to adapt in similar ways to similar changes in external conditions. In essence, the approach assumes and seeks to explain convergence of organizational practices, and three distinct mechanisms are introduced through which this process may come about. These they call 'mimetic', 'normative' and 'coercive'. The basis of the typology here is the reason, or motivation, for the similarity or convergence. Very briefly, in the first case, mimetic isomorphism results from organizations responding to conditions of uncertainty about what is proper or appropriate practice in a particular situation by imitating, or copying, what is identified as successful practice. In the second case, normative isomorphism is brought about by adherence to common educational or professional socialization experiences and/or membership of professional networks and/or, for instance, being attached to particular epistemic communities. In this case, the learned norms provide guidance on how to act in new situations. And isomorphism through the 'coercive' mechanism occurs in response to external constraints or pressures such as may be required by state regulation. The key factor linking these three mechanisms is that they are all forms of *legitimation* of practice, in the first case through imitating acknowledged successful practice, in the second through appeal to the norms of an epistemic community, and in the third by following what is demanded. The distinction here is between learning as promoting *efficiency* through the identification and adoption of best practice, for instance (and as Radaelli (2000: 25) points out, where there are no examples of best practice in member states, this opens up the possibility of the Commission supplying them, thus 'inseminating' solutions into national political practices), and learning as finding means of *legitimation*.

This formulation: (1) seems to offer rather more purchase than a simple top-down/bottom-up learning distinction; (2) indicates a way of moving beyond seeing all 'learning' as cognitive; and (3) might be profitably applied to distinguishing the different types of learning that have been discussed in the context of the OMC (it does not, of course, exhaust them; for instance, it would be very valuable to examine in greater depth ideas of 'interactive learning', and their use in 'learning organizations'). It also, and most importantly in this context, provides another angle on the question of mechanisms; what mechanism(s) of isomorphism are followed in benchmarking, for instance, or peer pressure?

Conclusion

I want to make three brief points in conclusion. First, my central concern has been to provide a critical account of the possible contribution of a governmentality approach to the understanding of the OMC. I have taken Jens Henrik Haahr's paper as the basis for this account, and conclude that it does make a significant contribution, and moreover one that is different in its assumptions, procedures, purposes and implications from the 'orthodox' approach to the OMC in the literature, which I refer to as the governance approach. In particular, it makes clear that the 'rational' approach to the meaning of the OMC is not by any means comprehensive or enlightening in its understanding of the relationship between the OMC and Europeanization. Haahr's emphasis on the significance of the OMC opens up valuable new possibilities for understanding the processes of Europeanization, as well as deepening the analysis of the OMC itself.

Second, I have suggested that the main problems I find with Haahr's analysis are not confined to his article but are widely recognized in discussions of governmentality. I discussed three problems in particular. The first was the absence of agency and a very narrow conception of context, which together are associated with a depoliticized account of the nature and implications of the OMC. The second was the way that the issue of scale was handled, which seemed to transpose the typical national focus of governmentality studies to the regional level, rather than to investigate what might be involved in the differences in scale. The third was the lack of articulation of how mechanisms of governmentality work, how they bring about their effects and in what circumstances. Thus, while the point is very much taken that the purpose of governmentality approaches is to 'make explicit the thought that is largely tacit in the way we govern and are governed' (Haahr 2004: 6) rather than to directly attribute agency to those forms, it is also the case that 'the thought that is largely tacit' is itself the outcome of continuing struggle among differently located agents, including across the spheres of agency, scale and mechanism.

Third, I have tried to argue that far from being zero-sum alternatives, 'governmentality' and 'governance' are both crucial elements of any form of government (though not if we restrict governance to the 'rational' form in which it has often been deployed in studies of the OMC; as I argued above, governance is better seen as the coordination of coordination, a formulation in which there is no necessary contradiction between governance and governmentality). I have suggested that both are always present, albeit often taken for granted or obscured. And I would like to suggest further that considerable progress might be made through considering the metatheoretical and theoretical conditions under which the objects of focus of the two approaches might combine in particular circumstances – and that the OMC might be a useful topic of study in the first instance.

Notes

1 I refer to 'a' governance discourse deliberately, since there are many different understandings of the term in the literature. While in discussing the literature on the OMC I shall confine my comments to discussions of it that centre around its capacity and potentiality to provide 'new', or 'effective' means of governance in that context, I do not see these as the only, or theoretically most useful ways of approaching the concept (Dale 1997, 2003a, 2003b).
2 One way we might see this is in the conceptions of 'bureaucracy's other face' or of 'street-level bureaucrats'; both represent technologies of power exercised alongside, possibly in the interstices of, sovereignty and discipline.

3   On the concept of the functional and scalar division of education governance, see
Dale (2003a).

References

Dale, R. (1997) 'The state and the governance of education: an analysis of the restructuring of the state-education relationship', in A.H. Halsey, H. Lauder, P. Brown and
A.S. Wells (eds) *Education: culture, economy and society*, Oxford: Oxford University Press.
——(2003a) 'The Lisbon Declaration, the reconceptualisation of governance and the
reconfiguration of European educational space', paper presented to RAPPE
seminar, Governance, Regulation and Equity in European Education Systems, Institute of Education, London University, 20, March 2003.
——(2003b) 'Globalisation and the rescaling of educational governance: a case of
"sociological ectopia"', Keynote Address to International Sociological Association
meeting, Lisbon, September 18–20, 2003.
de la Porte, C. (2002) 'Is the open method of coordination appropriate for organising
activities at European level in sensitive policy areas?', *European Law Journal*, 8(1):
38–58.
de la Porte, C. and Pochet, P. (2002) *Building Social Europe through the Open Method of Coordination*, Brussels: P I E/ Peter Lang.
DiMaggio, P.J. and Powell, W.W. (1983) 'The iron cage revisited: institutional isomorphism and collective rationality in organizational fields', *American Sociological Review*,
48(2): 147–160.
Esping-Andersen, G., Duncan, G., Hemerijk, A. and Myles, J. (2002) *Why We Need a
New Welfare State*, Oxford: Oxford University Press.
European Council (2000) Conclusions of the European Presidency Council in Lisbon,
March 23–24, 2000.
Ferrara, M., Matsagainis, M. and Sacchi, S. (2002) 'Open coordination against poverty:
the new EU "social inclusion process"', *Journal of European Social Policy*, 12(3):
227–239.
Foucault, M. (1991) 'Questions of method', in G. Burchell, C. Gordon and P. Miller
(eds) *The Foucault Effect: studies in governmentality*, Hemel Hempstead: Harvester.
Fraser, N. (2003) 'From discipline to flexibilization? Rereading Foucault in the shadow
of globalization',*Constellations* 10(2): 160–71.
Haahr, Jens Henrik (2004) 'Open coordination as advanced liberal government',
Special Issue on OMC, *Journal of European Public Policy*, 11(2).
Hindess, B. (2000) 'Divide and govern', in R. Ericson and N. Stehr (eds) *Governing
Modern Societies*, Toronto: University of Toronto Press.
Hodson, D. and Maher, I. (2002) 'The open method of coordination as a new method
of governance: the case of soft EU policy coordination', *Journal of Common Market
Studies*, 39(4): 719–746
Jacobsson, K. (2001) 'Employment and social policy coordination. A new system of EU
governance', paper presented at Scancor workshop on 'Transnational regulation and
the transformation of states', Stanford, June 22–23, 2001.
——(2003) 'Soft regulation and the subtle transformation of states; the case of EU
employment policy', paper presented at seminar on the OMC, Center for European
Studies, Harvard, 28, April 2003.
Jenson J. and Pochet, P. (2002) 'Employment and social policy since Maastricht:
standing up to the European monetary union', paper prepared for The Year of the

Euro, Nanovic Institute for European Studies, University of Notre Dame, 5–8, December.

Jessop, B. (2003) 'The future of the state in an era of globalisation', *Internationale Politik und Gesellschaft/International Politics and Society*, 3: 30–46.

Larsson, Alan (2002) 'The new Open Method of Coordination – a sustainable way between a fragmented Europe and a European supra state? A practitioner's view', lecture delivered at Uppsala University, 4 March. Downloaded 22, July 2003.

Lemke, T. (2001) "The birth of bio-politics": Michel Foucault's lecture at the Collège de France on neo-liberal governmentality', *Economy and Society*, 30(2): 190–207.

——(2003a) 'Comment on Nancy Fraser: rereading Foucault in the shadow of Globalization', *Constellations* 10(2): 173–179.

——(2003b) 'Foucault, governmentality, and critique', *Re-Thinking Marxism*, 14(3): 49–64.

Pawson, R. (2002) 'Evidence-based policy: the promise of "realist synthesis"', *Evaluation*, 8(3): 340–358.

Pochet, P. (2002) 'From subsidiarity to the open method of coordination in social policy issues'. Online. Available at:
http://www.uni-bamberg.de/sowi/europastudien/dokumente/pochet.doc (accessed 9, December 2002).

Power, M. (1997) *The Audit Society: rituals of verification*, Oxford: Oxford University Press.

Radaelli, C. (2000) 'Policy transfer in the European Union: institutional isomorphisms as a source of legitimacy', *Governance*, 13(1): 25–43.

——(2003) 'The open method of coordination: a new governance architecture for the European Union Research Report', Swedish Institute for European Policy Studies.

Rhodes, M. (2000) 'Lisbon: Europe's Maastrict for welfare?', *ECSA Review*, 13(30): 2–7.

Rodrigues, M.J. (ed.) (2002) *The New Knowledge Economy in Europe: a strategy for international competitiveness and social cohesion*, Aldershot: Elgar.

Rosamund, B. (2002) 'Imagining the European economy: "competitiveness" and the social construction of "Europe" as an economic space', *New Political Economy*, 7(2): 157–177.

Rumford, C. (2003) 'Rethinking the state and polity-building in the European Union: the sociology of globalization and the rise of reflexive government'. European Political Communication Working Paper Series, Issue 4/03, Centre for European Political Communications.

Scharpf, F.W. (2001) 'European governance: common concerns vs. the challenge of diversity', MPIfG Working Paper 01/6, September, 2001.

——(2002) 'The European social model: coping with the challenges of diversity', *Journal of Common Market Studies*, 40(4): 645–665.

Scott, C. (2002) 'The governance of the European Union: the potential for multi-level control', *European Law Journal*, 8(1): 59–79.

Sisson, K., Arrowsmtih, J. and Marginson, P. (2002) 'All benchmarkers now? Benchmarking and the "Europeanisation" of industrial relations'. Working Paper 41/02, 'One Europe or Several?' Progamme Brighton: University of Sussex.

Teague, P. (2001) 'Deliberative governance and EU social policy', *European Journal of Industrial Relations*, 7(1): 7–26.

Trubek, D. and Mosher, J. (2003) 'New governance, EU social policy, and the European social model', in J. Zeitlin and D. Trubek (eds) *Governing Work and Welfare in a New Economy: European and American experiments*, New York: Oxford University Press.

Vandenbroucke, F. (2002) 'The EU and social protection: what should the European Convention propose?', paper presented at the Max Planck Institute for the Study of Societies, Cologne, 17, June 2002.

Wincott, D. (2003) 'Beyond social regulation? Social policy at Lisbon: new instruments or a new agenda?' *Public Administration*, 81(3): 533–554.

Zeitlin, J. (2002) 'Opening the open method of coordination', presentation prepared for the Committee of the Regions Conference on 'The Open Method of Coordination: Improving European Governance?', Brussels, 30 September–1 October.

10 Ethical capitalism

Andrew Barry

The world of global business is marked by a remarkable and growing concern with ethics. This is an era when notions of corporate social responsibility, ethical audit, ethical consumption, and environmental sustainability have become commonplace. Global corporations are now expected to be ethical and expect themselves to be ethical. Moreover, many go to great lengths to make their ethical concerns public and open to a limited degree of scrutiny. Ethical behaviour is promoted through ethical brands, and inspected through ethical audit. At the same time, corporations are frequently criticized because the effects of their activities on the environment, their involvement in corruption, the greed of their executives, and their lack of concern with human rights. Both corporations and their critics frequently adopt the language of ethics.

What are we to make of the extraordinary growth of ethical concern on the part of business? Is it the latest phase in the development of marketing, intended to extract profit from the contemporary preoccupation with the politics of lifestyle? Is this discourse simply a way of muffling the counter-discourse of the critics of contemporary business? Should we be cynical about the degree of interest that business now appears to be showing in ethics? Do notions such as business ethics and corporate social responsibility simply obscure the harsh reality of contemporary capitalism, and should they not detain us before we move on to examine capitalism's deeper structural dynamics?

In this chapter, however, I suggest that we should treat the contemporary corporate concern with ethics seriously, and that there is value in analysing the ethicalization of business in terms of some of the conceptual tools associated with the analysis of governmentality. Such an approach has four general implications for the analysis of what I shall term ethical capitalism. First, it means that we understand corporate ethics not as an abstract set of ethical principles, but as a practical and heterogeneous set of techniques directed towards a specific set of issues. How do corporations become ethical? What methods do they use? Can a corporation embody ethics, or do corporations derive ethical resources from bodies that are exterior to the business? What problems and issues are made visible as ethical and what are not? Viewing corporate ethics in terms of governmentality means that we bracket the question of whether this form of ethics measures up to the standards of the moral philosophy, and focus instead on what it does.

Second, viewing ethics in the context of an analysis of governmentality means interrogating the relations between ethics and the forms of knowledge that are associated with it. What kinds of knowledge show that a corporation is ethical, or demonstrate that it is unethical? Rather than a concern with the ideological character of corporate 'ethics' in general, such an approach focuses attention on the way that the contemporary concern with ethics entails the generation of empirical knowledge about ethical behaviour. The contemporary concern with corporate ethics has little to do with moral philosophy and a lot to do, as Tom Osborne has argued, with the visibility of ethical conduct (Osborne 2003).

Third, the notion of governmentality directs attention to the variable practice of non-state actors, including experts, non-governmental organizations (NGOs), businesses and citizens in the conduct of international government. However, such a perspective does not ignore the continuing importance of the nation state (Hirst and Thompson 1999). However, it recognizes that citizens, businesses, professionals and others all engage in forms of governmental activity, both in relation to themselves and others. Although, as we shall see, international organizations such as the World Bank have played a role in establishing a global benchmark against which ethical decisions might be taken, it would be a mistake to view the contemporary ethicalization of business as directed primarily by international institutions.

Finally, the notion of 'ethical capitalism' implies nothing about capitalism as a system in general. It does not imply that capitalism is necessarily more moral than it was in the past. Rather, I use the notion to refer to a cluster of techniques that have been developed to make the ethical or unethical conduct of businesses *explicit*. Ethical capitalism refers not to a system, or a stage in the evolution of system, but to a set of ways of acting on the conduct of business activity.[1] Moreover, ethical capitalism does not imply an achieved result, but rather points to a process of ethicalization. It is the form of this process that is new. Ethical problems have generally been reckoned to be external to the market. The potential ethical dilemmas business corporations might have to confront have been traditionally resolved elsewhere (by the political system) and have been then translated into the form of legal regulations and taxation that impact on the conduct of business. Ethical concerns have informed the frame within which businesses have operated, but they are not reckoned to be the explicit concern of business.[2] Increasingly, however, ethical concerns are directly addressed by business. Corporations are expected explicitly to address ethical issues themselves and not to anticipate that they will first be translated by the political system into a purely economic or legal form. Corporations have become entangled in ethical concerns.

Studies of governmentality have tended to take an historical approach, tracing the broad path of development of rationalities and technologies of government over time. In examining the ethicalization of global business, however, I focus on a specific case. The case study concerns a particular multinational – British Petroleum (BP) – which has positioned itself at the cutting edge

of the wider movement towards higher standards of business ethics and corporate social responsibility.[3] BP prides itself on its ethics, its capacity to act
ethically, and its role in fostering ethical practice. The chapter focuses also on a
particular BP project, a major oil pipeline that is planned to run from Baku in
Azerbaijan   to   Ceyhan   on   the   Turkish   Mediterranean   coast: the
Baku–Tbilisi–Ceyhan (BTC) pipeline. In examining a case study, I say little about
the history of the ethicalization of business,[4] and instead focus on specific issues
(such as environmental and human rights impacts) and ignore others (such as
corporate governance). However, a case-study approach has the advantage in
that it makes it possible to analyse the relation, which is often ignored in studies
of governmentality, between government, political action and political events.[5]

Business, ethics and government

In his book *Professional Ethics and Civic Morals* Émile Durkheim doubted that business was a good place to find ethics. If one looked at business, he noted:

> there is nowhere any organ with the duty of seeing that they [ethical princi-
> ples] are enforced. They have no sanctions other than those which a
> diffused public opinion has at hand, and since that opinion is not kept lively
> by frequent contact between individuals and since it therefore cannot exer-
> cise control over individual actions, it is lacking in both stability and
> authority.
>
> (Durkheim 1957: 10)

Durkheim's interest in the location of ethics in social institutions was a governmental one. He was alert to what he saw as a moral crisis in European societies,
and sought to find institutions and practices that could foster an appropriate
level of direction to moral activity. While business provided limited resources for
the solution to this crisis, the state had conversely an important role: 'the fundamental duty of the State is laid down in this very fact: it is to persevere in
calling the individual to a moral way of life' (1957: 69). In the twentieth century
institutions such as public broadcasting and museums and the education system
have played a key governmental function, both in fostering the development of
a responsible and ethical public and in promoting a vision of national identity
(for example, Donald 1992; Bennett 1995). They acted, to use Deleuze's term,
as ethical assemblages (*agencements*): spaces within which ethical forms of action
might be produced (Deleuze 1988).

But what of the location of ethics in the era of globalization? Does business,
an institution of which Durkheim once seemed so sceptical, possess the ethical
resources that it previously did not? Can business supplement – or even displace
– the governmental role of the state beyond the boundaries of the nation state?
And, if so, how? In the context of globalization, is the weakness of business
ethics a problem? Or is business part of the solution to the problem that the
capacity of the state to act is limited by the existence of national territorial

boundaries? What organs, to use Durkheim's terms, have a duty to enforce ethical principles on business at a global level?

In answering these questions three problems arise. First, there is the problem of the constitution of a corporation as an ethical assemblage. How does a corporation, such as BP, come to be a place where ethical action is generated and sustained? How does it come to be that the projects associated with the name of BP come to be in some way ethical? The general problem of ethics and business takes a particular form within the context of the project of globalization.[6] For in relation to globalization, the ethical values which business is expected to embody and extol are reckoned to be global values. These include, in particular, international commitments to environmental sustainability and a respect for human rights.[7] In these circumstances, the problem is whether the aspiration by many to foster such global values can or cannot be embodied in business. Through what practices and procedures can global values actually become operationalized in the world of global business? Through what network of institutions and organizations can ethical principles be realized?

The second problem is the problem of demonstration. How is it possible for a firm, a government, or a political movement to *demonstrate* that an action or project is or is not ethical?[8] How is it possible to show that certain ethical practices (such as public consultation and fair compensation) are carried out and others (corruption and human rights abuse) are not? What forms of knowledge and practice are required to demonstrate the existence or lack of existence of such practices? On what basis, do certain actors claim to be able to demonstrate facts about such ethical matters while others are unable to do so?[9] In the context of the project of globalization it is particularly difficult to solve these problems. Governments, firms and NGOs all have the task of demonstrating the existence (or absence) of ethical action outside the territorial boundaries of the nation state.[10] How is it possible to demonstrate the performance of ethical or unethical actions at a distance?[11]

The focus in this chapter on visibility, knowledge and demonstration can be contrasted with the work of those writers who stress the role of 'global civil society' in contemporary global politics (for example, Lipschutz and Mayer 1996; Scholte 2000; Anheier *et al.* 2001; Keane 2003). Of the writers on global civil society, Ronnie D. Lipschutz, in particular, has sought to make a connection between the notion of global civil society and global governmentality. According to Lipschutz, global civil society has to be understood as an 'element in an expanding liberal regime of power, expressed through particular forms of global governmentality, which helps to legitimize that which would otherwise be legitimate' (Lipschutz 2003: 1–2). In his analysis, Foucault's conception of governmentality offers a way of understanding how political action is constrained within a global market society and limited in its effects. There is according to Lipschutz:

> [a framework] of discursive power which, ultimately, organizes and maintains the structures of governmentalities, agencies, institutions, and practices. The

power of the market lies in the invisibility of its power, which normalizes behaviour within market society and marginalizes behaviour outside of its confines.

The difference between the approach developed here and that of Lipschutz corresponds to two different ways of reading Foucault. For Lipschutz, Foucault provides a set of categories that can be assimilated into a general account of global society. Lipschutz assumes the view of classical social theory that 'society' can be grasped from a privileged external vantage point (cf. Haraway 1997; Barry 1998; Latour 2003). In his particular account of global society, the notion of global governmentality is used to indicate the existence of a network such as a political system within which the possibilities for collective political action are restricted.

Foucault's writings on governmentality suggest, however, a different reading. In this account, the notion of governmentality is not an element of a general social theory at all. Instead it points, amongst other things, to the multiplicity of ways in which social science and political thought have rendered social and political forms visible to others (Foucault 1989; Barry *et al.* 1996). Rather than imagine that sociology has the key to understanding what society is, this interpretation indicates the need to examine how actors themselves, including social scientists, construct specific social forms.[12] And rather than viewing the activities of NGOs and other actors merely as an expression of something else ('global civil society', 'global social movements' or 'global governmentality'), such an approach implies the need to focus on the practices through which objects and issues are rendered visible. This reading of Foucault is a constructivist one, but not in the sense that the intention is to show that particular objects and issues (such as the ethical conduct of particular firms) are merely 'social constructions' (Hacking 1999). On the contrary, the notion of construction should be understood in a positive sense to refer to the ways in which social objects are assembled.

The third problem is the problem of political events. One of the undoubted weaknesses of many early studies of governmentality was the lack of concern with political conflict and negotiation. Studies emphasized the specificity of particular forms of governmental thought and practice, but not the political events with which they were associated (cf. Barry *et al.* 1995). The effect, unintended or not, was to imply the existence of an opposition between the more-or-less routine exercise of forms of rule and the more or less unroutinized emergence of resistance. Yet, it is precisely in conjunction with specific political conflicts, scandals, accidents and other events that new forms of governmental practice often develop. Studies of governmentality should not ignore the study of political events but recognize their critical role in changing the direction of the history of government.[13] Here I stress how the concern with corporate ethics has to be seen, part, in its relation to political events.

The ethical assemblage

Philosophical accounts of ethics raise the question of how one moves between abstract and general ethical principles and concrete particulars. Often this is posed as a problem of where it is possible to locate or *embody* ethical principles. Some contemporary moral philosophers want to embody ethical principles in the capacities of particular ethical individuals – such as doctors, scientists and judges.[14] Such individuals can be trusted to act – to use their freedom – ethically. In this way, the notion of ethics becomes connected to *freedom* and *trust* – only those individuals who are free need to be trusted to act ethically. And only those who can be trusted to act ethically can be fully free. Furthermore there is generally an unequal distribution of trust, and the presumption that ethical conduct is possible. Only certain categories of persons are generally reckoned to be capable of acting ethically in certain situations. One sociological account of ethics is to describe the relation between the unequal distribution of ethical responsibility and the unequal distribution of social power. Bourdieu's *Pascalian Meditations* provides a scathing critique of the way in which moral philosophy articulates 'disinterested' and universal ethical principles which can only be realized fully in very specific elite and autonomous institutions (Bourdieu 2000). Although there is much to be said for this account of the interest of expressions of disinterestedness, it says little about the existence of more practical forms of ethics. In the context of a study of governmentality, ethical forms of conduct might be better understood as a practical matter. Rather than examine ethics as an abstract set of principles, such an approach would focus on the specificity of the discursive and non-discursive assemblages that are expected to generate ethical forms of conduct.[15] In a court, for example, the jury – a representative sample of citizens who are expected to make disinterested judgements – are restrained from the dangers of corruption or external influence. Their ethical capacity to judge a crime on the basis of the evidence that is presented before them depends on the spatial and procedural organization of the court. Although the law assumes that all citizens have, in principle, the capacity to make disinterested judgements, this capacity is not intrinsic to the citizen but is an effect of the ethical assemblage of which he or she comes to play apart. A similar account could be given of institutions such as hospitals where particular forms of ethical action are expected and inculcated. Doctors are expected to act ethically, but their capacity do so is (increasingly) thought to depend on the existence of an institutional and procedural environment within which they will act.[16] But if institutions such as hospitals are intended to operate as ethical assemblages, then what of businesses? How can businesses possibly provide an environment for ethical forms of action?

In the case of BP – as with other companies – ethics is both an internal and an external matter. Externally, ethical concerns (with the environment, corruption and human rights, and with the effects of the development of the oil industry on local communities) are a central feature of the BP brand.[17] Activists and commentators date the rebranding of the oil industry – and, in particular, Royal Dutch Shell and BP – to a specific political event: Brent Spar. In the case of Brent Spar, Shell suffered extensive public criticism as a result of a campaign by Greenpeace against the dumping of an oil rig (the Brent Spar) in the North Sea, despite what the company (and prevailing scientific opinion) believed to be a sound analysis of the environmental impact of its intended action.[18] According to the scientific journal *Nature*, 'Shell Oil's decision not to sink an oil rig is a needless dereliction of rationality' (in Huxham and Sumner 1999: 350). Nonetheless, following Brent Spar, Shell and BP both made green concerns central to their brand identity, performing what environmentalists came to call 'greenwash'. The Chief Executive of BP, Lord Browne, is said to have played a leading role in rebranding BP as a 'green' ethical company with a new logo and a new identity ('Beyond Petroleum') and an advertising campaign that placed stress on the company's support for renewable energy sources. At one level, the ethical rebranding of the oil industry was intended to have anti-political effects, reducing the destabilizing effect of events such as Brent Spar.[19] A concern with ethics was not a turn away from politics. On the contrary, ethical concerns emerged in the middle of political events, and as a way of dealing with them. In this way, 'ethics' became central to the interface between the world of BP and other companies and a global public political realm, which itself was being fostered by the actions of NGOs such as Greenpeace.[20]

But if the brand is central to the ethical assemblage of BP, Shell and other companies, ethics is not just a matter of external image. An explicit concern with ethics emerges at the same time as a broader concern with the importance of brands in business in the context of globalization (Franklin *et al.* 2000), but it also is coincident with the growth of audit (Owen and Swift 2001; Power 1997). Increasingly, public accounts of ethical conduct and corporate social responsibility are demanded by governments and shareholders, and these demands are anticipated by companies themselves.[21] In its public presentation of itself the company ties these two trends together:

> Each year, all employees in positions of responsibility are asked to person- ally attest that the teams have complied with our ethical conduct policy. In all cases, action plans are put in place ... and unethical behaviour is not tolerated ... unfortunately, breakdowns of our policy do occur. These may be recognized and raised by those concerned; issues could be identified following routine audit activity.[22]

According to BP, forms of unethical conduct revealed through such procedures consist mainly of minor examples of corruption and conflicts of interest in the award of subcontracts. Along with the company's internal controls, ethical conduct is formally audited. BP's auditors, Ernst and Young, provide a public assurance of the implementation of the ethical policy. Furthermore, the company is audited not just by Ernst and Young but also encourages interactivity with the public itself. Visitors to the BP web-site are encouraged to answer a specific ques- tion: 'Do you think we take our environmental and social responsibilities seriously?'

How then does a company such as BP seek to become an ethical assemblage? Certainly, topics such as business ethics and corporate social responsibility figure increasingly in the curricula of management schools and internal company training programmes. Contemporary capitalism is characterized by a remarkable growth in 'soft' forms of business knowledge in topics such as human resources, leadership, branding and business ethics.[23] Yet it would be wrong to imagine that individual members of the company are expected to be ethical merely on account of their professional training. Rather, individuals in the company act ethically in so far as their ethical behaviour is also monitored, disciplined and made visible. Ethical conduct is reckoned to be *internal* to the company, but this depends on the possibility of making this ethical (or unethical) conduct *external* (Strathern 2002). The external image (the brand) of the company is not just an external image. Not only is it more or less perfectly internalized, but its internalization depends on the extent of its public display. Public display has internal effects. Internal control depends on the public performance of control. Corporate ethics is, above all, about observability (Osborne 2003).

Lacking the kinds of persons (such as GPs, judges, scientists, priests, and honest and disinterested citizens) who have been conventionally thought to embody ethics in their own persons, business has adopted two intersecting strategies.[24] One, as we have seen, is to make ethical (and unethical) conduct observable. The other, in conjunction with this, is to create explicit connections with sources of ethical authority – through, for example, establishing links with NGOs and by employing academics as consultants. As Richard Rogers and Noortje Marres have shown, the analysis of web-sites provides a good starting point for analysing the increasingly complex network relations between business, government, NGOs and academia. In part this is because the web itself has become a key space for political debate between multinational corporations and their critics. In part, also, because the web (with the use of windows and hyperlinks) provides a very clear display of the institutional network of relations which form part of the constitution of ethical assemblages. By contrast to the web-sites of other oil companies, the web-sites of 'ethical' oil companies such as Shell and BP include links to NGOs such as the World Wildlife Fund for Nature, Greenpeace and Friends of the Earth, for example (Rogers and Marres 2000; Rogers 2002).

Writers on governmentality, following Foucault, have long emphasized that the activity of government cannot be reduced to the actions of the state. In an era when direct state control and ownership has declined (because of privatization and re-regulation), or is difficult (because of the transnational organization of companies), international institutions, NGOs, auditors, consultants and multinational corporations are together expected to perform the job of government at a distance. Global governmentality has been associated with the dispersion of governmental functions amongst a network of international and non-state institutions. Within this network, clear distinctions between the identities and functions of different institutions may sometimes be difficult to make. Ethical principles are expected to be realized by government, by NGOs *and* by business together. Amnesty International business network, for example, aims to: 'make the human rights policies [of companies] explicit, ensuring that these are integrated across all functions, monitored and audited'.[25] More controversially, according to one senior BP executive, both NGOs and business should be viewed as simply part of the same 'human rights community': 'why imply that human rights organizations are somehow different in value terms or in terms of their ethical principles from business?' (Rice 2002: 134).

Durkheim was concerned that business was a poor place to find ethics. Certainly, it remains the case that few would trust a business manager solely on the basis of his or her professional qualifications as a manager or on the basis of a membership of a professional institution. But for those concerned with contemporary business ethics, this is not necessarily a problem. Business expects to become ethical by continually demonstrating, in conjunction with others, and to others, that it does act ethically.

Demonstration

The notion of ethical audit might suggest that constitution of a business as an ethical assemblage is something of a routine matter, or should become so. Yet what I have termed the ethicalization of business has been, in part, a response to specific political events and public criticism of specific actions and technologies. In the oil industry, Brent Spar and Exxon Valdez have had particular salience. In other industries, companies such as Nestlé, Nike, Starbucks, Monsanto, Barclays, McDonalds and others have been the object of public political protest in relation to specific actions and events.

In accounts of contemporary forms of political protest, theorists have rightly pointed to their 'disorganized' character. Individual protests against capitalist enterprise often occur without the existence of any common political ideology or unified organization to direct them. Indeed, their existence may rely on the capacity of a campaign or action to mobilize the energies of quite diverse concerns, identities and interests (Barry 2001; Lash 2002; Thoburn 2002). Yet, despite the disorganization of political opposition, and the multiciplicity of its forms and identities, it would be a mistake to draw a clear dividing line between the more or less routinized and bureaucratic procedures of ethical audit and inspection, and the more anarchic and spontaneous actions associated with contemporary forms of protest.

There are three reasons for this. First, many NGOs, such as Friends of the Earth, World Wildlife Fund for Nature and Amnesty International, occupy an ambiguous and shifting position in relation to the conduct of companies and more disorganized forms of political activism. They may both engage in negotiations with companies concerning their ethical conduct, *and* form loose alliances with less compromising and organized oppositional groups. There is no clear point at which government ends and resistance begins. Moreover, the identities and positions of established political institutions and NGOs may be as uncertain and multiple as those of less organized forms of protest.

Second, auditors, shareholders and campaigning groups may *all* frame their criticisms in broadly similar (ethical) terms. Many may accept, in public at least, that the conduct of a company can be assessed in relation to global ethical standards.[26] All may agree that companies should not be corrupt, should not be directly or indirectly responsible for abuses of human rights, and should accept the need for policies that support environmental sustainability.[27] Political disagreement does not occur over the question of whether it is acceptable to frame criticism of a company's actions in ethical terms or not, but rather concerning whether a company is or is not acting ethically. Is the visibility of a company's commitment to ethics merely part of its marketing strategy and/or an effective defence against possible public criticism? Or does it create a catalytic surface on which more or less radical forms of political opposition react, and have effects?

Third, there is no clear dividing line between the forms of 'technical' demonstration commissioned by companies and government to show whether particular actions are ethical or not, and the forms of 'political' demonstration associated with the actions of campaigners and protestors. On the one hand, there are significant similarities in the form of scientific and political demonstrations (Barry 2001, 2002). The notion of demonstration – in both science and politics – denotes an activity oriented towards pointing out or showing the existence of a problem, an object or an effect to a wider audience. As such, all demonstrations are forms of publicity, although both the audience and mechanisms of publicity may vary considerably. The success of a demonstration depends, in part, on whether it is *not* viewed by its audience as simply a manifestation of the political and economic interests of the demonstrators, or as an expression of a given political identity. In politics, as in science, the political effectiveness and significance of a demonstration may depend on the extent to which it is not reducible to politics. On the other hand, protestors and campaigners may try be as 'rigorous' in their research on the ethical conduct of companies as those commissioned to carry out formal evaluations of company conduct. Rather than assuming that the studies commissioned by companies and governments are more 'scientific' than those of NGOs or campaigners we must assume, as sociologists of scientific knowledge have long argued, that the scientificity and rigour of conflicting accounts is the outcome of a process of debate rather than the basis of an explanation of why one account is true and another is not (Latour 1987).

Some common concerns

Consider, for example, the conduct of a campaign to stop the construction of Baku–Tbilisi–Ceyhan. a pipeline which is planned to carry oil from the Caspian Sea in Azerbaijan to the Turkish Mediterranean coast.

At one level, the plan to construct the pipeline has been subject to a form of routine ethical inspection. BP, leading a consortium of companies, commissioned a social and environmental impact assessment of the pipeline development. This assessment was necessary because the consortium applied to a number of international financial institutions, including the World Bank and the European Bank for Reconstruction and Development, for financial support.[28] In 2000, the World Bank adopted guidelines for the financing of international development projects that recommended that such projects be assessed not only in terms of their environmental impact but also their social impacts and human rights implications.[29] In effect, global (World Bank) benchmarks inform the development of specific procedures, widely adopted by other international financial institutions, from which ethical outcomes are the expected result. The procedures envisaged are intended to make both the facts and (global) norms of ethical conduct visible and measurable.

A key document of the campaign against the pipeline development is a short book called *Some Common Concerns*. The book, produced by a London-based art organization, PLATFORM, in collaboration with Friends of the Earth, the Central and Eastern Europe Bankwatch project, the Kurdish Human Rights Project, along with other organizations, is descriptive. It takes the form of a detailed report on the conduct and organization of BP, both in relation to the construction of earlier pipelines and in relation to the planned construction of the BTC pipeline. It examines every aspect of the pipeline development, including its legal framework, its likely impact on human rights and its immediate environment, and its wider geopolitical implications. In effect, it presents itself as an alternative to BP's own assessment of the possible social, human rights and environmental impact of the pipeline project. It questions, on the basis of the past record of BP, and its future plans, whether the company can be trusted to act in the interests of others.

How does *Some Common Concerns* attempt to demonstrate that the actions of BP and the companies and governments with which it is associated are unethical? First, as a form of demonstration, the book was addressed to a public audience. It was launched in a political institution, the House of Lords. The institution was appropriate given the form of the book's argument. For in the British system the House of Lords occupies a particular position: both at the centre of the political system and yet also, in a certain respect, on the margins of it. The Lords, in so far as they are politicians who are not elected, are reckoned to have the capacity to take decisions on 'ethical' or 'scientific', rather than on narrowly political, grounds. In the British Parliamentary system the Lords has rather weak formal powers, but its views often have weight precisely because it is not so easy for opponents to accuse them of being motivated by party political interest. Along with institutions such as Royal Commissions, government advisory bodies and ethics committees, the House of Lords is clearly connected to politics, but framed as partly outside of it. The historical links between the Lords and institutions of ethical authority – the church, the ancient universities, the judiciary – is significant in this respect. By its launching in the House of Lords, the report could draw upon and address these sources of ethical authority.

Second, the book both reflected and interrogated the frame of the company's own ethical audit, intending to make visible the existence of effects (pollution, human rights abuse, etc.) which had not been acknowledged by the company. Through its own ethical audit, BP continues to reveal specific minor instances of corruption associated with the company. The report expanded the frame much further, arguing that corruption is on a much wider scale than BP admitted.[30] For example, it noted that Azerbaijan was judged to be the third most corrupt country in the world according to an international audit of corruption by an organization called Transparency International. This global governmental institution, itself funded by national government and multinational business, has the explicit aim to attack corruption not through exposing individual cases but by encouraging the development of 'systems' which make corruption visible: 'a principle tool in the fight against corruption is access to information'.[31]

Third, the authors of the report interrogated BP's own assessments of the social and human rights impacts of its operations and, thus, its capacity to represent the interests of local populations:

> BP's 1998 report of the social impact of its operations in Colombia proudly stated that consultants found in 1996 that BP's environmental standards and performance ... 'equaled or exceeded' international expectations. The BP report did not refer, however, to a 20-page report by the Colombian government's independent ombudsman, detailing hundreds of thousands of dollars of fines for serious environmental damage ... meanwhile, for the smallholders who have lost their land or whose land has been destroyed, BP is still refusing to compensate them and is, in effect, forcing them to take an expensive case to the courts.
>
> (PLATFORM 2002: 86)

This past, the report argues, informs the future. A fact-finding mission by campaigners to Turkey found patterns of land compensation disturbingly close to those for Colombia (2002: 88). If the ethical authority of BP depends on its capacity to represent its activities in Turkey, Colombia and Alaska to its banks and shareholders in London and New York, then the credibility of these representations can be undermined by alternative representations. If the ethical authority of BP depends on its capacity to enlist and represent the position of external others at a distance (such as affected local people), then these links can also be undermined through description. In the report, the 'ethical' concern of the company for the local population and environment are also reframed as themselves embodying political and economic motivations:

> [the work of social impact assessors] is not only vital as 'insurance' against opposition to the pipelines and the company, and against reputational damage in the future; it is also vital in the present as BP tries to secure financing from institutions such as International Finance Corporation and the European Bank of Reconstruction and Development.
>
> (PLATFORM 2002: 50)

At the time of writing, the controversy concerning the development of the BTC pipeline is unresolved. Here, I am less concerned with how this controversy will be closed, or whether particular claims made by the opponents of the pipeline are refuted or not, or simply ignored, than with the form that opposition to the pipeline has taken. The opposition has been, from one angle, disorganized. The coalition of 'organizations' involved in the campaign includes well-known NGOs and small anarchist groups, human rights and environmental organizations, researchers and direct activists. Yet this disorganization is associated with a remarkable attention to the detail of the pipeline project and its likely effects on its human and non-human environments. J.K. Gibson-Graham and others have sought to rethink Marx as something like a critical accountant.[32] Likewise one might view the authors of *Some Common Concerns* as engaging in a form of critical ethical audit, expanding, interrogating and reframing the forms of ethical assessment commissioned and performed by the company themselves.

Conclusions

To examine the globalization of ethics one might try to trace the progressive replication of general statements of ethical principles in the constitutions of international bodies and nation states. But while this process is not unimportant, it is at best only part of the story. One of the virtues of studies of governmentality is that they direct us away from statements of general political and ethical principles to the very practical ways in which particular domains of life come to be governed. In the case of corporate ethics this points us to the development of efforts to monitor, assess and make visible forms of ethical and unethical conduct. The globalization of corporate ethics certainly has involved the replication of commitments to the eradication of corruption and the defence of human rights on the part of national and international bodies, for example. But it has also been associated with the generation of detailed empirical knowledge about the conduct of business in other places. Both the ethical and unethical conduct of business have to be demonstrated to others elsewhere.

The production of knowledge about the ethical conduct of business might be thought to have a largely anti-political effect. For critical sociology, and for Foucault, expert knowledge is generally reckoned to be an instrument of rationalization. In relation to corporate ethics, however, the situation is more complex. Although there are efforts to make the assessment of ethical conduct a routine matter, this has not been successful. Claims regarding the ethical conduct of businesses are too uncertain, and too clearly self-interested, to be taken simply as true.[33] Rather, the field of ethics has become the terrain on which the conduct of specific corporations is contested. The ethical conduct of global business has become an object of both government and political action.

Notes

1 Thus, the concept connects to broader arguments concerning the diversity of forms of market organization (Slater and Tonkiss 2001).
2 Callon (1998) uses 'frame' to describe the ways in which a distinction is created and maintained between the market and what is exterior to the market.
3 For an indication of the growing importance of notions of business ethics and corporate social responsibility see Willmott (2001); Beckett (2003); Business for Social Responsibility (2003).

4 In tracing this history it would be necessary, for example, to examine the links between contemporary concerns and the long-standing tradition, particularly well developed in the United States, of philanthropy.
5 On this point see Barry *et al.* (1995). See Osborne (1999) for analysis of the importance of political events in Foucault's work.
6 Rather than view globalization as a cause, we may better view it as an aspiration which may or may not be embodied in specific actions or projects (Larner and Walters 2002; Franklin *et al.* 2000).
7 Such commitments to global values are found enshrined in international declarations and agreements such as the UN's Universal Declaration of Human Rights (1948) and the Brundtland report of the World Commission on Environment and Development (1987).
8 The notion of demonstration refers to all those scientific and political methods through which objects and issues are rendered visible to others. On the relation between scientific and political forms of demonstration see Barry (1998: chap 8; 2001).
9 Mitchell poses the relevant question in his study of colonialism in Egypt: 'What strategies, structures, and silences transform the expert into a spokesperson for what appears as the forces of development, the rules of law, the progress of modernity, or the rationality of capitalism?' (Mitchell 2002: 15).
10 In *Capital*, Marx was able to draw extensively on the reports of *national* government inspectors of factories (Marx 1976).
11 On the general problem of demonstrating facts about distant events, and the association between this and the history of empire, see Latour (1987) and Barry (1996).
12 The notion of social form needs to be expanded to include non-human as well as human actors (Latour 1999, 2003; Callon *et al.* 2001).
13 'Genealogy does not resemble the evolution of a species and does not map the destiny of a people. On the contrary, to follow the complex course of descent is to maintain passing events in their proper dispersion; it is to identify the accidents, the minute deviations – or conversely, the complete reversals – the errors, false appraisals, and the faulty calculations that gave birth to those things that continue to exist and have value for us; it is to discover that truth or being does not lie that the root of what we know and what we are, but the exteriority of accidents'. Foucault (1986: 81)
14 For a recent example, see O'Neill (2002).
15 On the notion of the assemblage, see Deleuze (1988).
16 On the difference between 'liberal' and 'neo-liberal' approaches to the government of medical practice, see Osborne (1993).
17 Some writers on management stress the intimate relations between notions of ethics and corporate responsibility on the one hand, and marketing and branding on the other: '...three critical issues facing business today – corporate citizenship, core values and branding – come together in an integrated way to form the concept of citizen brands' (Willmott 2001: 5).
18 The Greenpeace campaign was a form of public demonstration, using television and the Internet. 'The fact that television cameras recorded these events as they were unfolding created access to, and involvement with, events which, although they took place in a specific locality, came to impinge quickly and directly on many parts of the world' (Held *et al.* 1999: 59).
19 On the notion of anti-politics see Barry (2001, 2002). Other oil companies – most notably Exxon – have shown little concern with the movement towards greater corporate social responsibility and the environment.
20 See Yearley (1996) on the role of NGOs in constituting the environment as a global political problem.
21 In the UK, for example, the 2000 Pensions Act required the pensions fund industry to take into account social issues (Osborne 2003).

22 Available at: http://www.bp.com/environ_social/business_ethics/index.asp
23 This knowledge is theoretical and performative: it is intended to embodied in practice, and communicated through embodied practice: 'embodied performance
increasingly is central to the communication of business knowledge: the kind of
performance found in the management seminar is a fundamental part of business
life' (Thrift 1998: 181; see also Thrift 2002).
24 Of course, the capacity of such figures to claim to be able to embody ethics has
been considerably undermined in recent years and has itself become the object of
increasing levels of scrutiny.
25 Available at: http://www.amnesty.org.uk/business/objectives.shtml
26 This does not mean that there is agreement about what these values are, nor that all
criticisms of corporate behaviour are framed in ethical terms.
27 'Just a few years ago a conference about business and sustainable development would
have been focusing on whether it was a serious business issue and if there was a business case for responsible corporate behaviour. I would argue that this is no longer the
case. The questions today are not whether, but what can be done; not if there is a
business case, but just how far the case stretches' (Beckett 2003: 1).
28 Campaigners argue that this was necessary because the pipeline was a geopolitical
rather purely a commercial project. The planned route of the pipeline, backed by
the US and Turkish governments, avoided alternative routes via Iran, Afghanistan,
Armenia and Russia.
29 Available at: http://www.worldbank.org
30 On the notion that the constitution of markets involves framing certain objects and
problems as outside of the market, see Callon (1998).
31 Available at: http://www.transparency.org
32 'Like all systems of accounting, Marx's language of class highlights certain processes
and obscures others, potentiates certain identities and suppresses others, and has the
capacity to energize certain kinds of activities and actors while leaving others
unmoved' (Gibson-Graham *et al.* 2001: 9).
33 On the relation between scientific uncertainty and politics see Callon *et al.* (2001).

References

Anheier, H., Glasius, M. and Kaldor, M. (eds) (2001) *Global Civil Society*, Oxford: Oxford
University Press.
Barry, A. (1996) 'Lines of communication and spaces of rule', in A. Barry, T. Osborne
and N. Rose (eds) *Foucault and Political Reason*, London: UCL Press.
——(1998) 'Modest witnesses: Donna Haraway, science and international relations',
Millennium: Journal of International Studies, 27(4): 869–883.
——(2001) *Political Machines: governing a technological society*, London: Athlone.
——(2002) 'The anti-political economy', *Economy and Society*, 31(2): 268–284.
Barry, A, Bell, V. and Rose, N. (1995) ' "Alternative" political imaginations', *Economy and
Society*, 24(4): 485–488.
Barry, A., Osborne, T. and Rose, N. (eds) (1996) *Foucault and Political Reason*, London:
UCL Press.
Beckett, M. (2003) 'Keynote speech on corporate social responsibility', paper presented at
The Guardian and Observer Business and Society Conference, February, 2003. Online.
Available at: http://www.defra.gov.uk/corporate/ministers/speeches/ mb030206.htm
Bennett, T. (1995) *The Birth of the Museum: history, theory, politics*, London: Routledge.
Bishop. J.D. (2000) *Ethics and Capitalism*, Toronto: Toronto University Press.
Bourdieu, P. (2000) *Pascalian Meditations*, Cambridge: Polity.

Burchell, G., Gordon, C. and Miller, P. (1991) *The Foucault Effect: studies in governmentality*, Hemel Hempstead: Harvester Wheatsheaf.

Business for Social Responsibility. Online. Available at: *http://www.bsr.org*

Callon, M. (ed.) (1998) *The Laws of the Markets*, Oxford: Basil Blackwell.

Callon, M., Lascoumes, P. and Barthe, Y. (2001) *Agir dans un Monde Incertain: essai sur la démocratie technique*, Paris: Seuil.

Deleuze, G. (1988) *Foucault*, Minneapolis: University of Minnesota Press.

Donald, J. (1992) *Sentimental Education: schooling, popular culture and the regulation of liberty*, London: Verso.

Durkheim, E. (1957) *Professional Ethics and Civic Morals*, London: Routledge.

Export Credit Guarantees Department (2002) *ECGD's Business Principles*, London: ECGD.

Foucault, M. (1986) 'Nietzsche, genealogy, history', in P. Rabinow (ed.) *The Foucault Reader*, London: Penguin.

——(1989) 'An ethics of pleasure', in *Foucault Live*, New York: Semiotext(e).

Franklin, S., Lury, C. and Stacey, J. (2000) *Global Nature, Global Culture*, London: Sage.

Gibson-Graham, J.K., Resnick, S. and Wolff, R.D. (2001) 'Toward a poststructuralist political economy', in J.K. Gibson-Graham, S. Resnick and R.D. Wolff (eds) *Representing Class: essays in postmodern Marxism*, Durham, NC: Duke University Press.

Hacking, I. (1999) *The Social Construction of What?*, Cambridge, MA: Harvard University Press.

Haraway, D.J. (1987) *Modest_Witness@Second_Millennium.FemaleMan_Meets_OncoMouse. feminism and technoscience*. New York and London: Routledge.

Held, D., McGrew, A., Goldblatt, D. and Perraton, J. (1999) *Global Transformations: politics, economics and culture*, Cambridge: Polity.

Hirst, P. and Thompson, G. (1999) *Globalisation in Question: the international economy and the possibilities of governance*, 2nd edn, Cambridge: Cambridge University Press.

Huxham, M. and Sumner, D. (1999) 'Emotion, science and rationality: the case of Brent Spar', *Environmental Values*, 8: 349–368.

Keane, J. (2003) *Global Civil Society?* Cambridge: Cambridge University Press.

Larner, W. and Walters, W. (2002) 'Globalization as governmentality', paper presented at the International Studies Association Congress, Brisbane, July 7–13, 2002.

Lash, S. (2002) *The Critique of Information*, London: Sage.

Latour, B. (1987) *Science in Action*, Milton Keynes: Open University Press.

——(1999) *Politiques de la Nature: comment faire entrer les sciences en démocratie*, Paris: La Découverte.

——(2003) 'Is re-modernization occurring – and if so, how to prove it?: A commentary on Ulrich Beck', *Theory, Culture and Society*, 20(2): 35–48.

Lipschutz, R. (2003) 'Global civil society and governmentality: or, the search for politics and the state amidst the capillaries of power', paper presented at the International Studies Association Annual Meetings, March 2003, Portland, OR.

Lipschutz, R. and Mayer, R. (1996) *Global Civil Society and Global Environmental Governance: the politics of nature from place to planet*, Albany, NY: SUNY.

Marx, K. (1976 [1867]) *Capital: a critique of political economy vol. 1*, London: Penguin.

Mitchell, T. (2002) *The Rule of Experts: Egypt, techno-politics, modernity*, Berkeley: California University Press.

Munro, R. (1999) 'The cultural performance of control', *Organisation Studies*, 20: 619–640.

O'Neill, O. (2002) *Autonomy and Trust in Bioethics*, Cambridge: Cambridge University Press.

Osborne, T. (1993) 'On liberalism, neo-liberalism and the "liberal professions" of medicine', *Economy and Society*, 22(3): 345–356.

——(1999) 'Critical spirituality: on ethics and politics in the later Foucault', in D. Owen and S. Ashenden (eds) *Foucault Contra Habermas*, London: Sage.

——(2003) 'Ethical capital in the creation of human capital', paper presented at conference on Inside Ethics, Girton College, Cambridge, January, 2003.

Owen, D. and Swift, T. (2001) 'Social accounting, reporting and auditing: beyond the rhetoric?', *Business Ethics*, 10(1): 4–8.

PLATFORM *et al.* (2002) *Some Common Concerns: imagining BP's Azerbaijan–Georgia–Turkey pipelines system*, London: PLATFORM.

Power, M. (1997) *The Audit Society: rituals of verification*, Oxford: Clarendon Press.

Rice, D. (2002) 'Human rights strategies for corporations', *Business Ethics*, 11(2): 134–136.

Rogers, R. (2002) 'Operating issue networks on the web', *Science as Culture*, 11(2): 191–213.

Rogers, R. and Marres, N. (2000) 'Landscaping climate change: a mapping technique for understanding science and technology debates on the World Wide Web', *Public Understanding of Science*, 9: 141–163.

Rose, N. (1999) *The Powers of Freedom*, Cambridge: Cambridge University Press.

Scholte, J. (2000) 'Global civil society', in N. Woods (ed.) *The Political Economy of Globalization*, London: Macmillan.

Slater, D. (2002) 'Capturing markets from the economists', in P. du Gay and M. Pryke (eds) *Cultural Economy*, London: Sage.

Slater, D. and Tonkiss, F. (2001) *Market Society: markets and modern social theory*, Cambridge: Polity.

Strathern, M. (2002a) 'Externalities in comparative guise', *Economy and Society*, 31(2): 250–268.

——(forthcoming) 'Robust knowledge and fragile futures', in A. Ong and S. Collier (eds) *For Oikos and Anthropos: rationality, technology and infrastructure*, Oxford: Basil Blackwell.

Thrift, N. (1998) 'Virtual capitalism: the globalisation of reflexive business knowledge', in J. Carrier and D. Miller (eds) *Virtualism: a new political economy*, Oxford: Berg.

——(2002) 'Performing cultures in the new economy', in P. du Gay and M. Pryke (eds) *Cultural Economy*, London: Sage.

Willmott, M. (2001) *Citizen Brands: putting society at the heart of your business*, Chichester: John Wiley.

World Bank (2003) *Operational Manual*. Online. Available at: http://www.worldbank.org

Yearley, S. (1996) *Sociology, Environmentalism and Globalization*, London: Sage.

11 Global benchmarking

Participating 'at a distance' in the globalizing economy

Wendy Larner and Richard Le Heron[1]

Comparative quantitative techniques such as indicators, standards and bench-marks now play a central role in constituting globalizing economic spaces. These globalizing economic spaces are multiple; they include regions (both supra- and sub-national), networks, sectors, supply chains and the materials and people enrolled into these. While all of these globalizing economic spaces involve processes of production, distribution and consumption, they do not represent a 'spatial fix' (Jessop 1999) that replaces the national economy. Rather, they involve temporary resolutions based on the re-placing of capital and labour through global comparisons. In this chapter we explore how these global comparisons have come to make global imaginaries material. We use the example of supply chains – a space in which geographically distant producers and consumers are linked vertically and horizontally through industry and policy associations – to demonstrate that calculative practices, in their diverse forms, are integral to the constitution of these new globalizing geographies of economic connection.

Our preliminary observation is that these global comparisons involve interna-tional competitiveness aspirations. They are bound up with a growing preoccupation with participating 'at a distance' in globalizing economic processes. These 'at a distance' comparisons depend on a battery of calculative practices that now populate scientific, business, government and popular thought, and are influencing the very nature of contemporary political-economic initiatives. Of course, we are not the first to point to the significance of calculative techniques (Barry 2002; Hopwood and Miller 1994; Munro and Mouritsen 1996; Power 1997; Strathern 2000). Yet to date, discussions have tended to focus on national techniques identifying, for example, the role of statistics in constituting national populations and economies (Curtis 1997; Kalpagam 2000; Tomlinson 1996). The relative silence about the constitutive aspects of international comparisons is particularly striking given the centrality of the ethos of international competi-tiveness to neo-liberalism (Hindess 1998).

We argue that what is novel about the current period is that international comparisons now extend beyond the firm into economic and social life more generally. Increasingly, the neo-liberal citizen is expected to compare themselves and their organisations in a wider sphere of reference. Comparative practices themselves have mutated from firm- and industry-centred techniques to those that attempt to quantify multiple spatial configurations. Our contribution to broader discussions of 'global governmentality' is to demonstrate how the calculative technologies binding contemporary governmental practices are formative of new economic spaces. In particular, we argue that benchmarking is hybridising as an integral part of evolving systems of globalizing (not international) competition, and plays a key role in constituting new placements of capital and labour in new spaces of competition.

Our argument is presented in several parts. We begin by claiming that benchmarking, along with audit and contractualism, is a key technique of neo-liberalism. To demonstrate our argument about the new significance of benchmarking, we develop a genealogical account to show how benchmarking has shifted from being a technical to a governmental discourse, and how benchmarking itself has gradually become a different object. We identify three 'generations' of benchmarking techniques: quality, benchmarking, calculative practices. It is the most recent of these that interests us, where techniques previously developed in isolation are summoned, realigned and harnessed to do globally referenced competitive work. Finally, a discussion of global 'supply chain' thinking in New Zealand's land-based sectors illustrates why these calculative practices are so important. We conclude that the globalizing economy is being made manifest through these constitutive processes of calculation, and involves *multiple and changing spaces*.

Audit, contractualism and benchmarking

Governmentality and actor–network approaches draw attention to the practical aspects of governing, arguing that political discourses only become governmental to the extent that they become technical. This focus on the practical dimensions of power has revealed much about contemporary forms of rule. Whereas accounts of 'neo-liberalism' focus on particular political projects (Thatcherism, Reaganomics, Rogernomics and so on), analysts of 'advanced liberalism' draw attention to the more mundane aspects of this new way of governing. Governmentality analysts have shown that governmental technologies are imbued with multiple aspirations and can be linked to both left- and right-wing political projects (Dean 1999; Rose 1999). This helps explain why, as Peck and Tickell (2002: 380) recently observed, 'neoliberalism seems to be everywhere'. As they argue:

> neoliberalism has played a decisive role in constructing the 'rules' of inter-local competition by shaping the very metrics by which regional competitiveness, public policy, corporate performance, or social productivity are measured – value for money, the bottom line, flexibility, shareholder value, performance rating, social capital and so on.
>
> (2002: 387)

What is downplayed in their account, and indeed in the writings of political economists more generally, are the techniques through which these global 'rules' are constituted.

Notable amongst these is audit. Often assumed to be a relatively straightforward accounting technique, Power (1997) shows how audit now covers almost every branch of government from medical, to criminal justice, from charities to corporate control. Others have built on his claims to show how audit has become 'a now taken for granted process of neo-liberal government and contributing substantially to its ethos' (Strathern 2000: 3). Strathern and her colleagues argue that audit not only gives power and authority to numbers and abstract modelling, but also that it has begun to structure social expectations in such a way as to create new principles of organisation. They suggest that to understand the content of concepts such as society and culture today we need to look carefully at the workings of such techniques.

Another important contribution to this discussion is analysis of the 'new contractualism' (Yeatman 1995, 1997, 2002). This work shows how the language and practice of contract has moved from traditional legal domains into diverse fields including public administration, employment, education, private relationships, women's rights and minority rights. In governmentality analyses, this analysis is often used in discussions of the (contested) recasting of relationships between state agencies and citizen, whereby the state provides benefits in return for which individuals are required to fulfil obligations such as seeking paid work or entering counselling and/or training. More significantly for our purposes, Hindess (1997, 1998) also links contractualism to changing perceptions of the national economy, arguing there is now a generalised concern to promote the use of markets and quasi-market instruments in both economy and society.

Our claim is that benchmarking sits alongside audit and contractualism as another technique of advanced liberalism. Amongst management theorists, benchmarking techniques are well recognised, quite uncontroversial, and the emphasis is on improving their quality. In contrast, critical social scientists have paid very little attention to benchmarking. We think this is an oversight, particularly at the present moment. For example, in an otherwise useful collection on globalization, the only mention of comparative techniques is a brief discussion of 'best practice' that focuses on methodological flaws (McBride and Wiseman 2000: 107–109). The conclusion that such techniques are 'partial, incomplete and ultimately ideological' is entirely understandable, but misses their significance for the reconstitution of spaces and subjects. As Barry (2002: 277) has stressed, it is important to examine the 'inventiveness of measurement' and the 'performative and regulative consequences' that follow the circulation of new objects of measurement.

Just as audit and contractualism are associated with fundamental changes in governance, so too is benchmarking. If audit is about checking (Power 1997: 1), and contract is about performing, then benchmarking is about *comparison*. Moreover, whereas benchmarking began by comparing like with like, these techniques now make it possible to think of organisationally discrete and spatially disparate objects as comparable. It is this ability to make the 'incommensurable commensurable' that allows economic space to be represented as global, exemplifying a broader claim that numbers make up the object domains upon which government is required to operate (Rose 1999: 197). Benchmarking fabricates new fields of competition made up of 'best practice' peers that other individuals and organisations seek to emulate.

Modern economic activity has always involved comparisons: What should we charge? How much profit have we made? But benchmarking is of a different order. It does not involve passive comparisons. In a context where there are no more 'frontiers' for capitalist penetration, either in the form of untapped places or peoples, benchmarking sustains the accelerating momentum that underpins the relentless pursuit of international competitiveness. Unlike earlier comparisons, benchmarking involves a treadmill of incessant learning and feedback. Benchmarking encourages places and people to constantly reinvent themselves and remobilise their efforts, bringing new economic spaces and subjects into being. Differentiated hierarchies are thus being remade through these comparative techniques. In turn, this fosters new understandings of 'where' they/we are, the rise of globalizing points of reference, and an abiding concern with economic difference and differentiation.

Genealogy of benchmarking

Our argument is that new conceptions of economic space and subjectivity are being made through benchmarking. But it did not start off like that. Like contractualism, benchmarking has moved from being a narrow business technique, to a theory of management, to a policy/governmental agenda (Yeatman 1997). In this section we trace shifts in the discourse of benchmarking, showing how the technique itself has been transformed. Benchmarking initially involved comparisons within companies to ensure consistency of products, then between national companies to improve the quality of products and processes. Today, the language and practice of benchmarking is ubiquitous, and creates new forms of global inclusion and exclusion. The term encompasses an entire family of conceptually related techniques, and there is a shift from tactical to strategic interventions.[2] It is benchmarking that now sorts out those regions, organisations and individuals that are internationally competitive, and so can be linked into globalizing economic processes, and those who cannot.[3]

Quality

The earliest forms of comparison explicitly named as benchmarking were framed through the language of quality, were specific to manufacturing, and largely internal to companies. They included quality management norms first used by the United States Department of Defence during the 1950s to ensure that contractors of complex weapon systems consistently produced defect-free products (Brunsson *et al.* 2000). The term benchmarking was also used in the newly fledged computer industry as a means of measuring performance.[4] More generally, the so-called 'Quality Gurus' of the mid-1950s advocated statistical control of the manufacturing process (Bendell *et al.* 1993). Their ideas were particularly influential in the Japanese automobile industry, and then during the 1960s and 1970s spread to other manufacturing industries.

By the early 1980s quality techniques were widely used to measure performance in terms of cost/sales and investment ratios, allowing businesses within particular industries to identify their strengths and weaknesses through comparison with their peers. In particular, Total Quality Management (TQM) emerged as a hybrid of Japanese and American concepts and methods. Quantitative measures were integral to this new formulation: 'Facts and statistical data must be used to communicate throughout the organisation and measurements must be used as motivation' (Rehder and Ralston 1984: 24). The spread of these techniques was also associated with increasing computerisation, particularly the rise in storage capacity and the so-called 'software revolution', which allowed the development of more refined techniques to measure and compare performance.

Notable amongst the more sophisticated measures of quality control were standards.[5] In 1977 a proposal for an international committee to develop quality standards was made, leading to the establishment of the International Standards Organisation (ISO). The 1980s saw further development and refinement of ISO standards and their transfer to a wide range of commercial products (see, for example, Perry 1997). In time, cross-firm comparisons became more important, albeit in the same industry or sector. With the development of ISO 9000 certification, and then ISO 14000, standards came to be understood as techniques that could be used by third parties to compare results anywhere in the world (Busch 2000; Casper and Hancké 1999; Reardon *et al.* 2001; Wall *et al.* 2001). The development of standards marked a shift from static to dynamic conceptions of quality. Comparisons of the technical specifications of products and materials were increasingly complemented by those emphasising the production process itself. Thus, a technical device began to mutate into a managerial system (Hayward *et al.* 1998; Perry *et al.* 1997).

As a technical discourse, a key feature of benchmarking historically was that it tended to be inward looking and was not output focused. For example, total quality management, or TQM, was criticised as being too system oriented, in that it was possible to have a perfect operational process that resulted in an unsaleable product. Today, technical discourses of benchmarking are more likely to be outward focused. They focus on the identification of statistical similarities and differences amongst different firms in different places, thus providing industry actors with increasingly global points of reference. While this acceptance of global norms and standards is clearly an integral part of globalizing economic processes (Capmany *et al.* 2000; Jessop 1999), these are not simply neutral measurements. Storper (2000: 50), for example, draws attention to how the language of international standards is used by economic actors to confirm membership of international knowledge communities. He also argues that such knowledge flows may have important impacts on which activities can be deterritorialised. This suggests that the significance of benchmarking requires further consideration.

Benchmarking

The first text to explicitly frame benchmarking as a management tool appeared during the late 1980s (Camp 1989). This book also marked the beginning of the popularisation of the term, with fewer than twenty articles on benchmarking having been published previously (Warner 1997). It is probably significant that this publication followed a period of widespread American concern about the declining competitiveness of their auto companies in comparison to Japanese competitors (Womack *et al.* 1990).[6] Very quickly, benchmarking became an integral part of managerial discourse. Commentators observed: 'In the early 1990s it is almost impossible to read a management magazine or attend a management conference without some reference to benchmarking' (Bendell *et al.* 1993: 3). In this context the term benchmarking began to take on new meaning, and do new work.

Internal explanations of the rapid rise of benchmarking as a managerial strategy attribute it to the 'natural' evolution of concepts of competitor and market analysis, quality improvement programmes and performance measurement (Codling 1995). However, the new prominence of benchmarking is also linked to the increased importance of management training during the 1980s, particularly in the areas of planning, finance and human resources (Bryson 2000; Thrift 2000). It was during this period that the term benchmarking began to be used across industries and sectors, becoming the generic term *for the means of taking ideas from other companies and improving processes.* Thus whereas benchmarking was initially understood as a narrowly defined technical tool designed to ensure quality, by the late 1990s benchmarking had become the discursive framing for managers undertaking broad-based industry comparisons.

During this period benchmarking also moved from a focus on internal comparisons, to an external frame of reference explicitly linked to concerns about competitiveness. Consider, for example, the following observation:

> What does appear to be novel is the function which benchmarking is serving. Many benchmarking programmes represent specific attempts to bring the 'reality' of the outside world to within the boundary of the organization and therefore serve to provoke and legitimate change.
>
> (Oliver 1997: 43)

This change also saw benchmarking begin to be used for comparisons across nation-states. International benchmarking was pursued with particular intensity in Europe and the Asia-Pacific region, less so in Asia. Indeed, we note with interest that Tradenz, New Zealand's own export and foreign investment agency, made the first attempt at the international benchmarking of an entire industrial sector (Camp 1994). In these external comparisons benchmarking and 'best practice' were seen as closely related and the terms often used interchangeably (Keen and Knapp 1996).

In contrast to the inward focus of benchmarking as a technical discourse, benchmarking as a managerial strategy is outward looking, aimed at improving performance by comparing across organisations, industries and nation-states. As a managerial discourse, the rise of benchmarking was associated with the new centring of the consumer. As the discourse of customer satisfaction became increasingly ubiquitous, benchmarking began to be understood as being applicable to public sector organisations, including the non-profit sector, government and education (Camp 1994; Snell and Prasad 2001). Indeed, the current US 'top ten' of benchmarking organisations (those who are heavily involved in benchmarking) includes three government departments.[7] Today there is a huge range of 'how-to' industry and sector specific benchmarking books, with a random search in late 2001 identifying benchmarking as relevant to areas as diverse as health, pharmaceuticals, food services, software development, engineering, third-sector organisations, human resources, organ procurement organisations, financial forecasting, public libraries and trade promotion. Most recently, the possibility and benefits of benchmarking across economic sectors has begun to be promoted (Jayne 2002).

Calculative practice

Benchmarking is now transforming into a governmental strategy. This can be argued at two levels. Most immediately, benchmarking is now used as much in the public sector as it is in the private. Like audit and contract, this sectoral move can be associated with the rise of New Public Management (Osborne and Gaebler 1993; Hood 1998). As public services began to be understood as enterprises that could be run in a more business-like fashion, benchmarking began to be used to compare the effectiveness of governmental policies and programmes nationally and internationally. Significantly, the subject-specific reports produced by the OECD to allow for comparison and evaluation of New Public Management across countries disregarded the place-specific aspects of government reforms. Instead the measurements were 'distanced, disconnected from time and space, rendered generalisable' (Brunsson *et al.* 2000: 107).

But our point is more than simply an observation about the increased use of benchmarking techniques in the public sector. Benchmarking has now become both polyvalent and polysemic. There is a more general trend for indexes, indicators, categorisations, measurements, polls and surveys of all kinds to be understood as 'benchmarking studies'. These multiple forms of benchmarking encompass earlier technical and managerial incarnations and extend them into new terrains. At the heart of all these techniques is the idea that quantitative measures of performance can be used to compare spatially and organisationally discrete systems, activities and individuals. We are also seeing the popularisation of benchmarking. Not only has benchmarking become a 'buzzword' for industry and government, so too are community organisations 'benchmarking' themselves in the search of for 'best practice'. It is in this context, we would suggest, that benchmarking has become an integral part of contemporary forms of rule. It is a technique that has proved to be both flexible and mobile, and can be used to solve problems across a wide range of spaces and sectors.

The rise of benchmarking is associated with a new emphasis on knowledge, ideas and innovation in the context of new forms of international competitiveness. However, the impetus to compare appears to be pronounced in particular locations. We have been struck, for example, by the non-reaction to benchmarking in the United States. In this regard, benchmarking is aspirational; most likely to be utilised by those who are not already globally centred. Knowing the global through calculative practices is to place oneself a series of techniques and rationalities for engaging in the global economy on 'one's own terms' at a distance. This, as Lempert (2002: 689) contends, is part of 'giving measurements of performance new meaning'. Benchmarking is also highly selective. Most immediately, it redefines core and periphery by linking up those organisations and people understood to have 'value' and discarding the rest. It is a limited and liminal technique in that not everyone can be 'best-in-class' or 'world-class', and it is possible to both enter into and be pushed from these ranks. Thus, as we have argued elsewhere, '(P)ower works in part through its ability to name, to define and to describe certain people and places as being different from others and in a way that excludes other definitions' (Larner and Le Heron 2002).

The proliferation of benchmarking cannot be contested by claims for more rigour in the use of terminology and techniques. Indeed, even if the processes by which 'benchmarking studies' are produced can be shown to be dubious, once tabulated the numbers take on a life of their own (Larner 2001). Moreover, how the numbers are produced is less important for our argument than how they travel and the work they do. Contestation around benchmarking naturalises it, for even to engage in discussion about the inadequacy (flawed methodologies and so on) or inappropriateness (for example, quantitative versus qualitative measures) of benchmarking techniques is enough to give them some materiality. More significantly, benchmarking is not simply a neutral tool of measurement; *it is a technique that is bringing its own spaces and subjects into existence.* Specifically, the calculative practices now encompassed by the term benchmarking have allowed the emergence of a global economic imaginary.[8] In the next section we demonstrate through a New Zealand case study how benchmarking is part of the reconfiguration of economic governance that allows participation 'at a distance' in the globalizing economy.

Supply chains[9] as objects of governance: the New Zealand experience

On 12, February 2002 Craig Norgate, the recently appointed CEO of Fonterra,[10] the newly formed mega-company from the merger of New Zealand Dairy Group and Kiwi Dairies, was guest speaker at an American Chamber of Commerce breakfast in Auckland. Farmer anxieties and concern over the abolition of the New Zealand dairy producer board framework and the fate of the industry under corporate control were still at a peak. Obviously relieved that he was speaking to an audience of Auckland suits, he remarked, 'I was doing farm shed meetings last week and that set a benchmark in questioning'.[11]

Framing supply chains

Amongst other new spaces of competition, supply chains have recently become objects of industry/sectoral attention as well as federal, national and local policy (Wolfe and Gertler 2001; Pritchard 1999). With the push for free trade and structural adjustment, the field of relevant comparisons is rapidly widening and the problems of linking distant producers and consumers have been brought to the fore (Daviron and Gibbon 2002; Dolan and Humphrey 2000; Gereffi 1999; Hughes 2000; Mutersbaugh 2002; Rice 2001). Supply chains, or global production networks, are increasingly understood to be frameworks through which individuals and groups might recreate value through mutual associations (Henderson *et al.* 2001; Storper 2000). The concept is a relatively new spatialisation of the economic, a distinct imaginary that has the governmental effect of institutionalising conversations between vertically and horizontally linked actors around the expectations of distant consumers. Supply chains, as emerging sites of production, distribution and consumption, have become new economic spaces. In the short discussion that follows we develop a 'mapping' of supply chains originating from New Zealand to illustrate our claims about the increasing 'governmentalisation' of these globalizing economic spaces and explore the constitution of calculative practices in New Zealand's realigning of the sheep meat supply chain. We do so in the understanding that only from 'historically institutionalised spaces of political-economic intervention and action' (MacKinnon *et al.* 2002: 306) can analyses of different globalizing trajectories take us closer to their consequences.

In the context of New Zealand's restructuring experience the choice of the land-based sector for closer scrutiny of the emergence of supply chains makes particular sense.[12] During the 1980s a dramatic neo-liberalising reform process dismantled a highly interventionist state regulatory apparatus in favour of market processes, including the elimination of subsidies and assistance for the expansion of production, removal of exchange rate, tariff and interest rate controls, commercialisation and then eventual abolition of the producer–marketing board framework. An outcome was that the land-based sector found itself confronting in new terms the question of how to be internationally competitive in a geographical location removed from the metropolitan centres of the globalizing economy. Calculative practices now play an integral role in subsequent attempts to reposition New Zealand-based individuals and organisations into relationally intimate but physically distant and scattered webs of economic activity. More specifically, these practices have underpinned the emergence of a global economic imaginary that is constitutive of new spaces, subjects and forms of association.

Geography enters into our narrative in multiple ways. The reforms of the 1980s began with a profound reworking of external relationships involving both decoupling and recoupling with global networks. Links with the United Kingdom were severed, forcing a search for new market opportunities. Moreover, under the established regulatory framework spatial imaginaries had been framed in particular ways. Specifically, governance through state departments (forestry) or producer boards (apples, dairy, meat) tended to privilege commodity production and 'containerise' economic interactions. The primary link for the farmer, for example, was the processor who was the recipient of farm outputs such as milk or animals. Processed farm products were then exported by single-desk sellers, the producer boards, which paid guaranteed prices and attempted to sell produce offshore. Following the reforms agricultural actors met new conditions and expectations (that is, to maximise profit instead of volume of production). What began to ensue was the wholesale transformation of the previous relationships of land-based production. Existing arrangements at each stage in the physical chain from New Zealand-based production to international consumers were called into question.

In just over a decade the global supply chain was gradually envisaged and enshrined as a new object of governance in New Zealand's land-based system, usurping the earlier commodity and container imaginary. Growing recognition of interlinkages amongst diverse actors has seen the global supply chains emerge as a series of interconnected sites for new levels of performativity where these interdependencies are understood to exert tremendous pressures for quick and effective responses or initiatives. How has this come about? Who could have imagined such a comprehensive development?

Supply chains as arenas of calculation

We begin by providing a broad mapping of global supply chains in New Zealand land-based sectors. Our claims, summarised in Table 11.1, represent a broad argument only. We do not develop a genealogy of the individual chains, rather our aim is to demonstrate a general patterning across the chains based on the new centrality of calculative practices. Moreover, we are adopting the industry-led disposition to view the supply chain as the most valuable framework to coordinate interaction in each land-based sector. We go further, however, by recognising the influence of uneven power networks that frame the emerging supply chain world. Calculative practices are being driven by organisations occupying strategic sites in the supply chains, some in New Zealand, some abroad. The resulting dynamics harness supply chain interconnections into new spaces of (often-contested) interactions. Crucially, however, while the extent to which calculative practices have penetrated into and reshaped each supply chain is highly variable, the changes depicted reveal the explicitly spatial character of this globalizing activity.

New Zealand's land-based sectors are managing at least three 'at a distance' problems in their effort to participate in the globalizing economy. First, these sectors are rapidly transforming from a commodity base, with a steady increase in value added production. This has heightened awareness of consumer demands. It is increasingly accurate to speak of a food economy instead of agri-cultural, pastoral and horticultural industries. With this shift has come unfamiliar requirements such as content and labelling regimes. Second, the management of market risk through supplier failure, including complete exclusion from partic-

Table 11.1: Supply chain developments in New Zealand

New Zealand industries	Emergent practices	Key organising concepts	Strategic sites in supply chain	Reterritorialisation through supply chain dynamics (examples)
Apples	Biosecurity standards. Production standards.	Integrated Production Management. Organic production.	UK supermarkets ENZA (vertically integrated corporate).	USDA officials inspecting in New Zealand.
Dairying	Dairy effluent management. Mastitis management.	Clean green farming. Milk quality.	Fonterra (vertically integrated corporate). Dexcel (dairy research corporation).	Joint ventures to launch into or penetrate further 'region' markets.
Kiwi fruit	Production standards. Intellectual property.	Branding. Licensing of new cultivars.	UK supermarkets. ZESPRI (vertically integrated corporate).	Licensing of Kiwi Gold in different countries.
Meat	Contracts for production to precise specification.	Performance-based verification in supply chain.	Meat processors. UK supermarkets.	Real-time supermarket product sales information to meat processing plant in New Zealand.
Wine	Labelling standards.	Regionalisation of grape growing.	Foreign wine-making companies. New Zealand Wine Institute	Entry of foreign capital into New Zealand grape-growing and wine production.
Forestry	Forestry standards.	Chain of custody of wood. Forest certification.	Trading chaebol / sogo shosha. Forestry MNCs.	Entry of foreign capital links into USA via US DIY companies.

ular countries because of phytosanitary and biosecurity 'events', is shaping government policy, food company strategies and on-farm behaviours. These risks take many forms. Recent problems include accidental contamination by genetically modified corn, fireblight in apples, noxious weeds in imported grain, foot and mouth scares, the rabbit calcivirus disease, tuberculosis levels in the possum population, painted apple moth, various diseases in Pinus radiata and so on. Third, New Zealand's image as a 'clean green' producer of food products is threatened by effluent disposal practices (discharges from dairy farms, food-processing facilities including dairy factories and meat-freezing works, and pulp mills) and some livestock handling practices (Thull and Kissling 2002). In each of these issues, calculative practices play a central role in efforts to find long term governance solutions to perceived, anticipated and actual coordination problems, and to serve to insert land-based actors in new ways into globalizing economic spaces.

Such spatial transformations are emerging through the restructuring of historical links between local producers and overseas consumers. In the case of the apple and kiwi fruit sectors, the New Zealand marketers (ENZA and ZESPRI) are introducing integrated fruit production, while some growers are converting to organics production (Hayward and Le Heron 2002; McKenna and Campbell 1999). Sheep meat has seen efforts to extend production to precise specification through the use of new contracts in an effort to meet the quality assurance codes and standards of UK supermarkets (Sainsbury, Waitrose, Tesco) first introduced in the early 1990s (Penny and Le Heron 2002). More recently, forestry companies have adopted forest certification under the NGO-driven Forest Stewardship Council from Mexico, to ensure timber exports to the USA meet the performance specifications of that country's DIY importers. The wine sector, in contrast, is proceeding with a system of regional authentication similar to that of the French AOC (Moran *et al.* 2000).

Although a diverse set of organisations are driving change, supply chain realignment rests upon a different order of calculative practices to those of the recent past. Foremost, audit processes are central. For example, the meat industry has embarked on the creation of a system which will clearly distinguish 'sellers, certifiers and verifiers' (Lynch 2001). The organics sector is actively reconfiguring the landscape of certification, a process that involves attempting to second guess the best international organic standard(s) to adopt, leading to what one commentator calls, a 'market of competing benchmarks' (Davis 2001).[13] Second, realignment presupposes a consideration of all dimensions of the global supply chain. Thus, the perspective is neither looking immediately up or down the chain, but increasingly taking into account the ramifications of changes everywhere. In sheep meat, for example, the growing concentration accompanying a shift in ownership from foreign companies (the 1980s) to New Zealand cooperatives and private companies (the 1990s), together with processes resulting from internal dynamics as well as pressures from government-led restructuring, saw pronounced attitudinal changes at the management level and a greater willingness to engage in farmer–processor dialogue with a view to understanding how traditionally antagonistic farmer–processor relations might be altered (Le Heron *et al.* 2001). A recent study of farmer–processor relationships showed that both parties are trying on the one hand to calculate their risks and returns, while on the other hand they are aspiring to develop the performance of the sheep meat supply chain to the UK (Penny and Le Heron 2002). Third, a reorientation of science and R&D infrastructure has occurred, in response to government (and industry) funding of research into supply chain realignment issues such as compliance, behaviour change, learning processes, innovation adoption and conflict resolution. The new emphasis on performativity embodied in this reorientation differs from the pre-reform objective of state-funded science which was to extend the productivity of the grassland–livestock ecosystem and increase the volume of exports.

Governmental dimensions of sheep meat supply chain realignment

According to Lynch (2003) the sheep meat sector is 'getting used to being a New Zealand industry … The (now) New Zealand companies, previously oriented to procurement, skipped adolescence, moving instead to adulthood', where they are 'seeking to differentiate themselves, through new supply chain relationships'. A study of the learning challenges associated with realignment in the sheep meat sector carried out between 1998 and 2001 (Le Heron *et al.* 2001; Penny 2003; Penny and Le Heron 2000, 2002) reveals many barriers and tensions arising from different expectations and needs on the part of those in the emerging chains. The evidence sketches how a bundle of practices such as benchmarking, best practice, standards and audit are integral to the supply chain ethos that has flourished in New Zealand's neo-liberalising environment.

At the centre of the sector's transformation from of a commodity production culture are changes in the farmer–processor relationship, driven very much by pressure to differentiate lamb, for the first time in 150 years. The reworking involves a number of dimensions: a shift from commodity frozen carcasses to chilled lamb cuts, the introduction of a schedule system specifying meat qualities to replace the purchase of meat 'by the head' under the previous volume-based system, new drafting skills to identify lambs meeting specification, the revaluing of the role of the company livestock representative, the widespread use of scales on farms to weigh fattening lambs to gauge progress, accurate diary keeping to record information on animal growth, use of killing sheets to check lamb and farm 'hit rates', and the adoption of contracts to stipulate broad performance expectations on the part of farmers and processors. The new context also sets new demands. A world of contracts requires farmers to ask: 'What do our customers need and what do we need to do and then deliver it?' (Farmer interview, April 1999). Measures of performance are aptly captured in the acronym DIFOTA – Deliver In Full On Time Accurately – coined to emphasise the value attached to delivery of stock with consistent attributes suitable for eventual presentation as chilled meat cuts.

From the perspective of the meat processor, the aim has been to 'change the way they think' (Processor manager, April 1999), because:

> our customers around the world they couldn't give a continental about what happens in this country. They have customers or consumers that want to put their hand in the supermarket cabinet every week of the year. And they will not hear of supply shortages, they just don't want to know. If the weather is no good here, that's our problem. You're either supplying us or you're not.

Yet, as one farmer observed, the 'companies expect us to tell them what we can supply but they are not telling us the information we need!' (Group meeting comment, October 1998). Farmers leaving the 'production mentality' and committing to the demands of supplying differentiated product under contract, are 'moving out of the pack', and are finding they are able to participate in the increasing range and number of contracts being run by the meat companies each season. The 'them' and 'us' antagonisms that typified the past are gradually receding, as the 'trust gap has been bridged somewhat' (Processor interview, May 1999). The same processor manager reflected,

> do we recognize excellence and the answer I guess in terms of by the way we pay [for] things, yes, but do we acknowledge it and the answer is no, we are still not good at that. We are very good at showing people where they went wrong and telling them how. We give hit rates and all that but actually saying to someone 'well hey, you are exceptional. Thank you, it's really appreciated', no, we are not good at that.

Conversely, a farmer remarked that it is 'nice to feel an important part of the supply chain' (Farmer interview, October 1998), citing the fact that the contracting company had 'Tesco here talking to Tesco suppliers. We had Waitrose last year' (Processor interview, April 1999).

The new realities of supplying to more precise specification have meant that farmers and processors are concluding 'there is no such thing as a normal year' (Farmer interview, October 1998). In an effort to respond to the uncertainties and risks of changing world markets, actors are being aligned into collaborative relationships; on the one hand *farmer*, banker, farm adviser and accountant and, on the other hand, *processor*, livestock representative and drafter. These relationships facilitate new practices such as being more 'analytic' as farmers, or developing more round-about-ness to production by moving lambs between areas and farms in order to maximise animal performance and returns. While one farmer regarded benchmarking in the supply chain, through comparative experience with multiple contracts, companies, regions and seasons, as 'the most exciting thing to happen (in the new conditions)' (Farmer interview, October 1998), such individualistic but probably warranted enthusiasm needs to be tempered by the remark of a livestock representative, who stated, 'there's been two significant targets I've had as livestock manager (1) building a good core of suitable suppliers and the other is getting hands on management of our business – getting control' (Processor manager, April 1999). Indeed, the mid-point assessment of realignment provided by the study was salutary. Speaking from frustration that the 'chain is only as good as its weakest link', a manager signalled the unfinished business when he posed the challenging question: 'How do we get them (farmers) to find out how much they really understand about the game other than "I got rid of the lambs"?'

Reflections on supply chain development

This brief discussion identifies the shifts in what is being governed (from a national industry to a global supply chain), and reveals a little of how this governing activity is constituted, evaluated and reconstituted (see also Le Heron 2003; Le Heron and Roche 1999). In particular, it foregrounds how calculative practices are now being used as a basis for knowing the global in the land-based sectors. The frames involve a temporary freezing of people and places into an imaginary space so that the calculative work can be performed. This global disposition is understood to be relational rather than linear. Finally, while audit, contracts and benchmarking should all be seen as contributing to governing at a distance, and as constituting globalizing subjects, it is the calculative practices that explicitly position New Zealand land-based sectors in globalizing economic spaces.

However, even given the coarse heuristic and single example used, we cannot dismiss the multiplicity of spatial imaginaries that emerge from contemporary forms of governance. Even in the case of global supply chains the processes of reterritorialisation are not unitary. New economic spaces are constructed through continuing reassessments by the chain actors in terms of their engagement in globalizing economic processes. The political work of enshrining contracts should not be understated. Thus, the Foundation of Research Science and Technology and the Crown Research Institutes have sought to influence the direction and detail of supply chain realignment. On the farm, decisions are made in the context of farm management and farm business strategies. At the interface between companies and farmers/growers, translators such as farmer/grower and chemical company representatives and professionals such as veterinarians and so on are working with farmers to make practical sense of rulings connected with supply chain involvement and are thereby integrally involved in remaking and reshaping these economic spaces.

Finally, while we have considered what is being resolved in supply chain frameworks, we might also ask what supply chain thinking hides? Under the earlier producer board system, market relations were often less visible, as the focus was on expanding productivity of the land. In contrast, the calculation-based enrolment of actors into global supply chain processes potentially masks concentration tendencies in each chain, as each constituency attempts to deploy standards, benchmarking and other practice to their own ends, and in doing so, ignores or sidelines the implications of structural trends in the supply chains.

Conclusion

Our discussion of benchmarking highlights the crucial role of calculative practices in constituting globalizing economic spaces. We stress the importance of these apparently mundane techniques, convinced that by comprehending such activities we will gain more sense of their significance and implications. It is the potential to assemble and translate measurements relating to the performance of others in near and far places that marks out benchmarking as a globalising practice. Through our discussion we illustrate these claims, offering a stylised account of how global economic space is known through calculative practices in this particular context. Being included in calculations, and therefore named as an international competitor, is an instance of simultaneous individualisation at different geographic scales. Any such comparison always asks: where do we sit in relation to others, in different countries, in regions or our country and within our organisation? In this regard, benchmarking initiates a game of constant learning in which there is no single or ultimate solution. But more often than not the centrality of spatial relations in this process is assumed unconsciously.

We conclude by stressing that the new centrality of calculative practices has other consequences. Whereas nation-centred imaginaries could and did encourage the development of progressive traditions, global imaginaries drawing on calculative practices may be less likely to prioritise social agendas. The main reason for this is that calculative practices are enterprise-centred, despite being framed in wider systems such as industries, sectors, supply chains or regions. Spatially referenced calculations aimed at achieving levels of performance that ensure continued and profitable insertion into globalising processes is unquestionably an activity and imagining that privileges *economic* spaces.

Yet these new economic geographies are fluid and multiple – hence our disinclination to use scale as a point of entry into our analysis and interpretation of calculative practices (Amin 2002). If calculative practices are mutating in the ways we argue, then understanding this feature of contemporary economic life upsets the notion of an eventual new unitary 'spatial fix', whether that be at regional or global levels. Our argument points instead to new forms of governance as a composite of spatialities reaching back into and out from the webs and circuits of the nation-state. Our claim that these socially constructed interactions amongst multiple places are shaped in important ways by calculative practices is to give a more grounded account of contemporary re-territorialisation processes.

Finally, it is important to stress that the analysis outlined in this chapter remains emergent knowing in at least three senses. First, the actual construction of globalizing economic spaces is very particular to context. Those in the land-based sectors of New Zealand view globalizing economic and political processes through their experiential frame. While hardly new, the significance of this claim is that it implies a cumulative engagement with other parts of the world that is drenched in a specific history and geography. Second, we surmise that the global apprehended from the New Zealand context articulates with the global as understood by others. We have not dealt with this here, but consider that research into this relational and relativistic question should be a high priority. Third, it is empirically clear, even from the sketchy evidence we have used, that constructing the global is not independent of local or national projects of various kinds. Thus, we cannot say the national and local are less relevant. Rather they are co-constitutive, though in ways that we know little about. We suspect that the calculative dimensions of benchmarking are pushing a new level of sensitivity to the question of 'where we are situated'. We contend that to both pose and to try to answer *this* question is made more possible having worked themes of globalizing economic spaces through the portal of calculative practices.

Notes

1   This chapter was supported by the New Zealand Royal Society Marsden Fund Project 'Spaces and practices of the global economy' and the Foundation for Research Science and Technology Project 'APEC's agenda, Asia-Pacific integration and New Zealand's competitive advantage'. Eugene Rees and Erena Le Heron provided research assistance. William Walters gave very generous comments and insightful feedback.

2   We find it useful to distinguish wider mobilising frameworks of intervention (strategic) from initiatives with limited and immediate intent (tactical).

3   In the late 1980s some writers asked how places could revalorise themselves (Conti 1993; Harvey 1989). The mutation of benchmarking forms an illustrative answer to this line of questioning.

4   The broader interface between practices in the IT industry and other areas of the economy should not be underestimated.

5   We do not offer a genealogy of standards per se even though these might also be conceptualised as calculative practices.

6   In the major US and European management journals of the 1980s the dominant world view was nation-centred, perhaps best summarised as 'American firms abroad'.

7   Available at: www.benchnet.com/bppf2002.htm

8   We utilise this theoretical concept with caution. The disposition to imagine activities and imaginaries elsewhere is not uniform. We suspect New Zealand's relatively open borders, migrant heritage and trade relations heighten such an imaginary. Second, we would hasten to add that we do not suggest that there is a singular or unchanging imaginary. The crucial point is that being able to imagine the global has been facilitated by calculative practices that have accelerated the interest in and ability to envisage 'here and there' simultaneously.

9   Several other concepts are roughly equivalent. Global commodity chains, global value chains and filiere are categories of political economy aimed at revealing the wider connectivity of economic processes, while the business concept of value chain is normally limited to firms and inter-firm networks. Supply chain is the term that has the most visibility in the worlds of industry and policy, at least in Australia and New Zealand.

10 Fonterra accounts for 95 per cent of New Zealand dairy production and is ranked, by different criteria, as high as fourth amongst the world dairy companies.

11 In his speech, Norgate spoke of Fonterra as an established global corporate, whose latest strategic alliance was a development with food giant Nestlé to increase their South American market. He also referred to the external evaluation process facing Fonterra, the 'new discipline of Standards and Poors' and claimed that 'our people enjoy facing measurable targets'.

12 New Zealand's profile as a leading exporting nation means the interest in supply chains *as an object of governance* lies with the export sector.

13 See Campbell and Liepins (2001) for further details.

References

Amin, A. (2002) 'Spatialities of Globalization', *Environment and Planning A*, 34: 385–399.

Barry, A. (2002) 'The anti-political economy', *Economy and Society*, 31(2): 268–284.

Bendell, T., Boulter, L. and Kelly, J. (1993) *Benchmarking for Competitive Advantage*, London: Pitman Publications.

Brunsson, N., Jacobsson, B. and Associates (2000) *A World of Standards*, Oxford: Oxford University Press.

Bryson, J. (2000) 'Spreading the message: management consultants and the shaping of economic geographies in space and time', in J. Bryson, P. Daniels, N. Henry and J. Pollard (eds) *Knowledge, Space, Economy*, Routledge: London.

Busch, L. (2000) 'The moral economy of grades and standards', *Journal of Rural Studies*, 16(3): 273–283.

Camp, R. (1989) *Benchmarking: the search for industry best practices that lead to superior performance*, Milwaukee: Quality Press.

——(1994) *Business Process Benchmarking: finding and implementing best practices*, Milwaukee: ASQC Quality Press.

Campbell, H. and Liepins, R. (2001) 'Naming organics: understanding organic standards in New Zealand as a discursive field', *Sociologia Ruralis*, 41: 21–39.

Capmany, C., Hooker, N., Ozuna, T. and van Tilburg, A. (2000) 'ISO 9000 – a marketing tool for U.S. agribusiness', *International Food and Agribusiness Management Review*, 3: 41–53.

Casper, S. and Hancké, B. (1999) 'Global quality norms within national production regimes: ISO 9000 standards in the French and German car industries', *Organization Studies*, 20(6): 961–985.

Codling, S. (1995) *Best Practice Benchmarking: a management guide*, Gower, Aldershot.

Conti, S. (1993) 'The network perspective in industrial geography: towards a model', *Geografiska Annaler*, 75B(3): 115–130.

Curtis, B (1997) 'Official documentary systems and colonial government: from imperial sovereignty to colonial autonomy in the Canadas 1841–1867', *Journal of Historical Sociology*, 10(4): 389–417.

Daviron, B. and Gibbon, P. (2002) 'Global commodity chains and African export agriculture', *Journal of Agrarian Change*, 2(2): 137–161.

Davis, P. (2001) Green Party Parliamentary Secretary, Interview, July 2001.

Dean, M. (1999) *Governmentality: power and rule in modern society*, London: Sage.

Dolan, C. and Humphrey, J. (2000) 'Governance and trade in fresh vegetables: the impact of UK supermarkets on the African horticultural industry', *Journal of Development Studies*, 37(2): 147–176.

Gereffi, G. (1999) 'International trade and industrial upgrading in the apparel commodity chain', *Journal of International Economics*, 48: 3–70.

Harvey, D. (1989) *The Condition of Postmodernity*, Oxford: Blackwell.

Hayward, D. and Le Heron, R. (2002) 'Horticultural reform in the European Union and New Zealand: further developments towards a global fresh fruit and vegetable complex', *Australian Geographer*, 33(1): 9–27.

Hayward, D., Le Heron, R., Perry, M. and Cooper, I. (1998) 'Networking, technology and governance: lessons from New Zealand horticulture', *Environment and Planning A*, 30: 2025–2040.

Henderson, J., Dicken, P., Hess, M., Coe, N. and Yeung, H.W.-C. (2001) 'Global production networks and the analysis of economic development', working paper 433, Manchester School of Business, Manchester.

Hindess, B. (1997) 'A society governed by contract?', in G. Davis, B. Sullivan and A. Yeatman (eds) *The New Contractualism*, Sydney: Macmillan Education.

——(1998) 'Neo-liberalism and the national economy', in M. Dean and B. Hindess (eds) *Governing Australia: studies of contemporary rationalities of government*, Cambridge: Cambridge University Press.

Hood, C. (1998) *The Art of the State: culture, rhetoric and public management*, Oxford: Clarendon Press.

Hopwood, A. and Miller, P. (1994) *Accounting as Social and Institutional Practice*, Cambridge: Cambridge University Press.

Hughes, A. (2000) 'Retailers, knowledges and changing commodity networks: the case of the cut flower trade', *Geoforum*, 31: 175–190

Jayne, V. (2002) 'Looking for higher benchmarks', *New Zealand Herald*, January 23, D1.

Jessop, B. (1999) 'Reflections on globalization and its (il)logic(s)', in P. Dicken *et al.* (eds) *The Logic of Globalization*, London: Routledge.

Kalpagam, U. (2000) 'Colonial governmentality and the economy', *Economy and Society*, 29(3): 418–438.

Keen, P. and Knapp, E. (1996) *Every Manager's Guide to Business Processes*, Boston: Harvard Business School Press.

Larner, W. (2001) 'Governing Globalization: the New Zealand Call Centre attraction initiative', *Environment and Planning, A*, 33: 297–312.

Larner, W. and Le Heron, R. (2002) 'From economic globalization to globalizing economic processes: towards post-structuralist political economies', *Geoforum*, 33(4): 415–419.

Le Heron, R. (2003) 'Creating food futures: reflections on food governance issues in New Zealand's agri-food sector', *Journal of Rural Studies*, 19: 111–125.

Le Heron, R. and Roche, M. (1999) 'Rapid reregulation, agricultural restructuring and the reimaging of agriculture in New Zealand', *Rural Sociology*, 64: 203–218.

Le Heron, R., Penny, G., Paine, M., Sheath, G., Pederson, J. and Botha, N. (2001) 'Global supply chains and networking: a critical perspective on learning challenges in the New Zealand dairy and meat commodity chains', *Journal of Economic Geography*, 1: 439–456.

Lempert, D. (2002) 'Review of audit society: rituals of verification and audit cultures: anthropological studies in accountability, ethics and the academy', *American Anthropologist*, 104(2): 689–692.

Lynch, B. (2001) Interview with Executive Director of the Meat Industry Association, July, Wellington.

——(2003) Interview with Executive Director of the Meat Industry Association, August, Wellington.

MacKinnon, D., Cumbers, A. and Chapman, K. (2002) 'Learning, innovation and regional development: a critical appraisal of recent debates', *Progress in Human Geography*, 26(3): 293–311.

McBride, S. and Wiseman, J. (eds) (2000) *Globalization and its Discontents*, New York: St. Martins Press.

McKenna, M. and Campbell, H. (1999) 'Strategies for 'greening' the New Zealand pipfruit export industry: the development of IFP and organic systems', *Studies in Rural Sustainability, Research Report No. 6*, Department of Anthropology, University of Otago, Dunedin.

Moran, W., Perrier-Cornet, P. and Traversac, J.-B. (2000) 'Economic organisation and territoriality within the wine industry of quality: a comparison between New Zealand and France', in B. Sylvander, D. Barjoile and F. Arlini (eds) *The Socio-economics of Origin-*

labelled Food Products in Agrifood Supply Chains: spatial, institutional and coordination aspects, Versailles: INRA Editions.

Munro, R. and Mouritsen, J. (eds) (1996) *Accountability: power, ethos and the technologies of managing*, London: International Thomson Business Press.

Mutersbaugh, T. (2002) 'The number is the beast: a political economy of organic-coffee certification and producer unionism', *Environment and Planning A*, 34: 1165–1184.

Oliver, N. (1997) 'Benchmarking', in *Concise Encyclopaedia of Business and Management*, London: International Thomson Business Press.

Osborne, D. and Gaebler, T. (1993) *Reinventing Government*, New York: Plume.

Peck, J. and Tickell, A. (2002) 'Neoliberalizing space', *Antipode*, 34(3): 381–404.

Penny, G. (2003) 'Networks for agricultural supply chain (re)alignment in New Zealand dairy and sheep meat industries', paper presented to the IGU Commission on 'The Dynamics of Economic Spaces', Vancouver BC, August, 2003.

Penny, G. and Le Heron, R (2000) 'Comparative perspectives on farmer–processor networking in the dairy and meat sectors', Proceedings 18th New Zealand Geographical Conference.

——(2002) 'Contract issues in New Zealand's lamb supply chain', Proceedings 19th New Zealand Geographical Conference, Dunedin.

Perry, M. (1997) 'The Baldrige quality competition in New Zealand: a critical assessment', *International Journal of Quality Science*, 2(2): 70–86.

Perry, M., Le Heron, R., Hayward, D. and Cooper, I. (1997) 'Growing disciplines through total quality management in a New Zealand horticultural industry', *Journal of Rural Studies*, 13(3): 289–304.

Power, M. (1997) *The Audit Society: rituals of verification*, Oxford: Oxford University Press.

Pritchard, B. (1999) 'Australia as the supermarket to Asia? Governance, territory and political economy in the Australian agri-food system', *Rural Sociology*, 64(2): 284–301.

Reardon, T., Codron, J-M., Busch, L., Bingen, J. and Harris, C. (2001) 'Global change in agrifood grades and standards: agribusiness and strategic responses in developing countries', *International Food and Agribusiness Management Review*, 2(3): 421–435.

Redher, R. and Ralston, F. (1984) 'Total quality management: a revolutionary management philosophy', *Advanced Management Journal*, 49(3): 24–34.

Rice, R. (2001) 'Noble goals and challenging terrain: organic and fair trade coffee movements in the global marketplace', *Journal of Agricultural and Environmental Ethics*, 14: 39–66.

Rose, N. (1999) *Powers of Freedom: reframing political thought*, Cambridge: Cambridge University Press.

Snell, D. and Prasad, S. (2001) ' "Benchmarking" and participatory development: the case of Fiji's sugar industry reforms', *Development and Change*, 32: 255–276.

Storper, M. (2000) 'Globalization and knowledge flows: an industrial geographer's perspective', in J. Dunning (ed.) *Regions, Globalization and the Knowledge Based Economy*, New York: Oxford University Press.

Strathern, M. (ed.) (2000) *Audit Cultures: anthropological studies in accountability, ethics and the academy*, London: Routledge.

Thull, J.-P. and Kissling, C. (2002) 'Mitigating stock effluent discharges from trucks: Stakeholder consultation and environmental education', Proceedings of the Third Joint Conference of the New Zealand Geographical Society and the Institute of Australian Geographers.

Thrift, N. (2000) 'Performing cultures in the new economy', *Annals of the Association of American Geographers*, 90(4): 674–692.

Tomlinson, J. (1996) 'Inventing "Decline": the falling behind of the British economy in the postwar years', *Economic History Review*, XLIX(4): 731–757.

Wall, E., Weersink, A. and Swanton, C. (2001) 'Agriculture and ISO 14000', *Food Policy*, 26: 35–48.

Warner, M. (ed.) (1997) *Concise International Encyclopedia of Business and Management*, London: International Thomson Business Press.

Wolfe, D. and Gertler, M. (2001) 'Globalization and economic restructuring in Ontario: from industrial heartland to learning region?', *European Planning Studies*, 9(5): 575–592.

Womack, J., Jones, D. and Roos, D. (1990) *The Machine that Changed the World*, New York: Rawson Associates.

Yeatman, A. (1995) 'Interpreting contemporary contractualism', in J. Boston (ed.) *The State Under Contract*, Wellington: Bridget Williams Books.

——(1997) 'Contract, status and personhood', in G. Davis, B. Sullivan and A. Yeatman (eds) *The New Contractualism*, Sydney: Macmillan Education.

——(2002) 'The new contractualism and individualized personhood', *Journal of Sociology*, 38(1): 69–73.

12 Insecurity and the dream of targeted governance

Mariana Valverde and Michael Mopas

Scholars working with tools borrowed or adapted from Foucault's 'Governmentality' essay and from the rich body of theoretical and empirical research that has developed in loose connection with that essay (for example, Burchell *et al.* 1991) have brought about major changes in how security, safety, policing, punishment and crime are being analysed and theorized. A popular database, the Criminal Justice Abstracts, lists sixty recent articles in which Foucault appears as a keyword. And influential theoretical works written by scholars who are not Foucauldian nevertheless acknowledge the way in which the field has been transformed by the spread of 'governmentality' analysis. A notable example is David Garland's *The Culture of Control*, arguably the most influential recent theoretical overview of criminal justice issues (Garland 2001), which incorporates many of the key insights of studies of policing, punishment, and crime prevention undertaken by Foucauldian criminology into a synthesis with broad intellectual and policy appeal. Along similar lines, 'governmentality' is now a routine component of the theoretical training of many criminology graduate students, in Australia, the UK, and Canada – and it is beginning to make some inroads in the United States.[1]

Why should this be of interest to scholars working in the 'global' field? Criminology is, arguably, the least global of the social sciences. There are now studies of efforts to coordinate policing internationally, particularly in the case of organized crime, the smuggling of migrants, and issues in illicit drug and arms control. But the emergence of new, 'trendy' areas of empirical – and usually very narrowly policy-oriented – research has not been accompanied by any collective soul-searching about the statist origins and mission of criminology. As a matter of textual fact, studies of policing, punishment, safety and security have been historically tethered to the nation-state, specifically to the state's machinery of criminal law and criminal justice policy. Even in countries with strong traditions of academic freedom (such as the UK, Australia, and New Zealand), states have funded, and to some degree controlled, not only specific criminological research projects but even whole research institutes. So why would a volume such as this include an article about recent developments in a field that is still known as 'criminology', a term redolent of Durkheimian statist science?

Statist no more? Redefining policing as governance, not government

The statist tradition of criminology began to be challenged in the 1970s by the emergence of a self-described 'critical' criminology that was located in sociology departments as much as in criminology research institutes, and which drew most of its theoretical and political inspiration from critical sociological studies conducted on purely academic lines, without criminology's traditional state strings. A foremost leader in this critical turn, Stanley Cohen, persuasively redefined criminology as the study of *social control* – a 180-degree turn from the old concern with studying the causes of crime with a view to normalizing criminals and minimizing disorder.[2] Nevertheless, despite its oppositional politics, critical criminology was still focused on the state – albeit to denounce it. The statist focus, it could perhaps be argued, began to be seriously challenged by the emerging 1980s literature on 'private policing' (Shearing and Stenning 1987). These studies of the private security industry's growing importance were not taken up in mainstream social and political theory, but within criminology they were highly influential, and prompted much theorizing about the inadequacy of the old categories of 'public' and 'private', 'state' and 'civil society'. With the benefit of hindsight (and somewhat speculatively), it can be argued that this contingent feature made criminology open to the governmentality perspective, since one of the key concerns of early English-language governmentality studies was precisely to de-centre state governance and to encourage a mapping of actually existing relations that is faithful to new, hybrid developments in governance.

The Toronto Centre of Criminology had been a crucial player in the 'private policing' research programme, and it is, in our view, not coincidental that this Centre also became, during the 1990s, a significant site for the 'translation' into criminological research concerns of the 'governmentality' texts appearing, largely outside of criminology, in the UK and Australia. In 1992, when governmentality was a new perspective, a very influential article by Nikolas Rose and Peter Miller (Rose and Miller 1992) argued that Foucault's work can help inspire us to study *governance* networks as they actually exist, mapping the networks of the kind of small-p political power that is not identified with state apparatuses. A few years earlier, some political theorists had enthused about 'civil society' as a new object for political science, but governmentality work did not take sides in the state versus civil society debate, encouraging instead an agnostic stance from which governance relations could be documented without presupposing the pre-given containers of political science ('the state'; 'civil society'; 'the family'). This helped researchers concerned with security and policing to pay theoretical attention to phenomena such as the neoliberal managerial moves by which some public police forces were encouraged or forced to engage in 'partnerships' with private sector actors and with community groups and to market their services to municipal and other governments.

In part under the influence of studies of governance and governmentality, the study of 'policing' was redefined in the 1990s in quite a radical manner: as the study of the provision of security or the maintenance and governance of order, rather than the study of one state institution. That the provision and guaranteeing of order, including basic physical security, is a function that can and is carried out by a whole host of actors and institutions, with the modern public police being merely one of these, is now a generally accepted insight. An indicator of the success of the project to redefine policing in a non-statist manner is the fact that as the Law Commission of Canada focused research resources and legal policy attention on the issue of security, it organised a major international conference in February of 2003, in Montreal, whose co-sponsors included two large private security firms, as well as police and government representatives. If even a national 'Law Commission' has come to think of security in non-statist, non-legalistic terms, Foucauldian academics can be forgiven for concluding that 'govern*ance*' has indeed won out over 'govern*ment*' and 'state' in at least one field of policy-relevant intellectual work.

The de-centring of the state in and by researchers working on policing and security has been most evident in the inclusion of private, for-profit institutions within the ambit of criminological research. Some work has also been done, mostly at the urban level, analysing the relations between state bodies and non-profit community groups in the delivery of security and safety services (for example, Crawford 1997). By contrast, much less has been done to explore a different dimension of the extra-state governance of security, namely the international dimensions of order maintenance. A few specific issues – illegal drugs, money laundering – are regarded, without much discussion, as naturally belonging within the 'global'. At present, these issues, though important in law enforcement circles, have a relatively low profile in theoretical and critical studies of crime and security. Nevertheless, the intellectual revolution discussed above (the rethinking of policing as a governmental rather than a government function) makes it increasingly likely that research attention will focus on law-breaking, law enforcement, and, more generally, security-enhancing activities that cross national boundaries. Peacekeeping, for example, has recently come to the fore as a subject for criminological research in Canada, rather belatedly given Canada's long history of specializing in this particular dimension of international order and security. Any study of peacekeeping, which will necessarily focus on military personnel and on NGO activity rather than on the public police, will sooner or later help to bridge the rather outdated barriers separating criminology from political science and international law – boundaries that have thus far kept the study of crime and law enforcement artificially separate from the study of war and the study of human rights.

Thus, a potential space for research and thought has been opened up by the fact that studies of policing and security that are influenced by Foucauldian work on governance are no longer tethered to the nation-state even when their particular focus is a national police force or a national criminal justice programme. Even in the case of scholarship which does not explicitly theorize extra-state relations or dimensions of security work, findings from the literature on the governance of security, we would argue, can still be very relevant to readers of this anthology interested in understanding the current transformations of the processes by which non-state and state organizations attempt to achieve and to guarantee security, in whatever context.

It is worth noting that if governmentality studies helped many criminologists to stop taking the boundaries of the state and of 'law' for granted, encouraging us to study governance relations across the conventional boundaries separating public from private, state from economy, and state from community, this analytic shift to de-centre the state had a different character from the de-centring of 'the state' effected (or advocated) in the work of many 'globalization' theorists. While Foucault's work did not directly address 'the global' (not surprisingly, since during Foucault's lifetime terms such as 'international', 'imperialist', and so on were still the currency of both politics and theory), it would be quite inconsistent with Foucault's general approach to flee from the frying pan of statism only to fall into the fire of generalizations about globalization.

The Foucault-influenced research on recent shifts in the work of providing and guaranteeing basic physical security and enforcing laws and regulations does not provide any evidence to back up any general thesis about the coming of 'globalization'. In the field of political economy, some excellent work has undercut the grand claims made both by the neoliberal right and the left about the relentless march of a globalization regarded as consisting of unimpeded capital mobility and smooth socioeconomic homogenization (for example, Hirst and Thompson 1999). In keeping with Hirst and Thompson's realistic and nuanced analysis of how the complexities of economic governance emerging at the beginning of the twenty-first century belie any generalities about the global, we too would like to highlight the persistently, unfashionably *non-global* character of much policing, even of supposedly *international* policing.[3]

A key but little-known fact regarding international policing is that despite the changes in cross-national governance structures in spheres from commerce to illegal drugs to foreign policy, the number of international covenants or agreements conferring international powers on police is exactly zero. There is much rhetoric about information sharing, and possibly a growing amount of actual information sharing (the character and extent of which is unlikely to be visible to the public, or even to researchers). But this information sharing merely serves to enhance the action of nationally based police forces (Gill 1998; Sheptycki 1998). Any form of inter-country police cooperation must be done in accordance with the domestic laws of each of the states, and is limited by the fact that international organizations – of which Interpol is one of the very few examples[4] – are not, contrary to some crime-novel representations, international bodies linking states or existing above states, but rather are professional organizations, comparable to international organizations of academics. Police cooperate only by exchanging information as they see fit. And, most importantly, the flow of this information is such as to reinforce rather than threaten state-based police jurisdictions. The exchanged information, we stress, is given not to another government but rather to other police forces, who then use it to enforce national law (Anderson 1989; Walker 2000; Deflem 2000). And as revelations arising from the US inquiry into the intelligence failures surrounding September 11 suggest, sometimes the information flowing from one police force in one region goes only to one particular agency, which jealously guards it, rather than to 'the state' as a whole. Thus, while there are developments in international law enforcement that one could cite if one wanted to write about the globalization of policing, nevertheless, close attention needs to be paid to the shape of actual networks of power and knowledge. Occasional, discretionary collaboration between different national police forces (for example, in the pursuit of users of Internet child pornography) should not be mistaken for 'globalization'. States and local municipalities remain the key venues for, and jurisdictions of, law enforcement, even when law enforcement processes are qualitatively different in that they crucially involve 'community' agencies, for-profit security firms and other non-state actors.

It is not necessarily an exercise in intellectual imperialism to argue that the findings from studies of new technologies (including political technologies) of security used at the urban level may be of use to scholars analysing security programmes beyond the sphere of traditional urban-focused policing – programmes that, while still centrally relying on state actors and resources, nevertheless exceed the physical boundaries of the state, for example, international peacekeeping operations. At a higher level of abstraction, we would argue that there is no good reason, either intellectual or political, for continuing to maintain the old boundaries that keep 'crime' – that old Durkheimian statist object – separate from such phenomenologically similar entities as 'human rights violations', 'terrorism', 'smuggling' and 'war'. Just to give one example, 'war' is not what is used to be: while during the Cold War it was often thought that the end of the Cold War would mean a drying up of the political and military roots of Third World wars, wars have in recent years multiplied rather than decreased. And while the 'new wars' 'dissolve conventional distinctions between 'people', 'army', and 'government'' (Duffield 2001: 136), so too recent developments in the US-led 'war on terrorism' also blur the lines formerly separating (non-political) crime from 'terrorism' and from (statist) war.

What this has meant for international relations and for theories of war is being explored by others; for our purposes, what is important is to reflect on the significance of the fact that the line separating political from non-political crime and insecurity seems thinner than ever, in a wide variety of different settings. As people experienced in 'development' work constantly remind us, today's 'humanitarian' crises are generally complex events with multiple dimensions: the situations that have arisen in places such as the former Yugoslavia, Rwanda, and the Congo cannot be slotted neatly into any one of the old categories (war; crime; migration; cultural conflict; economic conflict; natural disaster). Given that policing researchers – and for that matter, policy-makers – are now focusing not so much on particular crimes that need detection and apprehension, but rather on the overall, future-oriented process of ensuring security, the insights of analyses of recent trends in the governance of (urban) security could thus be of use to those concerned with other dimensions and other venues of order maintenance and security provision. Or, to put it more academically, perhaps criminology and political science could begin to undo or at least question the institution-building work of the past decades, work which has made it difficult to remember that in the end, both enterprises are fundamentally concerned with the Hobbesian problematic of insecurity. With Hobbes, we could say that neither crime nor war, these days:

> consisteth of Battell only, or the act of fighting: but in a tract of time, wherein the Will to contend by Battell is sufficiently known: and therefore the notion of Time, is to be considered in the nature of Warre [and lack of safety]; as it is in the nature of the Weather. For as the nature of Foule weather lyeth not in a showre or two of rain, but in an inclination thereto of many dayes together: So the nature of War [and crime] consisteth not in actual fighting; but in the known disposition thereto, during all the time there is no assurance to the contrary.
>
> (Hobbes 1968: 186)

If the study of policing – one of the key subfields for the international Anglophone criminological research programme that emerged during the 1970s as the study of criminal justice *institutions* came to overshadow classical questions about 'the criminal' and 'criminality' – found in governmentality a key theoretical resource to help explain what many saw as the key empirical issue of the time (namely, the growing interpenetration of private and public security personnel and resources), so too theoretical resources loosely linked to Foucault, or more accurately to some of his collaborators, were also important in the theoretical transformation of the study of the other keystone of current criminological thought: punishment.

From discipline to risk: the new penology

The literature on 'the new penology', one of the key theoretical innovations in criminology of the past fifteen or so years, relied on some Foucauldian resources (if one can include under that label the work of Francois Ewald and Robert Castel) to analyse some important recent changes in the way that authorities govern offenders and deliver state punishment. While the sort of modern penalty associated with the nineteenth-century penitentiary focused on the offender as a soul or as a psyche, aiming to normalize if not the individual at least the population of offenders, in the last third of the twentieth century, neoliberal and managerial moves to displace therapy, to cut back state budgets, and to impose new knowledges more amenable to performance assessment, found the new logic of 'risk' more useful than the older, more ambitious and totalizing logic of 'discipline.' The psyche of the offender, long the key object of penological discourse and practice, came to be if not replaced at least displaced by a new set of entities – among which risk assessment scales were most prominent. Disciplinary tools and diagrams of rule (for example, prison labour, psychotherapy) have been in many places replaced by tools that to a large extent can govern subpopulations without governing through the person or seeking to shape the soul.[5] Low-level correctional officers can check off items on a risk assessment scale and generate an auditable assessment that can be quickly used to move offenders into one or another facility or programme. Psychiatric and social work professional discretionary judgement is thus sidelined, in much penal practice, in ways that parallel what has happened in many other settings.

The literature on governing penal issues and penal populations through risk could be of use to anyone studying contemporary developments in global security along a number of different dimensions. The sophisticated literature on governing criminality through risk has thus far remained, to our knowledge, uncited and unused by those examining global security (for example, Duffield 2001), and even by scholars studying immigration law and policy. Airport screening, for example (both that done by state immigration and customs officials and that done by security guards), follows the same 'risk profiling' logic that has become ubiquitous in correctional and police settings, but we are not aware of studies of airport security or other international processes that use the insights of the new penology.

With the aim of facilitating analytic experimentation and the borrowing of analytical tools across disciplinary and field boundaries, let us here provide a brief overview of the key findings of the literature on penality and risk, together with very sketchy suggestions on how they might be useful in other contexts. In the last section of the chapter we will then develop our own theoretical argument about the way in which risk management is part of a wider shift in governance that we call 'targeted governance'. There, we will make some tentative suggestions about the potential uses, for scholars of the global, not only of the 'risk' literature arising out of criminology but also of other studies that support the thesis that our particular present is dominated by a utopian governance dream – a 'smart', specific, side-effects-free, information-driven utopia of governance that in policing circles takes the form of 'intelligence-led policing' and in medical circles is known as 'evidence-based medicine'.

But first, let us look at the new penology and the rise of 'risk management'. Since the late 1980s, researchers documenting developments in penal policy and practice have noted a trend away from nineteenth-century concerns to normalize deviants that originally gave rise to criminology. The harsh regimes of early penitentiaries and the more benevolent regimes of mid-twentieth century welfarist rehabilitation programmes diverged sharply in political orientation: but they shared a common epistemology. This was the fundamental opposition between 'normal' and 'deviant', most famously explored by Foucault in his studies on prisons and on sexuality, and the consequent belief that at least for reformable 'deviants', the state and various expert bodies should devote resources to normalizing them, reforming their habits, and rehabilitating their souls.

Whether they were being harshly disciplined in workhouses and asylums, or benevolently reformed in welfarist institutions, the ill, the ignorant, the unfortunate and the deviant had to be personally known to the authorities. Hence the great nineteenth-century technologies of personal knowledge – the case file, the family history, the diagnostic analysis (see Rose 1990, 1996; Poovey 1998) – and the related information systems, from censuses to epidemiological statistics, in which individual-level data were centrally collected so that the aggregate data, as tables of numbers and as statistics, were disseminated to help rationalize the governance of populations and the management of a variety of problems.

The normalization project, with its dual objective of identifying problem individuals and improving biopolitical aggregates, was never abandoned. But with the rise of neoliberal and neoconservative projects to change governance, for instance by having the private sector or philanthropies provide public services, with the state 'steering but not rowing', new ways of visualizing and governing deviant populations emerged. Within the correctional setting – prisons, probation, parole – the biggest trend of the past thirty years has undoubtedly been the rise of risk measurement and risk management. As David Garland puts it, offenders, 'rather than clients in need of support, are seen as risks that must be managed. Instead of emphasizing rehabilitative methods that meet the offender's needs, the system emphasizes effective controls that minimize costs and maximize security' (2001: 175).

What came to be called 'the new penology' was a reflection on the profound changes involved in shifting away from discipline to risk. Discipline (and rehabilitation) governs individuals *individually* while simultaneously forming and normalizing populations. Risk management, by contrast, breaks the individual up into a set of measurable risk factors. This of course is not unique to criminal justice: in health care too, patients being diagnostically examined by a clinician using old fashioned clinical judgement appear to have given way to bundles of test results. Each test generates, automatically, a particular risk profile, determined by existing aggregate data. Clinical judgement – the original prototype of the individualizing gaze of the disciplines, according to Foucault – now consists mainly of juxtaposing and synthesizing the risk profiles generated by different tests.

The most influential exposition of 'the new penology' was that of Malcolm Feeley and Jonathan Simon, who argued that modern penal policies have shifted away from individualized rehabilitation and towards administrative, risk-factor-driven, population management approaches (Feeley and Simon 1992). This was very close to the analysis of the shift 'from dangerousness to risk' provided by the French sociologist of medicine Robert Castel:

> The new strategies dissolve the notion of a subject or a concrete individual, and put in its place a combinatory of factors, the factors of risk … The essential component of the intervention no longer takes the form of the direct face-to-face relationship between the carer and the cared … It comes instead to reside in the establishing of flows of population based on the collation of a range of abstract factors deemed liable to produce risk in general.
>
> (Castel 1991: 281)

Initially, risk management was identified with bureaucratic techniques for identifying and isolating problem populations (for example, offenders with a high risk of recidivism, as determined by scales derived from previous aggregate data). However, later contributions to the literature on risk showed that risk techniques are not tied to any particular way gaze (bureaucratic versus clinical, impersonal versus individualized), or to any particular political project. Social insurance and universal health coverage, for example, are well-known ways of using risk technologies to spread risks among the whole population, thus achieving a democratic effect. This use of risk has the opposite political effect to the use of risk-measuring tools to 'redline' uninsurable poor neighbourhoods or to segregate and warehouse certain offenders.

Risk, then, as Pat O'Malley has influentially argued as against Ulrich Beck, is a flexible, multivalent technique of governance (O'Malley 2000). It is even possible to continue delivering certain welfare-state services to needy populations, if one cleverly redefines people's 'needs' as 'risks' (Hannah-Moffat 2003). The risks that generally matter, in a neoliberal universe, are risks to property and to the respectable; but it is possible to redefine people's own risks (poverty, illiteracy, alcohol dependence, hunger) as factors that lead to or predict future risks to 'society', to capitalism, or to global security, and thus as requiring attention and perhaps even state funding. Social services to homeless youth or to released convicts are now rationalized, in Canada at any rate, as helping vulnerable populations to learn to monitor and manage their risks, thus protecting 'society' from criminal and from fiscal dangers.

There are a number of new initiatives in and around criminal justice that show the amazing flexibility of risk talk and risk-measurement tools. On the more coercive side, we have the rise of 'Megan's laws' – sex-offender community notification statutes (Levi 2000). These begin by classifying sex offenders into different risk groups – and it is a given of risk analysis, here as elsewhere, that there is no such thing as zero risk, only high or low risk – and then communicating the presence of high-risk released offenders to 'the community', so that the community can protect itself. This is a good example of risk information being used to heighten social exclusion, in contrast to the ways in which welfarist programmes use risk information precisely to direct resources for prevention and inclusion purposes.[6]

The sex-offender notification statutes are interesting theoretically because they articulate risk information technologies with somewhat independent neoliberal discourses of community empowerment. In previous decades risk information about offenders was monopolized by the state (and in certain countries, such as Germany or France, information about criminal risks is still largely monopolized by the state, with community agencies and philanthropies having a much smaller role than in the common-law world). The state gathered the information and the state acted. But in the neoliberal universe, particularly in the common-law neoliberal universe, which relies on local authorities and sub-state powers more than is the case in many more centralized states, state bodies such as the police are not given the monopoly over the task of actually securing the community even when they have a monopoly on the process of generating the risk *information* (Levi 2000; Ericson and Haggerty 1997). Communities (an amorphous term that often amounts to businesses and/or traditional families) are regarded as having the duty and the right to use the government-provided risk information to take their own risk precautions.

The same goes for private homeowners, who are constantly addressed by authorities (including insurance companies as well as the police) with the Hobbesian discourse of eternal homeowner vigilance, and enjoined to become active providers of their own security.[7] This reconfiguration of the risk of crime is in keeping with the neoliberal reconfiguration of medical risks: we go to experts to get our risk assessment, but we are then enjoined to take up exercise, eat certain foods, and so on, so as to act upon our own risk factors. Similarly, the welfarist recipient of universal old-age insurance has given way to the enterprising holder of individual pension plans, an individual who carefully scans the financial pages and chooses his or her own way of balancing the risks inherent in stock-market investment against the risks of an old age dependent only on dramatically scaled back state provisions.

Along similar lines, we have the proliferation of crime prevention and urban safety initiatives that encourage citizens to know, monitor, and manage everyday risks to their own safety and that of their neighbourhoods. These initiatives are by no means limited to wealthy gated communities; many poorer neighbourhoods, in the Third World particularly, have developed innovative ways to manage risks to their safety with minimal involvement from the often-discredited and sometimes downright hostile public police (see, for example, Brogden and Shearing 1993).

Given these widespread trends, it is not surprising that recent research highlights the growing use of 'risk profiling' within police work, and the ways in which risk information, rather than being hoarded by public authorities, is constantly transferred out, to some extent to communities but mainly to private insurance companies, employers, and other organizations that use this police-supplied risk information for their own purposes. Ericson and Haggerty's influential and voluminous study of police work, which shows that most police time is spent not fighting crime but rather gathering and communicating risk information, shows that the well-publicized logic of racial profiling is only one of a wide range of risk communication practices:

> For example, the RCMP has a Security Fraud Information Centre that risk-profiles securities transactions. The centre's mandate is 'to maintain a national repository of criminal intelligence information on fraudulent and illegal activities in the security field and disseminate information to security commissions across Canada'.
>
> (Ericson and Haggerty 1997: 218)

The growing tendency to use risk information formats (such as the ubiquitous 'risk assessment scales' used in child protection work through to community safety audits to addiction counselling) in order to govern security and safety through risk factors – rather than directly through persons – has been closely linked, in the criminal justice field, to the growing influence and prestige of private security tools and concerns. The Canadian Mounted Police did not suddenly come up with the idea of risk-profiling securities, obviously, and neither did it design the tools with which to do this: the financial industry did. Similarly, private-sector agents concerned more to prevent employee fraud and theft than to bring offenders to justice have devised a number of innovative surveillance techniques – not only the well-known high-tech innovations of the modern office, such as tracking employees' computer use or requiring computerized plastic cards to enter buildings, but also a welter of low-tech ad hoc solutions, such as placing the reception desk in a location designed to maximize 'natural surveillance' of activities resulting in a loss of profit, from taking too many cigarette breaks to pilfering office supplies. These measures to manage and mini-mize risks to corporations have been adapted for use in public spaces, partly by public police and partly by the fast-growing industry of crime prevention through environmental design (CPTED) consultants.

That the private sector would lead the way in risk technologies of security is not surprising. For the private sector the goal was, and is, to minimize risks and losses; going after wrongdoers is often not a rational goal, either financially or from the point of view of organization morale. Risks are often best minimized through impersonal techniques acting on the environment so as to lower the opportunities for wrongdoing. This impersonal way of maximizing security treats everyone as a rational actor; it is uninterested in drawing lines separating the normal from the deviant, the criminal from the honest worker.

And yet, the focus on the private-enterprise origins and uses of much infor-mation technology and risk management technology should not be allowed to obscure the still not outdated old Marxist insights about the coercive apparatus of the state. Much of the technology currently used in both public policing and private sector surveillance originated in military research. And of course, the Internet itself, while hailed as a great neoliberal space of consumer and intellec-tual freedom, was originally developed by the American military. (Americans who see the Internet as a great space of freedom might do well to reflect on why it is that American email addresses exist in and help to constitute a virtual impe-rial space, in which the relevant divisions are merely those between 'gov', 'com', 'edu' and 'org', functioning like so many independent states – 'ca', 'uk', 'au', 'fr' and so on.) Apart from the American military-industrial complex's unique ability to actually realize, in practice, dreams of governance that other organizations could never render technical, one could note that the use of CCTV cameras in the UK is historically rooted in the British Army's experiments with electronic counter-insurgency and city planning in Belfast (Haggerty and Ericson 2001: 55). The emergence of what is known as 'database policing', where officers search not persons or vehicles but databases on the basis of certain risk profiles or specific information, is but one additional example of the trickle-down effect of military technology on daily police practice.

Nevertheless, despite the undeniable deep roots of policing rationalities and technologies in both military and corporate needs and concerns, the most recent literature on the policing of risks also reminds us that risk management is a pragmatic and highly mobile affair. Risk techniques developed by state security systems or by corporations can, at least theoretically, be used in other contexts with different effects. The surveillance camera that maximizes the corporation's security by deterring employees as a group from pilfering tools from the storeroom can also be used to enhance women employees' safety by identifying a rapist. In general, governmentality writers try to avoid the paranoid style of writing and the conspiracy theories of causation that pervaded earlier schools of critical criminology. Although some of them sometimes fall back into the 'Big Brother is watching' school of sociology, probably due to the persistent drag of the 'social control' paradigm, nevertheless, much governmentality work on security demonstrates the flexibility and unpredictability of technologies of surveillance and risk management. For example: one recent study by Foucault-influenced criminologists documents the invention of gadgets sold over the Internet allowing American parents to drug-test their own children, gadgets marketed as helping white suburban nuclear families to stay out of state sight. Instead of decrying the relentless march of state control into the heart of the family, however, the study shows that the same firms that make the devices allowing parents to unknowingly test their own children for illicit drug use also market equally effective gadgets that drug users can buy to fool their parents' or their employers' drug-screening efforts (Moore and Haggerty 2001).

Indeed, one of the recurring themes of governmentality studies of crime and security is that there is no one-to-one, fixed relationship between particular political projects and sets of governance tools or techniques. Statistics aren't always 'the state's facts' even if that is their empirical origin. And surveillance cameras placed outside a women's shelter have a different political effectivity than the same cameras placed outside a government building. In keeping with Foucault's own radical refusal of grand narrative of Big Brother oppression, future work in the area of security technologies and rationalities is likely to emphasize the flexibility and unpredictability of the effects of governing through risk. Political determinism is as problematic, from a Foucauldian perspective, as technological determinism.

Risk security techniques are not uniquely linked to neoliberal capitalism or to any other macroeconomic or political project since poor neighbourhoods taking autonomous measures to protect themselves, or women fearing abusive husbands, can and do use risk technologies as well as corporations. It is an inescapable conclusion that the military and corporations have been the most inventive and prolific providers of new risk techniques, and that these techniques are still generally used to protect profits and to measure and enhance state security. But a governmentality analysis would suggest that it is important to try to document alternative, creative uses of risk techniques – not to romanticize 'resistance', but simply to show that governance is often more heterogeneous and unpredictable in practice than would be suggested by looking at general 'models' or by determining the actual historical 'origin' of this or that technology. Innovations in governance are usually to be found in the unheralded front lines, not among theorists. The criminology of social control tended to see every innovation in policing or punishment as another ruse of power, another instance of 'net widening', yet more fuel for the runaway train of social control. Foucauldian studies, by contrast, try to walk a fine line, on the one hand acknowledging the circuits of 'big power,' and on the other hand being attentive to the creativity, fluidity and dynamism of governance on the ground (O'Malley 1996).

Targeted governance

Governing security and safety through risk techniques that identify and evaluate the presence and the magnitude of risk factors in people, spaces, and activities is connected to – and is sometimes just a part of – a very generalized way of governing that has been called 'targeted governance' (Valverde 2003).

One way of visualizing the shift towards targeted governance is to reflect on what 'smart drugs', smart bombs, and targeted social programmes have in common. In all three cases, the ideal of targeting governance effectively and economically arises out of a general disenchantment with more universalistic or totalizing strategies. Smart drugs zero in on a very specific process – a particular neuron receptor site on the brain, for instance – and seek to use data from scientific studies to act upon a single process (for example, raising the serotonin levels in the brain), rather than attempting to cure a (whole) person of a (whole) disease such as depression. Smart bombs, on their part, are supposed to once more use expert knowledge (intelligence data, in this case) to isolate a target and act upon that with a minimum of collateral damage.

In the sphere of the social, many universal social programmes have been replaced by 'targeted' programmes, often by deploying the same justifications and rationales used to promote 'smart drugs'. Popular as well as expert neoliberal discourses in the era of Thatcher and Reagan managed to convince large numbers of people that the collateral damage or the side effects of welfare – dependency on the state, mainly – were so severe as to justify cuts that in many cases brought back conditions, such as large-scale homelessness, not seen in many cities since the Great Depression. Once more, the idea of 'targeting' programmes was linked to the idea of efficient, apolitical, knowledge-driven, 'evidence-based' policy. Studies would show who really needed this or that programme; the lazy welfare bum would be differentiated from the deserving poor; the middle class would no longer benefit from child benefits and other universal programmes developed during the 1950s and 1960s. The dream of knowledge-driven targeted governance was, in this sphere as in many medical contexts, linked to a disappointment with or outright rejection of more totalizing dreams of governance that had come to be seen as hubristic and dysfunctional.

The policing field shows the same kind of transformation. The Peelian idea of policing as universal surveillance and total security through prevention came to seem as old fashioned and as fiscally irresponsible as universal, non-contributory social insurance. Street patrols covering a whole city equally were never totally abandoned, but they were minimized, with more and more resources devoted to 'targeted' policing.[8]

Targeted policing is not synonymous with racial profiling – racial profiling is merely one, not very representative, form of targeted policing. Policing has been and remains targeted along several different axes: (1) the targeting of problem *spaces*; 2) the targeting of problem *populations*; and (3) the targeting of particularly risky *activities*. Patrols around public housing projects exemplify the first; racial profiling is a notorious example of the second strategy; and airport security is a current example of the third strategy for the targeting of security resources.

Targeted governance (in its contemporary neoliberal form at any rate) is thoroughly pessimistic insofar as it arises out of a widely shared feeling that the totalizing transformations envisaged by the pioneers of the welfare state were not only too expensive but also inherently ill-advised.[9] We cannot cure poverty or cure schizophrenia, we are now told, and the state cannot provide total security for the citizenry: people have to be taught to manage their own risks, with the help of information from state and expert bodies and perhaps some, limited, material resources. And the provision of resources is usually made contingent on submitting oneself or one's organization to a lifetime of monitoring, evaluation, auditing, and assessment (Power 1994). The welfare-era idea that one could actually cure both medical and social conditions, abolish poverty or abolish insecurity, once and for all, is dismissed as utopian.

But targeted governance is simultaneously highly optimistic in believing that good information can and will be collected to enable managers of all types to target their organization's resources efficiently and with maximum benefit. The manic side of the schizophrenic project that is targeted governance is particularly evident in self-help books on financial success: armed with the right information and with a positive attitude, anyone can ride the waves of marketplace or personal misfortunes and emerge happy, healthy, and successful. But even in genres less prone to bootstrapism, such as expert writing on security, one sees a lingering utopian optimism about total information providing total security coexisting with a neoliberal fear of governing too much. Targeted policing, for example, is closely intertwined with what is known as 'intelligence-led' policing, a project that has an implicit utopia of total security underwriting it – while in the medical field, targeted interventions and smart drugs are closely intertwined with what is known as 'evidence-based medicine'. In medicine too, the modesty that speaks about lifelong management of one's own discrete, incurable but manageable health risks coexists with the (often-disavowed) utopia of preventive therapies for everything, a governance utopia facilitated by the mapping of the human genome, with its attendant myth of ultimate biological knowledge, and by the increasingly sophisticated techniques for seeing – or at least visualizing, through mediating technologies – the biochemical secrets of every little neurone.

It may be that the contradictory dream of information-driven targeted governance – a dream which begins with neoliberal modesty but is dialectically intertwined with a vision of successfully targeting *everything* and thus returning to totalizing governance – applies at least in part to the international arena, specifically, to the recent history of disarmament projects. The CND-era ideal of bilateral disarmament, a project which assumed that there were only two sides, and that once those two sides saw reason and engaged in a dialogue to disarm, the world's security would be assured, seems hopelessly utopian now. We now know that there are multiple causes of wars and multiple reasons why wars continue, and we do not necessarily think we can understand, much less solve, all of them. The dream of the 1970s peace movement was 'turning swords into ploughshares' – the military equivalent of normalizing all deviants. But nobody talks about universal peace now, outside of New Age circles concerned only with psychic peace. Social democratic parties that during the 1970s promoted disarmament in general are now happy to talk about 'just wars' and about military action in other countries to prevent or halt human rights violations.

Disarmament efforts now do not invoke the kind of totalizing peace rhetoric associated with the anti-Vietnam war movement ('What if they gave a war and nobody came?' 'War is bad for children and other living things', and so on). What we see now are mostly uncoordinated efforts to achieve targeted, partial disarmament – applying only to nuclear weapons, or only to 'weapons of mass destruction', or only to 'the axis of evil', or only to one country, or one 'terrorist' organization, or only to a particular list of 'terrorist' organizations, or only to a particular state apparatus. Like targeted governance generally, these efforts are justified as information-driven – and hence as not ideological. Before invading Iraq in March of 2003, US Secretary of State Colin Powell gave a widely publicized presentation at the UN in which Powerpoint slides purported to let the world see 'with its own eyes' (as Bruno Latour would say) Saddam Hussein's arsenal of chemical weapons. Of course critics pointed out that we – and Colin Powell – could only see trucks and roads and buildings; but nevertheless, the point is that invading another country was supposed to be justified through information, through 'hard facts', rather than simply through political ideology. This is the international equivalent of intelligence-led policing.

And yet, the projects for the targeted governance of world security, like targeted policing at the urban level, also reveal the persistence of a certain utopian dream of total, non-targeted security. Many of those who urge the Israeli government to disarm just a little bit in some parts of the occupied territories are motivated not by a bureaucratic notion of what's most efficient and pragmatic, but by a deeply held commitment to the 'perpetual peace' ideal of Arabs and Jews living in harmony. And the targeting of 'the axis of evil' by the US government is clearly linked to a rather apocalyptic notion of 'manifest destiny' and total world domination. These days wars are usually fought one country at a time; but there are always more tyrants to be deposed, more geopolitical objectives to be secured.

Liberalism has been defined as arising out of a concern not to govern too much (Rose 1999). But the new neoliberal strategies for the governance of security could be seen as suggesting that liberalism is perhaps only a fear of governing too much *all at once*. 'Targeting' does not necessarily mean governing less. There are always more targets; and there are endless ways of fiddling with existing 'smart' weapons, smart drugs, and targeted social programmes. The logic of targeted governance is in its own way as endless, as utopian, as the better-known logic of totalitarian control.

Notes

1   Perhaps the key vector for Foucauldian influences in American criminology and sociolegal studies is Jonathan Simon (cf. his forthcoming book, *Governing Through Crime*).
2   See Cohen (1985), and the influential anthology edited by D. Garland and P. Young, *The Power to Punish* (1983).
3   We adopt here Hirst and Thompson's useful distinction between multinational entities, which function around the world but nevertheless work through and in states, and the much-touted but much rarer stateless 'global' or 'transnational' processes and entities. Peacekeeping in Afghanistan today is indeed a multinational endeavour, but it is hardly a state-less project.
4   The International Criminal Police Commission, and its French-based successor, the International Criminal Police Office (Interpol), have supplied a network of communication among participating national police organizations. But Interpol is not so much an instance of global governance as a fancy 'policeman's club' (Anderson 1989: 43) where important professional contacts are made by senior officers from around the world. There is no such thing as global or even international policing, strictly speaking, although there are of course some legal and political tools that translate policing priorities from one country to another (most notably the US war on drugs, which has been forcibly exported to various Latin American countries, but even in that case US police officers cannot be directly involved in the way that US military advisers are directly involved).
5   Jonathan Simon, John Pratt, Kevin Stenson, Pat O'Malley and Kelly Hannah-Moffat are among the main contributors to this literature.
6   We thank Pat O'Malley for many discussions on the issue of whether the most useful categorization of risk technologies is that which would separate exclusionary from inclusionary risk measurement techniques, although he is not responsible for anything we claim here.
7   Addressing a hypothetical (optimist) critic, Hobbes justifies his argument that people will trade in all rights for security with evidence drawn from the field of crime prevention: 'let him therefore consider with himselfe, when taking a journey, he armes himselfe, and seeks to go well accompanied; when going to sleep, he locks his doors; when even in his house he locks his chests, and this when he knows there be Lawes, and publike Officers, armed, to revenge all injuries shall bee done him...' (Hobbes 1968: 186–187).
8   In the city of Toronto, the density of police patrols is determined – in a curious example of consumer-driven targeting – by the number of phone calls to police originating from the area. Thus, poorer areas, which in Toronto as elsewhere generate more calls to police per household than upper-class neighbourhoods where problems are usually solved without recourse to the police, end up being more heavily policed. Complaint-driven targeting is common in other fields (liquor licensing inspections, for example, or police raids on street prostitutes); its logic appears similar to that of targeted governance driven by expert-compiled data, but it could be argued that it is actually the opposite of information-driven, 'evidence-based' targeting.
9   One could cite here the immense popularity, among ordinary people as well as experts, of the 'small is beautiful' school of urban design and planning that replaced the Le Corbusier-influenced grander projects of the 1950s and 1960s.

References

Anderson, M. (1989) *Policing the World: Interpol and the politics of international police cooperation*, Oxford: Clarendon Press.

Brogden, M. and Shearing, C. (1993) *Policing for a New South Africa*, London: Routledge.

Burchell, G., Gordon, C. and Miller, P. (eds) (1991) *The Foucault Effect: studies in governmentality*, Chicago: University of Chicago Press.

Castel, R. (1991) 'From dangerousness to risk', in G. Burchell, C. Gordon, and P. Miller (eds) *The Foucault Effect: studies in governmentality*, Chicago: University of Chicago Press.

Cohen, S. (1985) *Visions of Social Control*, New York: Polity Press.

Crawford, A. (1997) *The Local Governance of Crime: appeals to community and partnerships*, New York: Oxford University Press.

Deflem, M. (2000) 'Bureaucratization and social control: historical foundations of international police cooperation', *Law and Society Review*, 34(3): 739–778.

Duffield, M. (2001) *Global Governance and the New Wars: the merging of development and security*, New York: Zed Books.

Ericson, R. and Haggerty, K. (1997) *Policing the Risk Society*, Toronto: University of Toronto Press.

Feeley, M. and Simon, J. (1992) 'The new penology: notes on the emerging strategy for corrections and its implications', *Criminology*, 30: 49–74.

Garland, D. (2001) *The Culture of Control: crime and social order in contemporary society*, Chicago: University of Chicago Press.

Garland, D. and Young, P. (eds) (1983) *The Power to Punish: contemporary penality and social analysis*, London: Heinemann Educational Books.

Gill, P. (1998) 'Making sense of police intelligence? A cybernetic model in analyzing information and power in police intelligence processes', *Policing and Society*, 8: 289–314.

Haggerty, K. and Ericson, R. (2001) 'The military technostructures of policing', in P. Kraska (ed.) *Militarizing the American Criminal Justice System: the changing roles of the armed forces and the police*, Boston: Northeastern University Press.

Hannah-Moffat, K. (2003) 'Risk and need', unpublished paper submitted to *British Journal of Criminology*.

Hirst, P. and Thompson, G. (1999) *Globalization in Question: the international economy and the possibilities of governance*, 2nd edn, Cambridge: Polity Press.

Hobbes, T. (1968 [1651]) *Leviathan*, London: Penguin Books.

Levi, R. (2000) 'The mutuality of risk and community: the adjudication of community notification statutes', *Economy and Society*, 29(4): 578–601.

Moore, D. and Haggerty, K. (2001) 'Bring it on home: home drug testing and the relocation of the war on drugs', *Social and Legal Studies*, 10(3): 377–395.

O'Malley, P. (1996). 'Risk and responsibility', in A. Barry, T. Osborne, and N. Rose (eds) *Foucault and Political Reason: liberalism, neo-liberalism and rationalities of government*, London: UCL Press.

——(2000) 'Uncertain subjects: risks, liberalism and contract', *Economy and Society*, 29(4): 460–484.

Poovey, M. (1998) *A History of the Modern Fact: problems of knowledge in the sciences of wealth and society*, Chicago: University of Chicago Press.

Power, M. (1994) 'The audit society', in A. Hopwood and P. Miller (eds) *Accounting as Social and Institutional Practice*, New York: Cambridge University Press.

Rose, N. (1990) *Governing the Soul: the shaping of the private self*, London: Routledge.

——(1996) *Inventing Our Selves: psychology, power, and personhood*, New York: Cambridge University Press.

——(1999) *Powers of Freedom: reframing political thought*, New York: Cambridge University Press.

Rose, N. and Miller, P. (1992) 'Political power beyond the state: problematics of government', *British Journal of Sociology*, 43(2): 173–205.

Shearing, C. and Stenning, P. (eds) (1987) *Private Policing*, Newbury Park: Sage.

Sheptycki, J. (1998) 'Policing, postmodernism and transnationalization', *British Journal of Criminology*, 38(3): 485–503.

Valverde, M. (2003) 'Targeted governance and the problem of desire', in R. Ericson and A. Doyle (eds) *Risk and Morality*, Toronto: University of Toronto Press.

Walker, N. (2000) 'Transnational contexts', in F. Leishman, B. Loveday and S. Savage (eds) *Core Issues in Policing*, New York: Longman.

Index

Printed in the United Kingdom
by Lightning Source UK Ltd.
120764UK00001B/12